V&R

Journal of Ancient Judaism Supplements

Edited by
Armin Lange, Bernard M. Levinson
and Vered Noam

Volume 11

Vandenhoeck & Ruprecht

Rainer Albertz / Jakob Wöhrle (ed.)

Between Cooperation
and Hostility

Multiple Identities in Ancient Judaism
and the Interaction with Foreign Powers

Vandenhoeck & Ruprecht

With 16 figures

Bibliographic information published by the Deutsche Nationalbibliothek

The Deutsche Nationalbibliothek lists this publication
in the Deutsche Nationalbibliografie;
detailed bibliographic data available online:
http://dnb.d-nb.de.

ISBN 978-3-525-55051-9
ISBN 978-3-647-55051-0 (e-book)

Printed and bound in Germany by CPI buchbücher.de, Birkach
Printed on non-aging paper.

Preface

The question of why the cooperation of Jews with the Persian and Ptolemaic empires achieved some success and why it failed with regard to the Seleucids and the Romans, even turning into military hostility against them, has not been sufficiently answered. The present volume intends to show, from the perspectives of Hebrew Bible, Judaic, and Ancient History Studies, that the contrasting Jewish attitudes towards foreign powers were not only dependent on specific political circumstances. They were also interrelated with the emergence of multiple early Jewish identities, which all found a basis in the Torah, the prophets, or the psalms. The wide range of theological and ethical concepts, which were already enshrined in the Torah and even enlarged by the prophets, helped different Jewish groups to construct their identities in a way that enabled them to conform to or put up resistance against the demands of foreign rule in a non-violent way. Their different interpretations, however, involved likewise the danger of violent internal and external quarrels, which became apparent under specific social and political conditions, especially when any public control of interpretation failed.

This volume evolved out of the papers presented at an international conference that took place on June 1-3, 2011, at the University of Münster. It was organized by the research group "Distinction and Integration in the Foundational Document of Israel" at the Cluster of Excellence "Religion and Politics in Pre-Modern and Modern Cultures".

We want to thank all those who enabled the conference to take place and the conference volume to appear. The Cluster of Excellence generously sponsored the conference. Our students and doctoral candidates Ruth Ebach, Dagrun Pflüger and Svenja von Rönn provided magnificent help during the conference.

We thank the editors of the Supplements to the Journal of Ancient Judaism, Prof. Dr. Arming Lange, Prof. Dr. Bernard Levinson and Prof. Dr. Vered Noam, for accepting this volume in the series, and Vandenhoeck & Ruprecht for publishing it. We are very grateful for all the work Prof. Dr. Bruce Wells invested in correcting the English of this volume. Finally, we thank Vera Bongert and Corinna Pfannkuche for compiling the index.

Münster, November 2012   Rainer Albertz
                                                        Jakob Wöhrle

Contents

Abbreviations 9

Judeans, Jews, and their Neighbors:
Jewish Identity in the Second Temple Period
Daniel R. Schwartz 13

Conflicting Models of Identity and the
Publication of the Torah in the Persian Period
Thomas Römer 33

Joseph in Egypt:
Living under Foreign Rule according to the Joseph Story
and its Early Intra- and Extra-Biblical Reception
Jakob Wöhrle 53

The Adversaries in Ezra/Nehemiah – Fictitious or Real?
A Case Study in Creating Identity in
Late Persian and Hellenistic Times
Sebastian Grätz 73

"Genocide" in the Book of Esther:
Cultural Integration and the Right of Resistance against Pogroms
Reinhard Achenbach 89

Are Foreign Rulers Allowed to Enter and Sacrifice
in the Jerusalem Temple?
Rainer Albertz 115

The Construction of Samari(t)an Identity
from the Inside and from the Outside
Stefan Schorch 135

Manifest Identity: From *Ioudaios* to Jew:
Household Judaism as Anti-Hellenization in the Late Hasmonean Era
Andrea M. Berlin 151

Honor and Humiliation as a Factor in Hasmonean Politics
according to the Narrator of 1 Maccabees
Doron Mendels 177

From the "Master of the Elephants"
to the "Most Ungracious Wretch":
The Image of Foreign Commanders in the Second Book of Maccabees
Johannes Schnocks 205

Seduced by the Enemy or Wise Strategy?
The Presentation of Non-Violence and Accommodation
with Foreign Powers in Ancient Jewish Literary Sources
Catherine Hezser 221

The High Priests and Rome:
Why Cooperation Failed
Kai Trampedach 251

Index of Ancient Sources 267

Index of Authors 277

Abbreviations

AB	Anchor Bible
AGJU	Arbeiten zur Geschichte des antiken Judentums und des Urchristentums
AJEC	Ancient Judaism and Early Christianity
ANET	*Ancient Near Eastern Texts Relating to the Old Testament*, ed. J.B. Pritchard
ANRW	*Aufstieg und Niedergang der römischen Welt: Geschichte und Kultur Roms im Spiegel der neueren Forschung*, ed. H. Temporini/W. Haase
AOAT	Alter Orient und Altes Testament
AP	Anthologia Palatina
ASOR	American Schools of Oriental Research
ATANT	Abhandlungen zur Theologie des Alten und Neuen Testaments
ATD	Das Alte Testament Deutsch
atm	Altes Testament und Moderne
BBB	Bonner biblische Beiträge
BE	Biblische Enzyklopädie
BETL	Bibliotheca ephemeridum theologicarum lovaniensium
BKAT	Biblischer Kommentar. Altes Testament
BN	*Biblische Notizen*
BThSt	Biblisch-theologische Studien
BZAR	Beihefte zur Zeitschrift für Altorientalische und Biblische Rechtsgeschichte
BZAW	Beihefte zur Zeitschrift für die alttestamentliche Wissenschaft
BZNW	Beihefte zur Zeitschrift für die neutestamentliche Wissenschaft
CBQMS	Catholic Biblical Quarterly. Monograph Series
CEJL	Commentaries on Early Jewish Literature
CRINT	Compendia rerum iudaicarum ad Novum Testamentum
CSJH	Chicago Studies in the History of Judaism
EHS.T	Europäische Hochschulschriften. Theologie
EvT	*Evangelische Theologie*
FAT	Forschungen zum Alten Testament
FGH	*Die Fragmente der griechischen Historiker*, ed. F. Jacoby
FoSub	Fontes et Subsidia ad Bibliam pertinentes
FRLANT	Forschungen zur Religion und Literatur des Alten und Neuen Testaments

HAT	Handbuch zum Alten Testament
HBSt	Herders biblische Studien
HCS	Hellenistic Culture and Society
HKAT	Handkommentar zum Alten Testament
HTKAT	Herders theologischer Kommentar zum Alten Testament
HTR	*Harvard Theological Review*
HUCA	*Hebrew Union College Annual*
ICC	International Critical Commentary
IEJ	*Israel Exploration Journal*
INJ	*Israel Numismatic Journal*
JAJ	*Journal of Ancient Judaism*
JAJSup	Journal of Ancient Judaism. Supplements
JAOS	*Journal of the American Oriental Society*
JBL	*Journal of Biblical Literature*
JBTh	*Jahrbuch für biblische Theologie*
JJS	*Journal of Jewish Studies*
JNES	*Journal of Near Eastern Studies*
JQR	*Jewish Quarterly Review*
JSHRZ	Jüdische Schriften aus hellenistisch-römischer Zeit
JSJ	*Journal for the Study of Judaism*
JSJSup	Supplements to the Journal for the Study of Judaism
JSOT	*Journal for the Study of the Old Testament*
JSOTSup	Journal for the Study of the Old Testament. Supplement Series
JSP	*Journal for the Study of the Pseudepigrapha*
JSQ	*Jewish Studies Quarterly*
JTS	*Journal of Theological Studies*
KAT	Kommentar zum Alten Testament
LCL	Loeb Classical Library
MGWJ	*Monatsschrift für Geschichte und Wissenschaft des Judentums*
MoBi	Le Monde de la Bible
NEchtB	Neue Echter Bibel
NRTh	*La Nouvelle Revue Théologique*
NSK.AT	Neuer Stuttgarter Kommentar. Altes Testament
NTOA	Novum Testamentum et Orbis Antiquus
NTS	*New Testament Studies*
OBO	Orbis biblicus et orientalis
OTL	Old Testament Library
OTM	Oxford Theological Monographs
PEQ	*Palestine Exploration Quarterly*
PVTG	Pseudepigrapha Veteris Testamenti Graece
QD	Quaestiones disputatae
RB	*Revue biblique*

RechBib   Recherches bibliques
RGG   *Religion in Geschichte und Gegenwart*
RTP   *Revue des théologie et de philosophie*
SAA   State Archives of Assyria
SAGA   Studien zur Archäologie und Geschichte Altägyptens
SBA   Studies in Biblical Archaeology
SBLDS   Society of Biblical Literature. Dissertation Series
SBLSCS   Society of Biblical Literature. Septuagint an Cognate Studies
SBLSP   *Society of Biblical Literature. Seminar Papers*
SBS   Stuttgarter Bibelstudien
SCI   *Scripta Classica Israelica*
SJOT   *Scandinavian Journal of the Old Testament*
SNTSMS   Society for New Testament Studies. Monograph Series
SVTP   Studia in Veteris Testamenti pseudepigraphica
TAD   *Textbook of Aramaic Documents from Ancient Egypt*, ed. B.
                   Porten/A. Yardeni
TANZ   Texte und Arbeiten zum neutestamentlichen Zeitalter
TDNT   *Theological Dictionary of the New Testament*, ed. G. Kittel/G.
                   Friedrich, transl. G.W. Bromiley
Teubner   Bibliotheca scriptorum Graecorum et Romanorum Teubneriana
THAT   *Theologisches Handwörterbuch zum Alten Testament*, ed. E.
                   Jenni/C. Westermann
TRE   *Theologische Realenzyklopädie*, ed. G. Krause/G. Müller
TSAJ   Texte und Studien zum antiken Judentum
UTB   Uni-Taschenbücher
VT   *Vetus Testamentum*
VTSup   Supplements to Vetus Testamentum
VWGTh   Veröffentlichungen der wissenschaftlichen Gesellschaft für
                   Theologie
WA   Weimarer Ausgabe
WMANT   Wissenschaftliche Monographien zum Alten und Neuen
                   Testament
WUNT   Wissenschaftliche Untersuchungen zum Neuen Testament
ZAR   *Zeitschrift für Altorientalische und Biblische Rechtsgeschichte*
ZAW   *Zeitschrift für die alttestamentliche Wissenschaft*
ZBK   Zürcher Bibelkommentare
ZDMG   *Zeitschrift der deutschen morgenländischen Gesellschaft*
ZDPV   *Zeitschrift des deutschen Palästina-Vereins*
ZRGG   *Zeitschrift für Religions- und Geistesgeschichte*

Daniel R. Schwartz

The Hebrew University of Jerusalem

Judeans, Jews, and their Neighbors

Jewish Identity in the Second Temple Period

In 1856 one of the greatest Jewish historians of all time, Heinrich Graetz (1817–91), published volume III of his *Geschichte der Juden von den ältesten Zeiten bis auf die Gegenwart*. This volume, devoted to the period from 160 BCE to 70 CE, was entitled, *Geschichte der Juden von dem Tode des Juda Makkabi's bis zum Untergang des jüdischen Staates*. Graetz was fascinated by this period, as is evident from the fact that the volume went through four editions in his lifetime, growing by 50% from 572 to 858 pages – more editions, and much more growth, than any of the other ten volumes of his eleven-volume *Geschichte der Juden*.[1] Indeed, that is only proper for, as Graetz wrote in the *Vorwort* to this volume, the period to which it is devoted is the richest and most interesting of all periods of Jewish history ("*die interessanteste und anziehendste, aber auch die reichste der ganzen jüdischen Geschichte*").

I have taken Graetz's work as a point of departure because of a change he made in its title beginning with its third edition. If the first edition, in 1856, was dedicated to the history of the *Juden* since the death of Judas Maccabaeus and until the downfall *des jüdischen Staates*, and things were the same in the second edition (1863) too, beginning with the third edition, which appeared in 1878, the volume's title-page labeled it as dedicated to the history of the *Judäer* from the death of Judas Maccabaeus until the downfall *des judäischen Staates*. Correspondingly, throughout the hundreds of pages of the volume all occurrences of *Juden*, and of the corresponding adjective, *jüdisch*, were replaced by *Judäer* and *judäisch*. And that's the way, full of Judeans instead of Jews, Judean instead of Jewish, that the volume remained in subsequent editions. Graetz offers no explanation for this change, indeed, he makes no comment on it at all. But it is obvious that it points to an issue that was serious in his eyes.

I will return to Graetz later on, but first will note that the issue reflected here, in these deliberations in the middle of the nineteenth century, is one

---

[1] For a bibliography of Graetz's writings, including information on the editions of his *Geschichte*, see Brann, "Verzeichnis".

that is alive and well today, particularly in a context in which it is of very practical import – the translation of ancient texts. For a prominent example, note that the Loeb Classical Library edition of Josephus' works, published between the 1920s and the 1960s, includes volumes of Josephus' *Jewish War* and *Jewish Antiquities*, but the new "Flavius Josephus: Translation and Commentary" series, being published by Brill since 2000, has volumes of *Judean Antiquities* and one on the *Judean War*. I myself am currently working on preparing another volume for that series, on Books 18–20 of Josephus' *Antiquities*, and the present lecture is, among other things, part of my debate, with myself and with others, as to whether I should leave my files as they are, with "Jew" and "Jewish" throughout, or perhaps change those references, or some of them, to "Judean".[2]

One can approach this issue in different ways. The most obvious way to begin seems to be with dictionaries of our modern languages. What does "Jew" (or *Jude*) mean, in contrast to "Judean" (*Judäer*)? Answering that should help us decide which best corresponds to what the ancient texts meant when they used *Yehudi* in Hebrew, *Iudaios* in Greek, or *Iudaeus* in Latin.

If we go that route, we will easily discover that "Jew"/"Jude" denotes a person of a particular descent and/or religion (Judaism), while "Judean" denotes a person of a particular place (Judea). Thus, for some very standard and authoritative examples:

Judæan, Judean. [adjective:] Of or pertaining to Judæa or southern Palestine. [noun:] A native or inhabitant of this region.[3]

Jew. A person of Hebrew descent; one whose religion is Judaism; an Israelite.[4]

Judean, also *Judaean.* [adjective]: Of, relating to, or characteristic of ancient Judea. [noun]: An inhabitant of ancient Judea.[5]

Jew. A person belonging to the worldwide group constituting a continuation through descent or conversion of the ancient Jewish people and characterized by a sense of community; esp. one whose religion is Judaism.[6]

Judean. [adjective:]: of or pertaining to Judea. [noun:] a native or inhabitant of Judea.[7]

---

[2] The editor of the Brill series, Steve Mason, points to this "Judean" vs. "Jew" issue as an example of differences among various translators; see his "Series Preface", xi–xii.

[3] Simpson/Weiner (ed.), *Oxford English Dictionary*, 8:291.

[4] Simpson/Weiner (ed.), *Oxford English Dictionary*, 8:228.

[5] Grove (ed.), *Webster's Third New International Dictionary*, 1222–3.

[6] Grove (ed.), *Webster's Third New International Dictionary*, 1215.

[7] Stein (ed.), *Random House Dictionary*, 772.

Jew. 1. A person whose religion is Judaism. 2. one of a scattered group of people that traces its descent from the Biblical Hebrews or from post-exilic adherents of Judaism; Israelite.[8]

Jude. Angehöriger eines semitischen Volkes, einer religons- u. volksmässig zusammengehörenden, über die ganze Erde verstreuten Gemeinschaft.[9]

These definitions clearly indicate that when translating ancient Greek texts that refer to *Ioudaioi* we should use "Judean" when the text means to identify the person as a resident of Judea, or perhaps as a visitor or immigrant from Judea, but otherwise use "Jew". Sometimes this is simple. Thus, for example, when Josephus has someone report that Herod's grandson, Agrippa, was a *Ioudaios* and one of the most prominent people "there" (Ant. 18.196), it is evident that Josephus meant "Judean". When, on the other hand, numerous passages in Josephus (such as B.J. 2.487 and Ant. 18.257, and Ant. 19.278ff) refer to the troubles experienced by the *Ioudaioi* in Alexandria although they were century-long residents of that city, it would seem obvious that Josephus meant they were Jews, not Judeans. After all, the whole point of his stories about the *Ioudaioi* of Alexandria is that they encountered difficulties despite the fact that they had lived in Alexandria for centuries. They, and Josephus, would probably be quite miffed if we were to term them Judeans rather than Alexandrians.[10]

True, there is nothing impossible or unnatural about describing someone by the use of two geographical identifiers. Thus, for example, when we encounter texts that refer to Thracians in Alexandria or Athenians in Rome we have no trouble in understanding or translating them that way, no more than we have with modern texts that refer to Americans in Paris or Pakistanis in London, for example. What makes Judeans in Alexandria problematic is the fact that, as opposed to Thracians, Athenians, Americans, and Pakistanis, for which our languages have only one term each, our modern languages supply us, for *Ioudaioi*, with *two* words – "Jews" and also "Judeans". That means that any choice of one term amounts to a statement rejecting the other, especially since the word Judean is so rare in our modern languages (see note 9!) that anyone who chooses to use it, instead of Jew, is making a demonstrative statement, comparable, for example, to the statement made by someone who refers to a chairman as a "chairperson". That is: If I refer to a Thracian in Alexandria or an Athenian in Rome I have not

---

[8] Stein (ed.), *Random House Dictionary*, 767.

[9] Drosdowski (ed.), *Duden Deutsches Universalwörterbuch*, 650. This dictionary has no entry for *Judäer* or *judäisch*.

[10] Compare the case of one Helenos, who in an official petition of 5/4 BCE (*Corpus Papyrorum Judaicarum* II, no. 151) first termed himself an Alexandrian but then thought better and changed it, or was forced to change it, to "*Ioudaios* from Alexandria". See Modrzejewski, *Jews*, 164–5.

made any demonstrative statement about identifying the person in question in relation to his or her country rather than his or her ancestry or culture, because I did not have any choice about how to term the person. But if I choose to refer to ancient *Ioudaioi* as Judeans, as many urge us to do today, I am asserting that what made them *Ioudaioi* was their country, not their descent or their religion.

Indeed, the main exponents of using Judean throughout, in our discussion of ancient *Ioudaioi*, also argue that there was no such thing as religion in antiquity – not religion in general, and not Judaism in particular. Thus, for the prime examples, we find Steve Mason, who edits the Brill Josephus series that includes the volumes of *Judean Antiquities*, arguing in an important study in 2007 that it is not legitimate to speak of religion or of Judaism prior to the fourth century CE, when the Roman Empire adopted Christianity.[11] Daniel Boyarin goes even further and argues that Judaism as a "religion" did not exist in the premodern period.[12]

One type of response to these arguments is a very philological one. It entails a review of occurrences of the term *Ioudaios*, in Josephus and elsewhere, and an assessment, in each case, of what word available to us, today, best conforms to what the word connotes. Similarly, such a philological analysis would focus on the meaning of the term *Ioudaismos* in the few places it appears in ancient literature, asking whether its sense is not the same as that of our term "Judaism", which denotes a religion. I have undertaken something of those tasks elsewhere.[13]

Here, in contrast, I would attack the subject another way, one that is suggested by Graetz's experience.[14] Namely, Graetz's introductions to the successive editions of vol. 3 of his *Geschichte* all focus on the following question: Was the period of Jewish history covered by the volume, from the death of Judas Maccabeus until 70 CE, mainly religious in character or, rather, mainly political? That is, the question focuses not on the use of the word *Ioudaios* in any particular context but, rather, upon the types of issues that interested *Ioudaioi* qua *Ioudaioi*, and asks whether they are of the type of issues we normally understand as issues of state or, rather, as issues of religion. Graetz debates this question, very obviously preferring to define the period as religious but realizing that there was a lot of political orientation as well. At first he thought he could resolve the problem by saying the *Grundcharakter* of the period was religious but nevertheless qualifying that by characterizing the period as "political-religious". Eventually, apparently,

---

[11] Mason, "Jews".

[12] Boyarin, "Rethinking", esp. 8–12.

[13] See my "'Judaean'", and the appendix to my *Judeans*.

[14] For details about Graetz, see the fourth chapter of my *Judeans*.

Graetz realized that so much of what was happening in the period bespoke a political orientation – exemplified by the Hasmonean state, the Herodian state, and Jewish rebelliousness against Rome – that (beginning with the third edition) he changed all the *Juden* in the volume into *Judäer*.

Following in Graetz's footsteps, I propose that we revisit the question as to whether the *Ioudaioi* of whom we are speaking understood themselves more as residents of a country or as adherents of a religion. As a contribution to that, I propose to ask how some ancient works portrayed the *Ioudaioi* in contrast to others. I will focus on the first two Books of Maccabees, 1 Maccabees and 2 Maccabees – books that are full of reports of conflict between *Ioudaioi* and others, indeed, books that center upon Jewish rebellion and war against non-Jews and foreign powers. It seems likely that books with such contents will supply clear indications as to how their protagonists are defined, and upon examination it seems that the two books in fact give quite different answers.[15]

There is, of course, some basic similarity between the two books. They both begin by telling the story of the Hellenism, persecution, and rebellion – led by the Hasmoneans – in the days of the Seleucid king, Antiochus IV Epiphanes, down to the death of that king in 164 BCE and the Jewish restoration of the Temple of Jerusalem around the same time. After that, however, the respective scopes of the narratives differ greatly. While 2 Maccabees takes events down no further than 161 BCE, ending its story with Judas Maccabaeus's last great victory, 1 Maccabees gets to that point by ch. 7, but then continues, in chs. 8–16, to take the story down until the mid-130s, when the Hasmonean dynasty manages to achieve stability and more or less full independence. Thus, the first half of 1 Maccabees deals with the same period, and therefore with many of the same events, as the entirety of 2 Maccabees.

Apart from overlapping period and events, however, the differences between the two books are quite impressive. Here I would focus on some of those differences, and suggest that they culminate in the distinction between a Judean book and a Jewish book. Let us start with a very basic distinction. 1 Maccabees was originally in Hebrew, biblical Hebrew. That is plain from its Greek style, which is slavish translationese, as well as from other considerations. 2 Maccabees, in contrast, was originally composed in Greek. In fact, the editor (so-called Epitomator) who produced the work tells us (at 2 Macc 2:23) that it is based on a five-volume history by one Jason of Cyrene – a Jew of the Hellenistic Diaspora, part of the Ptolemaic kingdom, so the Greek is quite natural. 1 Maccabees, in contrast, was very evidently written by someone in Judea. That is clear both from the book's great interest in

---

[15] For a general comparison of the two books, see Nickelsburg, "1 and 2 Maccabees".

details of Judean geography as well as from the obvious closeness to the Hasmonean throne: 1 Maccabees is, basically, a dynastic history, that shows its readers how it happened, and why it is justified, that the Hasmonean family came to defeat the Seleucids and to rule Judea. The whole structure of the book is built to make that case. Thus, after ch. 1 presents the problem (foreign rule), chs. 2–16 tell the story of the Hasmonean solution, with successive sections of the book devoted to the tenures of the successive Hasmonean leaders: ch. 2 on Mattathias, chs. 3–9 on Judas, chs. 9–12 on Jonathan, and finally chs. 12–16 on Simon, including the long account in ch. 14 of how the people formally appointed Simon and his descendants to rule the country. When Simon was killed in ch. 16, he is succeeded by his son, John Hyrcanus, and with that the book ends – with the notice, in the work's very last words, that John inherited rule from his father. Thus, after a few rounds in which brother succeeded brother, the dynasty was finally established stably. Q.E.D.

2 Maccabees, in contrast, is not about the Hasmonean dynasty. Nor is the problem it addresses that of foreign rule. On the contrary, if the author of 1 Maccabees is very clear about just how bad foreign rule is, from its inception in the days of Alexander and especially in the period of Antiochus Epiphanes, the author of 2 Maccabees is just as insistent about Gentile rulers being, as a rule, just fine – and so Antiochus Epiphanes was just an unfortunate exception, a glitch. A comparison of the opening of the stories of the two books shows this clearly.[16]

Rather, the problem addressed by 2 Maccabees is one of sin, and the solution is one of atonement. After the first three chapters include introductory material and a story in ch. 3 about just how well God protects Jerusalem, ch. 4 reports Hellenization in Jerusalem, and that it led to negligence in the fulfillment of religious duties, and announces that this led to swift punishment, "for it is no trivial matter to be impious vis à vis the divine laws, as shall be shown by the next period" (4:17). Indeed, ch. 5 reports that Antiochus' forces attacked Jerusalem, murdering and enslaving tens of thousands of Jews, and robbing the Temple, and that is followed by Antiochus' decrees against Judaism, which result in much Jewish martyrdom – narrated in detail in chs. 6–7. The death of those martyrs worked atonement, and so, beginning in ch. 8, God again became reconciled with His people; 8:5, which announces that God's wrath had turned into mercy, is the turning-point of the entire book. From this point on, the rest of the book is a story of

---

[16] Compare 1 Macc 1:1–10, where Greek kings in general are terrible, a century and a half of their rule being summarized as "and they caused many evils on the earth" (v. 9) and so the wicked Antiochus Epiphanes was a natural outgrowth of such antecedents (v. 10), to 2 Macc 3:1–3 – the idyllic beginning of the story (after two chapters of introductory material), in which the Greek kings' benevolence, and respect for Judaism, is underlined.

how the Jews' fortunes improved: they became victorious in their wars against the Seleucids, Antiochus died a horrendous death, his successor revoked the decrees against Judaism, and after some more successful campaigning the Jews lived happily ever after. Thus, as Jan Willem van Henten put it in the title of his book about Second Maccabees, the Maccabean martyrs – not any rebels – were "the saviors of the Jewish people".[17] It was the martyrs' deaths that made God's wrath turn into mercy (as is said in 8:5), and from that point on events on the ground just have to work out the details, as it were: Judas wins his first victories in ch. 8, Antiochus dies a terrible death in ch. 9, Judas' forces retake Jerusalem and restore the Temple cult in ch. 10, etc., on down to the final victory in ch. 15.

1 Maccabees, in contrast, has no use for martyrs. They do not bring about any solution to the Jews' problems. Rather, they only illustrate, by being killed, how bad those problems were. If for 2 Maccabees the spilt blood of martyrs is effective, comparable to a sacrifice that works atonement,[18] for 1 Maccabees it's just spilt blood.[19] For 1 Maccabees, after all, the problem is not sin; the problem is foreign rule, and the way to put an end to that is not by being killed but, rather, by killing and otherwise defeating the foreigners. There is no reference at all in 1 Maccabees to Jewish sin engendering Jewish suffering, or atonement for such sins reversing the Jews' fortunes. Rather, the Jews' troubles are caused by Gentiles. That point, however, brings us to our topic: who *are* those Gentiles, and who, accordingly, are the *Ioudaioi*?

Turning first of all to 1 Maccabees, it is clear that the Gentiles are foreigners in the most basic, geographic sense. At several points, the book refers to the Jews' enemies as "the Gentiles roundabout".[20] Thus:

1 Macc 1:11   Come let us make a covenant with the Gentiles who are around us ...

     3:25   Fear and terror of Judas and his brothers began to fall upon the Gentiles around them.

     5:1   When the Gentiles roundabout heard ... they became very wrathful.

    5:10   The Gentiles roundabout us have gathered together against us to wipe us out [cf. 5:38].

---

[17] See van Henten, *Martyrs*.

[18] See especially 7:37–38 – the hope that the martyrs' death will bring about reconciliation with God.

[19] See esp. the contrast of the suffering at the end of ch. 1 to the rebellion in ch. 2, also the way the pious who die in 2:29–38 and 7:13–16 are contrasted to the Hasmonean rebels. On this theme, see my "Foils".

[20] On this theme, and its implications for the dating of 1 Maccabees, see Schwartz, "Israel".

>   5:57 Let us too make ourselves a name; let us go and fight the Gentiles
>   around us.
>
>   12:53 And all the peoples who were around them sought to wipe them out ...

Thus, the basic way this book defines non-*Ioudaioi* is as those who do not live in Judea, but only around it. Judea is conceived of as an isolated land, with borders, surrounded by regions inhabited by others who are very different from the *Ioudaioi*, and hostile to them. That implies that the *Ioudaioi* are what we would call Judeans.

However, things are more complicated than that, for 1 Maccabees is also very taken by the importance of *birth* in defining people. Thus, on the one hand, the Hasmoneans are the "seed" (*sperma*) that was chosen to save Israel (5:62), whereas those who are not of that "seed" are therefore doomed to defeat in battle; the Jews and the Spartans are said to be "brothers" because they are of "the *genos* of Abraham" (12:21). Similarly, on the other hand, when ch. 5 wants to explain what the Idumeans hoped to do, it refers to them as the sons of Esau and says they wanted to wipe out the seed (*genos*) of Jacob; etc.

If, then, we were to state what makes others others, for 1 Maccabees, the answer would be that they live elsewhere and are of different descent. That implies a world in which people who share common descent typically live each in their own lands. Probably "ethnic" or "national" is, accordingly, the best term to use for the criteria that distinguish people from one another.

If we now turn to the translation issue, however, and ask whether "Jew" or "Judean" best fits *Ioudaioi* whose world is defined that way, we get no clear answer. That is because, as we have seen, of the two parameters we are considering, geography and descent, English usage associates one, all by itself, with Judean, and the other, together with religion, with Jew. This requires us to go on and ask which of the two is more salient for 1 Maccabees. When we do that two criteria point to the geographic one:

1) *1 Maccabees makes no reference at all to the Jews of the Diaspora.* This is really quite striking: A book of history, which records delegations sent by the Hasmoneans as far as Rome and Sparta, and reports the Hasmoneans' involvement in events in Syria and awareness of events in Egypt, makes no reference at all to *Ioudaioi* living abroad – neither generally nor specifically. The closest we get to anything of the kind is the citation, in ch. 15, of a Roman letter in support of the Judeans, which was circulated to the rulers of various regions; some scholars have suspected that the choice of cities reflects the fact that there were Jewish communities in them.[21]

---

[21] So, for example, Gruen, *Diaspora*, 110.

Perhaps they are right. But 1 Maccabees makes no mention of such, and I see no logic that urges us to infer them despite that silence.[22]

Now, in contrast, I should explain that the definition of the Jews as sharing common birth is something that became particularly apposite, and, therefore, particularly popular, in the Persian period – the period that saw the restoration of the Second Temple but also the continued existence of a large Diaspora. In such circumstances, the easiest way to explain how they could all be members of the same collective was by pointing to the fact that they were all of the same "seed". Hence, it is no surprise to find, in the Persian period, Ezra calling the Jews "the holy seed" (Ezra 9:2), the Book of Esther referring to them as "the seed of the Jews" (Esther 6:13), and a prayer in the book of Nehemiah, that reviews biblical history, skipping directly from Creation to God's selection of Abraham, thus focusing its story on his descendants (Neh 9). If 1 Maccabees makes no reference to the Diaspora, it had no need to define the Jews by their descent. Or perhaps we should phrase that the other way around, and suggest that the author of 1 Maccabees was bespeaking a point of view that so unambiguously defined *Ioudaioi* with reference to Judea that it simply left Jews of the Diaspora beyond its horizon and, therefore, out of its scope. True, there are plenty of passages in the Bible that do the same, but by and large they reflect the First Temple period, when indeed there was no Diaspora. What is remarkable about 1 Maccabees is that it bespeaks the same point of view at a time when there was a huge Diaspora.

2) The lack of interest in the Diaspora goes hand in hand with a second factor. 1 Maccabees is very much focused on the land of Israel.[23] This is obviously the case insofar as its story is one of the establishment of Hasmonean rule in that country. Thus, for a salient example, the poem that opens ch. 14, which summarizes Simon's accomplishments, first summarizes that "And the land was quiet all the days of Simon" (14:4) and then goes on, later, to report that "he spread out the borders of his people, and conquered the land" (14:6), "and they were tending the land in peace, and the land gave its produce, the trees of the plain – their fruit" (14:8), "he made peace in the land, and Israel was joyous with great joy" (14:11). And so on; it is very clear that "Israel" and "the land" are essentially synonymous and coterminous. The same is also clear at the beginning of the story as well, where, in ch. 2, the author first reports that Mattathias and his men forcibly circumcised "all the uncircumcised children that they found within the

---

[22] As van Unnik roundly notes in his *Selbstverständnis*, 121: "In den Makkabäerbüchern spielt die Diaspora keine bedeutende Rolle. Aus dem Schreiben der Römer in I Makk. 15:16–24 lässt sich für unsere Frage nichts entnehmen …". That's all van Unnik discusses with regard to 1 Maccabees.

[23] On the land in 1 Maccabees see Mendels, *Land*, 47–50.

borders of Israel" (2:46), just as at 3:35–36 Antiochus is said to have given
orders "concerning the residents of Judea and Jerusalem", namely, to "destroy the strength of Israel and ... settle foreigners in all their borders" –
here too it is quite clear that "Israel" has its borders, and those are defined
as "Judea and Jerusalem". Similarly, when at 1 Macc 9:72–73 Jonathan
came to an arrangement with the Syrian general, Bacchides, ideal circumstances were again restored:

> 1 Macc 9:72 And [Bacchides] returned to him the captives he had earlier taken in
> the land of Judah, and he departed, returning to his land; he never
> again came within their borders.
>
> 73 And the sword ceased in Israel, and Jonathan resided in Michmash;
> and Jonathan began to judge the people and make the impious disap-
> pear from Israel.

All of these passages make it very clear that "the people", also known as
"Israel", has its territorial borders. And that corresponds, of course, to 1
Maccabees' failure to relate to the Jews of the Diaspora. Accordingly, if
above we saw that for this book *Ioudaioi* are defined by their land and their
descent, now we may add that the land is the primary category, so Judeans
would seem to be the appropriate term to use.

For 2 Maccabees, in contrast, things are very different. True, the book
focuses, formally, upon the history of a place, Jerusalem. The story opens
(in ch. 3) with everything being fine in the Holy City, and it ends with the
restoration of wonderful conditions there; as the author puts it, at the very
end of the story, "since ... ever since the city was taken over by the Hebrews
it has been in their hands, here I too will conclude this account" (15:37).[24]
But that should not mislead us into thinking that the main way the author
understands his protagonists is as residents of a land. Rather, he refers to
them as devotees of *Ioudaismos*, "Judaism" – a term for which this book is
the earliest evidence. Three times in the book he characterizes his heroes as
those who remained faithful to Judaism:

> 2 Macc 2:21 ... and the heavenly apparitions which occurred for those who nobly
> fought with manly valor for Judaism, so that although they were few
> in number they plundered the entire country and chased away the bar-
> baric hordes.
>
> 8:1 Judas Maccabaeus and those with him ... had been going in and out
> and around secretly to the villages, summoning their kinsmen and
> those who remained in Judaism; growing in numbers, they gathered
> together about 6000 men.

---

[24] On the translation of this verse, see my *2 Maccabees*, 556–7.

14:38 In the foregoing times of strife he had brought in a decision for Judaism and with complete intensity had risked body and soul for Judaism.

That, on the face of it, and along with the fact that the author was a *Ioudaios* of the Diaspora, should be enough to tell us that, for this book, *Ioudaioi* are not Judeans but, rather, what we call *Jews*, adherents of Judaism.

There has been, however, some recent debate about the meaning of *Ioudaismos* in 2 Maccabees. Namely, in the context of the increasing populari-
ty of the use of *Judeans*, a few scholars have claimed that *Ioudaismos* does
not refer to what we call Judaism, namely the Jewish religion, but, rather,
something else: Mason suggests it refers to the forcing of others to adopt
Jewish practices or support the Jews' cause,[25] and Boyarin suggests that it
"it doesn't mean Judaism the religion but the entire complex of loyalties
and practices that mark off the people of Israel" – a more general conglom-
erate of Jewish practices and characteristics, perhaps what we call Jewish
"culture".[26] I have no real quarrel about that with Boyarin; I consider the
Jewish religion to be a part of Jewish culture, what Cohen calls "Jewishness",[27] and so as long as we agree that "Judaism" refers to the things Jews
do because they are Jewish we can leave aside the question which of those
things are part of their religion and which of other parts of their culture.
Mason's argument, in contrast, appears to me to be unjustified, supported
by little more than the demands of his general theory. In fact, "Judaism" in
2 Maccabees seems to mean what it means for us; something which one can
practice, to which one can remain devoted; something to which a wicked
king might forbid people to declare allegiance (6:6) but to which some,
especially in villages outside of the king's supervision, might nonetheless
remain loyal (8:1). There is no reason to turn it into doing something to
others.

I have written about that elsewhere.[28] Here, in contrast, I would point to a
few aspects of 2 Maccabees that illustrate just how religiously-oriented the
book is. And I will do this by indicating, down the line, the contrast with 1
Maccabees, a contrast so thoroughgoing that it itself justifies, or perhaps
demands, the use of different nomenclature for the protagonists of the two
stories:

1) *Sin and atonement*: As noted above, 2 Maccabees tells a story of sin
and atonement; 1 Maccabees has neither.

2) *Miracles and apparitions*: 1 Maccabees reports nothing supernatural –
no miracles, no divine apparitions. 2 Maccabees is full of them: From the

---

[25] Mason, "Jews", 465–8.
[26] Boyarin, "Rethinking", 8.
[27] Cohen, *Beginnings*.
[28] For a detailed discussion, see the appendix to my *Judeans*.

horse and rider who descend from heaven (along with two handsome ruffians) to punish Heliodorus in 3:25–26 to the heavenly army over Jerusalem in 5:2–4, the heavenly horsemen that descend to protect Judas in 10:29–30 and another who leads his troops in 11:8, and finally to the appearance of Onias and Jeremiah in Judas Maccabaeus' dream reported at 15:12–16, which dream was so real that Judas actually received from Jeremiah the sword he then goes on to use to defeat the Syrian general, God is visibly active in the story from beginning to end. Nothing like those episodes appears in 1 Maccabees, and although it too reports that Judas acquired a special sword, it says he took it from a fallen enemy general after valiantly defeating him in battle (3:11–12).

3) *Poetic justice*: The assertion that the fate of villains corresponds to their crimes is a more subtle way of asserting God's providential and just control of events – and it too is absent from 1 Maccabees but frequently found in 2 Maccabees. Thus, for some examples: A temple-robber was killed by an angry Jewish mob near the Temple treasury (4:42);[29] Jason was exiled because he had exiled others (5:9);[30] Antiochus had persecuted the innards of others (by forcing them to eat impure foods) and so he died "very justly" with great pains in his innards (9:6); the only Jews who died in battle were discovered to have been wearing idolatrous amulets under their tunics, which shows that God "judges righteously and makes the hidden things visible" (12:40–41); and Menelaus died "very justly" in ashes because he had defiled the ashes of the altar (13:7–8).

4) *Prayer*: Here the picture is not as totally one-sided, for there are some prayers and references to prayer in 1 Maccabees. However, beginning with ch. 5 they are very few and far between, and usually no more than a brief reference that is not much more than pro forma.[31] In 2 Maccabees, in contrast, prayers are numerous and often long, throughout the book, and they

---

[29] For a similar point elsewhere in Jewish Hellenistic literature, note Philo's *In Flaccum* 115: the wicked Flaccus, who had destroyed innumerable hearths of his innocent victims, was arrested at his own hearth. See also ibid., 170–4 and esp. 189: "Justice" saw to it that the number of Flaccus' wounds, in being executed, corresponded precisely to the number of his victims.

[30] Here the author uses paronomasia to underline the irony: *apoksenōsas epi ksenēs apōleto*.

[31] Prayers or references to prayer in 1 Maccabees after ch. 4: 5:33; 7:36–38, 40–42; 9:46 (a call to prayer); 11:71; 12:11 (mention of prayer in a diplomatic missive); 13:47, 51 (psalms in the wake of military success), 16:3 (a banal expression of hope for help from heaven). Note especially the contrast between the news of invasion in 3:42, which engenders twelve verses of prayer, and the prayer-less reception of similar news at 5:16, 6:28ff, 9:6, 10:74, 12:24, and 13:1; the closest we get to prayer in such contexts is the banal "may help from heaven be with you" in 16:3. Similarly, contrast the post-victory prayer at 4:24 with its absence at 7:47 (contrast the prayers at same occasion according to 2 Macc 15:34!), 10:87, 11:74, 12:33–35, and 16:10. As for why things change beginning with ch. 5 (although note the sacrifices at 5:54), see below, note 35.

are answered.[32] This, of course, corresponds to the book's emphasis upon God's active providence; time and again the book points out, explicitly, that it was God who made things happen.[33]

5) *"Luck/fate"*: In contrast, 1 Maccabees clearly states, at three important junctures, that something blind exerts control over events. The term it uses for such luck or fate is *kairos*, literally "point in time, moment". Thus:

– at 9:10 Judas refuses to flee the field of battle despite overwhelming odds against him, saying that if his *kairos* had come to die he would rather do so without staining his honor;

– at 12:1 Jonathan realizes that the *kairos* was going his way and so he seized the opportunity to send ambassadors to Rome; and

– at 15:33–34 Simon notes that at some past *kairos* others had conquered the Judeans' ancestral lands and now when "we have the *kairos*" his forces had retaken them.

Whether this *kairos* is conceived of as blind uncontrolled luck or rather astrologically, or some other way,[34] what is important for the contrast with 2 Maccabees is that *kairos* has nothing to do with a providential God.

What all these points amount to is quite simple: 2 Maccabees, a work bespeaking the circumstances of diasporan Jews who, qua Jews, have no army and can depend only upon God to protect them, tells a story that focuses on the Jews' covenant with God and His protective care of them so long as they observe His laws or, if they sin, when they see to atoning for their sins via suffering and martyrdom. 1 Maccabees, in contrast, written on behalf of a dynasty that undertook to put an end to foreign domination of Judea, successfully did so, and was very impressed with its own accomplishments and saw them as justifying its claim to rule the newly established Judean state, tells a story that focuses upon that dynasty and leaves God, by and large, out of the picture. Indeed, beginning with ch. 5 the book hardly mentions Him.[35] But if 2 Maccabees is a book about God and those who are

---

[32] Prayers or references to prayer in 2 Maccabees 3–15 (the body of the story): 3:14–15, 18–21, 30; 5:4; 7 passim; 8:2–4; 10:16, 25–26, 38; 11:6; 12:6, 28, 41–44; 13:10–12; 14:15, 34–36, 46; 15:21–24, 26–27, 29, 34.

[33] Suffice it to say that the great power of God, and His providential care for the Jews, is the lesson learned by all those who attacked the Jews: 3:36–39; 8:36; 9:11–17; 11:13. For another dramatic presentation of the same point in another Hellenistic Jewish work, see Philo's *In Flaccum* 170.

[34] On the senses of *kairos* in the Septuagint see Delling, *"kairos"*, 458–9. Finkelstein, *"Kairos"* points especially to Polybius 3.30.4 and 18.22.8 (another historiographical work of the second century BCE), where *kairos* appears in the sense of "fate"; the formulation of 3.30.4 is quite similar to that in 1 Macc 15:33–34.

[35] *Theos* ("God") is not mentioned at all in 1 Maccabees, and after the first few chapters, which may reflect a generation that was still more biblically oriented, there is hardly any other reference to the Deity ("the Lord" [*Kyrios*] appears for the last time in ch. 5, and even "Heaven" is mentioned only three times after that chapter). The difference between the first four chapters of the

faithful to Him, while 1 Maccabees is a book that ignores Him and focuses upon a dynasty that founded a state, the former has what we would term a religious orientation while the latter focuses upon a country – which means that although the Greek text of both books uses *Ioudaioi* it is appropriate for us, when translating these works into English, which offers two words, to use "Jews" for 2 Maccabees but "Judeans" for 1 Maccabees.

In moving toward a conclusion, I would like to enlarge a bit upon this conclusion. What I have just now suggested is that these two works of the second century BCE point to a fundamental distinction between the orientation of ancient Judeans and that of Jews of the Diaspora. While it is of course difficult to know how representative these two works are, of their respective contexts, there is no reason to think they are exceptional. 1 Maccabees, certainly, was written to be a representative work; it is a dynastic history, prepared by the court historian, and obviously reflects that dynasty's orientation. As for 2 Maccabees, the religious and universal nature of its values are very similar to those of the more or less contemporary *Letter of Aristeas* and the somewhat later 3 Maccabees (which has nothing to do with the Maccabees); all three of these works of the Hellenistic Diaspora (presumably – of Alexandria) bespeak similar attitudes that we may characterize as religious and universal, focusing upon God and religious values and not upon any particular state (a point that is particularly striking about 2 Maccabees since its story does focus upon Judea). Moreover, 2 Maccabees serves, in its current form, to invite its readers to celebrate the Hanukkah festival (see the two opening letters), and the end of the work seems to show the original work too was meant to justify the celebration of a holiday;[36] that is, the book was meant for a broad audience. Now I would add, however briefly, that the same basic distinction we have noted, between 1 and 2 Maccabees, between Judeans and Jews, maintains itself in other contexts as well, in the Second Temple period. I will point to two other expressions of the same distinction, and thus, I hope, further clarify its basic nature.[37]

The contrast between priestly Judaism and Pharisaic/rabbinic Judaism is widely recognized. Priestly religion – represented for us by the ancient Sadducees and the Qumran sect – focused upon a particular place and upon

---

book, which culminate with the dedication of the Temple, and the story of the wars thereafter (chs. 5–16), which we have noticed above (note 31) with regard to prayers and now with regard to reference to God, seems to indicate a difference in sources: whoever edited the book, in the last third of the second century BCE, perforce used earlier materials in preparing the first part of his story, and, as we see, in those pre-state years the religious elements were more salient. For more such differences between early and late in 1 Maccabees, see my "Mattathias' Final Speech".

[36] See Momigliano, "Second Book", 88, and my *2 Maccabees*, 7–10.

[37] These two contexts are discussed in some detail in chs. 2–3 of my *Judeans and Jews*.

people of a particular pedigree: it claimed that all the most important tasks assigned to religion, including atonement – the maintenance of a proper relationship with God – could only be fulfilled at the Temple of Jerusalem and must be mediated by Aaronite priests. Rabbinic religion, in contrast, claimed that God was equally accessible everywhere, and that any man, regardless of his descent, including a convert, could be a rabbi. That means, however, that priestly religion corresponds well to 1 Maccabees – which is, indeed, a book about the rise of a dynasty of high priests, a dynasty that, at the height of its flourishing, became Sadducean.[38] Pharisaic-rabbinic religion, in contrast, corresponds well to 2 Maccabees, which emphasizes that God resides in heaven (3:39; 14:34–35), which is spread over all people equally, and that it is the individual's choice to remain faithful to Judaism, not his birth, that makes the difference. Indeed, if 2 Maccabees is a book of the Diaspora, rabbinic Judaism flourished in the Diaspora – in contrast to priestly Judaism, which basically disappeared, understandably, with the destruction of the Second Temple.[39]

The other context upon which I would focus is that of the writings of Flavius Josephus, especially upon the contrast between his War, written in the 70s of the first century, and his Antiquities, written in the 90s. Josephus, who was born in 37 CE and lived the first half of his life as a priest of Jerusalem, accompanied Titus to Rome after the destruction of Jerusalem and lived the rest of his life there, devoting his time to chronicling his people's past. As it happens, the first two books of his first work, War, which lead up to the outbreak of the rebellion in 66 CE, cover ground that he again covered twenty years later, in his Antiquities. This allows us to make numerous comparisons between his values and orientation shortly after he got off the boat after decades in Judea, and those to which he subscribed after twenty years in the Diaspora. Such comparisons can be quite instructive, and often they indicate, I believe, that those decades saw the transformation of Josephus from a Judean into a Jew. I will offer three brief examples:

---

[38] For the mid-Hasmoneans' turn to Sadduceeism see esp. Josephus Ant. 13.296 and 401; Geller, "Alexander". For the Sadducee-(high-)priest nexus, see e.g. Acts 5:17.

[39] Cf. Goodman, "Religious Variety".

War 1 (trans. Thackeray [LCL])	*Antiquities* 14 (trans. Marcus [LCL] and D.R.S.)
(146) Indeed, the labors of the Romans would have been endless, had not Pompey taken advantage of the seventh day of the week, on which the Jews, from **religious scruples (*thrēskeia*)**, refrain from all manual work ...	(63) But if it were not our ancestral custom to rest on the Sabbath day, the earthworks would not have been finished, because the Jews would have prevented this; for the **Law (*nomos*) permits** us to defend ourselves against those who begin a battle and strike us, but it does not **allow** us to fight against an enemy that does anything else.
(148) Just as if the city had been wrapt in profound peace, the daily sacrifices, the expiations and all the ceremonies of **worship (*thrēskeia*)** were scrupulously performed to the honor of God. And at the very hour when the temple was taken, when they were being massacred about the altar, they never desisted from the **religious rites (*thrēskeia*)** for the day.	(65) And one may get an idea of the extreme piety which we show toward God **and of our strict observance of the laws (*nomoi*)** from the fact that during the siege the priests were not hindered from performing any of the sacred ceremonies through fear, but twice a day, in the morning and at the ninth hour, they performed the sacred ceremonies at the altar, and did not omit any of the sacrifices even when some difficulty arose because of the attacks.
(150) Then it was that many of the priests, seeing the enemy advancing sword in hand, calmly continued their sacred ministrations, and were butchered in the act of pouring libations and burning incense; putting the **worship (*therapeia*)** of the Deity above their own preservation.	(67) ... nor were they compelled, either by fear for their lives or by the great number of those already slain, to run away, but thought it better to endure whatever they might have to suffer there beside the altars than to neglect any of the **ordinances (*nomima*)**.[40]

---

[40] On the use of *nomima* for legal requirements of a status less than that of laws (*nomoi*), hence my "ordinances", see Ant. 13.296–7 and especially the way that text is echoed at Ant. 13.408: the former says that Hyrcanus abrogated the Pharisees' *nomima* and the latter says that "if there was anything, even (!) of the *nomima*", that the Pharisees had introduced and Hyrcanus had abrogated, Salome restored it. Note also Plato Laws 7.793a-d and Philo's very explicit statement in Hypothetica 7.6, where he distinguishes between unwritten *ethē* (customs), *nomima*, and "the *nomoi* themselves". Thus, by using *nomima* here Josephus is praising the priests for their perseverance in fulfilling even the least of their legal obligations.

War 1 (trans. Thackeray [LCL])	*Antiquities* 17 (trans. D.R.S.)
(648) There were in the city two wise men who were thought to be especially accurate concerning the ancestral (customs), and for that reason they enjoyed the highest respect in the entire nation. (650) For it is (they said) not allowed[41] that there be **in the Temple** any image or bust or any work representing a living being.	(149) There were ... the most learned of the Jews and unparalleled expounders of the **ancestral laws**, men who were loved by the people due to the education (which they supplied) the youth ... (151) For **the law forbids** those who choose to live according to it to imagine setting up images and to prepare dedications of any living beings.

War (trans. Thackeray [LCL])	*Antiquities* (trans. Marcus [LCL] and D.R.S.)
(1.287) (Herod's brother, Joseph) was on the point of leaving the fortress, when on the very night fixed for his departure, rain fell in abundance ...	(14.390–1) But he was stopped by a rain which **God** sent in the night, for once the cisterns were filled with water, they no longer needed to flee ...
(1.340–1) That evening, Herod, having dismissed his companions to refresh themselves after their fatigues, went himself just as he was, yet hot from the fight, to take a bath, like any common soldier, for only a single slave attended him. Before he entered the bath-house one of the enemy ran out in front of him ...	(14.462) At this point the king ordered his soldiers to have their supper, as it was late, and he himself, being tired out, went into a room to bathe. And here he came into very great danger, but **by the providence of God** escaped it ...
(1.656) From this point on onwards Herod's malady began to spread to his whole body and his sufferings took a variety of forms ...	(17.168) But Herod's illness became more and more acute, for **God** was afflicting just punishment upon him for his lawless deeds ...
(2.183) Yielding to these solicitations, Herod presented himself to Gaius, who punished him for his cupidity by banishing him to Spain.	(18.255) Gaius, angered by her high spirit, exiled her together with Herod and gave her possessions to Agrippa. This, then, was the judgment with which **God** punished Herodias for her envy of her brother, and Herod for having listened to frivolous womanly words.

---

[41] According to Danker, *Lexicon*, 24, *athemitos* "refers primarily not to what is forbidden by ordinance but to violation of tradition or common recognition of what is seemly or proper".

Here we see Josephus, after twenty years in the Diaspora, formulating devotion to cult as an instance of devotion to Law; law is the major category, and is one that is quite functional for Jews abroad. Similarly, he recognizes that being Jewish is a matter of choice; if a baby born in Judea is Judean by nature, a baby born in Rome is a Roman by nature and it is only the parents' decision, or eventually that of the individual him- or herself, that will make the individual Jewish despite Roman birth. And, most thoroughly, Josephus introduces God into the story. In all of these ways, therefore, Josephus's writings testify to his transformation from Judean into Jew, and if Josephus' *War* should be called the *Judean War*, his *Antiquities* should be termed the *Antiquities of the Jews*.

Thus, it seems that the distinction between 1 and 2 Maccabees is just an example, if a salient and relatively early example, of a basic dichotomy in Judaism of the Second Temple period – one between the values and orientations that typified Judeans and functioned well for them, and those that typified Jews of the Diaspora. It was this dichotomy that made it so difficult for Graetz to decide how to characterize the period: Within his basic scheme of the First Temple period being state-oriented and the period after 70 being that of exile, he couldn't pin the Second Temple period down one way or the other, so in the end he settled for a bit of legerdemain. Namely, between the Israelites of the First Temple period and the Jews of the post-70 period he eventually inserted Judeans, beginning with his 1878 edition, as if the use of the new term could give a unified definition to the *Ioudaioi* of the period. In fact, however, they cannot be defined in a unified way, and it is that which makes the period so rich and interesting, as Graetz put it. It seems, therefore, that we are better served, if, taking advantage of the fact that our modern languages offer us two terms, Jews and Judeans, *Juden* and *Judäer*, we indeed use both. I propose, accordingly, that we use *Judeans* when dealing with such contexts and phenomena as 1 Maccabees, as the priestly sects, and the early Josephus, but *Jews* when dealing with such diasporan phenomena and contexts as 2 Maccabees, Pharisaic and rabbinic Judaism, and Josephus' later works. Such non-unified nomenclature has its prices, but it seems best to correspond to the facts as they present themselves. The prices may well be outweighed by the way that the use of such differentiated nomenclature points to real differences and encourages students of this formative period to study their implications.

References

Boyarin, D., "Rethinking Jewish Christianity: An Argument for Dismantling a Dubious Category (to which is Appended a Correction of my *Border Lines*)", *JQR* 99 (2009/10) 7–36.

Brann, M., "Verzeichnis von H. Graetzens Schriften und Abhandlungen", *MGWJ* 61 (1917) 444–91.

Cohen, S.J.D., *The Beginnings of Jewishness: Boundaries, Varieties, Uncertainties* (HCS 31; Berkeley: University of California, 1999).

Danker, F.W. (ed.), *A Greek-English Lexicon of the New Testament and Other Early Christian Literature* (based on W. Bauer's Griechisch-deutsches Wörterbuch; Chicago: Chicago University, [3]2000).

Delling, G., "*kairos*", *TDNT* 3 (2004) 458–9.

Drosdowski, G. (ed.), *Duden Deutsches Universalwörterbuch* (Mannheim: Dudenverlag, 1983).

Finkelstein, A., "*Kairos* in I Maccabees: A Non-Biblical Concept in a Biblically-Styled Book" (unpublished M.A. thesis, Hebrew University of Jerusalem, 2004).

Geller, M.J., "Alexander Jannaeus and the Pharisee Rift", *JJS* 30 (1979) 202–11.

Goodman, M., "Religious Variety and the Temple in the Late Second Temple Period and Its Aftermath", in S. Stern (ed.), *Sects and Sectarianism in Jewish History* (IJS Studies in Judaica 12; Leiden/Boston: Brill, 2011) 21–37.

Grove, P.B. (ed.), *Webster's Third New International Dictionary of the English Language, Unabridged* (Springfield: Merriam, 1976).

Gruen, E., *Diaspora: Jews Amidst Greeks and Romans* (Cambridge: Harvard, 2002).

Mason, S., "Series Preface", in L.H. Feldman, *Flavius Josephus: Judean Antiquities, Books 1–4* (Flavius Josephus: Translation and Commentary 3; Leiden: Brill, 2000) ix–xii.

–, "Jews, Judaeans, Judaizing, Judaism: Problems of Categorization in Ancient History", *JSJ* 38 (2007) 457–512.

Mendels, D., *The Land of Israel as a Political Concept in Hasmonean Literature* (TSAJ 15; Tübingen: Mohr, 1987).

Modrzejewski, J.M., *The Jews of Egypt from Rameses II to Emperor Hadrian* (Philadelphia/Jerusalem: Jewish Publication Society, 1995).

Momigliano, A., "The Second Book of Maccabees", *Classical Phililogy* 70 (1975) 81–8.

Nickelsburg, G.W.E., "1 and 2 Maccabees – Same Story, Different Meaning", *Concordia Theological Monthly* 42 (1971) 515–26.

Schwartz, D.R., "'Judaean' or 'Jew'? How Should We Translate *Ioudaios* in Josephus?", in J. Frey et al (ed.), *Jewish Identity in the Greco-Roman World: Jüdische Identität in der griechisch-römischen Welt* (AJEC 71; Leiden: Brill, 2007) 3–27.

–, *2 Maccabees* (CEJL; Berlin: de Gruyter, 2008).

–, "Foils or Heroes? On Martyrdom in First and Second Maccabees", *AJS Perspectives* (Spring 2009) 10–11.

–, "Mattathias' Final Speech (1 Maccabees 2): From Religious Zeal to Simonide Propaganda", in A.M. Maier et al. (ed.), *"Go Out and Study the Land" (Judges 18:2): Archaeological, Historical and Textual Studies in Honor of Hanan Eshel* (Leiden: Brill, 2012) 213–23.

–, *Judeans and Jews: Four Faces of Dichotomy in Ancient Jewish History* (forthcoming).

Schwartz, S., "Israel and the Nations Roundabout: I Maccabees and the Hasmonean Expansion", *JJS* 42 (1991) 16–38.

Simpson, J.A./Weiner, E.S.C. (ed.), *The Oxford English Dictionary* (Oxford: Clarendon, [2]1989).

Stein, J. (ed.), *The Random House Dictionary of the English Language* (New York: Random House, 1971).

van Henten, J.W., *The Maccabean Martyrs as Saviours of the Jewish People: A Study of 2 and 4 Maccabees* (JSJSup 57; Leiden: Brill, 1997).

van Unnik, W.C., *Das Selbstverständnis der jüdischen Diaspora in der hellenistisch-römischen Zeit* (ed. P.W. van der Horst; AGJU 17; Leiden: Brill, 1993).

Thomas Römer

Collège de France Paris

Université de Lausanne

Conflicting Models of Identity and the Publication of the Torah in the Persian Period

Introduction:
The Positive View of the Persians in the Hebrew Bible

If you read the three parts of the Hebrew Bible you get the impression that it ends with the Persian period. In the *Nebiim* Haggai, Zechariah and Malachi, the last of the twelve Prophets, are situated under the Persians, and the *Ketubim*, according to most Hebrew manuscripts, end with the permission of the Persian king for rebuilding the Temple and the appeal to come back to Jerusalem: "Thus says King Cyrus of Persia: Yhwh, the God of heaven, has given me all the kingdoms of the earth, and he has charged me to build him a house at Jerusalem, which is in Judah. Whoever is among you of all his people, may the Lord his God be with him! Let him go up" (2 Chron 36:23).

As in Second Isaiah, Cyrus appears to have been chosen to restore Judah and to invite the Babylonian Diaspora to do their *Aliyah*. It is interesting that this "open end" of the *Ketubim* does not respect chronology since the story about restoration of Jerusalem, its Temple and the promulgation of the Law is told in the books of Ezra and Nehemiah which were placed before Chronicles.

It might be possible that Chronicles was written later than the oldest parts of Ezra and Nehemiah, perhaps during the Hellenistic period, as suggested by Welten and others.[1] Still it is interesting that there are no direct allusions to events from the Greek period.

The same holds true for the Latter Prophets. Several European scholars have argued that the latest redactions of many prophetic books were undertaken during the Hellenistic period,[2] and that the scroll of Jonah was written at that time, but here again the redactors did not introduce clear allusions to

---

[1] Welten, *Geschichte*; Willi, *Chronik*.
[2] See for instance Steck, *Abschluß*.

that time. To this one can compare the idea found in the Talmud that prophecy ended in the Persian period.[3]

The Persian period is apparently considered as an accomplishment of sorts. This fits well with the fact that the Persian kings and the Persian Empire are, in the Bible, never said to be an abomination and are never condemned, as is the case for the Egyptians, the Assyrians and the Babylonians. There may be some Persian individuals who act badly, as narrated in the book of Esther, but once their intrigues are thwarted, the Persian king will act favorably with regard to the Jews.

Even if there is little extra-biblical evidence for the theory of the so-called Imperial Authorization in order to explain the publication of the Torah, the fact remains that the biblical accounts about the promulgation of the Law present Ezra as acting in conformity with the will of the Achaemenid ruler. According to Ezra 7, Ezra is sent by order of the Persian king in order to publish a Law, which is the law of Ezra's god and also the law of the Persian ruler (v. 28), and Ezra's God is also the God of heaven (v. 23: אלה שמיא).

Should Ezra's accreditation letter be a creation from the early Hellenistic period, as argued by Grätz,[4] it is all the more interesting that it reveals an attempt to identify Ezra's law with the law or at least the will of the Persian king.

What are the reasons for this very positive view of the Persians? The answer may be twofold. First, the Judeans considered them as "liberators" since they had vanquished the Babylonians, who had destroyed the temple and deported important parts of the population. Second, the Persians were apparently quite liberal with regard to the internal affairs of the people incorporated into the Empire, as long as they were loyal and paid their taxes.

The pro-Persian attitude of an important segment of Judean intellectuals can be detected in the different reactions to the events of 587, which were written down at the beginning of the Persian period and which can be labeled as "crisis literature".

---

[3] Babylonian Talmud, Sanhedrin 11a: "Our Rabbis taught: Since the death of the last prophets, Haggai, Zechariah and Malachi, the Holy Spirit [of prophetic inspiration] departed from Israel"; Baba Batra 12b: "Since the day when the Temple was destroyed, prophecy has been taken from the prophets and given to the wise".

[4] Grätz, *Edikt*.

The Origins of the Hebrew Bible:
A reaction to the Crisis of the Loss of the Temple and the Land

In his book "Krisensemantik: Wissenssoziologische Untersuchungen auf einem Topos moderner Zeiterfahrung" Steil investigates the concept of crisis in the context of the French revolution and delineates three reactions to this crisis that he characterizes in the following way, using a terminology inspired by the work of Max Weber.[5]

	Prophet	Priest	Mandarin
Situation	Marginal	Representative of the former power	Belonging to the high officials
Legitimization	"Personal knowledge"	Tradition	Intellectual instruction
Semantic of crisis	Hope for a better future	Return to mythical origins	Construction of a history
Reference	Utopia	Myth	"History"

The attitude of the "Prophet" considers the crisis as the beginning of a new era. The representatives of this view are people who stand somewhat at the margins of society, but who are nevertheless able to communicate their views. They legitimate their discourse by appealing to personal inspiration. The "priestly attitude" reflects the position of representatives of the collapsed social, political and religious structures. Their approach to overcoming the crisis is to valorize the time of "origins" and the God-given institutions that reflect the divine will. The so-called "mandarin position" sums up the attitude of high officials who try to construct a discourse in order to understand the irruption of the crisis. They also try to maintain their former privileges through the construction of a historiography that provides the reasons for the breakdown of the former structures and that makes them appear as the experts of "history".

Interestingly, Steil created this terminology without any allusion to the Bible. It seems to me a very helpful model for discerning the construction of post-587 identities in different intellectual groups.

As far as we can see in Ancient Near Eastern texts there are mainly two ways to explain military disasters. Either the national god has become angry with his people and abandons them (Mesha stela, poem of Erra) or the na-

---

[5] Steil, *Krisensemantik*; for the following see also Römer, "L'Ancien Testament".

tional deity has been defeated by the more powerful gods of the invaders (Assyrian propaganda; see 2 Kings 18). The first model is adopted in the prophetic discourse, while the second is denied in different ways by the "Mandarins" and the "Priests".

The Prophetic Discourse of the Early Persian Period

Isaiah chapters 40–55 were perhaps originally conceived as an independent collection of (anonymous) salvation oracles that arose at the end of the Babylonian or the beginning of the Persian era and that were later added to the scroll of Isaiah. Like the "Deuteronomists", Second Isaiah understands the fall of Jerusalem as a sign of divine wrath, which leads Yhwh to hide himself and not to intervene in favor of his people: "I was angry with my people, I profaned my heritage" (Isa 47:6). This idea comes close to the Nabonidus Inscription where the destruction of Harran and the sanctuary of Sîn is explained as follows: "Sîn, the king of all gods, became angry with his city and his temple, and went up to heaven and the city and the people became desolate".[6]

An inscription of Esarhaddon also relates exile to divine wrath but insists that the deity changes quickly from anger to mercy: "Seeing this, the Enlil of the gods, Marduk, got angry. His mind became furious, and he made an evil plan to disperse the land and its people ... Though he had written 70 years as the length of its abandonment the merciful Marduk quickly relented, reversed the order of the numerical symbols, and ordered its resettlement for the 11th year" (Inscription of Esarhaddon).[7]

Similarly, texts in Second Isaiah claim that Yhwh's anger does not last for a long time ("For a brief moment I abandoned you, but with great compassion I will gather you. In overflowing wrath for a moment I hid my face from you, but with everlasting love I will have compassion on you, says Yhwh, your Redeemer", Isa 54:7–8) and that this time of wrath has definitely come to an end. The crisis is a turning point here towards a new creation, the arrival of Cyrus being compared to a messianic era.

Interestingly the attitude of the author(s) of Isa 40–55 is to take on the official rhetoric of the Cyrus cylinder and to proclaim him, by doing so, Yhwh's messiah for Israel and the world.[8]

---

[6] Harran Inscription, quoted according to ANET, 560–2.

[7] Quoted after Parpola, *Assyrian Prophecies*.

[8] www.britishmuseum.org/research/search_the_collection_database/search_object_details.aspx ?objectid=327188&partid=1 (08/11/2011).

Cyrus Cylinder		Second Isaiah	
12	He (Marduk) took under his hand Cyrus, ...	45:1	Cyrus, whose right hand I took
	and called him by his name	45:3	I, Yhwh, the God of Israel, call you by your name.
13	He made the land of the Qutu and all the Medean troops prostrate themselves at his feet	45:1	to subdue nations before him
	while he shepherded in justice and righteousness the black-headed people	44:28	who says of Cyrus, 'He is my Shepherd',
15	like a friend and companion, he (Marduk) walked at his side.	45:2	I will walk before you
32	I collected together all of their people and returned them to their settlements, ...	45:13	I have aroused Cyrus ... and I will make all his paths straight; he shall build my city and set my exiles free ...

The Persian ruler is praised as Yhwh's liberator who will inaugurate a new future, which, according to another passage, shall make everyone forget the "former events":

Isa 43:16 Thus says Yhwh, who makes a way in the sea, a path in the mighty waters,

17 who brings out chariot and horse, army and warrior; they lie down, they cannot rise, they are extinguished, quenched like a wick:

18 Do not remember the former things, or consider the things of old.

19 I am about to do a new thing; now it springs forth, do you not perceive it? I will make a way in the wilderness and rivers in the desert.

20 The wild animals will honor me, the jackals and the ostriches; for I put water in the wilderness, rivers in the desert, to give drink to my chosen people,

21 the people whom I formed for myself so that they might declare my praise.

According to Jean-Daniel Macchi this passage was added in the 5th or 4th century BCE into the Isaianic corpus.[9] The "first things" (ראשנות) allude to the divine judgments and especially to the destruction of Jerusalem. The author claims that they are not worth any longer to be remembered since a new era has arrived and the page of remembering the past can now be

---

[9] Macchi, "Ne ressassez plus".

turned. This is in fact an anti-Dtr position because, as we will point out, for the Deuteronomists the fall of Jerusalem and the exile are at the very center of their theological reflection.

Contrary to Second Isaiah where the new era that follows the crisis is understood to happen immediately, the majority of the prophetic books underwent an "eschatological" or a "salvation" oriented redaction, which often added a new positive ending to the scrolls, suggesting that the oracles of doom had been realized and that the era of disaster can now be turned into a better future. This is, for instance, the case with the book of Amos in which the two last verses announce the restoration of Yhwh's people in their land, or equally the book of Joel, which ends with the promise that Judah and Jerusalem will be inhabited forever and that Yhwh will dwell on his holy mountain.

One may conclude that many prophetic books were revised during the Persian period from an eschatological perspective; this may partially be understood as a reaction to the fact that the revolutionary announcement of a paradise-like situation in Second Isaiah did not come true. Contrary to most of the prophetic books, which have a future-oriented perspective, the "mandarin attitude" of the Deuteronomists maintains a focus on divine judgment and exile.

The So-Called Deuteronomistic History and its Revision in the First Half of the Persian period

Noth's idea that the books of Deuteronomy through Kings constitute a historiography written shortly after the catastrophe of 587 (around 560)[10] has known several modifications and has even been recently rejected, especially in German scholarship. A significant number of scholars now argue that a "Deuteronomistic History" never existed.[11] It is impossible here to comment in a detailed way on the present debate. Suffice it to say that the opponents of the theory do not present an alternative solution for the presence of Dtr texts in the former Prophets. Moreover, the idea of several seemingly random and unrelated insertions that reflect Dtr thought creates, in my view, not an advancement in scholarship but a regression of a sort, back to Wellhausen.[12] For our present purposes we do not need to discuss the question of the starting point of the Dtr History (DtrH), which in my

---

[10] Noth, *Studien*; English translation: *Deuteronomistic History*.

[11] For a presentation of the current debate see Römer, *Deuteronomistic History*, 27–43.

[12] Wellhausen argued that there were many Dtr editorial modifications in the books of Judges, Samuel and Kings; see Wellhausen, *Composition*, 301.

view lies at the end of the 7th century BCE. Contrary to Noth, one must emphasize that the so-called DtrH underwent several editions and that it was not the work of a single author but resulted from a school of scribes. We will focus on the last redactions of this history that took place during the early Persian period.

Noth is still right, in that he understands the Dtr History as an etiology for exile.[13] The Deuteronomists from the Babylonian and Persian periods correspond in this respect to the "Mandarin" attitude identified by Steil. The Deuteronomists belong to the class of high officials of the Judean court, who (perhaps in Babylon) attempted to edit a comprehensive history in order to understand why the disaster happened. They wanted to provide a rationale for the exile by showing that, even though the people and the kings were constantly warned, they disregarded those warnings. Several actors are held responsible for the catastrophe: the whole people, the (bad) kings, or Manasseh alone, the worst of all kings. This diversity may be explained by the assumption of different Dtr redactors. It may also be understood as an attempt to suggest different possibilities for identifying the causes of the exile. Interestingly, the high Judean court officials are never directly blamed, probably because the DtrH arose within this milieu. If the DtrH is an explanation of the exile, it is also a theodicy. Like some prophetic books (Second Isaiah, Jeremiah) the Deuteronomists affirm that the exile is not due to Yhwh's weakness but that he provoked the Babylonian invasion in order to punish Judah (2 Kings 24:3, 20).

Interestingly, the DtrH does not end with a proper conclusion but with a short notice about Jehoiachin's release from his Babylonian exile (2 Kings 25:27–30). This "open end" is somewhat intriguing. For Noth it was added because "it belongs in the account of the fate of the Judean kings", although it "lacks any intrinsic historical significance".[14] In no way it should be understood "to herald a new future".[15] This is probably a very minimalistic interpretation, but it is true that the Deuteronomists' main goal concerning the crisis was to provide an explanation for it. One may also find, however, some subtle strategies directed at the time period after the fall, by pointing to the literary parallels between the description of Jehoiachin's destiny and the Diaspora-novels in Gen 37–50 (Joseph), Dan 2–6 (Daniel) and Esther. In all these texts an exiled person is brought out of prison, becomes in a way second to the king (2 Kings 25:28; Gen 41:40; Dan 2:48; Esther 10:3) and the accession to this new status is symbolized by the changing of clothes (2 Kings 25:29; Gen 41:42; Dan 5:29; Esther 6:10–11; 8:15). Each

---

[13] Noth, *Deuteronomistic History*, 122.
[14] Noth, *Deuteronomistic History*, 117.
[15] Noth, *Studien*, 143.

of the stories insists on the fact that the land of deportation has become a land where Jews can live and even have interesting lives and careers. 2 Kings 25:27–30 could be interpreted similarly: Exile is transformed into Diaspora. This idea is brought forward discreetly through the strategy of an open-ended ending. It shows that the Deuteronomists accepted the new geo-political situation and probably tried to come to terms with Babylonian domination and then with that of the Persians.

The notion of an "ongoing exile" can also be detected in the Persian pe-riod revisions of the account of Josiah's reform in 2 Kings 22–23. The importance of the "discovered" book and its public reading seems best explained by a time when the temple lay in ruins, or more generally, by a Diaspora situation where access to the Jerusalem sanctuary was difficult for Jews living outside the land. Interestingly, Josiah's reform consists mainly in the cleansing of the temple from all kinds of cultic symbols. The temple is emptied in order to become a place where the book is read to the people. The replacement of the temple cult by the reading of the Torah in 2 Kings 22–23 can be understood as the ideological foundation behind the formation of synagogues and the foundation of Judaism as a "book religion".[16] In the last revision of Solomon's prayer at the inauguration of the temple (1 Kings 8), the king gives the built or rebuilt temple a new role: it becomes a *qibla*. The Dtr redactor envisions that Yhwh will listen from heaven but will not bring the people back from exile; rather, he will allow those who deported them to treat them with compassion. The root רחם is rare in the writings of the DtrH;[17] the closest parallel occurs in Deut 30:3, which also belongs to a Persian period text.

Deut 30:3	ושב יהוה אלהיך את־שבותך ורחמך ושב וקבצך מכל־העמים
1 Kings 8:50	ונתתם לרחמים לפני שביהם ורחמום

In Deut 30 the divine compassion leads to the return to the land, whereas in 1 Kings 8, Yhwh provokes compassion among Israel's vanquishers in order that the exiles can live in the foreign land. This parallel underlines how the Persian edition of the DtrH tries to combine the interests of the returnees and of those who remained in Babylonia.

---

[16] Sonnet, "Livre 'trouvé'"; Römer, "Transformations"; Smyth, "Josiah".

[17] It occurs in the sense of compassion only in Deut 13:18, which presupposes the Achan story in Josh 7 and which speaks of Yhwh's compassion leading to the multiplication of offspring. 2 Kings 13:23, which mentions Yhwh's compassion for Israel because of his covenant with the Patriarchs, is clearly an insertion into the notice about Hazael's succession and may stem from a post-Dtr redactor; see Römer, *Israels Väter*, 387–8.

Competing Origin Myths: Exodus versus Abraham

The ideology of the Dtr school represents the interests of the Babylonian Golah, those who stayed in Mesopotamia, as well as of those who returned. For this reason the Dtr school also edited the Moses story in the book of Exodus, integrating it with the so-called D-composition. The foundation of Yhwh's history with Israel lies for the Deuteronomists in the story of the Exodus. The Exodus and conquest story affirm the right to possess the land through an ideology of colonization: Yhwh brought Israel out of Egypt to give them the land; he will also bring back the members of the "true Israel" from Babylon, and they will possess the land again.

It is difficult to estimate the percentage of the deported Judean population. The idea of the "empty land" and the exile of "all Judah", which can be found at the end of the book of Kings (2 Kings 25:21: "So Judah was carried away captive out of his land"), does not reflect historical reality, as shown already by other biblical accounts such as Jer 40–42 or the book of Lamentations.[18] Recent archaeological work on the situation in Judah after 597 suggests that the Judean population decreased significantly.[19] Contrary to earlier estimations, which allowed for a very low percentage of exiled Judeans, recent publications tend to increase this amount; those estimations vary currently between 20% and 60% (this, by the way, shows that the interpretation of archaeological data can be as speculative as exegesis).[20]

There was clearly an ideological and perhaps also an economic conflict between the Babylonian Golah and the population that had remained in the land. The text of Ezek 33:23–29 reflects this conflict from the perspective of the Golah.

This passage, Ezek 33:23–29, contains a *disputatio* against the inhabitants of the land (Jerusalem?) who were not exiled and who claimed possession of the land.[21] It begins by quoting one of the claims of this group:

Ezek 33:23 The word of Yhwh came to me:
24 "Son of man, the inhabitants of these ruins (ישבי החרבות) in the land of Israel are saying, 'Abraham was only one (אחד), yet he possessed the land (ויירש את־הארץ), but we are many; to us the land has been given (לנו נתנה) for a possession (למורשה)'".

---

[18] Barstad, *Myth*.

[19] Lipschits, "Achaemenid Imperial Policy".

[20] See for instance the different estimations of Lipschits (foregoing footnote) and Finkelstein, "Territorial Extent"; see also the discussion in Albertz, *Exilszeit*, 73–80; English translation: *Israel*.

[21] Zimmerli, *Ezechiel*, 817.

This claim is heavily rejected by the prophet and further destruction is announced:

> Ezek 33:27   This is what you must say to them: "This is what the Lord Yhwh says: 'As surely as I live, those living in the ruins (אשר בחרבות) will die by the sword, those in the open field I will give (נתתיו) to the wild beasts for food, and those who are in the strongholds and caves will die of disease.
> 28   I will turn the land into a desolate ruin (ונתתי את הארץ שממה) ...
> 29   Then they will know that I am Yhwh when I turn the land into a desolate ruin (בתתי את־הארץ שממה) because of all the abominable deeds they have committed.'"

This rejection uses a play on words through the root נתן: Instead of giving the land to the people, Yhwh will "give" the land's inhabitants to death and their land to desolation. This might point to a conflict between the deportees of 597 and those who remained in the land.

Verses 25–26, which mention cultic reasons for the divine judgment against the inhabitants of the land, are missing in LXX*[22] and are therefore probably a very late addition.[23] It is disputed whether this oracle should be attributed to the prophet Ezekiel himself[24] or a "golah-oriented" redaction[25] revising the original message of the prophet in order to strengthen the claim that the first Babylonian Golah represented the true Israel. Even if the passage is the work of a later redaction, it is very plausible that Ezek 33:24 quotes an existing saying of the non-deported Judean population. Their claim about the land is probably directed against the exiles; this is clearly the case in a parallel passage in 11:14–18 (Ezek 11:15 contains a parallel formulation – לנו [היא] נתנה הארץ למורשה – but without reference to Abraham).[26]

The reference to Abraham is particularly interesting. Firstly, it is assumed that he is a known figure, which clearly indicates that the oldest Abraham traditions are not an invention from the Babylonian period. Secondly, he is presented as אחד, as "one". This adverb creates an opposition with the רבים. It is also noteworthy that the link with Jacob or a land promised to Jacob is apparently unimportant (or unknown?). Thirdly, the text

---

[22] In LXX the messenger formula at the beginning of v. 25 introduces the oracle of v. 27–29. There is also a change between the second person singular in v. 25–26 to the third person plural in v. 27.

[23] Against Zimmerli, *Ezechiel*, 815.

[24] See Zimmerli, *Ezechiel*, 818, and most commentaries.

[25] So especially Pohlmann, *Hesekiel*, 454–6; similarly Garscha, *Studien*, 298–302.

[26] Another possibility would be that the adage refers to Edomite occupation of the land after the fall of Judah (see the root ירש in Ezek 35:10 and the substantive מורשה in 36:2–3, 5). So Pohlmann, *Hesekiel*, 454–6. But the polemical context makes it more plausible that here we witness an inner-Judean conflict between the Babylonian Golah and the "people of the land".

says that Abraham possessed or took possession of the land, which indicates that the saying of the non-deportees is based upon an Abraham tradition – one that told how the patriarch came to possess the land. Interestingly, there is no allusion to a divine gift or the promise of the land. Furthermore, there is no indication of a 'Mesopotamian' origin of the patriarch. Abraham appears as an autochthonous figure. A tradition about Abraham's immigration from Mesopotamia would have been seen as contrary to the claims of the people who remained in the land.[27] The redactors of Ezek 33 thus rejected the claim of the non-exiles by presenting the members of the Babylonian Golah as the true Israel.

Somewhat later, a text in Second Isaiah tries to bring about a reconciliation between the exiles and the "autochthonous" population. The exact date of Isa 51:1–3 is difficult to assess. What is clear, however, is that the invoking of Sarah and Abraham seems to presuppose and to "correct" the passage of Ezek 33:23–29.

Ezek 33:23–24	Isa 51:2–3
Son of man, the inhabitants of these *ruins* (ישבי החרבות) in the land of Israel are saying, '*Abraham was one* (אחד), yet he possessed the land, but *we are many* (רבים); to us the land has been given for a possession.'	Look to *Abraham your father* and to Sarah who bore you; for *he was one* (אחד) when I called him, I blessed him *and made him many* (וארבהו). For Yhwh will comfort Zion; he will comfort all her *ruins* (כל־חרבתיה).

Both texts share common features. They present Abraham as "one" and contrast him with his "many" descendants. Both texts mention the "ruins", even if for a different purpose. Whereas Ezek 33:24–29 is extremely hostile to the inhabitants of the "ruins", Isa 51:3 announces the consolation of Zion's ruins. It looks as if the author of Isa 51:1–3[28] wanted to resolve the conflict between the inhabitants of the land and the exiles. Therefore he promises consolation for the ruins of Zion (v. 3) as well as the return of the exiles (v. 11), emphasizing the unity of "all Israel". In Isa 40–55, as already observed, there are also allusions to a new exodus, and the addressees are often called "Jacob". Exodus traditions and patriarchal traditions are both known, but the first literary link between them was probably created by priestly authors.

---

[27] This supports the hypothesis that the idea of Abraham's origin in Mesopotamia only occurs in the latest layers of the Abraham tradition; see also Köckert, "Geschichte", 106.

[28] The parallels between Ezek 33:24 and Isa 51:2–3 invalidate van Oorschot's assertion in *Babel*, 248, that v. 3 has nothing to do with v. 2.

The Priestly School and the Idea of a Separation
between Religious Identity and Political Power

The existence of "Priestly texts" in the Pentateuch is probably with very few exceptions the most stable theory of Pentateuchal research since Graf and Wellhausen. Most scholars would agree to locate P either at the end of the Babylonian period, or, probably the better option, at the beginning of the Persian era. I will not take up the current discussion regarding whether P was originally written as an independent document, a view held by the majority of scholars, or whether P was a work of redaction from the very start that was intended to supplement the older non-priestly material.[29] More relevant for our purposes is the question of the extent of the original P account. One's identification of the end of P carries significant theological import. Does the P document (or redaction) end with the establishment of the people in the land (somewhere in Josh 18:1 or Josh 19:51)[30] or with Moses' death in Deut 34*?[31] Or is P much more limited, with a conclusion at the end of Exodus or more logically after the establishment of the cult in Lev 9 with the consecration of the priests and the first sacrifices followed by the appearance of Yhwh's glory to the whole people (Zenger),[32] or in Lev 16, where Aaron is allowed to enter the adytum and where Yhwh's encounter with Israel has become a permanent feature in the cultic acts of purification and sacrifices (Köckert, Nihan).[33]

There is however a priestly text in Exod 6:2–8, where Yhwh promises to Moses that he will bring the people into the land. This land that Yahweh gave to the ancestors is called in 6:4 ארץ מגריהם, the land in which they resided as aliens (see also Gen 17:8 and 28:4). This implies that, according to P, the Israelites are "resident aliens" in the land, which is given to them as אחזה; this probably means that Yhwh gives to the Israelites the usufruct of the land but that it remains God's exclusive possession.[34] P's conception of the land comes close to the idea of that expressed in the Holiness Code: "the land is mine; with me you are but aliens (גרים) and tenants" (Lev 25:33). One may therefore conclude that the gift of the land after the exodus is basically the same as the gift of the land to the ancestors.[35] One may even

---

[29] A good overview of the present discussion can be found in Shectman/Baden, *Strata*.

[30] Blenkinsopp, *Pentateuch*, 237; Knauf, "Priesterschrift".

[31] The still quite popular, but in my opinion unconvincing, view that P ended in Deut 34* with the death of Moses depends on Noth's idea that P covered the whole extent of the Pentateuch. For this view, see especially Frevel, *Blick*; Schmidt, "P".

[32] Zenger, "Priesterschrift".

[33] Köckert, "Leben"; Nihan, *Priestly Torah*, 379–94.

[34] Bauks, "Begriffe".

[35] Nihan, *Priestly Torah*, 85.

go further and argue that for P it makes little difference whether Israel is living in the land or in "exile", since it effects no change in the people's *ger*-status.

P constructs its "history of revelation" in three steps characterized by three divine names: *elohim* for all humans, *el shadday* for all descendants of Abraham and *yhwh* for Moses and Israel. In Exod 6:3 Yhwh states: "I appeared to Abraham, Isaac and Jacob as El Shadday but by my name Yhwh I did not make myself known to them"; this is a clear reference to Gen 17:1 ("... Yhwh[36] appeared to Abraham and said to him: I am El Shadday ..."). Here P creates a clear link between the patriarchs and the Exodus, by presenting Abraham as an "ecumenical ancestor", who is not only the ancestor of Isaac and Jacob but also the forefather of most of the populations with whom the Judeans had to live together in the Persian period. In the priestly version of the Abraham narrative, the text of Gen 11:27–32 presents Abraham and his family as coming from Mesopotamia, trying to construct Abraham also as an identity marker for the Golah.

The priestly school advocates – contrary to the Deuteronomists – an inclusive monotheism: its three stages divine revelation suggest that all people of the earth venerate the same god, irrespective of whether they address him as elohim, el, or el shadday. For P, there is no need to struggle against the worship of other gods, since these gods represent only partial manifestations of Yhwh. The Diaspora situation and the contact with other people do not represent a threat for "Israel".

This kind of theology, moreover, seems quite compatible with the Persian worldview of a supreme God presiding over all the nations of the empire, as can be seen in the Persian royal inscriptions or in the representation of Persian rule in Behistun.

Furthermore P also insists that all major "identity markers" for the nascent Judaism are given during the origins stage, before entering the land and before the creation of an Israelite or Judean state. The *Sabbath* is the result of God's creation of the world (Gen 2:1–4) before it is discovered by Israel in the wilderness (Exod 16). The rite of *circumcision* is given to Abraham for all his descendants and those who are closely related to him (Gen 17). Circumcision, which was quite commonly practiced in the Levant, becomes an identity marker in the Babylonian Golah, since the Babylonians did not observe this ritual. It may be that P began something new by changing the moment of circumcision, transforming it from a puberty ritual into a birth

---

[36] Some commentators have thought that the name Yhwh in Gen 17:1 does not fit with P's theory of the divine revelation. But this is not true: The narrator uses the tetragrammaton in order to inform the reader about the identity of El Shadday. In the narrative, of course, Abraham is not privy to this information.

ritual (as can be seen in the fact that Ishmael is circumcised at the age of thirteen and Isaac on his eighth day). The *Passover* is instituted in Egypt (Exod 12) and seems to become a major festival also in the Egyptian Diaspora as shown by the so-called Passover letter. *Regulations about licit and illicit food* are given already in Noah's time (e.g., the prohibition on eating blood) and then more specifically for Israel during the time in the desert. And even the sanctuary is constructed in the desert according to a model that Yhwh revealed to Moses. The idea of a mobile sanctuary may constitute an attempt to redefine the Dtr notion of cult centralization and perhaps to signal the acceptance of different Yhwh sanctuaries (e.g., Jerusalem, Gerizim, Elephantine).

By situating all rituals and religious institutions in a mythical past, P claims that there is no need for a king or a state to enforce the cult; everything is founded in the original revelation. In a sense, P is therefore the first to invent the separation of "religion" and "state". The creation of a religious identity, which is not based on the idea of the state or the land or political autonomy is the very basis of the construction of the Pentateuch and also the foundation of Judaism as a religion, which is able to accept life under foreign rulers and to accept this rule as God-given.

Hexateuch or Pentateuch?

The decision to promulgate the Pentateuch in the middle of the Persian period was in a certain sense also based on an anti-eschatological perspective. As Frank Crüsemann has already observed,[37] the Torah does not allot much space to prophecies of salvation. It is mainly the work of a compromise between the priestly and the Dtr circles. In my view the Pentateuch came into being thanks to the decision to separate the book of Deuteronomy from the books of Joshua through Kings in order to combine it with the pre-priestly and priestly traditions in Genesis–Exodus* and to make it the conclusion of the Torah.[38]

There are also a few hints concerning the existence of a Hexateuch project, which would have had the "Torah" end with the book of Joshua. As has often been observed, the last chapter of Joshua (Josh 24) clearly presents itself as the conclusion of a Hexateuch, and a Hexateuch would certainly have also been acceptable to the Samaritans (see especially the loca-

---

[37] Crüsemann, "Pentateuque".
[38] The book of Numbers would then have been created as a bridge of sorts between the "Triateuch" and the book of Deuteronomy. See Römer, "Israel's Sojourn"; Albertz, "Numeri".

tion of Joshua's final discourse in Shechem).[39] Biblical scholarship has so far largely neglected the question of the role and the participation of the Samaritan authorities with regard to the process that led to the promulgation of the Torah.[40] One can imagine that there was a minority coalition of priests and lay people, which may have included Samaritan authorities, a coalition that might well have been in favor of Israel's political restoration.

There is indeed a major ideological difference between a Pentateuch and a Hexateuch. The theological focus of the Hexateuch is undoubtedly the land, promised by Yhwh to the Patriarchs and conquered by Joshua. A Hexateuch would have constructed a post-exilic identity centered on the possession of or the claim to the land. For political, sociological and theological reasons, such an idea was difficult to maintain. The majority of Judean intellectuals accepted Judah's integration into the Persian Empire and would have been unhappy with a foundation document that ends with a narration of a military conquest of regions that did not even belong to the provinces of Yehud and Samaria. For the members of the Babylonian – but also Egyptian – Diaspora, the idea that living in the land is a constitutive part of Jewish identity was unacceptable.

The central figure in the Pentateuch is Moses, and its central concern is the Law, of which Moses is the mediator. Theologically, the Pentateuch has an inconclusive ending: Moses is allowed only to contemplate the land; he will not enter it. The divine promise is repeated in Deut 34, but inside the Torah it is not fulfilled. This literary strategy opens up different possibilities for understanding the fulfillment of the promise; it can be read as fulfilled with the arrival of the Achaemenids or still to be accomplished in a more eschatological sense. The story of Moses' death outside the land clearly betrays a Diaspora perspective. It is a message to the Jews of the Diaspora who were very concerned about having a burial place within the land. Probably since the Persian period wealthy Jews were very eager to be buried in Jerusalem or in the "land of their ancestors".[41] In contrast to this, Deut 34 claims that one may live and die outside the land, as long as one respects the Mosaic Torah. Moses thus becomes a symbol for an exilic identity, based on the reading and observance of the Law.

---

[39] Römer/Brettler, "Deuteronomy 34".

[40] Especially since we know that there was already a sanctuary on Gerizim; see Stern/Magen, "Archaeological Evidence"; Nihan, "Torah".

[41] Lichtenberger, "Im Lande Israel".

The Integration of Minority Voices

Although the Pentateuch is mainly a product of the priestly and the Dtr schools, which represent above all the interest of the Babylonian Golah (those returned to Palestine and those who remained in Babylon), it integrates nevertheless discordant voices. The Joseph narrative, which was probably inserted at a very late stage of the formation of the Torah, represents the interests of the Egyptian Diaspora and its more "liberal" perspective.

In Num 11, a discrete place was provided for ecstatic prophetic groups.[42] There, Moses complains to be the only mediator between the people and Yhwh. Therefore God takes some of Moses' spirit and places it on 70 elders of the people, who are thus enabled to prophesy. Over the protests of Joshua, Moses legitimates the idea of independent prophetic groups who receive the divine spirit directly. This idea corresponds to prophetic and charismatic milieus of the Persian era according to which all of the people could become Yhwh's prophets (Isa 44:3; Ezek 36:27; 39:29; Joel 3:1–2). However, prophetic voices are rare in the Pentateuch, and the narrative in Num 11 claiming the democratization of prophecy was immediately corrected in Num 12 by the demonstration of a qualitative difference between Moses and all other prophets (12:6–8). Only much later were the prophetic scrolls added to the Torah. Interestingly, the collection of the *Nebiim* opens with the books of Josh through Kings, in which the task of the prophets is by no means eschatological but to warn their addressees to respect the divine law.

The Pentateuch is not only cautious with regard to prophecy but also anti-royalist in a way. The construction of Moses as a royal figure suggests that there is no more need for a king because the whole Law is already given through Moses, and even in the book of Kings the Israelite and Judean monarchs are not lawgivers anymore. One text however, Deut 17:14–20, concedes the possibility that Israel might be ruled by a king, although in quite a restrictive way. The statement that Israel should not be governed by a foreign king (17:15) might be a concession to nationalistic groups, which struggled for the continuation of the Davidic dynasty. On the other hand, the law of the king summarizes negatively the story of the origins of the Israelite monarchy (especially 1 Sam 8–12 and 1 Kings 3–10) and transforms the king into a reader and promoter of the book of the Law.

---

[42] For the following see with more details Römer, "Nombres 11–12".

Conclusion: The Persian Period as "Fulfillment of History"

When the Torah was edited, prophetic and eschatological expectations were somewhat excluded because the redactors of this document accepted Persian rule. The books of Joshua through Kings, as well as other prophetic scrolls, were now retained as a kind of "deutero-canonical" section within a constantly growing prophetic library. When Kings became part of the *Nebiim*, 2 Kings 25 was not an absolute ending anymore but rather a transition to the prophetic oracles, which contained all the prophecies of doom to which Israel and Judah had not listened; but the oracles of judgment are followed by oracles of restoration, so that the history from the conquest to the loss of the land is followed by an eschatological perspective.[43] Both historiography and prophetic literature are from now on under the authority of the Mosaic Law, to which both are related. This is probably the reason why biblical historiography only covered the time until the Persian period, since the Torah was considered to be the fulfillment of history.

References

Albertz, R., *Die Exilszeit: 6. Jahrhundert v. Chr.* (BE 7; Stuttgart et al.: Kohlhammer, 2001); English translation: *Israel in Exile: The History and Literature of the Sixth Century B.C.E.* (Studies in Biblical Literature 3; Atlanta: Society of Biblical Literature, 2003).

–, "Das Buch Numeri jenseits der Quellentheorie: Eine Redaktionsgeschichte von Num 20–24 (Teil I)", *ZAW* 132 (2011) 171–83.

Barstad, H.M., *The Myth of the Empty Land: A Study in the History and Archaeology of Judah during the 'Exilic' Period* (Symbolae Osloenses; Oslo: Scandinavian University Press, 1996).

Bauks, M., "Die Begriffe מורשה und אחזה in Pᵍ: Überlegungen zur Landkonzeption in der Priestergrundschrift", *ZAW* 116 (2004) 171–88.

Blenkinsopp, J., *The Pentateuch: An Introduction to the First Five Books of the Bible* (The Anchor Bible Reference Library; New York et al.: Doubleday, 1992).

Crüsemann, F., "Le Pentateuque, une Tora: Prolégomènes à l'interprétation de sa forme finale", in A. de Pury/T. Römer (ed.), *Le Pentateuque en question* (MoBi 19; Genève: Labor et Fides, ³2002) 339–60.

Finkelstein, I., "The Territorial Extent and Demography of Yehud/Judea in the Persian and Early Hellenistic Periods", *RB* 117 (2010) 39–54.

Frevel, C., *Mit Blick auf das Land die Schöpfung erinnern: Zum Ende der Priestergrundschrift* (HBSt 23; Freiburg et al.: Herder, 1999).

Garscha, J., *Studien zum Ezechielbuch: Eine redaktionskritische Untersuchung von Ez 1–39* (EHS.T 23; Bern/Frankfurt: Lang, 1974).

Grätz, S., *Das Edikt des Artaxerxes: Eine Untersuchung zum religionspolitischen und historischen Umfeld von Esra 7,12–26* (BZAW 337; Berlin/New York: de Gruyter, 2004).

Knauf, E.A., "Die Priesterschrift und die Geschichten der Deuteronomisten", in T. Römer (ed.), *The Future of the Deuteronomistic History* (BETL 147; Leuven: University Press/Peeters, 2000) 101–18.

---

[43] Schmid, "Historiographie", 42–3.

Köckert, M., "Leben in Gottes Gegenwart: Zum Verständnis des Gesetzes in der priesterschriftlichen Literatur", *JBTh* 4 (1989) 29–61.

–, "Die Geschichte der Abrahamüberlieferung", in A. Lemaire (ed.), *Congress Volume Leiden 2004* (VTSup 109, Leiden/Boston: Brill, 2006) 103–28.

Lichtenberger, H., "'Im Lande Israel zu wohnen wiegt alle Gebote der Tora auf': Die Heiligkeit des Landes und die Heiligung des Lebens", in R. Feldmeier/U. Heckel (ed.), *Die Heiden, Juden, Christen und das Problem des Fremden* (Tübingen: J.C.B. Mohr, 1994) 92–107.

Lipschits, O., "Achaemenid Imperial Policy, Settlement Processes in Palestine, and the Status of Jerusalem in the Middle of the Fifth Century B.C.E.", in idem/M. Oeming (ed.), *Judah and the Judeans in the Persian Period* (Winona Lake: Eisenbrauns, 2006) 19–52.

Macchi, J.-D., "'Ne ressassez plus les choses d'autrefois!' Esaïe 43,16–21, un surprenant regard deutéro-ésaïen sur le passé", *ZAW* 121 (2009) 225–41.

Nihan, C., *From Priestly Torah to Pentateuch: A Study in the Composition of the Book of Leviticus* (FAT II/25; Tübingen: Mohr Siebeck, 2007).

–, "The Torah between Samaria and Judah: Shechem and Gerizim in Deuteronomy and Joshua", in G.N. Knoppers/B.M. Levinson (ed.), *The Pentateuch as Torah: New Models for Understanding Its Promulgation and Acceptance* (Winona Lake: Eisenbrauns, 2007) 187–223.

Noth, M., *Überlieferungsgeschichtliche Studien: Die sammelnden und bearbeitenden Geschichtswerke im Alten Testament* (Darmstadt: Wissenschaftliche Buchgesellschaft, [1943] 1967); English translation of the first part: *The Deuteronomistic History* (JSOTSup 15; Sheffield: Sheffield Academic Press, 1991).

Parpola, S., *Assyrian Prophecies* (SAA 11; Helsinki: Helsinki University Press, 1997).

Pohlmann, K.-F., *Das Buch des Propheten Hesekiel (Ezechiel): Kapitel 20–48* (ATD 22/2; Göttingen: Vandenhoeck & Ruprecht, 2001).

Römer, T., *Israels Väter: Untersuchungen zur Väterthematik im Deuteronomium und in der deuteronomistischen Tradition* (OBO 99; Fribourg/Göttingen: Universitätsverlag/Vandenhoeck & Ruprecht, 1990).

–, "L'Ancien Testament: Une littérature de crise", *RTP* 127 (1995) 321–38.

–, "Nombres 11–12 et la question d'une rédaction deutéronomique dans le Pentateuque", in M. Vervenne/J. Lust (ed.), *Deuteronomy and Deuteronomic Literature* (FS C.H.W. Brekelmans; BETL 133; Leuven: Peeters, 1997) 481–98.

–, "Transformations in Deuteronomistic and Biblical Historiography: On 'Book-Finding' and Other Literary Strategies", *ZAW* 109 (1997) 1–11.

–, *The So-Called Deuteronomistic History: A Sociological, Historical and Literary Introduction* (London/New York: T&T Clark/Continuum, 2005).

–, "Israel's Sojourn in the Wilderness and the Construction of the Book of Numbers", in R. Rezetko et al. (ed.), *Reflection and Refraction: Studies in Biblical Historiography in Honour of A. Graeme Auld* (VTSup 113; Leiden/Boston: Brill, 2007) 419–45.

Römer, T./Brettler, M.Z., "Deuteronomy 34 and the Case for a Persian Hexateuch", *JBL* 119 (2000) 401–19.

Schmid, K., "Une grande historiographie allant de Genèse à 2 Rois a-t-elle un jour existé?", in T. Römer/K. Schmid (ed.), *Les dernières rédactions du Pentateuque, de l'Hexateuque et de l'Ennéateuque* (BETL 203; Leuven: Peeters, 2007) 35–46.

Schmidt, L., "P in Deuteronomium 34", *VT* 59 (2009) 475–94.

Shectman, S./Baden, J.S. (ed.), *The Strata of the Priestly Writings: Contemporary Debate and Future Directions* (ATANT 95; Zürich: TVZ, 2009).

Smyth, F., "When Josiah Has Done his Work or the King Is Properly Buried: A Synchronic Reading of 2 Kings 22.1–23.28", in A. de Pury et al. (ed.), *Israel Constructs its History: Deuteronomistic Historiography in Recent Research* (JSOTSup 306; Sheffield: Sheffield Academic Press, 2000), 343–58.

Sonnet, J.-P., "Le livre 'trouvé': 2 Rois 22 dans sa finalité narrative", *NRTh* 116 (1994) 836–61.

Steck, O.H., *Der Abschluß der Prophetie im Alten Testament: Ein Versuch zur Frage der Vorgeschichte des Kanons* (BThSt 17; Neukirchen-Vluyn: Neukirchener Verlag, 1991).

Steil, A., *Krisensemantik: Wissenssoziologische Untersuchungen zu einem Topos moderner Zeiterfahrung* (Opladen: Leske und Budrich, 1993).

Stern, E./Magen, Y., "Archaeological Evidence for the First Stage of the Samaritan Temple on Mount Gerizim", *IEJ* 52 (2002) 49–57.

van Oorschot, J., *Von Babel zum Zion: Eine literarkritische und redaktionsgeschtliche Untersuchung* (BZAW 206; Berlin/New York: de Gruyter, 1993).

Wellhausen, J., *Die Composition des Hexateuchs und der historischen Bücher des Alten Testaments* (Berlin: de Gruyter, [1899] 1963).

Welten, P., *Geschichte und Geschichtsdarstellung in den Chronikbüchern* (WMANT 42; Neukirchen-Vluyn: Neukirchener Verlag, 1973).

Willi, T., *Chronik.* Vol 1: *1 Chronik 1,1–10,4* (BKAT 24/1; Neukirchen-Vluyn: Neukirchener Verlag, 2009).

Zenger, E., "Priesterschrift", *TRE* 27 (1997) 435–46.

Zimmerli, W., *Ezechiel* (BKAT 13; Neukirchen-Vluyn: Neukirchener Verlag, 1969).

Jakob Wöhrle

Westfälische Wilhelms-Universität Münster

Joseph in Egypt

Living under Foreign Rule according to the Joseph Story and its Early Intra- and Extra-Biblical Reception

Introduction

Joseph was the first Israelite, who lived in a foreign land for a sustained period of time. According to the biblical story, Joseph was sold by his brothers into Egyptian slavery. In Egypt he first came into prison, but then he rose up to a high position at Pharaoh's court. He became the second highest authority in the state of Egypt. In this position he was able to save the life of his family, who followed him to Egypt.

Thus, the Joseph story describes different facets of Joseph's life in a foreign land: from slave to regent, from the outcast to the savior of his people. It is therefore not a coincidence that within the intra- and the extra-biblical tradition the Joseph story was often adopted in order to treat general aspects of life in a foreign land or, more generally, life under foreign rule. Through the character of Joseph it was possible to describe the prospects but also the risks of such a life.

In the following it will be shown that the biblical story itself is characterized by different views concerning life in a foreign land. In a second step, then, it will be shown how different Jewish groups in the later Hellenistic period adopt these different views in order to legitimize their particular attitude towards life in a foreign land and under foreign rule.

1. The Biblical Joseph Story

In recent research scholars often describe the biblical Joseph story as a "diaspora novel".[1] According to their view, by recounting the example of Joseph, his life and his advancement in Egypt the Joseph story shows that

---

[1] Meinhold, "Gattung", 311–24; Niditch/Doran, "Success Story", 179–93; Römer, "La narra-tion", 23; Wahl, "Motiv", 59–74; Lux, *Josef*, 234; Schmid, "Josephsgeschichte", 109–11; Ebach, *Genesis 37–50*, 39, 692–3; cf. Kratz, *Komposition*, 285–6.

living in a foreign land and under foreign rule is possible and that one can succeed in that situation.

It has to be recognized, however, that the Joseph story is the product of a long-term redactional development.[2] The original, independently transmitted Joseph story, encompassing already the range of Gen 37:3–50:21*, has been expanded in several steps to its present form.[3] Different redactors added, for example, larger units like the account of Judah and Tamar in Gen 38, the account of Joseph in Potiphar's house in Gen 39, the blessing of Ephraim and Manasseh in Gen 48 and Jacob's testament in Gen 49.[4] Additionally, they added some smaller sections like the priestly passages in Gen 37:1, 2aα; 41:46a; 46:6–7; 47:7–11, 27b, 28; 48:3–7; 49:1a, 29a, 33aαb; 50:22, the promise to Jacob in Gen 46:1aβ–5a and the last words of Joseph in Gen 50:24–26.[5]

Against recent trends of globally defining the Joseph story as a "diaspora novel" these different redactional levels of the Joseph story present very different views on life in a foreign land and among the people of a foreign

---

[2] Reviews of current research on the formation of the Joseph story are presented by Schmid, "Josephsgeschichte", 87–93; Albertz, "Josephsgeschichte", 12–14.

[3] In older research scholars commonly divided the Joseph story, like the preceding parts of the patriarchal narratives, among the different Pentateuchal sources. However, since Donner, "Gestalt", 79–94, it is widely recognized that the Joseph story originally was an independent piece; cf. for example Redford, *Study*, 245–8; Schmitt, *Josephsgeschichte*, 127–9; Dietrich, *Josephserzählung*, 45–6; Blum, *Komposition*, 244–57; Schmid, "Josephsgeschichte", 93–4; Weimar, "Josef", 10–11 note 6; Albertz, "Josephsgeschichte", 19–23. The assumption put forward by Kratz, *Komposition*, 281–2, that the Joseph story – in several steps – has been composed as a continuation of the preceding patriarchal narratives, is contradicted by obvious differences between these two units. There is, for example the fact that Gen 37:10, in contrast to Gen 35:16–20, presupposes that Joseph's mother is still alive; cf. Schmid, "Josephsgeschichte", 93–4.
More controversial is the extent of the original Joseph story. Due to the fact that the Joseph story twice mentions the reconciliation of the brothers and twice gives a theological interpretation of the preceding events (Gen 45:1–5; 50:15–21), many scholars, since Dietrich, *Josephserzählung*, 37–40, presume that the original version extended only to Gen 45; cf. Kebekus, *Joseferzählung*, 149–52; Levin, *Jahwist*, 303; Kratz, *Komposition*, 284. However, Gen 45 is not a convincing conclusion to the Joseph story, since at this point of the narrative the emigration of Jacob to Egypt has not been told. Coats, *Canaan*, 52–3; Albertz, "Josephsgeschichte", 21–3, thus think that Gen 47:12, 27a, where Jacob comes to Egypt, is the original end of the story. But this is not a solid conclusion for the conflict between the brothers, which is of general importance for the Joseph story. More likely, therefore, is the oft-proposed solution that the original Joseph story – or rather the oldest attainable form of the story – extended to Gen 50:21; cf. Blum, *Komposition*, 241; Römer, "La narration", 20; Schmid, "Josephsgeschichte", 95–106, and Ebach, *Genesis 37–50*, 691.

[4] That Gen 38; 48; 49 are secondary additions to the original Joseph story is widely recognized; cf. Blum, *Komposition*, 244–57; Römer, "La narration", 20; Schmid, "Josephsgeschichte", 102–6; Albertz, "Josephsgeschichte", 21–6. For Gen 39 see note 13 below.

[5] For the priestly passages, cf. Wöhrle, *Fremdlinge*, 101–46; for the secondary nature of Gen 46:1aβ–5a see note 21 below; for Gen 50:24–26 cf. Gertz, *Tradition*, 361–2; Blum, "Verbindung", 150–1; Albertz, "Josephsgeschichte", 31.

land. This shall be shown by examining the original Joseph story, the account of Joseph in Potiphar's house in Gen 39, and the promise to Jacob in Gen 46:1aβ –5a.

1.1 The Original Joseph Story

The original Joseph story (Gen 37:3–50:21*) is the story of a conflict. It presents the conflict between Joseph and his brothers about the leadership among Jacob's sons.[6]

The Joseph story begins in 37:3 mentioning that Jacob loves Joseph more than his brothers. But even more: Jacob prepares Joseph a "long robe" (כתנת פסים).[7] Thus, he gives him a royal garment and by doing this he visibly documents the leading position of Joseph among his brothers.

The leadership of Joseph is also the subject of Joseph's dreams (37:5–11). He dreams in different pictures – the picture of sheaves and the picture of heavenly bodies – that the brothers prostrate themselves before him and so accept his leading position.

But the brothers oppose Joseph's leadership. They hate him (37:4, 5, 8) and as the opportunity arises they sell him to Ishmaelite traders, who bring him to Egypt (37:12–28).[8] There, Joseph comes into the house of Potiphar, a high official of Pharaoh (39:1*).

Because of his God-given ability to interpret dreams, Joseph escapes from slavery. He interprets Pharaoh's dreams about the seven years of plenty and the seven years of famine, and Pharaoh promotes him to a high position. Joseph becomes the second highest authority in Egypt (41:1–43).

In this position he finally saves the life of his brothers. When they come to Egypt at the time of the famine, he is able to provide a dwelling place as well as sustenance for his brothers and for his father Jacob.

---

[6] Crüsemann, *Widerstand*, 143–55; Dietrich, *Josephserzählung*, 53–66; Kebekus, *Joseferzählung*, 244–50; Weimar, "Josef", 10–12; Albertz, "Josephsgeschichte", 23.

[7] The only further occurrence of כתנת פסים within the Hebrew Bible is 2 Sam 13:18–19. There the "long robe" is presented as a garment worn by the daughters of the king. Thus, Gunkel, *Genesis*, 404; Jacob, *Genesis*, 697; Crüsemann, *Widerstand*, 146; Westermann, *Genesis*, 3:283, are right that Joseph's "long robe" is a royal garment and hence a visible sign that Jacob gives him the leadership among his brothers. The assumption of Ebach, *Genesis 37–50*, 60, that Joseph's robe is just a festive dress seems rather unlikely.

[8] In the present form of the Joseph story, however, it is not the brothers themselves who sell Joseph to the Ishmaelites. According to Gen 37:28, 36 a group of Midianite traders takes Joseph out of the cistern, into which the brothers had thrown him, and sell him to the Ishmaelites. But the statements about the Midianites in Gen 37:28aα, 36 seem to be secondary additions intending to relieve the brothers of some culpability; cf. Blum, *Komposition*, 244–5; Schmid, "Josephsgeschichte", 105–6; Albertz, "Josephsgeschichte", 25.

At the end of the story, the brothers have to accept the leadership of Joseph (50:18–21). As foreseen in the dreams at the beginning of the story they prostrate themselves before him and offer themselves as slaves.

From its beginning to the end the original Joseph story thus treats the subject of leadership.[9] It describes how under God's guidance and against all opposition Joseph's leadership is established, which in the end redounds to the brother's advantage.

In the original version of the Joseph story Egypt is simply the place where Joseph's leadership is established. The events in Egypt consequently result in the salvation of the brothers and thus in the establishment of Joseph's leadership among his brothers. A continuing or even permanent stay of Joseph and his brothers in the land of Egypt is not in the focus of the original Joseph story.

On the contrary, it can be shown that within the original Joseph story the stay in Egypt is restricted to the unique and temporally limited case of the current famine.[10] In Gen 45:7 Joseph says to his brothers that God sent him to Egypt in order to save their lives. Additionally, in Gen 45:11 Joseph says that he wants to support his father in the remaining five years of the famine, i.e. in a fixed and limited amount of time. Finally, in Gen 47:4 the brothers say to Pharaoh that they want to live in his land due to the ongoing famine.

Thus, the original Joseph story does not reflect life in Egypt. It does not treat the principal prospects of a permanent stay in a foreign land. It is not a "diaspora novel".[11]

The original Joseph story is rather concentrated on the person of Joseph. It reveals the significance of this son of Jacob. It describes how Joseph under God's guidance achieves leadership among his brothers, and it emphasizes that leadership's benefit for his brothers. The internal – one could also say domestic – relationships among the sons of Jacob, not their life in a foreign land dictate the unfolding of the original Joseph story.

At the very least, then, the core of the original Joseph story may go back to the time of the existing Northern Kingdom and may be understood as a legitimization of Joseph's dominance among the northern tribes.[12] After the

---

[9] Already Blum, *Komposition*, 237, emphasized that especially at its end the Joseph story treats the subject of leadership and not the prospects of a life in a foreign land.

[10] Albertz, "Josephsgeschichte", 22. In contrast, those scholars who understand the Joseph story as a "diaspora novel" often claim that this story – already on the primary level – presupposes that Joseph and his brothers permanently stay in the land of Egypt; cf. Meinhold, "Gattung", 321; Römer, "La narration", 27. This view, however, is undermined by the biblical passages presented below.

[11] Crüsemann, *Widerstand*, 145 note 27; Blum, *Komposition*, 235–7; Albertz, "Josephsgeschichte", 22, 27.

[12] Also Blum, *Komposition*, 243; Dietrich, *Josephserzählung*, 64–6, Kebekus, *Joseferzählung*, 250–7; Albertz, "Josephsgeschichte", 20. These scholars argue that the core of the Joseph story,

downfall of the Northern Kingdom the original Joseph story could well have been read as a general reflection on the importance of political leadership.

1.2 The Account of Joseph in Potiphar's House in Gen 39

In Gen 39, a short episode about Joseph's experiences in the house of his master Potiphar has been added to the original Joseph story.[13] The beginning of this episode illustrates that Yhwh is with Joseph and causes him to succeed in everything he does. Potiphar thus puts his whole household under Joseph's control (39:1–6). But Potiphar's wife lays an eye on Joseph. Several times she presses him to sleep with her. The situation escalates when Potiphar and the other members of the house are away: Potiphar's wife catches Joseph by his garment. Joseph wriggles himself out of the garment and flees (39:7–12). Potiphar's wife now calls the other slaves of the house and then Potiphar himself, and she alleges that Joseph was the one who wanted to lie with her (39:13–18). Potiphar becomes angry; he takes Joseph and throws him into prison (39:19–20).

In contrast to the original Joseph story, the account of Joseph in Potiphar's house focuses upon the circumstances that befall a member of the Israelite people in a foreign land. This can be shown by the very fact that Gen 39 – different from the rest of the Joseph story – mentions the protagonist's ethnicity.[14] It qualifies Potiphar, unlike any other individual person in Gen 37–50, as "Egyptian" (מצרי; 39:1, 2, 5), and it refers to Joseph as "He-

---

due to the prominent role of Joseph, stems from the time of the still existing Northern Kingdom. The alternative approaches dating the Joseph story into the exilic or even post-exilic era, are not convincing; contra Meinhold, "Gattung", 311–24; Römer, "La narration", 27; Lux, *Josef*, 234; Schmid, "Josephsgeschichte", 111; Ebach, *Genesis 37–50*, 693.

[13] The secondary nature of the Potiphar account in Gen 39 – or, more precisely, of Gen 39:2–23 – has often been recognized; cf. Eerdmans, *Studien*, 1:66–7; Redford, *Study*, 129–30; Schmitt, *Josephsgeschichte*, 81–9; Dietrich, *Josephserzählung*, 26–30; Weimar, "Jahwe", 61–124; Albertz, "Josephsgeschichte", 26–7. Several arguments speak for this assumption: Within the Joseph story, only Gen 39 uses the tetragrammaton Yhwh (Gen 39:2, 3, 5, 21, 23). Only this story gives the statement that Yhwh was with Joseph (יהוה את יוסף/אתו; Gen 39:2, 3, 21, 23). Only this story mentions and contrasts the ethnicity of its protagonists (מצרי; Gen 39:1, 2, 5 // עברי; Gen 39:14, 17). Finally, Gen 39 shows some terminological characteristics: In Gen 39:20, 22 the prison is called בית־הסהר, but משמר in Gen 40:3, 4, 7; 41:10; in Gen 39:21, 22, 23 the prison officer is referred to as שר בית הסהר, but as שר הטבחים in Gen 40:3, 4; 41:10, 12 (which is, astonishingly enough, in Gen 37:36; 39:1 the function of Potiphar). It thus seems very likely that Gen 39:2–23 is a secondary addition. Probably, the same hand responsible for Gen 39:2–23 added some further passages by which the Potiphar account was integrated into its context: Gen 39:1*(איש מצרי); 40:3aβb, 5b, 15.

[14] Gunkel, *Genesis*, 423; Dietrich, *Josephserzählung*, 27; Ebach, *Genesis 37–50*, 165–6, 183–4.

brew" (עברי; 39:14, 17). The Potiphar account is thus an exemplary description of the situation of a Hebrew man in the foreign land of Egypt.

The story begins by describing that Joseph, in the house of his Egyptian master, was under the special care of his God. Yhwh is with him and helping him to achieve success. But even more: According to Gen 39:3 his Egyptian master recognizes Yhwh's contribution to Joseph's success and thus gives everything into his hand. The special relationship to his God, which is recognized and respected even by the inhabitants of the foreign land of Egypt, brings Joseph into a comfortable position in this foreign land.

The subsequent events, however, are quite remarkable. After the unsuccessful attempts by Potiphar's wife to win Joseph over, she slanders him to the other slaves and to her husband. In Gen 39:14 she says to the slaves of the house:

> Gen 39:14 ... See, he has brought in to us (לנו) a Hebrew man (איש עברי) to mock us (בנו). He came in to me to lie with me, and I cried out with a loud voice.

Notably, in her speech to the slaves, Potiphar's wife puts herself on the same level as the slaves. She says that her husband brought "us" (לנו) a Hebrew man and that this man wanted to mock "us" (בנו). Potiphar's wife thus declares her solidarity with the slaves of the house and she sets herself and them in opposition to Joseph.[15] She presents the alleged assault committed by Joseph not only as an assault against herself, but as an assault against her and the group of the other slaves in the house.

Additionally, it is remarkable that Potiphar's wife explicitly refers to Joseph as a "Hebrew man" (איש עברי). By doing this, she relates the alleged assault to his ethnicity, to his being a Hebrew. Potiphar's wife thus puts forward a conscious stigmatization: As a Hebrew Joseph poses a risk for the other members of the household.[16]

The further progression of the story is also noteworthy: After Potiphar's wife tells her husband about the alleged events in his house, he reacts at once. He gets angry, takes his slave Joseph and throws him into prison (39:19–20).

The reaction of Potiphar is remarkable, since at the beginning of the story we are told that Potiphar himself saw that Yhwh was taking care of Joseph and bringing him success in everything he did (39:3–4).[17] Potiphar

---

[15] Thus already Jacob, *Genesis*, 731, and in more recent times Ebach, *Genesis 37–50*, 184–5.

[16] Not without reason, Gunkel, *Genesis*, 423, wrote: "sie macht ein wenig in Antisemitismus". Cf. Dietrich, *Josephserzählung*, 27; Lux, *Josef*, 103–4.

[17] It is noteworthy that at the end of the chapter, Gen 39:20–23, describing Joseph's time in prison, again mentions that Yhwh is with Joseph. But this passage does not say that his master,

recognized the special relationship between Joseph and his god and thus he gave his whole household into Joseph's hands. But after Joseph's defamation by Potiphar's wife, Joseph's special relationship to his god and its value for Potiphar's house is not worth anymore. Potiphar removes Joseph from his house immediately.[18]

The Potiphar account added in Gen 39 thus presents an ambivalent picture of Joseph's life in a foreign land. At first, it shows, how a Hebrew man, because of the special care of his god, acquires a comfortable position. But then it points out that this does not protect him from hostility. In cases of conflict, due to his being a Hebrew, he becomes the victim of arbitrary actions on the part of the citizens of the foreign land.[19]

By adding Gen 39, probably in the time of the exile, the original Joseph story focusing upon the conflict between Joseph and his brothers takes on a diaspora-critical overtone.[20] In its opening scenes the Joseph story now speaks to the unpredictable risks posed by the people of a foreign land, and it warns about life in such a foreign land.

1.3 The Promise to Jacob in Gen 46:1aβ–5a

In Gen 46:1aβ–5a another short episode has been added to the Joseph story.[21] According to this episode Jacob, on his way to Egypt, stops over in Beersheba, where Yhwh appears to him and speaks to him. Important are the following words to Jacob in Gen 46:3–4:

---

now the prison officer, sees Yhwh's care for Joseph. Thus, the statement given in Gen 39:3 is of special importance for the Potiphar episode.

[18] Some scholars presume, however, that Potiphar's anger is not directed against Joseph but against his wife. According to their view this is the reason why Joseph, though accused of rape, does not receive a worse punishment such as corporal punishment or the death penalty; cf. Jacob, *Genesis*, 732; Westermann, *Genesis*, 3:64; Lux, *Josef*, 104–5; Ebach, *Genesis 37–50*, 186. But according to Gen 39:19–20 Potiphar's first reaction out of anger is to throw Joseph into prison. Potiphar's thoughts about the role of his wife are not mentioned at all. Additionally, that Joseph does not receive a worse punishment is also caused by the mere fact that the Potiphar account was added before Gen 40 and thus had to end with the imprisonment of Joseph.

[19] Thus, the Potiphar account can not be read as a story about how life in the Diaspora can succeed under the special blessing of Yhwh; contra Meinhold, "Gattung", 313–14; Lux, *Josef*, 96–9; Ebach, *Genesis 37–50*, 166.

[20] Albertz, "Josephsgeschichte", 27.

[21] The secondary nature of Gen 46:1aβ–5a has often been recognized; cf. Donner, "Gestalt", 99; Westermann, *Genesis*, 3:169–70; Redford, *Study*, 18–19; Römer, "La narration", 20; Albertz, "Josephsgeschichte", 28. This view is corroborated by several observations. For example, Jacob's fear of the time in Egypt mentioned in Gen 46:3 has no basis in the preceding context. Additionally, the promise of Gen 46:3–4 reminds one of the promises given in the previous patriarchal narratives and thus, in contrast to the original Joseph story, presupposes the literary connection between the patriarchal narratives and the Joseph story.

> Gen 46:3 He said: I am God, the God of your father. Do not be afraid to go
> down to Egypt, for I will make you a great nation there.
> 4 I will go down with you to Egypt, and I will also bring you up again;
> and Joseph will put his hand on your eyes.

The promise given in Gen 46:3–4 responds to Jacob's fear of living in
Egypt. Interestingly, and in contrast to the original Joseph story, Gen 46:3–
4 presupposes that the time that Jacob and his sons will spend in Egypt is
not limited to the current famine. According to Gen 46:3, Jacob will become a great nation in Egypt. This promise implies that he and his descendants will stay in Egypt longer than the following five years of famine. Gen
46:3 thus expects Jacob and his descendants to stay permanently in this
foreign land.[22]

With respect to this permanent stay Yhwh says to Jacob that he should
not be afraid, since he, Yhwh, goes down with him to Egypt. Yhwh's assistance thus enables Jacob and his descendants to live in this foreign land for
a longer time.

While the Potiphar account added in Gen 39 points out that living in a
foreign land, despite Yhwh's assistance, is marked by unpredictable risks,
Gen 46:1aβ–5a notes that such risks need not be feared, precisely because
of Yhwh's assistance. Because of Yhwh's assistance Jacob and his descendants can not only exist but also develop and multiply in a foreign land.

With Gen 46:1aβ–5a – probably added in Persian times –[23] the Joseph
story gets a diaspora-friendly tone.[24] It counters the fear of risks and the
feeling of being threatened by the people of a foreign land, and it argues in
favor of living in a foreign land. With Gen 46:1aβ–5a the Joseph story can
now be read as a story of a successful permanent life in a foreign land. On
this redactional level, but only on this redactional level, it can be said that
the Joseph story is a "diaspora novel".

---

[22] Redford, *Study*, 19. It is a point of debate, however, whether the repatriation mentioned in
Gen 46:4 refers to Jacob alone (Gunkel, *Genesis*, 463; Levin, *Jahwist*, 305; Schmid, "Josephsgeschichte", 116 note 159; Albertz, "Josephsgeschichte", 28) or to the whole people descendent from
Jacob (Westermann, *Genesis*, 3:172; Gertz, *Tradition*, 277 with note 204). Due to the promise
given at the end of Gen 46:4 that Joseph will put his hands on Jacob's eyes, it seems more plausible that Gen 46:4 refers to the repatriation of Jacob's dead body (Gen 50:1–14). Thus, the repatriation mentioned in this verse does not speak against the assumption that Gen 46:3–4 expects a
permanent stay of Jacob's descendants in the land of Egypt.
[23] Due to the fact that Gen 46:1aβ–5a expects the multiplication of the people in Egypt, this
passage presupposes the literary connection of the Joseph story and the Exodus account. Contra
Blum, *Komposition*, 297–301; Schmid, "Josephsgeschichte", 116; Albertz, "Josephsgeschichte",
28–9, Gen 46:1aβ–5a is thus to be dated later than the priestly texts of the Pentateuch, by which
the literary connection between the Joseph story and the Exodus account has been established; cf.
Wöhrle, *Fremdlinge*, 103–6. Hence, Gen 46:1aβ–5a could not have been added before the postexilic period; cf. Römer, "La narration", 20 note 15; Gertz, *Tradition*, 273–7.
[24] Albertz, "Josephgeschichte", 28.

1.4 Conclusion

Because of its long-term redactional development the biblical Joseph story comprises very different views on life in foreign land. The original Joseph story does not focus on the possibility of a permanent stay in a foreign land. The original Joseph story rather focuses on the person of Joseph, the relationship to his brothers, and his leadership established under the guidance of God. On this literary level, Egypt is simply the place where Joseph's leadership is established.

With the account of Joseph in Potiphar's house, added in Gen 39, the Joseph story gets an additional focus against life in a foreign land. The Potiphar account shows how Joseph, because of his being a Hebrew, is exposed to hostility and arbitrariness from the people of the foreign land.

In contrast, the promise to Jacob added in Gen 46:1aβ–5a emphasizes that such risks are no reason to fear life in a foreign land. Yhwh's assistance also applies to those of Jacob's descendants who live in a foreign land, and there he makes them into a great nation.

The present form of the Joseph story thus comprises three different views on life in a foreign land: a more neutral view, a negative view and a more positive view. Remarkably enough, exactly these three different views on life in a foreign land are mirrored in the early extra-biblical reception of the Joseph story.

2. Joseph in the Early Jewish Literature

The early Jewish scriptures refer to Joseph quite often. The reception of the Joseph story ranges from short and isolated references to comprehensive retellings of the Joseph material.[25]

In the following, three examples of the reception of the Joseph story in early Jewish times will be examined: the Book of Ben Sira, the First Book of the Maccabees, and the Testaments of the Twelve Patriarchs. These three books stem from the same period, the later Hellenistic time, but they trace back to different Jewish circles. Consequently, these scriptures adopt the Joseph story in very different ways.

---

[25] Cf. Niehoff, *Figure*, esp. 38–53; Gruen, *Heritage*, 73–109; Hollander, "Portrayal", 237–63; Docherty, "Joseph", 194–216; Lisewski, *Studien*, 21–76.

2.1 Joseph in the Book of Ben Sira

One of the oldest adoptions of the Joseph story is found in the Book of Ben Sira.[26] Ben Sira was a Jewish scribe and teacher, who belonged to the upper-class of Jerusalem. The Book of Ben Sira stems from the beginning of the 2nd century, probably from the time between 190 and 175 BCE. Against the background of the upcoming orientation towards Hellenistic culture and religion, Ben Sira in his book develops a wisdom philosophy based upon the fear of God and obedience to the Torah.[27]

At the end of the Book, in Sir 44–49, Ben Sira brings forward the so-called "praise of the fathers". After a short introduction (44:1–15) Ben Sira, at first, gives a historical sketch mentioning prominent figures from Adam to Nehemiah. He emphasizes their wisdom, righteousness, their fear of God as well as their contributions to the people, and thus he presents them as paradigms for the Jewish people (44:16–49:13).[28] At the end of the "praise of the fathers" Ben Sira mentions some additional persons from Israel's prehistory (49:14–16).

Within the "praise of the fathers" Ben Sira also refers to Joseph. But, quite unexpectedly, he does not mention Joseph within the broad historical sketch put forward at the beginning of this section. Instead, he mentions Joseph only at the end in the section on additional individuals. Ben Sira's historical sketch omits Joseph. It segues from Abraham, Isaac, and Jacob to the time of Moses.

The fact that Joseph is not mentioned within the historical sketch of Ben Sira's "praise of the fathers" has led scholars to the conclusion that Ben Sira did not know the Joseph story or that he did not attach much importance to the person of Joseph.[29] It has to be recognized, however, that within the "praise of the fathers" not only is Joseph left unmentioned but so is the whole time in Egypt. The presentation of Moses does not mention one

---

[26] An edition of the Hebrew text of Ben Sira is provided by Beentjes, *Ben Sira*. For the different textual versions, the formation and date of the book, cf. for example Sauer, *Jesus Sirach*, 19–28; Reiterer, "Jesus Sirach"; Marböck, "Jesus Sirach", 408–16.

[27] Cf. Hengel, *Judentum*, 252–75; Sauer, *Jesus Sirach*, 29–34, or Marböck, "Jesus Sirach", 412–16.

[28] Cf. Gilbert, "Wisdom", 295–7.

[29] Due to the fact that the "praise of the fathers" does not mention Joseph, Lisewski, *Studien*, 37, supposes that Ben Sira did not know the Joseph story. Even more, he takes this to mean that Ben Sira had a version of the Pentateuch without the Joseph story. In contrast, Sauer, *Jesus Sirach*, 306–7, 335, presumes that Joseph was not of importance for Ben Sira. A further assumption is put forward by Lee, *Studies*, 208, and Collins, *Jewish Wisdom*, 105. They suppose that Ben Sira does not mention Joseph in Sir 44 because of his anti-Samaritan attitude (cf. Sir 50:26). But the mere fact that Joseph is mentioned in Sir 49:15 speaks against all of these assumptions.

single word about Moses' acts in Egypt. Moreover, the presentation of Moses even obscures that Moses appeared in a foreign land at all.[30]

This observation goes with the fact that Ben Sira rarely mentions foreign nations.[31] The Book of Ben Sira has only a few passages treating other nations, be it on the political or on the religious level. Ben Sira rather concentrates on his own history, his own religious and cultural traditions.

Thus, the "praise of the fathers" does not omit Joseph because Ben Sira did not know the Joseph story or because he did not attach much importance to the person of Joseph. It rather omits Joseph in order to omit the time in Egypt and thus the time of the people in a foreign land.[32]

At the end of the "praise of the fathers" Ben Sira refers to Joseph together with some figures from Israel's prehistory in Sir 49:14–16:[33]

> Sir 49:14 Few on earth have been like Enoch;
> he also was taken up within.
> 15 Was there born a man like Joseph?
> And also his dead body was cared for.
> 16 Shem, Seth, and Enosh were cared for;
> but above every living being was the splendor of Adam.

In Sir 49:14–16 Joseph is mentioned together with some important persons from the days of old, with Enoch, Shem, Seth, Enosh, and Adam. Joseph is described as a very significant person, with whom virtually no one can compare. With the mention of the special care for his dead body – referring to the biblical tradition about the transportation of the his body from Egypt to Canaan (Gen 50:25–26; Exod 13:19; Josh 24:32) – Joseph even gets a status near to the aforementioned Enoch, who ascended into heaven (Gen 5:22–24).

Thus, in Sir 49:15 the importance of Joseph, at first, lies in the fact that he, like Enoch, was in a special relationship with God. On this basis, the importance of Joseph may also lie in the fact that he, according to the bibli-

---

[30] Sir 45:3 says that Moses appeared before an unnamed king. Sir 45:18 mentions a struggle with foreign nations in the dessert. But Sir 45 gives no direct hints on Moses' function as liberator from Egyptian oppression.

[31] Cf. the overview given by Middendorp, *Stellung*, 164–6.

[32] Thus Middendorp, *Stellung*, 56. Less convincing are the considerations of Sauer, *Jesus Sirach*, 306–7. He thinks that the "praise of the fathers" does not mention the time in Egypt since Ben Sira's statements about Moses focus upon the giving of the Torah and its importance. Due to the fact that the whole Book of Ben Sira avoids treating the relationship to the nations, it is, however, much more likely that Ben Sira consciously omits any hint on the time in Egypt.

[33] Some scholars think that Sir 49:14–16 is a secondary addition to the Book of Ben Sira; cf. Middendorp, *Stellung*, 56; Mack, *Wisdom*, 201–3; Lisewski, *Studien*, 37–8. However, this notion is mainly based on the fact that Sir 44 does not mention Joseph. But this can be explained as a deliberate act. Thus, Collins, *Jewish Wisdom*, 106, or Witte, "Gebeine", 140, are right to oppose the idea that Sir 49:14–16 is a secondary addition.

cal narrative, saved the life of his brothers, under God's guidance, and thus
the existence of the Israelite people.[34] Not without reason the Septuagint
version of Sir 49:15 reads:

Sir 49:15 (LXX)   No one was ever born like Joseph,
                  leader of the brothers, sustainer of the people,
                  even his bones were cared for.

In the Septuagint version the importance of Joseph explicitly consists in the
fact that he saved the life of his brothers and therewith the existence of the
people – a view of the person of Joseph that seems to be inherent already in
the Hebrew version of Sir 49:15.[35]

Ben Sira thus refers to the biblical Joseph story. But he does this in a se-
lective way. Joseph's time in Egypt, his life in a foreign land and under
foreign rule, is not mentioned at all. Joseph is of paradigmatic importance
chiefly because of his special relationship with God and his commitment to
the life of his brothers and the existence of the later people of Israel.

As a member of the Jerusalemite upper-class Ben Sira thus takes into account the political circumstances of his time, the situation of Seleucid domination in Palestine. He avoids any statement about the relationship to foreign nations and the special circumstances of a life under foreign rule. Just
as in the original Joseph story, for Ben Sira the importance of Joseph lies in
his special relationship to God and in his acting for his brothers and the
people.

2.2 Joseph in the First Book of the Maccabees

One further reference to Joseph is documented in the First Book of the
Maccabees.[36] This book describes the Maccabees's revolt against Hellenistic pressure under Antiochus IV, their fight against the Seleucid rulers, the
adoption of the High Priest's office and further events up to the death of
Simon. The First Book of the Maccabees stems from the end of the 2nd
century. The author of the book belongs to the milieu of the Maccabean
movement.

---

[34] According to Witte, "Gebeine", 142, Gen 49:15 indicates "die Hochschätzung Josefs als Le-
bensretter der 'Söhne Israels'". Cf. Mulder, *Simon*, 97, who writes that Joseph functions in Sir
49:15 "as an ethical model, representing the ideal image of the good person".

[35] Cf. Witte, "Gebeine", 142, who argues that the Septuagint version of Sir 49:15 is an appropriate extrapolation of the Hebrew text.

[36] For the formation and the content of the First Book of the Maccabees, cf. for example Goldstein, *I Maccabees*, 4–160; Kaiser, *Apokryphen*, 17–20; von Dobbeler, "Makkabäerbücher"; Engel,
"Makkabäer", 313–21.

At the beginning of the book, 1 Macc 2:49–68 presents a longer speech of the dying Mattathias, the patriarch of the Maccabees.[37] In this speech, Mattathias, at first, reflects on some prominent figures from Israelite history, highlighting their obedience to the Torah. He then calls on his sons to adhere strictly to the Torah and to fight against their enemies. In this context, 1 Macc 2:53 says:

> 1 Macc 2:53 Joseph in the time of his distress (στενοχωρία) kept the law, and became lord of Egypt.

1 Macc 2:53 looks back to Joseph's stay in Egypt and mentions a time of distress, in which he kept the law and thus became lord of Egypt. Without doubt, the distress mentioned in this verse alludes to the events in Potiphar's house (Gen 39).[38] The distress is that brought about by Potiphar's wife, who tried to seduce Joseph. The command, which Joseph kept in this situation, is therefore the command against adultery.[39] Thus, 1 Macc 2:53 interprets Joseph's steadfastness, his refusal to get involved with Potiphar's wife – somewhat anachronistically – as a sign of his adherence to the Torah.

Interestingly enough, for the events in Potiphar's house 1 Macc 2:53 uses the term στενοχωρία. This term is, first of all, not a term for interpersonal – for example, sexual – animosities. Rather, στενοχωρία describes political threats, especially threats from external enemies.[40]

In 1 Macc 2:53 the events in Potiphar's house are thus set on a political level. Joseph's resistance against the assaults of Potiphar's wife is portrayed as resistance against distress of external enemies. Because of this resistance Joseph gets political power: he gets the regency over the land of Egypt.[41]

Correspondingly, the survey given in 1 Macc 2 presents some additional figures from Israelite history who distinguished themselves by their active or passive fight against external enemies. 1 Macc 2 mentions Phinehas, Joshua, Elijah, the three men in the furnace known from the book of Daniel, as well as Daniel himself. Mattathias' farewell address in 1 Macc 2 thus points out not only the ancestors' adherence to the Torah but also their resistance to outside enemies.[42]

---

[37] For 1 Macc 2 cf. Keel, "1 Makk 2", 123–33; Goldstein, I Maccabees, 6–8; Hieke, "Role", 61–74; Reiterer, "Vergangenheit", 75–100; Egger-Wenzel, "Testament", 141–9.

[38] Goldstein, I Maccabees, 240; Hieke, "Role", 66, and Reiterer, "Vergangenheit", 88. Thus, it cannot be said that 1 Macc 2:52–60 separates the ancestors from their historical context; contra Neuhaus, Studien, 168; Dommershausen, 1 Makkabäer, 26; von Dobbeler, 1/2 Makkabäer, 64.

[39] Cf. Hieke, "Role", 66.

[40] Deut 28:53, 55, 57; Isa 30:6; 1 Macc 13:3 (LXX); cf. Reiterer, "Vergangenheit", 88.

[41] Hieke, "Role", 66: "'Joseph' serves as a Biblical symbol for the idea that those who keep God's commandments are entitled to exercise political power."

[42] Thus, Dommershausen, 1 Makkabäer, 25, writes: "Mattatias ermahnt die Seinen, nach dem Vorbild ihrer berühmten Ahnen für das Gesetz ... kämpfend einzutreten." Cf. Hieke, "Role", 73–4.

Against this background, the further progress of Mattathias's speech is noteworthy. After his survey of the past Mattathias calls his sons to follow the ancestors' example. At the end of his speech, in 1 Macc 2:67–68, he gives the following command:

1 Macc 2:67   You shall rally around you all who observe the law, and take vengeance for your people.
        68   Pay back the gentiles, and obey the command of the law.

In 1 Macc 2:67–68, the command to keep the law is mentioned together with the call to take vengeance on the Gentiles. According to Mattathias' farewell speech, obedience to the Torah and resistance to the gentiles belong together.

This means that Joseph and the other ancestors mentioned in 1 Macc 2, who demonstrated their obedience to the Torah in times of political distress, are presented as paradigms for the resistance against Gentile enemies. Thus, Mattathias' farewell speech legitimizes the Maccabean revolt against the Seleucid rulers through the character of Joseph and the other ancestors of the people.

Like the author of the Potiphar account added in Gen 39 and based upon this account, the authors of the First Book of the Maccabees – and thus the sympathizers of the Maccabean movement – refer to Joseph in order to point out the distress to which the Israelite people are exposed among the nations. Additionally, and even beyond the biblical Joseph story, they use the figure of Joseph to issue a call to resist, a call to fight against the nations and to fight against a life under foreign rule.

2.3 Joseph in the Testaments of the Twelve Patriarchs

The last adoption of the biblical Joseph story, treated here, stands in the Testaments of the Twelve Patriarchs.[43] This scripture presents farewell speeches of the sons of Jacob, in which they look back on their lives and set forth ethical demands and eschatological promises. The Testaments of the Twelve Patriarchs originate from the later Hellenistic time, probably the 2nd or the 1st century BCE. They are – at the core – a document of the Egyptian Diaspora.[44]

---

[43] An edition of the Testaments of the Twelve Patriarchs is provided by de Jonge, *Testaments*; cf. the translations by Becker, *Testamente*, 32–158; Kee, "Testaments", 782–828. For the debated formation and content of this scripture, cf. Becker, *Testamente*, 23–9; Kee, "Testaments", 775–80; Collins, *Athens*, 174–85; Kugler, *Testaments*, 12–40; Tilly, "Testamente".

[44] The time and place of the Testaments' formation are, however, disputed. In its present form the Testaments of the Twelve Patriarchs are a Christian scripture. This led Hollander/de Jonge,

The Testaments of the Twelve Patriarchs mention Joseph several times. The following reflections focus upon the Testament of Joseph and especially upon the first section in T.Jos 1:3–10:4, in which Joseph describes his journey to Egypt (1:3–7) and the events in Potiphar's house (2:1–10:4). At the beginning of the remarks about Joseph's time in Potiphar's house, T.Jos 2:4–7 presents the following theological reflection:

> T.Jos 2:4 The Lord does not abandon those who fear him, neither in darkness nor in bonds nor in tribulation nor in necessities.
>
> 5 For God is not ashamed as a man, nor is he afraid as a son of man, nor is he weak or frightened as one born on the earth.
>
> 6 In all places he assists, and in different ways he comforts, though departing for a short time in order to test the disposition of the soul.
>
> 7 In ten temptations he showed that I was approved, and in all of them I endured; for endurance is a strong medicine and patience gives many good things.

T.Jos 2:4–7 describes the assistance of God in times of need and distress. Additionally, it emphasizes that God assists in all places. That means, the assistance of God also applies to those members of the people who live beyond the borders of their land.[45] Also those, who live like Joseph in a foreign land, in the Diaspora, may be certain of God's assistance and care.

But even more: According to T.Jos 2:6–7 hostilities and distress befalling the people in a foreign land are to be understood as divine testings. They are temptations in which the members of the people, like Joseph in the house of Potiphar, have to prove their patience and endurance.

This, the patience and endurance of Joseph, is illustrated in the subsequent sections of the Testament of Joseph (T.Jos 2:8–9:5).[46] It describes how Potiphar's wife demands again and again that Joseph become involved with her. She disrobes before him. She flatters him. She threatens him with

---

Testaments, 82–5, and Kugler, *Testaments*, 35–8, to suppose that the Testaments go back to Christian circles of the 2nd century CE. But following Becker, *Untersuchungen*, 129–372; Collins, *Athens*, 175–6, et al., it can be shown that the core of the Testaments has been written by Hellenistic Jewish groups and was re-edited in Christian circles. The original Jewish version of the Testaments may be dated in the 2nd or 1st century BCE; cf. Kee, "Testaments", 775; Mendels, *Land*, 89; Ulrichsen, *Grundschrift*, 338; Collins, *Athens*, 176–7; Tilly, "Testamente". Concerning the place of its origin Ulrichsen, *Grundschrift*, 340–2; Mendels, *Land*, 89–91, point to Palestine, probably Jerusalem. However, the Testaments give no reason to suppose that they can be traced back to a Hebrew *Vorlage*, they show some lack of knowledge about the geography of Palestine, they do not mention the cult of Jerusalem and they are not attested at Qumran. Thus, they were most probably written in the Diaspora, presumably in Egypt; cf. Becker, *Untersuchungen*, 374; Rengstorf, "Herkunft"; Collins, *Athens*, 176.

[45] Thomas, "Aktuelles", 113–14; Becker, *Untersuchungen*, 232–3.

[46] T.Jos 2:8–9:5 exactly describes the ten different temptations mentioned in T.Jos 2:7; cf. Becker, *Untersuchungen*, 234–5.

punishment, imprisonment, or with her own suicide. But Joseph resists all these temptations and hostilities.

At the end of the section, T.Jos 10:1–4 lays out the following admonition:

> T.Jos 10:1 You see, my children, how patience and prayer with fasting work great things.
>
> 2 You also, if you pursue chastity and purity with patience and humility of the heart, the Lord will dwell in you, because he loves chastity.
>
> 3 And where the Most High dwells, even if someone falls into envy or slavery or false accusation, the Lord who dwells in him, not only rescues him from these evils for the sake of his chastity, but also exalts him and glorifies him as he did for me.
>
> 4 For he unites with every man in deed, word or thought.[47]

In T.Jos 10:1–4 Joseph's behavior towards Potiphar's wife is presented as a positive example of endurance. In times of distress and hostilities Joseph's descendants will prove their patience and endurance just as he did. If they follow his example, the assistance and care of God also applies to them. God will live in them, and he will exalt them and glorify them as he did with Joseph.

The Testament of Joseph thus shows, by means of the character of Joseph, the circumstances and the prospects of life in a foreign land.[48] It concedes that hostilities can occur. But such hostilities are presented as temptations, in which the members of the people have to prove their patience and endurance. Additionally – comparable to the promise added to the biblical Joseph story in Gen 46:1aβ–5a – the Testament of Joseph points out that the assistance of God also applies to the members of the people who live in a foreign land. If they are patient and endure, their God cares for them, saves them and exalts them.

With the Testament of the Twelve Patriarchs the members of the Egyptian Diaspora thus illustrate that the life chosen by them, life in a foreign land and among a foreign people, can succeed. Due to the hostilities with which they are confronted in such a foreign land, they plead for an ethics of nonviolent resistance. They interpret such hostilities as divine testings in which they must prove their patience and endurance, and they demonstrate that it is possible to overcome such testings in the confidence that God will assist them.

---

[47] For T.Jos 10:4 cf. Becker, *Testamente*, 124 with note 4a.

[48] Cf. Rengstorf, "Herkunft", 38–44. Thus, the assumption of Pervo, "Testament", 22, or Hollander, *Joseph*, 41–2, that T.Jos focuses upon the ethical attitude of Joseph, falls short. They overlook that T.Jos describes Joseph's fate and his behavior under the circumstances of life in a foreign land.

Conclusion

The biblical Joseph story shows different or even contradictory views concerning life in a foreign land and under foreign rule. The original Joseph story focuses upon the person of Joseph, his special relationship to God, the leadership among his brothers and the salvation of his brothers. In contrast, the account of Joseph in Potiphar's house added in Gen 39 presents the hostilities and the arbitrariness with which the members of the people are confronted in a foreign land. The promise to Jacob added in Gen 46:1aβ–5a, however, shows that living in a foreign land, despite all risks, is possible due to the special blessing of God.

These different views on life in a foreign land, already documented within the biblical Joseph story, recur in the Jewish literature of the later Hellenistic time. The different Jewish groups of this time refer to the biblical Joseph story in very different ways and so again present, through the character of Joseph, a more neutral view, a negative view and a positive view on life in a foreign land.

As in the original Joseph story, Ben Sira, a member of the Jerusalemite upper-class, refers to Joseph because of his relationship to God and his commitment to the life of his brothers and the existence of the later people of Israel. As Gen 39 does, the sympathizers of the Maccabean movement present in the First Book of the Maccabees, through the character of Joseph, the hostilities of the nations that befall the members of the people, and they even issue a call to fight against foreign nations and against foreign rule. As is the case in Gen 46:1aβ–5a, the members of the Diaspora show in the Testaments of the Twelve Patriarchs, through the character of Joseph, that, despite all risks, life in a foreign land is possible thanks to the assistance of God.

The different adoptions of the Joseph story thus give insights into the attitudes of different Jewish groups in the later Hellenistic time towards life under foreign rule. The Jerusalemite upper-class, the sympathizers of the Maccabean movement and the members of the Diaspora all treat the question of how to live under foreign rule in very different ways.

What is remarkable, however, is that all these groups refer to the same biblical tradition. Due to the long-term redactional development of the biblical tradition it provides within a very small space very different views on life in a foreign land and under foreign rule. The later Jewish groups could all draw upon these different views documented within the biblical tradition. The Jerusalemite upper-class, the sympathizers of the Maccabean movement and the members of the Diaspora stand on one and the same biblical foundation. But due to their different social and political backgrounds they refer to different streams within the biblical tradition. The plurality of viewpoints among the different Jewish groups thus mirrors the plurality of the biblical tradition itself.

References

Albertz, R., "Die Josephsgeschichte im Pentateuch", in T. Naumann/R. Hunziker-Rodewald (ed.), *Diasynchron: Beiträge zur Exegese, Theologie und Rezeption der Hebräischen Bibel* (FS W. Dietrich; Stuttgart: Kohlhammer, 2009) 11–36.

Becker, J., *Untersuchungen zur Entstehungsgeschichte der Testamente der zwölf Patriarchen* (AGJU 8; Leiden: Brill, 1970).

–, *Die Testamente der zwölf Patriarchen* (JSHRZ 3; Gütersloh: Gütersloher, 1974).

Beentjes, P.C., *The Book of Ben Sira in Hebrew: A Text Edition of all Extant Hebrew Manuscripts and a Synopsis of all Parallel Hebrew Ben Sira Texts* (VTSup 68; Leiden et al.: Brill, 1997).

Blum, E., *Die Komposition der Vätergeschichte* (WMANT 57; Neukirchen-Vluyn: Neukirchener, 1984).

–, "Die literarische Verbindung von Erzvätern und Exodus. Ein Gespräch mit neueren Endredaktionshypothesen", in J.C. Gertz et al. (ed.), *Abschied vom Jahwisten: Die Komposition des Hexateuch in der jüngsten Diskussion* (BZAW 315; Berlin/New York: de Gruyter, 2002) 119–56.

Coats, G.W., *From Canaan to Egypt: Structural and Theological Context for the Joseph Story* (CBQMS 4; Washington: Catholic Biblical Association, 1976).

Collins, J.J., *Jewish Wisdom in the Hellenistic Age* (OTL; Louisville: Westminster John Knox, 1997).

–, *Between Athens and Jerusalem: Jewish Identity in the Hellenistic Diaspora* (Grand Rapids: Eerdmans, ²2000).

Crüsemann, F., *Der Widerstand gegen das Königtum: Die antiköniglichen Texte des Alten Testaments und der Kampf um den frühen israelitischen Staat* (WMANT 49; Neukirchen-Vluyn: Neukirchener, 1978).

de Jonge, M., *The Testaments of the Twelve Patriarchs: A Critical Edition of the Greek Text* (PVTG; Leiden: Brill, 1978).

Dietrich, W., *Die Josephserzählung als Novelle und Geschichtsschreibung: Zugleich ein Beitrag zur Pentateuchfrage* (BThSt 14; Neukirchen-Vluyn: Neukirchener, 1989).

Docherty, S., "Joseph the Patriarch: Representations of Joseph in Early Post-Biblical Literature", in M. O'Kane (ed.), *Borders, Boundaries and the Bible* (JSOTSup 313; Sheffield: Sheffield Academic Press, 2002) 194–216.

Dommershausen, W., *1 Makkabäer. 2 Makkabäer* (NEchtB 12; Würzburg: Echter, 1985).

Donner, H., "Die literarische Gestalt der alttestamentlichen Josephsgeschichte", in idem, *Aufsätze zum Alten Testament aus vier Jahrzehnten* (BZAW 224; Berlin/New York: de Gruyter, 1994) 76–120.

Ebach, J., *Genesis 37–50* (HTKAT; Freiburg: Herder, 2007).

Eerdmans, B.D., *Alttestamentliche Studien* (4 vol.; Gießen: Töpelmann, 1908–12).

Egger-Wenzel, R., "The Testament of Mattathias to His Sons in 1 Macc 2:49–70: A Keyword Composition with the Aim of Justification", in N. Calduch-Benages/J. Liesen (ed.), *Deuterocanonical and Cognate Literature: Yearbook 2006* (Berlin/New York: de Gruyter, 2006) 141–9.

Engel, H., "Die Bücher der Makkabäer", in E. Zenger et al., *Einleitung in das Alte Testament* (Kohlhammer Studienbücher Theologie 1,1; Stuttgart: Kohlhammer, ⁷2008) 312–28.

Gertz, J.C., *Tradition und Redaktion in der Exoduserzählung: Untersuchungen zur Endredaktion des Pentateuch* (FRLANT 186; Göttingen: Vandenhoeck & Ruprecht, 2000).

Gilbert, M., "Wisdom Literature", in M.E. Stone (ed.), *Jewish Writings of the Second Temple Period: Apocrypha, Pseudepigrapha, Qumran Sectarian Writings, Philo, Josephus* (CRINT 2; Assen/Philadelphia: Van Gorcum/Fortress, 1984) 283–324.

Goldstein, J.A., *I Maccabees: A New Translation with Introduction and Commentary* (AB 41; New York: Doubleday, 1976).

Gruen, E.S., *Heritage and Hellenism: The Reinvention of Jewish Tradition* (Berkeley et al.: University of California Press, 1998).

Gunkel, H., *Genesis* (HKAT 1,1; Göttingen: Vandenhoeck & Ruprecht, [6]1964).

Hengel, M., *Judentum und Hellenismus* (WUNT 10; Tübingen: Mohr, [3]1988).

Hieke, T., "The Role of 'Scripture' in the Last Words of Mattathias (1 Macc 2:49–70)", in G.G. Xeravits/J. Zsengellér (ed.), *The Books of the Maccabees: History, Theology, Ideology* (JSJSup; Leiden/Boston: Brill, 2007) 61–74.

Hollander, H.W., *Joseph as an Ethical Model in the Testaments of the Twelve Patriarchs* (SVTP 6; Leiden: Brill, 1981).

–, "The Portrayal of Joseph in Hellenistic Jewish and Early Christian Literature", in M.E. Stone/T.A. Bergren (ed.), *Biblical Figures Outside the Bible* (Harrisburg: Trinity Press, 1998) 237–63.

–/de Jonge, M., *The Testaments of the Twelve Patriarchs: A Commentary* (SVTP 8; Leiden: Brill, 1985).

Jacob, B., *Das Buch Genesis* (Stuttgart: Calwer, [1934] 2000).

Kaiser, O., *Die alttestamentlichen Apokryphen: Ein Einleitung in Grundzügen* (Gütersloh: Gütersloher, 2000).

Kebekus, N., *Die Joseferzählung: Literarkritische und redaktionsgeschichtliche Untersuchungen zu Genesis 37–50* (Internationale Hochschulschriften; Münster/New York: Waxmann, 1990).

Kee, H.C., "Testaments of the Twelve Patriarchs", in J.H. Charlesworth (ed.), *The Old Testament Pseudepigrapha* (vol. 1; Peabody: Hendrickson, 1983) 775–828.

Keel, O., "1 Makk 2 – Rechtfertigung, Programm und Denkmal für die Erhebung der Hasmonäer: Eine Skizze", in idem/U. Staub (ed.), *Hellenismus und Judentum: Vier Studien zu Daniel 7 und zur Religionsnot unter Antiochus IV.* (OBO 178; Fribourg/Göttingen: Universitätsverlag/Vandenhoeck & Ruprecht, 2000) 123–33.

Kratz, R.G., *Die Komposition der erzählenden Bücher des Alten Testaments* (UTB 2157; Göttingen: Vandenhoeck & Ruprecht, 2000).

Kugler, R.A., *The Testaments of the Twelve Patriarchs* (Guides to Apocrypha and Pseudepigrapha 10; Sheffield: Sheffield Academic Press, 2001).

Lee, T.R., *Studies in the Form of Sirach 44–50* (SBLDS 75; Atlanta: SBL, 1986).

Levin, C., *Der Jahwist* (FRLANT 157; Göttingen: Vandenhoeck & Ruprecht, 1993).

Lisewski, K.D., *Studien zu Motiven und Themen zur Josefsgeschichte der Genesis* (Europäische Hochschulschriften 23,881; Frankfurt a.M. et al.: Lang, 2008).

Lux, R., *Josef: Der Auserwählte unter seinen Brüdern* (Biblische Gestalten 1; Leipzig: Evangelische Verlagsanstalt, 2001).

Mack, B.L., *Wisdom and the Hebrew Epic: Ben Sira's Hymn in Praise of the Fathers* (CSJH; Chicago/London: University of Chicago Press, 1985).

Marböck, J., "Das Buch Jesus Sirach", in E. Zenger et al., *Einleitung in das Alte Testament* (Kohlhammer Studienbücher Theologie 1,1; Stuttgart: Kohlhammer, [7]2008) 408–16.

Meinhold, A., "Die Gattung der Josephsgeschichte und des Estherbuches: Diasporanovelle I", *ZAW* 87 (1975) 306–24.

Mendels, D., *The Land of Israel as a Political Concept in Hasmonean Literature: Recourse to History in Second Century B.C. Claims to the Holy Land* (TSAJ 15; Tübingen: Mohr, 1987).

Middendorp, T., *Die Stellung Jesu Ben Siras zwischen Judentum und Hellenismus* (Leiden: Brill, 1973).

Mulder, O., *Simon the High Priest in Sirach 50: An Exegetical Study of the Significance of Simon the High Priest as Climax to the Praise of the Fathers in Ben Sira's Concept of the History of Israel* (JSJSup 78; Leiden/Boston: Brill, 2003).

72   Jakob Wöhrle

Neuhaus, G.O., *Studien zu den poetischen Stücken im 1. Makkabäerbuch* (Forschungen zur Bibel 12; Würzburg: Echter, 1974).
Niditch, S./Doran, R., "The Success Story of the Wise Courtier: A Formal Approach", *JBL* 96 (1977) 179–93.
Niehoff, M., *The Figure of Joseph in Post-Biblical Jewish Literature* (AGJU 16; Leiden et al.: Brill, 1992).
Pervo, R.I., "The Testament of Joseph and Greek Romance", in G.W.E. Nickelsburg (ed.), *Studies on the Testament of Joseph* (SBLSCS 5; Missoula: Scholars Press, 1975) 15–28.
Redford, D.B., *A Study of the Biblical Story of Joseph (Genesis 37–50)* (VTSup 20; Leiden: Brill, 1970).
Reiterer, F.V., "Jesus Sirach / Jesus Sirachbuch", *WiBiLex* (2006).
–, "Die Vergangenheit als Basis für die Zukunft: Mattathias' Lehre für seine Söhne aus der Geschichte in 1 Makk 2:52–60", in G.G. Xeravits/J. Zsengellér (ed.), *The Books of the Maccabees: History, Theology, Ideology* (JSJSup; Leiden/Boston: Brill, 2007) 75–100.
Rengstorf, K.H., "Herkunft und Sinn der Patriarchen-Reden in den Testamenten der zwölf Patriarachen", in W.C. van Unnik (ed.), *La littérature juive entre Tenach et Mischna: Quelques problèmes* (RechBib 9; Leiden: Brill, 1974) 29–47.
Römer, T., "La narration, une subversion: L'histoire de Joseph (Gn 37–50*) et les romans de la diaspora", in G.J. Brooke/J.-D. Kaestli (ed.), *Narrativity in Biblical and Related Texts* (BETL 149; Leuven: Peeters, 2000) 17–29.
Sauer, G., *Jesus Sirach / Ben Sira* (ATD Apokryphen 1; Göttingen: Vandenhoeck & Ruprecht, 2000).
Schmid, K., "Die Josephsgeschichte im Pentateuch", in J.C. Gertz et al. (ed.), *Abschied vom Jahwisten: Die Komposition des Hexateuch in der jüngsten Diskussion* (BZAW 315; Berlin/New York: de Gruyter, 2002) 83–118.
Schmitt, H.-C., *Die nichtpriesterliche Josephsgeschichte: Ein Beitrag zur neuesten Pentateuchkritik* (BZAW 514; Berlin/New York: de Gruyter, 1980).
Thomas, J., "Aktuelles im Zeugnis der zwölf Väter", in W. Eltester (ed.), *Studien zu den Testamenten der Zwölf Patriarchen* (BZNW 36; Töpelmann: Berlin, 1969) 62–150.
Tilly, M., "Testamente der 12 Patriarchen", *WiBiLex* (2007).
Ulrichsen, J.H., *Die Grundschrift der Testamente der zwölf Patriarchen: Eine Untersuchung zu Umfang, Inhalt und Eigenart der ursprünglichen Schrift* (Acta Universitatis Upsaliensis: Historia Religionum 10; Uppsala: Almqvist & Wiksell, 1991).
von Dobbeler, S., *Die Bücher 1/2 Makkabäer* (NSK.AT 11; Stuttgart: Katholisches Bibelwerk, 1997).
–, "Makkabäerbucher 1–4", *WiBiLex* (2006).
Wahl, H.M., "Das Motiv des 'Aufstiegs' in der Hofgeschichte: Am Beispiel von Joseph, Esther und Daniel", *ZAW* 112 (2000) 59–74.
Weimar, P., "'Jahwe aber war mit Josef' (Gen 39,2): Eine Geschichte von programmatischer Bedeutung", in idem, *Studien zur Josefsgeschichte* (SBA 44; Stuttgart: Katholisches Bibelwerk, 2008) 61–124.
–, "Josef – Eine Geschichte vom schwierigen Prozeß der Versöhnung", in idem, *Studien zur Josefsgeschichte* (SBA 44; Stuttgart: Katholisches Bibelwerk, 2008) 9–26.
Westermann, C., *Genesis* (3 vol.; BKAT 1,1–3; Neukirchen-Vluyn: Neukirchener, 1974–82).
Witte, M., "Die Gebeine Josefs", in M. Beck/U. Schorn (ed.), *Auf dem Weg zur Endgestalt von Genesis bis II Regum* (FS H.-C. Schmitt; BZAW 370; Berlin/New York: de Gruyter, 2006) 139–56.
Wöhrle, J., *Fremdlinge im eigenen Land. Zur Entstehung und Intention der priesterlichen Passagen der Vätergeschichte* (FRLANT 246; Göttingen: Vandenhoeck & Ruprecht, 2012).

Sebastian Grätz

Johannes Gutenberg-Universität Mainz

The Adversaries in Ezra/Nehemiah – Fictitious or Real?

A Case Study in Creating Identity in
Late Persian and Hellenistic Times

There is no doubt that the present books of Ezra and Nehemiah intend to "rebuild identity" as Jacob Wright has put it very nicely.[1] The accounts of the rebuilding of the temple, the mission of Ezra, and the reconstruction of the city-walls appear at first glance to be accurate reports of the post-exilic history of Judah. They clearly display the aim of the authors to communicate valid information by displaying official texts, e.g., Aramaic letters of Persian kings, which should be adequate to underline the official character and the authenticity of the report.[2] On the other hand it is also clear that the accounts contain the perspectives of the authors who represent the interests of specific communities in the course of the rebuilding of Judah.[3] Thus, the accounts also serve to create aspects of identity by mentioning individuals by name or by defining specific groups, and it is, therefore, not astonishing that the presence of adversaries or enemies is described in every part of the books of Ezra and Nehemiah. To be more precise, the occurrence of adversaries or troublemakers is mainly connected to three specific features: first, the rebuilding of the temple in Ezra 4; 5–6; second, the rebuilding of the city-wall in the so-called Nehemiah-Memoir (Neh 1–6; 13); and third, the passage concerning the so-called mixed-marriages in Ezra 9–10. This last passage, however, deals not so much with adversaries who can be named as with specific circumstances in the post-exilic Judean society.[4] In my contribution I will thus focus only on Ezra 4–6 and the Nehemiah-memoir.

---

[1] Wright, *Identity*.

[2] See Grätz, *Edikt*.

[3] See among others Grabbe, "Persian Documents", 563, who holds that the compiler of Ezra reworked some original documents for apologetic and theological purposes.

[4] The case is labeled in Ezra 9:4 as "unfaithfulness of the golah" (*ma'al haggôlâ*). Thus, the case of "mixed marriages" represents a wrongdoing against the Torah (see Ezra 10:3) rather than a crisis caused by certain adversaries. The foreign peoples in Ezra 9:1 stem from Deut 7:1; 23:4, and they serve to illustrate the act of "unfaithfulness" of the Israelites.

1. The Book of Ezra: Ezra 4; 5–6

Ezra 4 consists of a Hebrew part in v. 1–5, and an Aramaic part in v. 6–24. The first verses read as follows:[5]

> Ezra 4:1 When the adversaries of Judah and Benjamin heard that the returned exiles were building a temple to the LORD, the God of Israel,
>
> 2 they approached Zerubbabel and the heads of families and said to them, "Let us build with you, for we worship your God as you do, and we have been sacrificing to him ever since the days of King Esarhaddon of Assyria who brought us here."
>
> 3 But Zerubbabel, Jeshua, and the rest of the heads of families in Israel said to them, "You shall have no part with us in building a house to our God; but we alone will build to the LORD, the God of Israel, as King Cyrus of Persia has commanded us."
>
> 4 Then the people of the land discouraged the people of Judah, and made them afraid to build,
>
> 5 and they bribed officials to frustrate their plan throughout the reign of King Cyrus of Persia and until the reign of King Darius of Persia.

V. 5 functions as a literary bridge to the following Aramaic part which ends in v. 24 with the conclusion that the work on the temple stopped until the reign of Darius. V. 1–4 are defined by the opposition of the "people of the land" (*'am hā'āreṣ*) and the "people of Judah" (*'am yĕhûdâ*). The context clarifies that the group called the "people of the land" is not at all a genuinely local group of people because they were imported by the Assyrian king Esarhaddon. Though they are worshippers of the Lord, the text makes a clear distinction between this *'am hā'āreṣ*[6] and the *'am yĕhûdâ*, the latter being identical to the *bĕnê haggôlâ*, rooted in the Babylonian Exile (v. 1). Even though the well-known text of 2 Kings 17, esp. v. 24–28,[7] with its anti-Samarian attitude may form the backdrop of our text, v. 1–5 function in the present context primarily to introduce the Aramaic letters of the following passage from v. 6 onward. However, it is not very easy to determine the sequence of letters presented in v. 6–11:

---

[5] All biblical passages are quoted from the NRSV.

[6] See Fried, "*'am hā'āræṣ*", 129ff, who argues for an identity of the *'am hā'āreṣ* with satrapal officials. If one takes Ezra 4:1–5 synchronously as an introduction to the letters that follow in v. 6ff, then this view seems to be plausible. On the other hand, it remains problematic that v. 5 and v. 6ff mention different kings and, thus, may suggest different stages of literary development. V. 1–5 and v. 24 put Darius together with the suspension of temple-building, whereas v. 6ff mention Xerxes and Artaxerxes in the context of the suspension of *city*-building. Therefore the identity between the *'am hā'āreṣ* in v. 1–5 and the personnel of v. 6ff is not assured. See also below.

[7] See Grätz, "Kommunikation?", 258–9.

Ezra 4:6   In the reign of Ahasuerus, in his accession year, they wrote an accusation against the inhabitants of Judah and Jerusalem.

    7 And in the days of Artaxerxes, Bishlam and Mithredath and Tabeel and the rest of their associates wrote to King Artaxerxes of Persia; the letter was written in Aramaic and translated.

    8 Rehum the royal deputy and Shimshai the scribe wrote a letter against Jerusalem to King Artaxerxes as follows

    9 then Rehum the royal deputy, Shimshai the scribe, and the rest of their associates, the judges, the envoys, the officials,[8] the Persians, the people of Erech, the Babylonians, the people of Susa, that is, the Elamites,

  10 and the rest of the nations whom the great and noble Osnappar deported and settled in the cities of Samaria and in the rest of the province Beyond the River wrote – and now

  11 this is a copy of the letter that they sent: To King Artaxerxes: Your servants, the people of the province Beyond the River, send greeting. And now ...

Here we find according to Schwiderski an accumulation of reports concerning four letters (1. v. 6; 2. v. 7a; 3. v. 8 [without *kĕnēmā'*]; 4. v. 8 [*kĕnēmā'*]–16). A fifth one, perhaps a part of a rescript, could be hidden in v. 7b.[9] Not until v. 11 do we come to know the content of the last of these letters which begins probably with v. 9. Additionally, the identification and the sequence of kings mentioned in Ezra 4:1–10 is puzzling: Ezra 4:5 mentions the time period from Cyrus to Darius whereas Ezra 4:6–8 notes the kings Xerxes and Artaxerxes. V. 10 refers to Osnappar/Assurbanipal(?), whereas v. 2 mentions Esarhaddon.[10] Finally, the content of the quoted letter deals clearly with the reconstruction of the city of Jerusalem. This is evident from v. 11–13, 16(, 21):

Ezra 4:11   ... And now,

    12 may it be known to the king that the Jews who came up from you to us have gone to Jerusalem. They are rebuilding that rebellious and wicked city; they are finishing the walls and repairing the foundations.

    13 Now may it be known to the king that, if this city is rebuilt and the walls finished, they will not pay tribute, custom, or toll, and the royal revenue will be reduced.

      ...

    16 We make known to the king that, if this city is rebuilt and its walls finished, you will then have no possession in the province Beyond the River.

---

[8] On the enumeration of the officials see Blenkinsopp, *Ezra–Nehemiah*, 105. Schwiderski, *Handbuch*, 348–9, assumes that the terms in question (v. 9bα) also denote persons.

[9] See Schwiderski, *Handbuch*, 345(ff).

[10] See Gunneweg, *Esra*, 84.

It is noteworthy that these events are dated to the reign of a certain Arta-xerxes, whereas the events reported in Ezra 4:1–5 are dated to the reign of Cyrus and focus on the rebuilding of the temple. Thus, it is unlikely that both parts, Ezra 4:1–5 and 4:6–23, originally belonged together. Only the last verse of chapter 4, v. 24, refers to 4:1–5 by mentioning king Darius again.[11]

> Ezra 4:1–5   Cyrus – Darius
> Ezra 4:6–23   Xerxes – Artaxerxes
> Ezra 4:24   Darius

Whereas Ezra 4:1–5 mentions generally the "people of the land" as adver-saries of the temple-builders, Ezra 4:7–10 offers a multitude of opponents, partly by name and partly in general. Unfortunately the adversaries who are mentioned by name are not identifiable as Blenkinsopp has shown.[12] Maybe the Tabeel (Aram. "god is good") in v. 7 could be identified with Tobiah who is well-known from the book of Nehemiah.[13] However, this identifica-tion remains extremely hypothetical. Otherwise it is obvious that v. 10 contains an anti-Samarian attitude. Here, the adversaries are identified with the peoples who were settled there by Osnappar. Thus far one can assume that the author of the last two letters in which Rehum, Shimshai and others are mentioned (letter 3 and 4) defines the Samarian population as foreign and considers them as the main adversaries of the Judeans. This presump-tion could be confirmed by Ezra 4:21–23 where Rehum and Shimshai are commanded to go to Jerusalem (apparently from outside of Judah) and to make the Judeans cease to work. The first letter (v. 6) names no sender. Therefore, the present text suggests that the sender is the "people of the land" of v. 4 who have already been labeled as adversaries in v. 1. Based on the allusion to Esarhaddon's resettlements in v. 2 and the fact that the "peo-ple of the land" worship YHWH, the author seems to identify these adver-saries as Samarians as well (cf. 2 Kings 17:24–34). Finally, the remaining second letter (v. 7a) names Bishlam, Mithredath and the aforementioned Tabeel. In the case of the first one, Bishlam, it is not clear whether it is a personal name at all. Thus, Blenkinsopp suggests the translation "in peace" or "in accordance with" (*bišlām*).[14] A certain Mithredath is also known as treasurer at the court of Cyrus in Ezra 1:8, and the third one, Tabeel, may be, as mentioned above, identified with Tobiah, although this remains very hypothetical. In sum, most of the adversaries in Ezra 4 are closely linked to the contemporary Samarian population which is said to have been the result

---

[11] See especially Böhler, *Stadt*, 119ff.
[12] See Blenkinsopp, *Ezra–Nehemiah*, 111–12.
[13] Blenkinsopp, *Ezra–Nehemiah*, 111–12. See below.
[14] Blenkinsopp, *Ezra–Nehemiah*, 110.

of the Assyrian policy of resettlement in the 8th and 7th centuries BCE.[15] The remaining figures of the second letter are hardly identifiable. Maybe they are drawn from elsewhere in the context of Ezra–Nehemiah. Gunneweg has supposed that the biblical pattern of the "Völkersturm" forms the backdrop of the multitude of adversaries in Ezra 4.[16] To put it more precisely, the hostile threat is created by the enumeration of foreign nations who constitute the one contemporary adversary, the Samarians. It is possible that the author draws his information from historical sources, but he arranges this information with the clear aim of describing an overwhelming hostility to the building-measures of the Judean people – and thus to the clear orders of God and the Persian king Cyrus (Ezra 1:2).

Ezra 5–6 form a distinct unit within the course of Ezra 1–6. Though Zerubbabel and Joshua are mentioned several times, it is mainly the group of the "elders of the Jews" who are in contact with the Persian officials (Ezra 5:5, 9; 6:7–8, 14).[17] The subject of the so-called Aramaic Chronicle is the legitimacy of the building of the second temple in the time of a certain Darius. In this way the text picks up where the last verse of Ezra 4 (v. 24), in which Darius is mentioned, leaves off. In Ezra 5 Persian officials make an inquiry regarding the temple-building:

> Ezra 5:1 Now the prophets, Haggai and Zechariah son of Iddo, prophesied to the Jews who were in Judah and Jerusalem, in the name of the God of Israel who was over them.
>
> 2 Then Zerubbabel son of Shealtiel and Jeshua son of Jozadak set out to rebuild the house of God in Jerusalem; and with them were the prophets of God, helping them.
>
> 3 At the same time Tattenai the governor of the province Beyond the River and Shethar-bozenai and their associates came to them and spoke to them thus, "Who gave you a decree to build this house and to finish this structure?"
>
> 4 They also asked them this, "What are the names of the men who are building this building?"

It is evident that the inquiry of the officials is not understood as an act of hostility. In the context of the Aramaic Chronicle the inquiry functions as a means to display the legitimacy of the second temple which is guaranteed by the rescript of Cyrus, rediscovered in Ezra 6:1–5. The appearance of officials who make official inquiries serves to underline the formal recognition of the sanctuary in Jerusalem by Persian kings. Thus, the text seems to

---

[15] For the historical background see Oded, "Deportation".

[16] See Gunneweg, *Esra*, 90; also: Karrer, *Ringen*, 342.

[17] See Grätz, "Chronik", 419ff.

have an apologetic attitude. As in the Elephantine letter, Cowley 30:13ff,[18] the legitimacy of the sanctuary is based on the positive attitude of a certain Persian king towards this sanctuary:

Cowley 30:13 And during the days of the kings of Egypt our fathers had built that temple in Elephantine the fortress and when Cambyses entered Egypt
14 he found that temple built. And they overthrew the temples of the gods of Egypt, all (of them), but one did not damage anything in that temple.

It is unknown to us whether the reported events are true or not. But it shows the aim of the author to legitimize the sanctuary which is, at the moment, lying in ruins.

Whereas Shetar Bosnai, bearer of a Persian name,[19] is not identifiable, a certain Tattenai appears in cuneiform sources. He is known from a text to have been governor of Ebir-Nari in 502 BCE. Because the region of Ebir-Nari did not form a satrapy distinct from Babylonia until the reign of Xerxes, he probably resided in Damascus.[20] Like the quotation of letters and rescripts, the reference to public officers serves to create an aura of authenticity and legitimacy. In the present context the intrusions and accusations by the numerous Samarian adversaries in Ezra 4 cannot survive the investigation carried out by the Persian officials in Ezra 5–6. Here it is undeniably demonstrated that the second temple is the only official and true sanctuary of the Lord and his Judean worshippers. The apparent fact that the author in Ezra 4:11–23 uses a record that deals with the reconstruction not of the temple but of the city during the reign of a certain Artaxerxes should be kept in mind.

2. The Nehemiah-Memoir

Recent investigations concerning the book of Nehemiah have challenged the classical view of a homogenous Nehemiah-memoir written in the first person singular. Wright in particular believes it possible to identify within the whole book of Nehemiah seven strata, corresponding to stages in the reception of the book.[21] According to Wright the core of the book consisted of a total of 15 verses or parts of verses, especially from chapter 2.[22] One wonders, however, whether such a short account written in the first person

---

[18] = *TAD* A4.7 // A4.8.

[19] Blenkinsopp, *Ezra–Nehemiah*, 120: Satibarzana.

[20] Blenkinsopp, *Ezra–Nehemiah*, 120.

[21] See Wright, *Identity*, 330ff; Blenkinsopp, *Judaism*, 90.

[22] See Wright, *Identity*, 340.

fits with any literary genre known to us. Moreover, the rebuilding of the
wall, the central aim of Nehemiah's journey to Jerusalem according to Neh
2:1–6 (which belongs to Wright's first stratum), would have been reported
in only two verses (3:38; 6:15). Therefore, Blenkinsopp focuses again on
the matter of the genre of the parts written in the first person singular.[23] His
starting-point is a thesis that in my opinion is correct: "First person narratives from early times are, for the most part, propagandistic and apologetic."[24] Following especially Mowinckel, Blenkinsopp holds that commemo-
rative inscriptions by Mesopotamian rulers share several important features
with the Nehemiah-memoir, e.g. the report of important deeds and the emphasis of the piety of the royal speaker.[25] In addition, he points out that the
salient feature of the first part of the memoir (1:1–7:5) was "the pattern of
opposition from the evil trio of Sanballat, Tobiah, and Geshem (Gashmu)
and the spirited reaction of Nehemiah."[26] In fact, the adversaries appear
throughout seven stages of Nehemiah's activities:[27]

2:9–10	Nehemiah's arrival
2:17–20	Nehemiah's decision to repair the wall
3:33–37	The work gets underway
3:38–4:3	The wall is half finished
4:17	Hostile plots are thwarted
6:1–9	The work is completed apart from the gates
6:15–16	The work is finally completed

Blenkinsopp stresses that the pattern seems to be deliberate, "with the notice that the wall was half finished appropriately at the center of the septe-
nary sequence. One would therefore think that the first person narrative was
put together with more care than might at first appear."[28] On the other hand,
it is not quite clear if 4:17 really belongs to such a pattern because here the
adversaries are not mentioned at all. In addition it should be mentioned that
Tobiah and Sanballat appear also in the second part of the memoir, Neh
13:4–9, 28–29. But it is striking that the adversaries are part of the whole
process involving Nehemiah's deeds in Neh 2–6, apart from chapter 5.

Now, who are these adversaries according to the portrayal of the memoir? Their first occurrence is reported in 2:9–10 when Nehemiah came to
Jerusalem:

---

[23] See Blenkinsopp, *Judaism*, 93ff.

[24] Blenkinsopp, *Judaism*, 93. This view, shared by many scholars, seems to challenge the ade-
quacy of the oldest stratum in Wright's analysis in which no apologetic tendency occurs. Nonetheless, Wright's analysis is, in my opinion, carried out with great perspicacity.

[25] See Blenkinsopp, *Judaism*, 99–100.

[26] Blenkinsopp, *Judaism*, 97.

[27] On these stages, see Blenkinsopp, *Judaism*, 97–8.

[28] Blenkinsopp, *Judaism*, 98.

Neh 2:9 Then I came to the governors of the province Beyond the River, and gave them the king's letters. Now the king had sent officers of the army and cavalry with me.

10 When Sanballat the Horonite and Tobiah the Ammonite official/servant heard this, it displeased them greatly that someone had come to seek the welfare of the people of Israel.

The stereotyped phrase "when Sanballat ... and Tobiah ... heard this" (*wayyišmaʿ Sanballaṭ wěṬôbiyyâ*), which occurs for several times in the pattern (Neh 2:10, 19; 3:33; 4:1; 6:1), suggests that the adversaries do not belong to the officials of the administration. The official correspondence is taking place between Nehemiah and the governors of the province – Sanballat and Tobiah are not involved in that correspondence and come to know what is going on only from hearsay. In addition, they oppose the explicit orders of the king. Thus, the adversaries are portrayed as hostile outsiders from the beginning. Especially curious is their declaration in Neh 2:19 when Nehemiah decides to begin the rebuilding:

Neh 2:19 But when Sanballat the Horonite and Tobiah the Ammonite official/servant, and Geshem the Arab heard of it, they mocked and ridiculed us, saying, "What is this that you are doing? Are you rebelling against the king?"

What is of interest here is the accusation of rebellion (*mrd*) against the king. The same word is used in Ezra 4:12 where the adversaries file a complaint against the Judeans. But here they refer to certain annals in which Jerusalem should have been described as a rebellious city (4:15). In the light of Neh 2:9 the accusation of 2:19 is, of course, baseless. Maybe it is possible that the accusation of rebellion (*mrd*) was taken as a stereotype from Ezra 4. This fits with the observation that the text of Ezra 4:11–23 deals originally with the rebuilding of the city, whereas the framing that deals with the temple seems to be secondary.[29] One may go even further and presume that Ezra 4:11–23, set in the time of a certain Artaxerxes, could have served as a paradigm for the Nehemiah-memoir, which is also linked to the reign of a certain Artaxerxes. All in all, there are significant similarities between the correspondence in Ezra 4 and the Nehemiah-memoir.[30]

The account denotes Sanballat stereotypically as the "Horonite", Tobiah as the "Ammonite servant", and Geshem as the "Arab". Three points about these descriptions are necessary.

---

[29] See ch. 1 above.

[30] This is true at least for the confrontation between Nehemiah and his adversaries from abroad. But it is important to note that this confrontation is, as Blenkinsopp has shown, constitutive for the memoir. On this topic, see also Karrer, *Ringen*, 342, who stresses the similarities between Ezra 4 and the Nehemiah-memoir as well.

First, it is not readily apparent what "Horonite" means. Most scholars believe that the name refers to the Ephraimite location *bêt ḥŏrōn*.[31] Besides this connection, Sanballat is clearly portrayed as a Samarian in the Nehemiah-memoir. In Neh 3:34 he speaks to his brothers and the "Samarian Army" (*ḥêl šōmrôn*).[32] Our historical knowledge of Sanballat tends to confirm this assumption. Apart from the references in Nehemiah, Sanballat is mentioned in the papyri from Elephantine (A4.7,29//A4.8,28) and from Wadi ed-Daliyeh (WD 22; WDSP 11r), although his appearance on Samarian coins is questioned by Dušek.[33] According to Kratz it is plausible to identify the Sanballat of the Elephantine-papyri with the one from the bulla of Wadi ed-Daliyeh.[34] Thus, our small epigraphic evidence seems to place the governor Sanballat in the historical context of the late fifth century or the beginning of the fourth century BCE and not in the middle of the fifth century BCE, as the majority of scholars, who base their view on the Nehemiah-memoir (both 1:1 and 2:1 point to the 20th year of Artaxerxes [I.], which was 445 BCE), suggest.[35] Josephus, in contrast, places Sanballat in the time of Darius III. and Alexander the Great. According to Ant. 11.309 he was related by marriage to the family of the High Priest and, together with his brother-in-law, was responsible for the erection of the sanctuary on Mt. Gerizim at the beginning of the Hellenistic era (Ant. 11.324).[36] This account may partly reflect Neh 13:28 where Sanballat also appears to be related by marriage to the family of the High Priest and is therefore driven out by Nehemiah.[37] In the face of the various literary traditions concerning the name of Sanballat, it is hardly possible to decide definitely if there existed one, two or more bearers of this name in the fifth and fourth centuries BCE. For our purposes, however, it is sufficient to conclude that the figure of Sanballat is linked closely to Samaria. In the Nehemiah-memoir this figure serves as a stereotypical adversary of Nehemiah and the Judean people during the re-building of the city of Jerusalem.

Second, Tobiah is described as the "servant from Ammon" or as simply the "Ammonite" (Neh 3:35). The definite *hā'ebed* may indicate a title, but

---

[31] See, e.g., Schunck, *Nehemia*, 46–7.

[32] Of course, this may be a secondary addition to the text. But it shows that the name of Sanballat has been associated with Samaria – an association that is, in fact, historically correct. See below.

[33] See Dušek, *Manuscrits*, 530–1.

[34] See Kratz, *Judentum*, 96.

[35] See, e.g. Schunck, *Nehemia*, 11ff.

[36] See Dušek, *Manuscrits*, 539ff.

[37] See the detailed analysis of Wright, *Identity*, 261ff, who assumes that Neh 13:28 reflects an historical event from the mid-fourth century BCE. It serves in the book of Nehemiah, as well as in the account of Josephus (Ant. 11.302ff), as a means to criticize the Judean nobility and Jerusalemite priesthood.

the Ammonite origin of Tobiah seems to be also important for the author. Apart from the book of Nehemiah a certain Tobiah is well-known from the Zenon-Papyri as a prosperous tenant in the Ptolemaic Ammanitis.[38] From the Zenon-Papyri it is also evident that Tobiah, even though he was Jewish, had broadly adopted Hellenistic customs. It is attested that he sold Jews as slaves and did not care about the circumcision of his bondsmen.[39] According to Josephus (Ant. 12.160) he was married to a sister of the High Priest Onias II. Thus, it may be not accidental that Tobiah is mentioned also in Neh 13:4–9 in the context of the Jewish separation from Moabites and Ammonites as well as in the context of the cultic contamination of the temple. After Nehemiah had driven Tobiah and his furniture out of his room in the courts of the temple, he purified (ṭhr) it. In sum, it is difficult to assume that the Tobiah who can be verified from the Ptolemaic Ammanitis had a "look-alike" in the times of Artaxerxes I, as portrayed in the book of Nehemiah and nowhere else.

Third, "Geshem, the Arab" is perhaps identical with sheik Guśam bin Šahr who, according to Knauf, controlled the southern parts of Palestine and the northern parts of the Heǧaz in the middle of the fifth century BCE.[40] In Neh 6:6 he is called Gashmu which seems to reflect the convention to write Arabian or Nabatean names in Imperial Aramaic with a waw at the end.[41] Controlling, among other areas, the Frankincense Road, he was surely a powerful neighbor of Yehud in Achaemenid times. Kellermann, however, has already pointed out that the dating of the relevant inscriptions[42] is quite uncertain and that the name in question was widespread during Achaemenid and Hellenistic times.[43] These cautions are supported by the Lihyanite dedicatory inscription, JS 89, from the first century BCE, in which a certain king named Gušam b. Lauḍān occurs.[44]

From a strictly historical point of view, it is unlikely that these three adversaries ever had any dealings with each other. They are prominent officials of their respective peoples in Achaemenid/Hellenistic times and seem to be symbols of the most important neighbors who now, in the narrative, act concertedly against the people of Judah and its representatives. Amplifying the Samarian issue of Ezra 4 the Nehemiah-memoir portrays Judah as surrounded by hostile neighbors in the vulnerable times of rebuilding.

---

[38] See Hengel, Judentum, 486ff.

[39] See Hengel, Judentum, 488–9.

[40] See Knauf, Ismael, 104ff; Lemaire, "Beitrag", 17.

[41] See Knauf, Ismael, 105.

[42] See Lemaire, "Beitrag", 17; Schwiderski, Inschriften, 169.

[43] See Kellermann, Nehemia, 170ff.

[44] See Caskel, Lihyan, 90.

The picture of the adversaries given in Neh 2–4 is amplified in Neh 6. The three scenes in Neh 6:1–9, 10–14, and 17–19 refer again to these well-known adversaries. Before the city-walls are completed (v. 15) they still make attempts to disrupt the progress and the completion of the work.

First, in v. 6–7 they renew the accusation of rebellion from Neh 2:19:

> Neh 6:6 In it [i.e. the letter from Sanballat] was written, "It is reported among the nations – and Geshem also says it – that you and the Jews intend to rebel; that is why you are building the wall; and according to this report you wish to become their king.
>
> 7 You have also set up prophets to proclaim in Jerusalem concerning you, 'There is a king in Judah!' And now it will be reported to the king according to these words. So come, therefore, and let us confer together."

Here, the accusation of rebellion (*mrd*) is explained with reference to Nehemiah's alleged ambition to become king. It is noteworthy that this assumption on the part of Sanballat and his colleague Geshem is also shared by the "nations" (*baggôyîm*).[45] However, the aim of this passage is not really clear until v. 8 where Nehemiah answers:

> Neh 6:8 Then I sent to him, saying, "No such things as you say have been done; you are inventing them out of your own mind."

Jacob Wright has made an interesting observation concerning the composition of the passage: "Although vv. 2–4 present Nehemiah, in analogy to royal building-inscriptions from the ancient Near East, as an 'indefatigable builder,' vv. 5–9 clarify that he did not arrogate to himself the kingship associated with the construction of a city wall."[46] In the light of prophetic statements such as Hag 2:23, where the governor Zerubbabel is proclaimed to be king,[47] Neh 6:1–9 makes good sense: by rejecting any claim of an indigenous kingship the author of the text asserts clearly his loyalty to the current regime. The adversaries function, therefore, implicitly as a means to emphasize this attitude of loyalty on the part of the Judean governor.[48] Whoever intends to reintroduce the kingship in Judah is, thus, labeled as hostile.[49] The focus, then, has shifted from the adversaries who are on the

---

[45] As in Ezra 4 one can correlate the "nations" with the non-believers in the songs of Zion within the Book of Psalms. Here the motif of hostile threats of foreign peoples also occurs. See Gunneweg, *Esra*, 90.

[46] Wright, *Identity*, 143.

[47] See Lux, *Prophetie*, 137.

[48] More carefully: Carroll, "Coopting", 90.

[49] Wright, *Identity*, 143, states: "In repudiating the claims and ascribing them to an assumption made by the enemy, he [i.e. the literary Nehemiah] effectively emphasizes the point that a monarchy is not a suitable form of government for the new Judah."

outside, i.e. the hostile neighbors, to threats from within, i.e. certain (prophetic) circles in Judean society who were interested in renewing the Judean kingship.[50]

Second, the passage in Neh 6:10–14 deals with the venality of the prophets.[51] Shemaiah, who is obviously a prophet (v. 12b), was hired by Sanballat
and Tobiah in order to discourage Nehemiah (v. 11, 13). Hence, this text
also seems to deal with internal – prophetical (see esp. v. 14) – issues, even
though the well-known adversaries serve again to introduce the case. In
sum, Neh 6:1–14 can be read as a rejection of internal doubts concerning
the leadership of Nehemiah.[52] We come to know that prophets are venal and
that prophets are dissatisfied with the political status of Judah and, thus,
oppose Nehemiah's claim of leadership. This is evident especially from v.
14, where the prophets are explicitly mentioned side by side with the noto-
rious adversaries:

> Neh 6:14 "Remember Tobiah and Sanballat, O my God, according to these
> things that they did, and also the prophetess Noadiah and the rest of
> the prophets who wanted to make me afraid."

Third, even after the completion of the city-walls (v. 15) it is Tobiah who
tries to intimidate Nehemiah further. The concluding scene in Neh 6:17–19
presents something of a dilemma: Tobiah is portrayed as an influential
obligee who has deep roots within Judean society. On the one hand, this
portrayal fits well with the historical image of Tobiah as a prosperous tenant in Hellenistic times, as discussed above. On the other hand, the domestic disturbances are again explained as occurring due to hostile external
influences – from abroad – as opposed to internal ones. This is in contrast to
Neh 5 where nothing is said about external forces being responsible for the
social problems within the province of Judah. Here, the nobles of Judah
($h\bar{o}r\hat{i}m$; $s\v{e}g\bar{a}n\hat{i}m$) are called to account for these problems (Neh 5:7), which
appear to be solved definitively (v. 13).[53] The dilemma of Neh 6:17–19 –
and, here, the problem remains unsolved – hints directly at Neh 13:4–9
where Nehemiah throws Tobiah out of his room in the courts of the temple
(i.e. out of the center of the Judean society).

Neh 6, therefore, shows an amplification and also a shift in how the foreign adversaries are portrayed.[54] Continuing the portrayal in Neh 2–4 but

---

[50] See Karrer, *Ringen*, 188.

[51] See Wright, *Identity*, 145–6.

[52] This issue is surely motivated by what is expressed in Neh 5:15, where Nehemiah's prede-
cessors are labeled as exploiters.

[53] See on this issue Wright, *Identity*, 159.

[54] This shifting view is surely the result of literary development on which I cannot focus here.
See esp. Wright, *Identity*, 133ff.

contrasting with that of Neh 5, the narrative has the adversaries function primarily to cause disturbances that appear, at least, originally to be home-made. But from the perspective of Neh 6 and its continuation in Neh 13, it becomes apparent that these disturbances ultimately are caused by foreign forces and that it is necessary to protect Judean society against these forces.

3. Conclusion

To sum up briefly, even if their historical existence can be proven, it is rather difficult to achieve a clear understanding of the adversaries of Nehe-miah. And it is yet more difficult to prove that they were all contemporaries acting together and sharing the same negative attitude toward the rebuilding of the city of Jerusalem in the time of Nehemiah. It seems therefore likely that, above all, these characters serve to illustrate the threats from without and, especially in Neh 6, from within during the fragile time of the rebuild-ing of Jerusalem, Judah and, last but not least, Judean society. Geshem and Sanballat act moreover as representatives or symbols for their people as Neh 3:34/4:1 ("army of Samaria") and Neh 4:1/4:7 ("the Arabs") clearly show. Additionally, Tobiah and Geshem also seem to represent the reli-gious (Neh 13:4–9) and mainly economic danger in which the Judean peo-ple find themselves: they face an enemy that surrounds them – a well-known figure in certain Psalms[55] – and must depend on the help of God. This supposition seems to be true also in Ezra 4 where a crowd of (Samari-an) adversaries accuse the people of Judah of rebellion against the king.[56] Hence, the adversaries in Ezra–Nehemiah seem, on the one hand, to be a means of illustrating the manifold difficulties of the restoration of Judah in post-exilic times and are, thus, portrayed in a more fictitious than real man-ner. On the other hand, this portrayal of the adversaries serves to define the limits of Judean society: the foreigners, even if they are YHWH-worshippers as is obviously true for Tobiah and Sanballat (and the Samari-ans), are essentially hostile toward Judean interests. They behave like ene-mies and are, therefore, not allowed to enter the center of Judean society (e.g. Ezra 4:1–5; Neh 13:4–9, 28–29). Neh 6 amplifies the issue of the adversaries from abroad by portraying certain Judean circles and persons acting as henchmen of the well-known foreign leaders who now have man-aged to penetrate the society deeply. The transfer of the three evil adver-saries from Neh 2–4 to Neh 6 is probably topical; that is, ch. 6 seeks to show that the threats will continue to remain until they are clearly labeled

---

[55] See Blenkinsopp, *Judaism*, 98, who alludes to Ps 118.
[56] See Gunneweg, *Esra*, 90.

and eliminated in a programmatic and thorough way. It is, then, the elimination of the threats that is suggested by the deeds reported in Neh 13.

References

Blenkinsopp, J., *Ezra–Nehemiah. A Commentary* (London: Westminster Press, 1988).
–, *Judaism: The First Phase. The Place of Ezra and Nehemiah in the Origins of Judaism* (Grand Rapids/Cambridge: Eerdmans, 2009).
Böhler, D., *Die heilige Stadt in Esdras a und Esra–Nehemia: Zwei Konzeptionen der Wiederherstellung Israels* (OBO 158; Fribourg/Göttingen: Universitätsverlag/Vandenhoeck & Ruprecht, 1997).
Carroll, R.P., "Coopting the Prophets: Nehemiah and Noadja", in E. Ulrich et al. (ed.), *Priests, Prophets and Scribes: Essays on the Formation and Heritage of Second Temple Judaism* (FS J. Blenkinsopp; JSOTSup 149; Sheffield: JSOT Press, 1994) 87–99.
Caskel, W., *Lihyan und Lihyanitisch* (Arbeitsgemeinschaft für Forschung des Landes Nordrhein-Westfalen. Geisteswissenschaften, Heft 4; Köln/Opladen: Westdeutscher Verlag, 1954).
Dušek, J., *Les manuscrits araméen du Wadi Daliyeh et la Samarie vers 450–332 av. J.-C.* (Culture and History of the Ancient Near East 30; Leiden/Boston: Brill, 2007).
Fried, L.S., "The *'am hā'āræṣ* in Ezra 4:4 and Persian Imperial Administration", in O. Lipschits/M. Oeming (ed.), *Judah and the Judeans in the Persian Period* (Winona Lake: Eisenbrauns, 2006) 123–45.
Grabbe, L.L., "The 'Persian Documents' in the Book of Ezra: Are They Authentic?", in O. Lipschits/M. Oeming (ed.), *Judah and the Judeans in the Persian Period* (Winona Lake: Eisenbrauns, 2006) 531–70.
Grätz, S., *Das Edikt des Artaxerxes: Eine Untersuchung zum religionspolitischen und historischen Umfeld von Esra 7,12–26* (BZAW 337; Berlin/New York: de Gruyter, 2004).
–, "Die aramäische Chronik des Esrabuches und die Rolle der Ältesten in Esr 5–6", *ZAW* 118 (2006) 405–22.
–, "Verweigerte Kommunikation? Das Verhältnis zwischen Samaria und Juda in der persischen Zeit im Spiegel der Bücher Esra und Nehemia", in F. Schweitzer (ed.), *Kommunikation über Grenzen* (VWGTh 33; Gütersloh: Gütersloher Verlagshaus, 2009) 252–68.
Gunneweg, A.H.J., *Esra* (KAT 19/1; Gütersloh: Gütersloher Verlagshaus Mohn, 1985).
Hengel, M., *Judentum und Hellenismus* (Tübingen: Mohr Siebeck, [4]1988).
Karrer, C., *Ringen um die Verfassung Judas: Eine Studie zu den theologisch-politischen Vorstellungen im Esra-Nehemiabuch* (BZAW 308; Berlin/New York: de Gruyter, 2001).
Kellermann, U., *Nehemia: Quellen, Überlieferung und Geschichte* (BZAW 102; Berlin: Töpelmann, 1967).
Knauf, E.A., *Ismael: Untersuchungen zur Geschichte Palästinas und Nordarabiens im 1. Jahrtausend v.Chr.* (Wiesbaden: Harrassowitz, [2]1989).
Kratz, R.G., *Das Judentum im Zeitalter des Zweiten Tempels* (FAT 42; Tübingen: Mohr Siebeck, 2004).
Lemaire, A., "Der Beitrag idumäischer Ostraka zur Geschichte Palästinas", *ZDPV* 115 (1999) 12–23.
Lux, R., *Prophetie und Zweiter Tempel* (FAT 65; Tübingen: Mohr Siebeck, 2009).
Oded, B., "Mass Deportation in the Neo-Assyrian Empire", *Shnaton* 3 (1979) 159–73.
Schunck, K.D., *Nehemia* (BKAT 23/2; Neukirchen-Vluyn: Neukirchener Verlag, 2009).
Schwiderski, D., *Handbuch des nordwestsemitischen Briefformulars: Ein Beitrag zur Echtheitsfrage der aramäischen Briefe des Esrabuches* (BZAW 295; Berlin/New York: de Gruyter, 2000).

–, *Die alt- und reichsaramäischen Inschriften.* Vol. 2: *Texte und Bibliographie* (FoSub 2; Berlin/New York: de Gruyter, 2004).

Wright, J., *Rebuilding Identity. The Nehemiah-Memoir and Its Earliest Readers* (BZAW 348; Berlin/New York: de Gruyter, 2004).

Reinhard Achenbach

Westfälische Wilhelms-Universität Münster

"Genocide" in the Book of Esther

Cultural Integration and the Right of Resistance against Pogroms[1]

1. The Problem

The oldest document about the existence of an ethnic entity named Israel is the memorial Stele of Pharaoh Merenptah from the year 1209/08 BCE, discovered by Petrie in the pharaoh's mortuary temple at Thebes 1896. In the description of the pharaoh's campaign to Palestine it says: *yyzr3r fk.w bn-prt=f – Israel is laid waste, its seed is no more* – stating that the danger from this ethnic group had been extinguished and – because they had no grain for further agricultural activities – they would not have any chance of survival in the future.[2] The problem of a threatening annihilation by war can be seen in certain practices such as the *ḥērem*, which was locally applied by the Moabites, as we know from the stele of king Mesha (KAI 181.17). The atrocities of Neo-Assyrian warfare, including the deportation of thousands of people into remote areas of the kingdom, caused fright and horror among the peoples of the ancient Near Eastern nations, especially because the military actions, the sieges and the sanctions against those who broke the vassal-treaties were cruel and devastating, so that the Assyrians remained in the memory of Israel as a people who have *"evil plans, his mind harbors evil designs, for he means to destroy, to wipe out nations, not a few!"* (Isa 10:7). It is – as far as I can see – the first time that a nation is reproached for committing genocide, in the form of a prophetic oracle with a divine accusation! The theorem of an ancient Israelite ban on the peoples of Canaan, as it was established in Deut 7:1–6 and in the book of Joshua, mirrors with its "language of violence" (Assmann) the ideological influence from the Assyrian era. It thus tries to give the quest for an inalienable right to live in the land of Israel's heritage a foundation legend during the Neo-Babylonian and early Persian periods, when the Judeans had lost all political sovereignty over the ancient areas of the kingdoms of Israel and Judah.[3]

---

[1] This article is the revised version of the former essay Achenbach, "Vertilgen", 282–314.

[2] For the text edition and interpretation cf. von der Way, *Göttergericht*, 98–9.

[3] For the problem cf. Assmann, "Monotheismus", 18–38; and Zenger, "Monotheismus", 39–73. Concerning the literary-historical function of the ban-theorem cf. Otto, *Krieg*, 86–107;

Interestingly enough, new analyses of the Exodus-Moses-Legend have shown that in the non-priestly shape of the text the salvation of Moses in a wicker-basket has a parallel to the foundation legend of the Assyrian Empire in the Sargon-Legend.[4] In the introduction to the Moses narrative we discover a radicalized form of the charge of genocide, when we are told that the pharaoh gives the commandment to kill all male newborn of the Israelites (Exod 1:22). He meant it as a preventive measure to diminish the Israelite population in order to preclude the possibility that "in the event of war they may join our enemies in fighting against us and rise from the ground" (Exod 1:10). The inhumanity of this despotic edict delegitimizes the imperial power of the king, so that the illegitimacy of genocide was inscribed into the foundation legend of Israel as an insight gained from the fundamental rights of slaves and of ethnic entities forced to live under conditions of corvée and dependence on another, more powerful ethnic group. The idea that it was the God of Israel who caused Israel's liberation from slavery and gave the people the fundamental and inviolable right to live in their own land under the condition of their own law of divine origin is influenced by the experiences of the Assyrian period. The theory of an occupation of the land due to the performance of the ḥērem-ritual is a pure legend. Its function was to express the thought that the right of a people to live in a land with sufficient supply of water and soil was not dispensable. The ḥērem-ritual was not part of regular historical warfare according to the laws of ancient Israel. In reflecting the experiences under Assyrian and Neo-Babylonian rule, the regulations for warfare in Deut 20–24 were the first such regulations introduced into an ANE law collection.[5] During the Achaemenid period we can observe that the legal rules on protection of foreigners and on integration and distinction with respect to aliens were discussed and developed in Israel but also among the Greek poleis and amphictyonies.[6] We can also observe that the international rules of warfare were under discussion, e.g. in the famous dialogue between the Athenians and Melians developed by Thucydides (Peloponnesian War 5.84–116).

In the novelette of Esther the issue has essentially a new quality, because it is not just the problem of atrocity and genocide in war that is discussed here, nor is it genocide against an ethnic group under governmental protection who is suspected of planning a war against the people of the land (as in the Exodus story). Instead, in Esther we find a consideration of the possibil-

---

Achenbach, "Warfare". For a close analysis of Deut 7 cf. idem, *Israel*, 212–88; Veijola, *5. Buch Mose*, 193–9; Otto, "Deuteronomiumstudien II", 96–7, 190–8.

[4] Lewis, *Sargon-Legend*; Otto, "Mose", 43–83; Gerhards, *Aussetzungsgeschichte*, 149–249; Kuhrt, "Making History", 347–61.

[5] Otto, *Krieg*, 86–106.

[6] Bederman, *International Law*, 120–36; Dihle, *Griechen*, 36–53.

ity that a mere resentment on the part of a despotic individual, who has the support of a tyrannical king, could lead to raising a movement of thousands prepared to extinguish the hated ethnos. I always have been astonished that the Esther story raised this difficult topic, especially since we know that a pogrom or a prosecution of Judeans or Jews did not take place under Achaemenid rule! And if we read commentaries on the book of Esther, we find how difficult it has been for authors to explain this very aspect of the story. What I want to do in this article is to argue for the thesis that the book of Esther is a narrative statement about the right of the Jewish people to defend their fundamental right to ethnic, cultural and religious integrity even when holding the status of an ethnic entity under foreign domination, and that there exists in general the right to resist the violation of human rights especially under the threat of genocide.

Although the problem of genocide was already known in antiquity it could not be defined in the form of an international law because of the lack of institutional backing.[7] The only way for this issue to come to a head came with the notion of indispensible human rights of integrity, based on a universal conception of monotheism as it was developed by the Jewish religion under the conditions of the Babylonian exile.[8] The seriousness of the conviction that there was no other God than Yhwh forced the scribes of the Pentateuch, as well as the scribal tradents of the prophetic scrolls, to reflect on the fate of the peoples under the universal principles of God's justice. Thus the priestly code defined the prohibition of bloodshed, a crime against life, as one of the fundamental and universal "Noahide" laws. In the book of Amos (Amos 1:3–2:3) atrocities in warfare such as genocide, human trafficking, violence against pregnant women and the mistreatment of corpses were condemned as outrageous assaults against the will of God.[9]

It took mankind a history of almost 2400 years until a legal definition was given in the United Nations "Convention on the Prevention and Punishment of the Crime of Genocide" (1948):[10]

Article I: The Contracting Parties confirm that genocide, whether committed in time of peace [sic!] or in time of war, is a crime under international law which they undertake to prevent [sic!] and to punish. Article II: In the present Convention, genocide means any of the following acts committed with intent to destroy, in whole or in part, a national, ethnical, racial or religious group, as such: (a) Killing members of the

---

[7] Reuter, "Völkermord", 1154–5; Otto, "Völkerrecht III", 1158–9; Schabas, *Genozid*.

[8] Cf. Isaiah 45:5 אני יהוה ואין עוד זולתי אין אלהים. From the multitude of literature I chose just one substantial treatment of the topic: Keel, *Geschichte Jerusalems*, 2:854–80.

[9] Barton, *Amos's Oracles*.

[10] Convention on the Prevention and Punishment of the Crime of Genocide. Adopted by Resolution 260 (III) A of the United Nations General Assembly on 9 December 1948 (according to www.hrweb.org/legal/genocide.html).

group; (b) Causing serious bodily or mental harm to members of the group; (c) Deliberately inflicting on the group conditions of life calculated to bring about its physical destruction in whole or in part; (d) Imposing measures intended to prevent births within the group; (e) Forcibly transferring children of the group to another group. Article III: The following acts shall be punishable: (a) Genocide; (b) Conspiracy to commit genocide; (c) Direct and public incitement to commit genocide; (d) Attempt to commit genocide; (e) Complicity in genocide.

In the third article the definition of punishable acts comprises not only the fulfillment of the act, but also the plan and the commitment. What these international conventions define as measures for international judgment corresponds to the moral measures explained in the Esther legend. The etiology of the Purim festival in Esther 9:20–28 declares the 14th–15th day of Adar every year to be a memorial day:

> Esther 9:22 The same days on which the Jews (יהודים) enjoyed relief from their foes ...
> 24 for Haman son of Hammedatha the Aggie, the foe of all the Jews, had plotted to destroy (אבד) the Jews, and had cast *pur* – that is, the log – with intent to crush and exterminate them (להמם לאבדם)."

The text refers to the edict of Ahasuerus (alias Xerxes), which authorized his servant Haman on the evening before Pesach (as a symbolic date), to execute all those members of the people of the province of Yehud who lived in the satrapies of the Persian kingdom. The formula used by the royal decree is ascribed to Haman, as well as the scope of the instruction:

> Esther 3:13 ... to destroy, massacre, and exterminate all the Jews, young and old, children and women, on a single day, on the 13th day of the 12th month – that is the month of Adar – and to plunder their possessions.

This is exactly what the modern text defines as the commitment to perform an organized genocide.[11] The text formulates with a remarkable brutality what the human mind is able to imagine and what quiets commentators, because it is impossible to find an adequate language for it. Adele Berlin has left this text without explanation in her commentary (2001).[12] Others seem to skirt around the passage, as Paton, who writes:[13] "There is not the least delay or hesitation on the part of the King in handing over the entire

---

[11] For the modern juridical definition of genocide cf. Lemkin, *Axis Rule*, 79–95; Huttenbach, "Editor", 167–75. Although in a strictly juridical sense law scholars hesitate to speak about the problem with respect to international law before the UN Convention of 9th December 1948, the phenomenon itself has existed before and has been discussed since antiquity; cf. Selbmann, *Tatbestand*, 17. Of course, the unique experience of the Shoah was decisive for the formulation of the UN text; cf. Katz, *Holocaust*; Korošec, *Inkriminierung*, 4.

[12] Berlin, *Esther*, 42–3.

[13] Paton, *Commentary*, 207.

Jewish race to destruction. Not merely the Jews in Susa and in the provinces of the Persian empire, but also those in Palestine are included in the edict. Despot as Xerxes was, it may well be questioned whether such an insane project ever met with his approval." – On the decisive formula in v. 13bα he is just able to note: "The heaping up of synonyms is in imitation of the legal style."[14] Even the narrator of the legend himself feels unable to give any explanation for the brutal formula. Gerleman speaks of "nicht ohne weiteres verständlichen Zügen der Erzählung".[15]

In earlier German commentaries we can hear the echo of an ice-cold language of the anti-Semitic Nazi administration. Haller (1940) treats the horrible issue of Esther 3:8, 12–14 with two short sentences:

"Hier wird nun auch klar gesagt, was die Juden im Reiche Ahasveros' verhaßt macht: ihre Absonderung von der Umgebung nach den Bestimmungen eines besonderen Gesetzes. – Gestützt auf solche königliche Vollmacht erläßt Haman die nötigen Ausführungsbestimmungen (12) und befördert sie auf schnellstem Wege [...] in alle Satrapien (13), wo sie sogleich Gesetzeskraft erlangen (14)."[16]

This is the language of the Shoah, and – what is even more unacceptable – this commentary was reprinted without correction in 1969 with only a new introduction by Ernst Würthwein.[17] The critical evaluation of the Esther legend in German Protestant exegesis had a long tradition, going back to Martin Luther himself.[18] The ambiguity is characteristic of the problems that Christian exegesis always had with the finale of the story, when it shows that 75.000 people lost their lives because they were guilty of planning and preparing the genocide. It is in 1983 that the East German scholar Arndt Meinhold found more proper formulations to describe what we have to consider here, that is a "demagogische, tödliche Verleumdung einer für das persische Weltreich verdienstvollen jüdischen Diaspora" by Haman and a "Vernichtungsverfügung über alle Juden".[19] Levenson (1997) speaks clearly of an "Edict of Genocide" – "in this post Holocaust era, frighteningly realistic". However, we should follow him when he concedes: "The truth

---

[14] Paton, *Commentary*, 209.

[15] Gerleman, *Esther*, 99.

[16] Haller, *Megilloth*, 125.

[17] Würthwein, *Megilloth*, 184.

[18] Martin Luther in "De servo arbitrio" expressed doubts about the legitimacy of the book as part of the canon (WA 18, 666:13–26), and in one of his "Tischreden" 1533 he said: "Ich bin dem Buch (2 Makk.) und Esther so feind, daß ich wollte, sie wären gar nicht vorhanden; denn sie judenzen zu sehr, und haben viel heidnische Unart" (WA Ti 1, 208:30). But on the other hand he referred rather often to the book by taking up its positive examples, such as the meekness of Esther who is not proud because of her crown or her external beauty etc.; cf. Bardtke, *Luther*, 53–70; Loader, "Ester", 203; Bush, "Esther", 39–54.

[19] Meinhold, *Esther*, 47; Crüsemann, "Gesetze", 9–10, on Esther 3:8–9: "Das ist die gezielte Planung einer Massenvernichtung. Und der wirtschaftliche Gewinn ist bereits berechnet."

is, however, that full scale genocide – that is, the annihilation of an entire ethnic group, wherever they are throughout an entire empire and without regard to their political or military status – is a Nazi innovation, lacking a strong precedent in the long, dreary history of human brutality and atrocity."[20] Daube describes the character of the book as follows: "It is precisely when we accept it on its terms that its earnest, desperately earnest, message and the magnificent, multifaceted artistry rendering it convincing and palatable are revealed ... The starting-point is a characterization of the Jews [i.e. Esther 3:8] which, let us note, though articulated by Haman in a distinctly malevolent tone and with the most evil intention, is nowhere substantially disputed ... When one of them offends, as Mordecai does in not prostrating himself before Haman, it tends to be held against all. Haman displays this inclination with shocking openness but we should not miss the hint that it already motivates those who report the slight to him. Again, once the state withdraws its protection, massive participation in organized excesses is forthcoming. The populace's response to Ahasuerus's initial edict allowing every kind of violence is reminiscent of the Kristallnacht in 1938."[21] Even in modern treatments of the matter exegetes still have their difficulties with the problem of violence and irrationality in the story.

2. Historical Background

There is a consensus among scholars that the Esther Legend is a mere legend and that it does not contain historical recollections of a conflict between Persians and Jews in Achaemenid times. We have no reports of the persecution of Jews in the Achaemenid empire.[22] The "perserie" of the novelette is typical of literature from the Hellenistic time.[23] Although there are reports

---

[20] Levenson, *Esther*, 73. Wahl, *Esther*, 105, describes the incident as the planning of a pogrom: "Der Inhalt der königlichen Briefe klingt vernichtend (V 13), die nur in Esther belegte dreigliedrige Formel להשמיד להרג לאבד auszurotten, zu töten und zu vernichten bekräftigt mit den drei ihrer Intention nach gleichbedeutenden Verben die geplante vollständige Vernichtung aller Juden." But also Wahl has no idea where the motif of the genocide has its origin.

[21] Daube, *Esther*, 2–3.

[22] Because of Persian loanwords, motifs and features that were considered to be "typical" for the Achaemenid era several scholars date the book into the pre-Hellenistic time (Talmon, "Wisdom", 419–55; Gerleman, *Esther*, 39; Meinhold, *Buch Esther*, 20; Berlin, *Esther*, xli–xliii; cf. also Hutter, *Iranische Elemente*, 51–66; Yamauchi, *Backgrounds*, 108); others look for historical evidence for a persecution of Jews at the Persian period, cf. Littman, "Policy", 145–55; Heltzer, "Mordechai", 119–21.

[23] Cf. Hagedorn, "Absent Presence", 39–66. For a dating to the Hellenistic Period cf. Bardtke, *Esther*, 252; Fox, *Character*, 140, 252; Zenger, *Einleitung*, 307; Levenson, *Esther*, 26; Macchi, "Le livre d'Esther", 97–135; Ego, "Esther", 279–302.

of Persian massacres at the Scythes[24] or about the regularly celebrated remembrance of the destroying of the rebellious Magaoi (cf. Herodotus History 3.79),[25] we have only rare notes about anti-Jewish measures from the Persian time.

Anti-Jewish *(cursive script)* and Pro-Jewish (recto script) Events in Antiquity[26]	
410 BCE	*Destruction of the temple in Elephantine*
404–398	*Baoji-incident (Josephus Ant. 11.297–301)*
	Jews had to leave Egypt
222–205	*Persecution under Ptolemaios Philopator IV (3 Macc 3)?*
198	Privileges for the Jews in Jerusalem by Antiochus III
168	*Persecution of Jews in Judea and Jerusalem under Antiochus IV Epiphanes* and Maccabean Rebellion (167–164)
100	Privilege of free trade for Jews in Pergamon
	Privileges for Jews in Sardes
63	*Pompeii conquers Palestine, end of the Hasmonean Kingdom*
63–40	John Hyrcanus High Priest
47	John Hyrcanus II is acknowledged as High Priest and as Ethnarch
46	Jews of Parium are allowed to live according to their own law
43	Privileges for the Jews in Ephesus
41	Restitution of old privileges for Jews in Tyre
27 BCE–14 CE	Allowance of freedom of religious practice for Jews in Rome and in the provinces
16–13 BCE	Confirmation of civil rights for Jews in Ionia
14 BCE	Confirmation of Privileges for Jews in Ephesus and in Cyrene
6 CE	*Augustus cancels privileges for Jews*
19	*Tiberius expels Jews from Rome*
	Pontius Pilate erects the standard of the Caesar in Jerusalem
38	*Persecution of Jews in Alexandria*
	Polemical anti-Jewish texts of Cicero, Seneca, Quintilian, Juvenal, Tacitus
41	*Caligula wants to erect a statue in the Jerusalem Temple area*
66–73	*Jewish Rebellion*
70	*Destruction of the Second Temple*
115–117	*Jewish rebellion in Alexandria*
132–135	*Rebellion under Bar-Kokhba*

The most famous exception are the anti-Jewish measures of the Egyptian soldiers led by Widranga who destroyed the Jewish sanctuary at Elephan-

---

[24] Herodotus Histories 1.106.

[25] Herodotus Histories 1.79.

[26] For a list with basic data cf. also Cuffari, *Judenfeindschaft*, 348, and his list on positive and negative judgments of authors from antiquity referring to Jews, ibid., 338–47; for further treatment of the topic cf. Yavetz, *Judenfeindschaft*.

tine 411 BCE,[27] and the measures of Bagohi/Bagoas, the Satrap of Transeuphratene, against the high priest and the temple of Jerusalem between 404 and 398 BCE, reported in Josephus Antiquities 11.[28] These measures might have caused the first serious fracture between the priesthood of the Second Temple and parts of the Persian leadership, but there is no trace of anything that could be compared to the plans of a pogrom at that time.[29] Even in the novelette itself the core of the conflict is the ancient antagonism between the lines of Haman the Agagite from the tribes of Amalek (cf. 1 Sam 15:8, 9, 20, 32, 33; Exod 17:8–16; Num 24:20; Deut 25:17–19)[30] and Mordecai of Kish from the tribe of Benjamin (Esther 2:5, 15).

The elements of the story that give the whole a historical color have no basis in reality: there is no testimony of a Jewish wife of Xerxes etc.;[31] everything is camouflage from a Jewish novelist with a message for Jewish people living in the Diaspora, offering wisdom, comfort and encouragement for people who might even have a high position and be well esteemed in their society but who, on the other hand, might experience hostility and anti-Jewish prejudices and antagonism. The invention of a pogrom against Jews serves to make an unthinkable possibility thinkable: that enmity and hatred could kindle up from a small origin and develop into a catastrophe, even at a time when Jews would not be thinking of that possibility and would see the menace of genocide as something out of the Exodus experience in the far remote past. Yet it is not clear at which point in time these particular thoughts were expressed. Levenson argued that the story could have its origin after the regime of the Seleucids had taken over Judah and Jerusalem in the 5th Syrian war under Antiochus III (about 200 BCE, peace contract with Ptolemaios V 194/3); the former pro-Ptolemaic Jews in the Diaspora were suddenly confronted with the danger that they could be seen as possible public enemies.[32] The narrative seems to react to a situation

---

[27] Porten, *Archives from Elephantine*, 278–98.

[28] Josephus Ant. 11.297–301. Scholars tend to assume a historical core behind the reports; cf. Rooke, *Zadok's Heirs*, 222–5, 235–6; Williamson, "Historical Value", 48–67; Achenbach, "Satrapie", 134–8; against this position cf. VanderKam, *Joshua*, 58–63.

[29] Yavetz, *Judenfeindschaft*, 53–63, stresses that the anti-Jewish position of the Egyptians at Elephantine found support from the corrupt Persian governor Widranga and that the protection of Jews by the satrap only lasted until the Persians had to leave Egypt. "Als Artaxerxes III. Ägypten wieder eroberte, gab es keine Juden mehr in Elephantine" (ibid., 63).

[30] The Greek tradition did not understand that, here, Haman is called βουγαῖος ("bully", "braggart"); Kottsieper, "Zusätze",145–6; Hagedorn, "Absent Presence", 54.

[31] Cf. Meinhold, *Esther*, 17–19; Levenson, *Esther*, 23–7; contra Zadok, "Historical Background", 18–23.

[32] For similar deliberations cf. Levenson, *Esther*, 26.

where ancient archenemies were suddenly in leading positions and ancient loyal Jews had to respect them.[33]

Cuffari in his dissertation on "Judenfeindschaft in Antike und Altem Testament"[34] has listed all possible historical events of anti-Jewish and pro-Jewish measures in antiquity from which the Esther novelette could have been motivated. With respect to this list we can surmise that the Esther story has its origins in the 1st half of the 2nd century BCE, either already at the time of Antiochus III, or after the Hasmonean kingdom had been established (around 150 BCE).

3. The Edict of Genocide in Esther 3 and Its Justification

The narrative tells that Haman ben Hammedatha the Agagaite was advanced to be head of the king's fellow officials (Esther 3:1). All courtiers showed their respect for Haman by kneeling and bowing before Haman, but Mordecai refused (v. 2):

Esther 3:1 Some time afterward, King Ahasuerus promoted Haman son of Hammedatha the Agagite; he advanced him and seated him higher than any of his fellow officials (וישם את־כסאו מעל כל־השרים אשר אתו).

2 All the king's courtiers in the palace gate knelt (כרעים) and bowed (משתחוים) low to Haman, for such was the king's order concerning him; but Mordecai would not kneel or bow low.

3 Then the king's courtiers who were in the palace gate said to Mordecai, "Why do you disobey the king's order?"

4 When they spoke to him day after day and he would not listen to them, they told Haman, in order to see whether Mordecai's resolve would prevail; for he had explained to them that he was a Jew.

5 When Haman saw that Mordecai would not kneel or bow low to him, Haman was filled with rage.

6 But he disdained to lay hands on Mordecai alone; having been told who Mordecai's people were, Haman plotted to do away with all the Jews, Mordecai's people, throughout the kingdom of Ahasuerus.

7 In the first month, that is, the month of Nisan, in the twelfth year of King Ahasuerus, *pur* – which means "the lot" – was cast before Haman concerning every day and every month, [until it fell on] the twelfth month, that is, the month of Adar.

---

[33] Herodotus Histories 1.134: "When one man meets another in the way, it is easy to see if the two are equals; for then without speaking they kiss each other on the lips; if the difference in rank be but little, it is the cheek that is kissed; if it be great, the humbler bows down and does obeisance to the other." (Translation Godley, *Herodotus*, 175).

[34] Cuffari, *Judenfeindschaft*, 348 (cf. above).

The *proskynesis* was the traditional ritual of obeisance with respect to the Persian kings. But – in contrast to the Diadochs after Alexander – the Persian Kings never claimed a divine status.[35] Thus Herodotus reports that Xerxes accepted when the Spartans refused the *proskynesis* before him (Herodotus Histories 7.136):

Thence being come to Susa and into the king's presence, when the guards commanded and would have compelled them to fall down and to do obeisance to the king, they said they would never do that, no not if they were thrust down headlong, for it was not their custom (said they) to do obeisance to mortal men, nor was that the purpose of their coming ... whereupon Xerxes of his magnanimity said that he would not imitate the Lacedaemonians; "for you", said he, "made havoc of all human law (τὰ πάντῶν ἀντρῶπον νόμιμα) by slaying heralds; but I will not do that which I blame in you, nor by putting you in turn to death set the Lacedaemonians free from this guilt".

The refusal of the *proskynesis* before the Persians was already a topos in Greek historiography and tradition.[36] Aischylos praised this attitude in the "Persians", when he described that after the battle of Salamis the Greeks refused to bow under the regency of Xerxes:

Aeschylus Persians 1.584–90	Translation (Weir Smyth)[37]
τοὶ δ'ἀνὰ γᾶν Ἀσίαν δὴν οὐκέτι περσονομοῦνται οὐδ' ἔτι δασμοθοροῦσιν δεσποσύνοισιν ἀνάγκαις οὐδ' ἐς γᾶν προπίτνοντες ἄζονται βασιλεία γὰρ διόλωκεν ἰσχύς.	They that dwell throughout the length and breadth of Asia will not for long abide under the sway of the Persians, nor will they pay further tribute at the compulsion of their lord, nor will they prostrate themselves to the earth and do him reverence, since the kingly power hath perished utterly.

Furthermore, in the story the demand to perform the *proskynesis* is extended to a servant of the king. At the time when Mordecai refused to perform this act of obeisance, he had already proven his loyalty to the regent by saving his life from a coup d'état (Esther 2:21–23), and – in analogy to the legendary Spartans – now proves his religious commitment: a Jew will only bow his knee (כרע) and prostrate himself (השתחוה) before Yhwh (Ps 95:6–7; 22:30; 2 Chr 7:3; 29:29;[38] cf. also 1 Kings 8:54 and Isa 45:23); this in-

---

[35] Paton, *Commentary*, 196, hints to Aischylos, Persians (see below), and to Quintus Curtius Rufus Histories of Alexander the Great 8.5–13; cf. also Xenophon Anabasis 3.2.13; Wiesehöfer, "Proskynese", 447–52; idem, "Proskynesis", 443–4.

[36] The same episode is reported by Plutarch, cf. Daube, *Esther*, 14–15.

[37] Smyth, *Aeschylus*, 158–9; Berlin, *Esther*, 40.

[38] To "bow the knee" (כרע) is considered as a ritual gesture of adoration (cf. 1 Kings 8:54; 19:7; Isa 45:23; Ps 72:9); to prostrate oneself (השתחוה) can be part of a cultic ritual adoration (Ps 5:8; 99:6, 9; 132:2; Deut 26:10; Neh 8:6; 9:3) or a gesture of rendering homage and honor to a

cludes the ritual act of *proskynesis* as well (cf. Neh 8:6 and Esther 4:17 C 5ff!).

Even according to the ancient Greek and Macedonian tradition the *proskynesis* was a privilege for the Gods and the Heroes,[39] and when Alexander the Great demanded it first from the Bactrians, this claim raised a heavy dispute, even among the Greeks; a famous critique against the ceremony of *proskynesis* was given by the historian Callisthenes.[40] Under the Ptolemeans the demand to perform the *proskynesis* caused problems for certain Diaspora Jews (cf. 3 Macc 3; Dan 3:3–13), but mostly the Ptolemeans accepted the special attitude of this religious group.[41] In general we can say that the Esther legend encourages Jews who share the same religious attitude as that of Mordecai and appeals to the understanding of the Greek society on that issue.[42]

The narrative clearly suggests that the reason for the measures against the Jew is beyond all legitimacy: Haman feels dishonored and reacts with a fury that is disproportionate. Behind the hatred against Mordecai a deep rooted animosity against all members of Mordecai's people is revealed.[43] The real reason for his actions is mere hatred and bias. He does not care about the raison d'état but misuses his position to carry out his personal revenge in a totalitarian way, where all Jews are concerned. His acts take an exaggerated and irrational shape. He abuses his political position for the sake of an extraordinarily huge intrigue. The notes on the Purim festival (Esther 3:7; 9:20–32) transform the novelette into a *hieros logos*, and they are often considered to be secondary.[44]

---

king (1 Sam 24:9; 2 Sam 1:2; 9:6; Ps 72:11) or a highly esteemed person (Gen 23:7; 33:3, 6, 7; Exod 4:31; 11:8; 18:7; Ruth 2:10). The use of both expressions here makes clear, that the gesture is considered to have a religious impact; cf. Ego, "Geschichtskonzeption", 89: "Gerade vor dem Hintergrund der Tatsache, dass sich im Esterbuch häufig implizit-theologische Anspielungen finden, spricht sehr viel dafür, dass Haman tatsächlich mit seiner Proskynese einen quasi-göttlichen Status für sich beanspruchte." Cf. also Bevenot, "Proskynesis", 132–9; Ego, "Esther", 289–90; contra Willi-Plein, "Ehrenbezeugung", 363–77, who argues that "proskynesis" describes just the pragmatic function of an act of veneration and does not mean an act of throwing oneself down upon the ground.

[39] Aeschylus Agamemnon 919–20, 925; Xenophon Anabasis 3.2.13; cf. Habicht, *Gottmenschentum*, 3–41; Schmitt, "Herrscherkult", 243–53.

[40] Arrian Alexandri Anabasis 4.11.8–9; Plutarch Alexander 52–5; cf. Cerfaux/Tondriau, *Culte*, 139–43; Mooren, "Nature", 223–4; Walbank, "Könige", 380; Wiemer, *Alexander*, 138.

[41] Cerfaux/Tondriau, *Culte*; Taeger, *Charisma*, 255–308.

[42] The Esther-Targum translates and explains the motif by an additional explanation: Mordecai rejected the *proskynesis* in front of an idol (Esther 3:5 MT: וירא המן כי אין מרדכי כרע ומשתחוה; Targ.: ‏(וחזה המן ארום לית מרדכי גהין לאנדרטא‏! The verb סגד is clearly ‏לו‎ connected to idolatry (cf. Targ. Exod 20:5; MT Isa 44:15–19; 46:6; Dan 3:5–28); for the Targum traditions of Esther cf. Ego, *Targum Scheni*, 2–8.

[43] For the inner connection between honor and violence, cf. Hettlage, "Gewalt", 121–49.

[44] Hagedorn, "Absent Presence", 49; Clines, *Esther Scroll*, 51–7; Levenson, *Esther*, 124–32.

Esther 3:8 Haman then said to King Ahasuerus, "There is a certain people, scattered and dispersed (מפזר ומפרד) among the other peoples in all the provinces of your kingdom, whose laws are different from those of any other people and who do not obey the king's laws; and it is not in Your Majesty's interest to tolerate them (להניחם).

9 If it pleases Your Majesty, let an edict be drawn for their destruction (לאבדם), and I will pay 10.000 talents of silver to the stewards for deposit in the royal treasury."

10 Thereupon the king removed his signet ring from his hand and gave it to Haman son of Hammedatha the Agagite, the foe of the Jews.

11 And the king said, "The money and the people are yours to do with as you see fit."

The author reveals the insidiousness and deceitfulness of Haman's speech, which is a mixture of correct and false statements, especially in not mentioning the ethnic group concerned (including the wife of the king himself and his savior Mordecai!). The legitimate character of the appeal is feigned.[45] The single case of a personal offense is generalized in the sense that the whole ethnic and religious group, the Jews, is described as criminal fundamentalists. Apparently Haman names some "facts", but already in the characterization of the people as "scattered" and "dispersed" in v. 8 he provokes the idea of a group that can only be localized with great difficulty and therefore does not fit into the Persian system of world order, where every people had its place on the basis of divine destination. Perhaps the Jews are even suspect as a people who are under a divine punishment or curse.[46] The formulation is able to cause suspicion and distrust.

That the Jews have a law distinct from the laws of all other people is a sentence that is in line with the self-awareness of the people of the Torah (cf. Deut 4:7–8).

Accordingly anti-Jewish polemics has often taken up this issue in order to discredit Jewish loyalty to a reigning regime.[47] The narrative has already shown for both protagonists, Esther and Mordecai, that they fully respect the Persian *dât* and that the accusation that they would not obey the king's law is wrong.[48] But under the government of Xerxes the royal edicts tended

---

[45] Meinhold, *Esther*, 46.

[46] Cf. also the epithet διεσπαρμένον, Esther 3:8 LXX, and the verb διασπείρω, LXX Lev 26:33; Deut 28:64; Ps 43:12; Isa 11:12; 56:8; διασπορᾶ, Deut 28:25 – Hebr.: עוה; cf. 2 Chr 29:8*.

[47] For a response to anti-Jewish polemics in the Midrashim, cf. Berman, "Aggadah".

[48] That the Persian *dât* had a special status in order to keep the peoples in the place where the regents had put them, according to Ahuramazda's world order, was a characteristic of the Persian empire; cf. Darius DB 1.20–24: "Saith Darius the King: Within these countries, the man who was loyal, him I rewarded well; (him) who was evil, him I punished well; by the favor of Ahuramazda these countries showed respect toward my law; as was said to them by me, thus was it done." (Kent, *Old Persian*, 119); cf. Xerxes Ph 46–56 (Kent, *Old Persian*, 152).

to be considered almost as an expression of divine law, as can be seen from an inscription of Persepolis (XPh 46–56):[49]

Thou who (shalt be) hereafter, if thou shalt think, "Happy may I be when living, and when dead may I be blessed," have respect for the law which Ahuramazda has established; worship Ahuramazda and Arta reverent(ly), The man who has respect for that law which Ahuramazda has established, and worships Ahuramazda and Arta reverently, he both becomes happy while living, and becomes blessed when dead.

When the narrative describes how the intrigue of Haman uses elements of Persian ideology, at the same time it discredits this ideology for the readers from Hellenistic times as exaggerated. As part aim of this argument it becomes clear that Haman wants the Jews to be extinguished from the empire as a people who are unwilling to adjust to the Persian ideology of regency, because they defy the royal world order and royal control. After all, the Achaemenid kings saw themselves as "Kings of all Peoples" (*xšāyaθiya dahyūnām vispazanānām;* vgl. DNa 10–11; DSe 9–10; DZc 5).[50]

According to Jewish law the accusation of Haman rests on false testimony and must be punished in a talionic way (Deut 19:16–19). According to Persian law it is *drauga* and therefore must be punished heavily, as Darius formulated it with respect to the end of the Magoi (DB 4.33–43):[51]

Saith Darius the King: These are the provinces which became rebellious. The *Lie* made them rebellious, so that these (men) deceived the people. Afterward Ahuramazda put them into my hand; as was my desire, so I did unto them. Saith Darius the King: Thou who shalt be king hereafter, protect thyself vigorously from the *Lie*; the man who shall be a *Lie-follower*, him do thou punish well, if thus thou shalt think, "May my country be secure!"

The offer to pay a huge amount of interest to the king gives the impression of Persian avarice. Consequently the king appears as a regent who hands over his own authority to a liar when he follows the suggestion of his servant. The edict is based on a lie![52]

Esther 3:12   On the 13th day of the 1st month, the king's scribes were summoned and a decree was issued, as Haman directed, to the king's satraps, to the governors of every province, and to the officials of every people, to every province in its own script and to every people in its own language. The orders were issued in the name of King Ahasuerus and sealed with the king's signet.

---

[49] Koch, "Weltordnung", 152; for the inscription Xerxes Ph 46–56 cf. Kent, *Old Persian*, 152.

[50] Koch, "Weltordnung", 150–1; for the inscriptions cf. Kent, *Old Persian*, 137, 141–2, 147.

[51] Kent, *Old Persian*, 129–32.

[52] It is not necessary to add that high religious ideals did not keep the Achaemenids from applying the strategy of lying to the reality of their political interrelations.

13 Accordingly, written instructions were dispatched by couriers to all the king's provinces to destroy, massacre, and exterminate all the Jews (להשמיד להרג ולאבד את־כל־היהודים), young and old, children and women, on a single day – on the 13th day of the 12th month – that is, the month of Adar – and to plunder their possessions.

14 The text of the document was to the effect that a law (דת) should be proclaimed in every single province; it was to be publicly displayed to all the peoples, so that they might be ready for that day.

15 The couriers went out posthaste on the royal mission, and the decree was proclaimed in the fortress Shushan.

The administrative procedure is described as efficient and exhaustive. Although the action has its roots in the difficult relationship with the Agagaite archenemy of the Jews, he is able to employ the power of a whole empire. Perhaps here is a bridge for non-Jewish readers to be aware that the reasons for anti-Jewish hatred may not lie within their own society itself. However, all other peoples of the empire are involved, and thus the case becomes a problem of the international community! The main issue of the edict is formulated as a subordinate clause, and the narrative refers to it several times: the edict concerns every member of the entire ethnic and religious entity of the Jews (את־כל־היהודים; Esther 3:6, 13; 4:8; 7:4; 8:11). The totality of the extinction goes even beyond the aims of the ancient Pharaoh in the Exodus narrative – although it has no basis in war or in law! The expression raises the cruelest of visions: to destroy, which reminds one of the ban-theology (Jos 7:12; 9:24; 11:14, 20; 23:15) and also of the destruction of the first temple (cf. Lev 26:30; Deut 28:48; cf. Deut 9:8, 14, 19–20, 25) and divine punishment (Isa 13:9; 14:23; 23:11; Ps 145:20). The intention is to make clear that this act has also a metaphysical dimension: the cult of the only God would be made impossible were the Jews to vanish from the earth.

The following verbs – killing and annihilating – are an explication of the first term and mark the activity of the killing and the aim of the persecution (להרג ולאבד); their connection with שמד hif. is unique in Esther 3:13; 7:4; 8:11.[53] LXX translates with ἀφανίζω (= to make vanish, to annihilate: ἀφανίσαι τὸ γένος τῶν Ἰουδαίων).[54] The idea of a genocide has found its paradigmatic expression in these lines of the Esther legend. Thus the teach-

---

[53] For similar wording cf. 2 Sam 14:7: "Then the whole clan confronted your maidservant and said, 'Hand over the one who killed his brother (מכה אחיו), that we may put him to death for the slaying of his brother (ונמתהו בנפש אחיו), whom he has murdered (אשר הרג), and so destroy the heir also (נשמידה גם את־היורש)!'" The aim of שמד hif. is to extinguish all possible claims of the enemy and his family.

[54] The verb appears in LXX in Esther 3:13; 9:24; 13:17; 14:8 and 1 Ezra 6:32 (edict of Darius); 1 Macc 9:73; 3 Macc 4:13!

ing of this wisdom narrative offers an exemplary reflection on the phenomenon, as such, and encapsulates the source of a stream of thought that found its destination in the UN declaration.[55] The inclusion of civilians is already known from the descriptions on Assyrian and Babylonian deportations (Isa 20:4; Lam 2:21; Ezek 9:6; Deut 29:10). Now they are explicitly named as intended victims,[56] including children and women.[57]

The fixed date may be associated with strategic deliberations, but also with the concept of a "doom's day" (יום נקם; Isa 34:8; 63:4).[58] The date is connected with Pesach (13th Nisan/13th Adar). The notion of plundering and booty is usually part of war, but here all rules of warfare seem to be set aside (cf. Deut 2:35; 3:7; 20:14; cf. Josh 8:2, 27; Isa 10:6).[59] Under the conditions of a time of peace when no one had even opened or declared a war (which was an act under dispute in Persian-Hellenistic times), the plundering was an offence against the protection of property even for the personae miserae (cf. Isa 10:2)! Here the very existence of the rule of law is under dispute. The possessions of a person condemned to death will go over to the crown, and the booty of war will partly go over to the soldiers. But the booty of a murderous act is simply illegal possession. After the ritual of vengeance the litigants have no further requests: the Jews do not demand part of the impure belongings of their dead foes.

The promulgation of the edict in all the provinces turns an illegal request into official law. A statutory order with legal force promotes a lie!

4. The Cancellation of the Edict and the Punishment of the Troops who are Prepared to Commit the Genocide and their Commanders

The story eventually marks the prodigious turn of Israel's fate through the help of Esther (הפך nif. Esther 9:1, 22) and the invisible support of God, who is never mentioned himself. Esther succeeds in saving her and her people's lives. The evil-doer suffers death by hanging, a punishment meant as an example for others (Esther 7:7–10; Deut 21:22–23).[60] The talionic

---

[55] Cf. above. For the background of narratives in Israelite wisdom teachings cf. Talmon, "Wisdom", 419–55.

[56] Cf. also Isa 3:5; Josh 6:21; Gen 19:4; Exod 10:9.

[57] Gen 34:29; 45:19; 46:5; Num 31:17, 18; 32:26; 2 Chron 20:13; 31:18.

[58] One day: 1 Sam 2:34; 1 Kings 20:29; Isa 9:14; 10:17; 47:9; Zech 3:9; 14:7, 9.

[59] Cf. Ezek 26:12; 29:19; 38:12, 13; 39:10; Isa 33:23; 2 Chron 20:25; 28:8.

[60] The exact way in which the death penalty was carried out is not clear; cf. Thornton, "Crucifixion", 419–26. For impalement and crucifixion as methods of execution among the Persians, cf. Herodotus Histories 3.159; 4.43; for the exhibition of corpses, Histories 7.238; cf. Wahl, *Esther*, 154–5.

punishment is in accordance with Persian and Jewish law.[61] The false edict of genocide is withdrawn (Esther 8:4–5); in fact, the king authorizes Mordecai to rescind the edict. Thus the fallibility of the Persian law has been proven by the Persians themselves, and the superiority or even moral supremacy of the Jewish law is attested.

Esther 3:13	Esther 8:10–12
13 ... and written instructions were sent by couriers into all the king's provinces, to destroy, massacre, and exterminate all the Jews, young and old, children and women, on a single day, on the 13th day of the 12th month, that is the month of Adar, and to take the spoil of them as booty.	10 ... and he sent written instructions by couriers ... 11 wherein the king granted the Jews that were in every city to gather themselves together, and to stand up for their lives, to destroy, massacre, and exterminate all armed forces of the people and provinces that would assault them, their children and women, and to take the spoil of them as booty 12 on a single day, in all the provinces of the king Ahasuerus, namely upon the 13th day of the 12th month, that is the month of Adar.

The new edict grants a series of new fundamental rights to the Jews, and thereby the narrative again fulfills its purposes of promoting certain exemplary principles. It gives the right to assemble in all cities and to form an own assembly. This assembly has the right to stand up for the lives of its members and to defend their rights. The defense is directed against all groups in the empire who are prepared to meet the Jews with weapons and

---

[61] Kratz, *Translatio imperii*, 241–3, has pointed out the legal aspects of the whole procedure, 241–2: "Ausfertigung (3,9–15) und Aufhebung (8,3–17) des Vernichtungsbeschlusses sind in Form der Ratifizierung und Entsendung eines königlichen Gesetzes gestaltet, welches einmal die vermeintlichen persischen Interessen gegen die 'jüdischen Gesetze' vertritt (vgl. דת in 3,14.15; 4,3aα8; 9,1), das andere Mal die jüdischen als die wahren Interessen des persischen Reiches anerkennt und darum die Existenz der nach ihren Gesetzen lebenden Judenschaft im Namen und mit dem Siegel des Königs, also 'unwiderruflich' (8,8) garantiert (vgl. דת in 8,13f.17; 9,14). In beiden Fällen, ebenso in 1,12ff, geht der gesetzgebenden Ausfertigung des Schreibens eine Beratung voraus, in deren Verlauf dem König zunächst ein Gesetzesentwurf unterbreitet wird (אם־על־המלך טוב, 1,19; 3,9; 8,5), bevor dieser, sofern er die Zustimmung des Königs findet, durch Niederschrift und Verschickung in Kraft gesetzt bzw. im Blick auf zukünftige Fälle gleicher Art in die Sammlung der unvergänglichen Gesetze der Meder und Perser aufgenommen wird (1,19). Demnach verdankt sich die Rettung, mithin die Existenz der jüdischen Bevölkerung im persischen Reich auch nach dem Zeugnis des Esterbuches einem juristischen Verfahren, das mit der Vergabe des großköniglichen Siegels an die wegen angeblicher Illoyalität ernstlich bedrohte Judenschaft die in 3,8 unter Anklage gestellten Gesetze sanktioniert."

with hostile intent to kill and to extinguish them,[62] i.e. those who are deter- mined and prepared to commit a genocide! Thus the Jews do not only have the right of self-defense, but also the right of resistance against everyone who targets them and their families with criminal intent. They are even granted the right of plundering in accordance to the rules of war. Thus the Jews exercise their new rights, as recounted in Esther 9, but they refrain from the right to take their enemies' possessions. They make this decision in order to avoid any danger of pollution[63] and they do not carry out talionic revenge by killing innocent civilians, young boys, old men, women and small children (as the first edict had allowed others to do with the Jews, according to Esther 3:13b).

Esther 8:11–12	Esther 9
11 ... the king granted the Jews that were in every city to gather themselves together, and to stand for their life, to destroy, massacre, and exter- minate all armed forces of the people and provinces that would assault them, their children and women, and to take the spoil of them for booty 12 on a single day, in all the provinces of the king Ahasue- rus, namely upon the 13th day of the 12th month, that is the month of Adar.	1 And so, on the 13th day of the 12th month, that is, the month of Adar, when the king's command and *dât* were to be executed, the very day on which the enemies of the Jews had expected to get them in their power, ... 2 the Jews gathered themselves together in their cities throughout all provinces of the king Ahasuerus, to lay hands on those who sought their hurt ... 5 So the Jews struck at their enemies with the stroke of the sword, with slaughter and de- struction, and they wreaked their will unto them that hated them. 10 ... but they did not lay hands on the spoil ... 16 The rest of the Jews, those in the king's provinces, likewise gathered themselves to- gether, and fought for their lives. Then they had rest from their enemies, and they killed those who hated them, 75.000; but they did not lay hands on the spoil.

---

[62] Meinhold, *Esther*, 101–2: "Die Judenfeinde entsprechen dem weisheitlichen Muster des Toren (vgl. z.B. Spr. 26,27a). Ihre Torheit erweist sich an dem besonderen Fall ihres Verhaltens einer Minderheit gegenüber, die allerdings über Beziehungen zum Hof verfügt. Die Judenfeinde treten schließlich massenweise auf, obgleich ein einzelner den Anfang gemacht hatte [...] Trotz eines erfolgversprechenden Kalküls werden die wirklichen Verhältnisse und Zusammenhänge vom Judenfeind nicht wahrgenommen [...] So fällt die Masse der Judenfeinde neben ihrer Verderbtheit auch ihrer Blindheit zum Opfer (9,5–16). Sie ist nicht (mehr?) erkenntnisfähig. Aber sie ist be- waffnet und zum Vernichten der ausersehenen Opfer entschlossen (8,11a)."

[63] According to Num 31:11–12, 21–24 a ritual of purification of booty was demanded in case of a war that was under the supervision of a priest. Those rituals would not have been thinkable under conditions in the Diaspora.

They organize themselves in a Qahal (Esther 9:2, 15, 16) in order to resist the assaults of the "killing-squads". Instead of the overall destruction of a people, now only those foes are targeted who attack the Jews with weaponry; the resistance is an act within the context of a real and public battle (Esther 9:5). Everyone who is officially prepared to execute the edict of genocide is met with the sword. In this situation most of the Persian officials back down and do not join the attack against the Jews, although not all of them, especially in the big cities. The divine terror supports the Jewish defense (פחד).[64] Only those who obviously intend to kill the Jews are treated as adversaries (מבקשי רעתם v. 2a; איביהם v. 5a,[65] cf. בקש נפש Ps 35:4; 38:13; 70:3; 1 Sam 20:1; 22:23; 23:14 and 1 Sam 24:10; 25:26; Jer 49:37; Ps 71:13, 24, passim). Haman's sons, who stand in a legal sense as the successors to Haman, are executed by hanging (Esther 9:7–10, 14), but there is no collective persecution of males! The number of those in the provinces who still were prepared to execute the genocide against the Jews is horrible: Esther 9:16 speaks about 75.000 enemies who were killed.[66]

The surprise is the number of foes. In ancient tradition the high number serves to exaggerate the glorious victory, but here the story acquires a new perspective: that the Jews could fight such a huge number of adversaries on one day is also an astonishing sign of divine support and – at the same time – a display of an amount of anti-Judaism that had been unbelievable until that time! In Christian exegesis, commentators often are stunned by the brutality of the Jews but not at all aware of the immensity of criminal potential among their foes! They read the story as an example of Jewish vindictiveness, but not as a parable for the right of resistance against immeasurable anti-Jewish prejudice and anti-Jewish, anti-religious zeal. By attacking despotism in general the novelette succeeds in formulating, for the first time in Jewish history, the idea of a right of resistance, of self-defense and of self-determination on the part of an ethnic and religious lower class minority.[67]

---

[64] Cf. Exod 15:16; Deut 2:25; 11:25; Isa 2:10; Jer 33:9; Ps 14:5.

[65] The words שׂנא and איב are synonymous (Ps 69:5; 106:10; Jenni, "איב", 118–22; idem, "שׂנא", 835–7.

[66] LXX B Esther 9:16, counts 15.000; LXX A Esther 8:46 (9:16) has 70.100. Wacker, "Tödliche Gewalt", 618, argues about the expansion of the second edict in the LXX E-version: "Sollte es doch zu Angriffen kommen, soll man den Juden in ihrer Verteidigung beistehen – Kampfhandlungen von jüdischer Seite sind hier nur für den äußersten Notfall vorgesehen und als Defensivaktionen bezeichnet (E 20)." Est 9:5 is omitted in this version. There is a tendency to diminish the amount of violence.

[67] Achenbach, "Vertilgen", 309.

5. The Text as Camouflage

The whole text is a camouflage that takes up elements of common knowledge about Persian culture and uses them for a wisdom teaching or parable about the danger of undermining fundamental laws by means of evil intrigues and intentional distortion. The lie of Haman the Agagite forms the basis of the Persian law and leads to the disguised injustice of genocide. The "Torah" of Mordecai and Esther turns the law into a true law in line with international convictions. The ancient Greek refusal of a *proskynesis* was shared by the Jews. The legend says that from the truth of the Jewish Torah – even though the name of the LORD is not mentioned – the Persians learned to overcome an excessive edict. The idea that there is a fundamental right of resistance to inhuman law and to genocide is established. There is no evidence that this novelette was developed during the existence of the Persian empire. On the contrary, the stylization of a Persian setting allows the reader the chance to identify the negative connotations of the hostile and despotic features with the disdained former enemy of the Greek world.

The Esther legend may have played an important role to legitimate Jewish existence in those areas that remained under Seleucid rule after the Maccabees had gained control over Jerusalem and Judah. The Hasmoneans celebrated the Day of Nicanor on the 13th Adar (1 Macc 7:49), in remembrance of their great victory in 161.[68] But what happened to the Jews who lived beyond their influence? It is not difficult to imagine that the internal pressure to integrate and to acknowledge especially the divine legitimation of Antiochus IV increased. It is not by chance that 2 Maccabees refers to martyrdom in several cases. When the Seleucids were forced to accept the political sovereignty of the Hasmoneans under Simon in 142 BCE (1 Macc 13:42), this might have also had the consequence of creating a great deal of pressure on the Jews in the Diaspora. When John Hyrcanus[69] I (134–104 BCE) achieved leadership over the Hasmonean kingdom and Antiochus VII died in a battle against the Parthians, the situation for the Jews under Seleucid rule may have become dangerous.

On the other hand, the political situation for Jews in the area under Parthian influence may have changed. In that case, the Esther narrative could be read as an example of positive relation between the Persians and the Jews of the Diaspora. When Mesopotamia became part of the Parthian Empire, Aramaic became again a popular language in the area[70] and the

---

[68] 1 Macc 7:26–43, 48–50; 2 Macc 14:11–15, 28, 31–37; Polybios Histories 31.14.4.

[69] The Epithet 'Hyrcanus' for the Jewish high priest is curious. Does it imply an allusion to Hyrcania, the area south of the Caspian sea, that was (re-)conquered by the Asrakides at that time?

[70] Wiesehöfer, *Persien*, 166–7.

book of Esther was translated into Aramaic. Along the Euphrates, Greek speaking groups remained in the area, e.g. in the cities of Seleucia and in Dura-Europos, which became a part of the Parthian empire in 114 BCE. The Greek version of Esther is influenced by the Aramaic versions[71] but stresses more the theological aspects (Esther 2:20; 6:1 LXX) and reduces the number of victims of Jewish vengeance (cf. Esther 9:1–2, 16 LXX). Perhaps it was at this time (between 134 and 104 BCE) that 2 Maccabees was written and the Nicanor Day was connected with the celebration of a festival of remembrance for "Mordecai" on the 14th of Adar (2 Macc 15:36)! Accordingly, we may assume that the book of Esther was written between the writing of 1 Maccabees and that of 2 Maccabees.

Perhaps we can find some indirect evidence for this assumption by comparing two parallel episodes in the books of Maccabees. In 1 Macc 6:1–16 the campaign of Antiochus IV to the east leads him to the area of the Elymais. There – according to Porphyrios – he plundered the temple of Diana.[72] The parallel account about Antiochus IV may have a historical background. The attempt of Antiochus IV to conquer the city fails (1 Macc 6:4). On the way back he receives the news about the successful Jewish reconquest of Jerusalem and falls into depression and contracts a disease. When he is about to die, he – according to the Jewish legend – has the deeper insight that his defeat by the Persians and his disease may be a divine punishment. 1 Macc 6:9–16 reads:

> 1 Macc 6:9 He lay there for many days, because deep grief continually gripped him, and he concluded that he was dying.
>
> 10 So he called all his friends and said to them, "Sleep departs from my eyes and I am downhearted with worry.
>
> 11 I said to myself, 'To what distress I have come! And into what a great flood I now am plunged! For I was kind and beloved in my power.'
>
> 12 But now I remember the evils I did in Jerusalem. I seized all her vessels of silver and gold; and I sent to destroy (to ban, to deliver to the curse)[73] the inhabitants of Judah without good reason (καὶ ἐξαπέστειλα ἐξᾶραι τοὺς κατοικοῦντας Ιουδα διὰ κενῆς).

---

[71] Kottsieper, "Zusätze ", 118–19.

[72] Porphyrios *FGH* 260 F 56; cf. Mittag, *Antiochos IV.*, 318–20. There are several divergent reports about Antiochus' attempts to plunder Persian temples. See ibid., 308: Polybios Histories 31.9 (a temple of Artemis in the area of the Elymais), 1 Macc 3:31, 37; 6:1–3 (a temple in the city of Elymais), 2 Macc 9:1–2 (a temple in Persepolis), Josephus Ant. 12.354–5 (a temple of Artemis in the city of Elymais in the area of the Persis), Appian Syriaca 66 (a temple of Aphrodite in the area of Elymais), Hieronymus Commentaria in Danielem 718 (a temple of Diana in the area of the Elymais). For further discussion of the problems, see Mørkholm, *Antiochus IV.*, 170–80; Schwartz, *2 Maccabees*, 148 (with other literature).

[73] ἐξᾶραι = to curse sb.

13 I know that it is because of this that these evils have come upon me; and behold, I am perishing of deep grief in a strange land." ...

16 Thus Antiochus the king died there in the one hundred and forty-ninth year.

According to the parallel account in 2 Macc 9 it was Persepolis that the king tried to conquer without success. The news of Nicanor's defeat reaches him in Ecbatana. He decides to go for warfare against the Jews in 2 Macc 9:4:

2 Macc 9:4 Transported with rage, he conceived the idea of turning upon the Jews the injury done by those who had put him to flight; so he ordered his charioteer to drive without stopping until he completed the journey. But the judgment of heaven rode with him! For in his arrogance he said (ὑπερηφάνως εἶπε), "When I get there I will make Jerusalem a cemetery[74] of Jews (πολυάνδριον Ιουδαίων Ιεροσόλυμα ποιήσω παραγενόμενος)!"

According to this version Antiochus is heavily punished by God for his hubris (v. 4–7), and the narrator explains the lesson to the reader in 2 Macc 9:8:

2 Macc 9:8 Thus he who had just been thinking that he could command the waves of the sea, in his superhuman arrogance (διὰ τὴν ὑπὲρ ἄνθρωπον ἀλαζονείαν), and imagining that he could weigh the high mountains in a balance, was brought down to earth and carried in a litter, making the power of God manifest to all.

Only when his spirit is broken he concedes in 2 Macc 9:12:

2 Macc 9:12 "It is right to be subject to God, and no mortal should think that he is equal to God (δίκαιον ὑποτάσσεσθαι τῷ θεῷ καὶ μὴ θνητὸν ὄντα ἰσόθεα φρονεῖν)."[75]

This insight comes too late. The punishment seems unavoidable and thus the "murderer and blasphemer" (ἀνδροφόνος καὶ βλάσφημος) has to die in a foreign land (2 Macc 9:28). Whereas 1 Maccabees depicts Antiochus as the one who committed the blasphemous assault against the sanctuary of Jerusalem and – as other cruel tyrants of the past, e.g. Nabonidus or Nebuchadnezzar – could have had the chance for a final conversion, in 2 Maccabees the despot cannot escape divine sanctions because he intended to extinguish the Jews from Jerusalem, i.e. to perform a genocide against the Jewish citizens of the holy city. Even if the writer of 1 Maccabees still

---

[74] The *polyandrion* can be a cemetery for people of all kind and a mass grave; cf. v. 15.
[75] Schwartz, *2 Maccabees*, 358–9; for further Greek parallels, cf. 2 Macc 5:21; Aeschylus Persians 744–51, 830.

could imagine that God could forgive the blasphemy of establishing an idol at the Jerusalem sanctuary, the intention to destroy the Jews from Zion is judged as an unforgivable sin. Consequently 2 Maccabees establishes a junction between the day of Nicanor and the day of Mordecai. The narrator of 2 Maccabees thus unites Jews in the Diaspora with the Jews from Zion. Somewhere, during that time, we may assume the origin of the literary form of the Esther Legend.[76] Its fundamental value as a parable about the origins of the human right to resist and to punish the planning and performing of genocide gives the book a preeminent place in ancient literature and makes it a treasure within the heritage of mankind.

References

Achenbach, R., *Israel zwischen Verheißung und Gebot. Literarkritische Untersuchungen zu Deuteronomium 5–11*, (EHS 23,422; Frankfurt a. M. et al.: Peter Lang, 1991).
–, "Vertilgen – Töten – Vernichten (Ester 3,13): Die Genozid-Thematik im Esterbuch", *ZAR* 15 (2009) 282–314.
–, "Satrapie, Medinah und lokale Hierokratie: Zum Einfluss der Statthalter der Achämenidenzeit auf die jüdischen Tempel und ihre Priesterschaft und zu dessen Folgen für die Gestalt sakraler Ursprungslegenden im Pentateuch", *ZAR* 16 (2010) 105–44.
–, "Divine Warfare and YHWH's Wars: Religious Ideologies of War in the Ancient Near East and in the Old Testament", in G. Galil et al. (ed.), *The Ancient Near East in the 12th and 10th Centuries BCE: Culture and History* (AOAT; Münster: Ugarit-Verlag, 2011, forthcoming).
Aeschylus (cf. Smyth, H.W./Sommerstein, A.H.).
Appian (cf. White, H.).
Arrian (cf. Wirth, G.).
Assmann, J., "Monotheismus und die Sprache der Gewalt", in P. Walter (ed.), *Das Gewaltpotential des Monotheismus und der dreieinge Gott* (QD 216; Freiburg et al.: Herder, 2005) 18–38.
Bardtke, H., *Das Buch Esther* (KAT 17,5; Gütersloh: Gütersloher Verlagshaus, 1963).
–, *Luther und das Buch Esther* (Tübingen: Mohr Siebeck, 1964).
Barton, J., *Amos's Oracles against the Nations: A study of Amos 1.3–2.5* (Cambridge et al.: Cambridge University Press, 1980).
Bederman, D.J., *International Law in Antiquity* (Cambridge/New York: Cambridge University Press, 2001).

---

[76] Macchi, "Esther. Esther Grec", 566–72, 610–14; idem, "Le livre d'Esther", 97–136, has already shown, that the similarities in Greek literature on the Persians with the Esther narrative "are so numerous that the book of Esther should be considered as a sort of a Jewish 'Persica', i.e. a standard form of Greek historical narrative about Persia." Ego, "Esther", 279, has confirmed these considerations "and a diaspora location for the origins of the book" from the inner perspective of the story: "Among the elements that contribute to this conclusion are the theological claims that underlie the Persian motifs, especially the rejection of *proskynesis* before a human ruler [...], the book's reversal structure, its treatment of Holy War, and the veiled speech of God. The negotiation of rule by foreign powers in light of the tension between Jewish law and the law of an external empire supports a pro-Hasmonean origin for the book." The last point could be disputed if one takes into consideration that the existence of Jews outside the reach of the Hasmoneans must have become extremely difficult after the success of the Maccabean revolt.

Berlin, A., *Esther* אסתר (The JPS Bible Commentary; Philadelphia: The Jewish Publication Society, 2001).

– et al. (ed.), *The Jewish Study Bible* (Oxford/New York: Oxford University Press, 2004).

Berman, J., "Aggadah and Anti-Semitism: The Midrashim to Esther 3:8", *Judaism* 38 (1989) 185–96.

Bevenot, H., "Die Proskynesis und die Gebete im Estherbuch", *Jahrbuch für Liturgiewissenschaft* 11 (1931) 132–9.

Bush, F.W., "The Book of Esther: Opus non gratum in the Christian Canon", *Bulletin for Biblical Research* 8 (1998) 39–54.

Cerfaux, L./Tondriau, J., *Le culte des souverains dans la civilisation gréco-romaine* (Bibliothèque de Théologie 3,5; Tournai: Desclée & Cie., 1957).

Clines, D.J.A., *The Esther Scroll: The Story of the Story* (JSOTSup 30; Sheffield: JSOT Press, 1984).

Crüsemann, F., "'... und die Gesetze des Königs halten sie nicht' (Est 3,8). Widerstand und Recht im Alten Testament", *Wort und Dienst. Jahrbuch der Kirchlichen Hochschule Bethel* NF 17 (1984) 9–25.

Cuffari, A., *Judenfeindschaft in der Antike und im Alten Testament. Terminologische, historische und theologische Untersuchungen* (BBB 153; Hamburg: Philo, 2007).

Daube, D., *Esther* (Oxford: Oxford Centre for Postgraduate Hebrew Studies, 1995).

Dihle, A., *Die Griechen und die Fremden* (München: C.H. Beck, 1994).

Ego, B., *Targum Scheni zu Ester: Übersetzung, Kommentar und theologische Deutung* (TSAJ 54; Tübingen: Mohr Siebeck, 1996).

–, "The Book of Esther: A Hellenistic Book", *JAJ* 1 (2010) 279–302.

–, "Die Geschichtskonzeption des Esterbuches als Paradigma historischer Sinnkonstruktion in der Spätzeit des Alten Testaments", in P. Mommer/A. Scherer (ed.), *Geschichte Israels und deuteronomistisches Geschichtsdenken*. (FS W. Thiel; AOAT 380; Münster: Ugarit Verlag, 2011) 85–105.

Fox, M.V., *Character and Ideology in the Book of Esther* (Studies on Personalities of the Old Testament; Columbia: University of South Carolina Press, 1991).

Gerhards, G., *Die Aussetzungsgeschichte des Mose: Literar- und redaktionsgeschichtliche Untersuchungen zu einem Schlüsseltext des nichtpriesterschriftlichen Tetrateuch* (WMANT 109; Neukirchen-Vluyn: Neukirchener Verlag, 2006).

Gerleman, G., *Esther* (BKAT 21; Neukirchen-Vluyn: Neukirchener Verlag, 1973).

Godley, A.D., *Herodotus with an English Translation in four volumes* (LCL; London/Cambridge: William Heinemann/Harvard University Press, [1926] 1966).

Habicht, C., *Gottmenschentum und Griechische Städte* (Zetemata 14; München: C.H. Beck, [2]1970).

Hagedorn, A.C., "The Absent Presence: Cultural Responses to Persian Presence in the Eastern Mediterranean", in O. Lipschits et al. (ed.), *Judah and the Judeans in the Achaemenid Period: Negotiating Identity in an International Context* (Winona Lake: Eisenbrauns, 2011) 39–66.

Haller, M./Galling, K., *Die fünf Megilloth: Ruth, Hoheslied, Klagelieder, Esther, Prediger Salomo* (HAT 1,18; Tübingen: Mohr Siebeck, 1940).

Heltzer, M., "Mordechai and Demoratus and the Question of Historicity", *Archäologische Mitteilungen aus Iran* 27 (1994) 119–21.

Herodotus (cf. Godley, A.D.).

Hettlage, R., "Gewalt der Ehre – Ehre der Gewalt: Über gesellschaftliche Zusammenhänge von Gewalt und Ehre in der Moderne", in K. Platt (ed.), *Reden von Gewalt* (München: Wilhelm Fink Verlag, 2002) 121–49.

Hieronymus (cf. Migne, J.-P.).

Huttenbach, H.R., "From the Editor: Towards a Conceptual Definition of Genocide", *Journal of Genocide Research* 4 (2002) 167–75.

Hutter, M., "Iranische Elemente im Buch Esther", in H.D. Galter (ed.), *Kulturkontakte und ihre Bedeutung in Geschichte und Gegenwart des Orients* (Grazer morgenländische Studien 1; Graz: Österreichische Urania, 1986).

Jacoby, F., *Die Fragmente der griechischen Historiker* (Berlin: Weidmann, 1923ff).

Jenni, E., "איב", *THAT* 1 (1978) 118–22.

–, "שנא", *THAT* 2 (1979) 835–7.

Josephus, F. (cf. Marcus, R.).

Katz, S.T., *The Holocaust in Historical Context*. Vol. 1: *The Holocaust and Mass Death Before the Modern Age* (New York: Oxford University Press, 1994).

Keel, O., *Die Geschichte Jerusalems und die Entstehung des Monotheismus* (3 vol.; Göttingen: Vandenhoek & Ruprecht, 2007).

Kent, R.G., *Old Persian: Grammar – Texts – Lexicon* (American Oriental Series 33; New Haven: American Oriental Society, 1953).

Koch, K., "Weltordnung und Reichsidee im alten Iran und ihre Auswirkungen auf die Provinz Jehud", in idem/K. Koch, *Reichsidee und Reichsorganisation im Perserreich* (OBO 55; Fribourg/Göttingen: Universitätsverlag/ Vandenhoeck & Ruprecht, ²1996) 133–317.

Korošec, D., *Kritisch über die Inkriminierung des Genozids* (Faculty of Law; University of Ljubljana 2003; www.law.muni.cz/edicni/dp08/files/pdf/mezinaro/korosec.pdf [10/01/2009]).

Kottsieper, I., "Zusätze zu Ester", in O.H. Steck et al., *Das Buch Baruch – Der Brief des Jeremia – Zusätze zu Ester und Daniel* (ATD Apokryphen 5; Göttingen: Vandenhoeck & Ruprecht, 1998) 111–207.

Kratz, R.G., *Translatio imperii: Untersuchungen zu den aramäischen Danielerzählungen und ihrem theologiegeschichtlichen Umfeld* (WMANT 63; Neunkirchen-Vluyn: Neukirchener Verlag, 1991).

Kuhrt, A., "Making History: Sargon of Agade and Cyrus the Great of Persia", in: W. Henkelman/A. Kuhrt (ed.), *A Persian Perspective* (Achaemenid History 13; Leiden: Brill, 2003) 347–61.

Landmann, G.P., *Thukydides: Geschichte des Peloponnesischen Krieges. Griechisch – Deutsch* (Sammlung Tusculum; Düsseldorf/Zürich: Artemis & Winkler, ⁴1993).

Lemkin, R., *Axis Rule in Occupied Europe: Laws of Occupation – Analysis of Government – Proposals for Redress* (Washington: Carnegie Endowment for International Peace [Division of International Law], 1944).

Levenson, J.D., *Esther. A Commentary* (OTL; Louisville/London: Westminster John Knox Press, 1997).

Lewis, B., *The Sargon-Legend: A Study of the Akkadian Text and the Tale of the Hero Who Was Exposed at Birth* (ASOR Dissertation Series 4; Cambridge: American Schools of Oriental Research, 1984).

Littman, R.L., "Religious Policy of Xerxes and the Book of Esther", *JQR* 65 (1975) 145–55.

Loader, J.A., "Das Buch Ester", in H.-P. Müller et al., *Das Hohelied. Klagelieder. Das Buch Ester* (ATD 16,2; Göttingen: Vandenhoeck & Ruprecht, ⁴1992) 203–81.

Luther, M., "De servo arbitrio" (1525) in *D. Martin Luthers Werke. Kritische Gesamtausgabe* (vol. 18; Weimar: Böhlau, 1883ff) 600–787.

–, "Tischreden aus der ersten Hälfte der dreißiger Jahre" in *D. Martin Luthers Werke. Kritische Gesamtausgabe. Tischreden* (vol. 1; Weimar: Böhlau, 1883ff).

Macchi, J.-D., "Esther. Esther Grec", in T. Römer et al. (ed.), *Introduction à l'Ancien Testament* (Geneva: Labor et Fides, 2004), 566–72, 610–14.

–, "Le livre d'Esther: Regard hellénistique sur le pouvoir et le monde perses", *Transeufratène* 30 (2005) 97–135.

Marcus, R., *Josephus in nine volumes VI: Jewish Antiquities, Books IX–XI* (LCL; London/Cambridge: William Heinemann/Harvard University Press, [1937] 1968).

Meinhold, A., *Das Buch Esther* (ZBK 13; Zürich: Theologischer Verlag Zürich, 1983).

Migne, J.-P., *Patrologiae cursus completus – Series latinae* (Paris: Garnier, 1841ff).

Mittag, P.F., *Antiochos IV. Epiphanes: Eine politische Biographie* (KLIO NF 11; Berlin: Akademieverlag, 2006).

Mooren, L., "The Nature of the Hellenistic Monarchy", in E. van't Dack et al. (ed.), *Egypt and the Hellenistic World: Proceedings of the international colloquium Leuven, 24–26 May 1982* (Studia Hellenistica 27; Leuven: Peeters, 1983) 205–40.

Mørkholm, O., *Antiochus IV. of Syria* (Kopenhagen: Gyldendal, 1966).

Müri, W., *Xenophon: Anabasis. Der Zug der Zehntausend* (Sammlung Tusculum; Düsseldorf/Zürich: Artemis & Winkler, [2]1997).

Otto, E., *Krieg und Frieden in der Hebräischen Bibel und im Alten Orient: Aspekte für eine Friedensordnung in der Moderne* (Theologie und Frieden 18; Stuttgart et al.: Kohlhammer, 1999).

–, "Mose und das Gesetz: Die Mose-Figur als Gegenentwurf politischer Theologie zur neuassyrischen Königsideologie im 7. Jh. v. Chr.", in idem (ed.), *Mose. Ägypten und das Alte Testament* (SBS 189; Stuttgart: Katholisches Bibelwerk, 2000) 43–83.

–, "Völkerrecht III: Alter Orient und Israel", *RGG⁴* 8 (2005) 1158–9.

–, "Deuteronomiumstudien II – Deuteronomistische und postdeuteronomistische Perspektiven in der Literaturgeschichte von Deuteronomium 5–11", *ZAR* 15 (2009) 65–215.

Paton, L.B., *A Critical and exegetical Commentary on the Book of Esther* (ICC; Edinburgh: T&T Clark, 1908).

Paton, W.R., *Polybius: The Histories* (6 vol.; LCL; London/Cambridge: William Heinemann/Harvard University Press, [1921] 1967).

Plutarch (cf. Ziegler, K.).

Polybios (cf. Paton, W.R.).

Porphyrios (cf. Jacoby, F.).

Porten, B., *Archives from Elephantine: The Life of an Ancient Jewish Military Colony* (Berkeley/Los Angeles: University of California Press, 1968).

Quintus Curtius Rufus (cf. Rolfe, J.C.).

Reuter, H.-R., "Völkermord", *RGG⁴* 8 (2005) 1154–5.

Rolfe, J.C., *Quintus Curtius in two volumes: II Books VI–X* (LCL; London/Cambridge: William Heinemann/Harvard University Press, [1946] 1985).

Rooke, D.W., *Zadok's Heirs: The Role and Development of the High Priesthood in Ancient Israel* (OTM; Oxford/New York: Oxford University Press, 2000).

Schabas, W.A., *Genozid im Völkerrecht* (Hamburg: Hamburger Ed., 2003).

Schmitt, H.H., "Herrscherkult", in idem/E. Vogt (ed.), *Kleines Lexikon des Hellenismus* (Wiesbaden: Harrassowitz, [2]1993) 243–53.

Schwartz, D.R., *2 Maccabees* (CEJL; Berlin/New York: de Gruyter, 2008).

Selbmann, F., *Der Tatbestand des Genozids im Völkerstrafrecht* (Schriftenreihe zum Völkerstrafrecht 1; Leipzig: Leipziger Universitätsverlag, 2002).

Smyth, H.W., *Aeschylus, Suppliant Maidens – Persians – Prometheus – Seven Against Thebes*, (LCL; London/Cambridge: William Heinemann/Harvard University Press, [1922] 1963).

Sommerstein, A.H., *Aeschylus: Oresteia. Agamemnon, Libation-Bearers, Eumenides* (LCL, London: William Heinemann Ltd./Cambridge: Harvard University Press, 2008).

Taeger, F., *Charisma: Studien zur Geschichte des antiken Herrscherkultes I* (Stuttgart: Kohlhammer, 1957).

Talmon, S., "Wisdom in the Book of Esther", *VT* 13 (1963) 419–55.

Thornton, T.C.G., "The Crucifixion of Haman and the Scandal of the Cross", *JTS* 37 (1986) 419–26.

Thukydides (cf. Landmann, G.P.).

VanderKam, J.C., *From Joshua to Caiaphas. High Priests after the Exile* (Minneapolis/Assen: Fortress Press/Van Gorcum, 2004).

Veijola, T., *Das 5. Buch Mose: Deuteronomium Kapitel 1,1–16,17* (ATD 8,1; Göttingen: Vandenhoeck & Ruprecht, 2004).

von der Way, T., *Göttergericht und "Heiliger" Krieg im Alten Ägypten: Die Inschriften des Merenptah zum Libyerkrieg des Jahres 5* (SAGA 4; Heidelberg: Heidelberger Orientverlag, 1992).

Wacker, M.-T., "Tödliche Gewalt des Judenhasses – mit tödlicher Gewalt gegen Judenhass? Hermeneutische Überlegungen zu Est 9", in F.-L. Hossfeld/L. Schwienhorst-Schönberger (ed.), *Das Manna fällt auch heute noch: Beiträge zur Geschichte und Theologie des Alten, Ersten Testaments* (FS E. Zenger; HBSt 44; Freiburg i.B.: Herder, 2004) 609–37.

Wahl, H.M., *Das Buch Esther: Übersetzung und Kommentar* (Berlin/New York: de Gruyter, 2009).

Walbank, F.W., "Könige als Götter. Überlegungen zum Herrscherkult von Alexander bis Augustus", *Chiron* 17 (1987) 365–82.

White, H., *Appian's Roman History with an English Translation in Four Volumes* (LCL; London/Cambridge: William Heinemann/Harvard University Press, 1962)

Wiemer, H.-U., *Alexander der Große* (München: C.H. Beck, 2005).

Wiesehöfer, J., *Das antike Persien: Von 550 v. Chr. bis 650 n.Chr.* (Düsseldorf/Zürich: Artemis & Winkler, 1993).

–, "Proskynesis", *Der Neue Pauly* 10 (2001) 443–4.

–, "'Denn ihr huldigt nicht einem Menschen als eurem Herrscher, sondern nur den Göttern': Bemerkungen zur Proskynese in Iran", in C.G. Cereti et al. (ed.), *Religious Themes and Texts of Pre-Islamic Iran and Central Asia: Studies in honour of Professor Gherardo Gnoli on the occasion of his 65th birthday on 6th December 2002* (Wiesbaden: Reichert, 2003) 447–52.

Willi-Plein, I., "השתחוה – Ehrenbezeugung oder Proskynese: Pragmatische Zugänge zur Bedeutung eines etymologisch umstrittenen hebräischen Verbs", in C. Karrer-Grube et al. (ed.), *Sprachen – Bilder – Klänge: Dimensionen der Theologie im Alten Testament und in seinem Umfeld* (FS R. Bartelmus; AOAT 359; Münster: Ugarit Verlag, 2009) 363–77.

Williamson, H.G.M., "The Historical Value of Josephus' Antiquities XI,297–301", *JTS* 28 (1977) 48–67.

Wirth, G./Roos, A.G., *Flavius Arrianus Scripta 1: Alexandri Anabasis* (BSGRT 1239; München: Saur, 2002).

Würthwein, E. et al., *Die fünf Megilloth: Ruth. Das Hohelied. Esther. Der Prediger. Die Klagelieder* (HAT 1,18; Tübingen: Mohr Siebeck, ²1969).

Xenophon (cf. Müri, W.).

Yamauchi, E.M., "The Archaeological Backgrounds of the Exilic and Postexilic Era. Part 2: The Archaeological Background of Esther", *Bibliotheca Sacra* 137:546 (1980) 99–117.

Yavetz, Z., *Judenfeindschaft in der Antike. Die Münchener Vorträge. Eingeleitet von C. Meier* (München: C.H. Beck, 1997).

Zadok, R., "On the Historical Background of the Book of Esther", *BN* 24 (1984) 18–23.

Zenger, E., "Der Mosaische Monotheismus im Spannungsfeld von Gewalttätigkeit und Gewaltverzicht: Eine Replik auf Jan Assmann", in P. Walter (ed.), *Das Gewaltpotential des Monotheismus und der dreieinge Gott* (QD 216; Freiburg et al.: Herder, 2005) 39–73.

–, *Einleitung in das Alte Testament* (Studienbücher Theologie 1; Stuttgart: Kohlhammer, ⁷2008).

Ziegler, K./Gärtner, H. (ed.), *Plutarchi vitae parallelae II,2: Philopoimen, Titus, Pelopidas, Marcellus, Alexander, Caesar* (Stuttgart/Leipzig: Teubner, 1994).

Rainer Albertz

Westfälische Wilhelms-Universität Münster

Are Foreign Rulers Allowed to Enter and Sacrifice in the Jerusalem Temple?

In the early summer of the year 66 CE Neapolitanus, the emissary of Cestius Gallus, Roman legate of Syria, venerated the Jewish god Yhwh in the temple of Jerusalem (B.J. 2.341).[1] By this gesture, he tried to pacify the violent conflicts that had taken place between Gessius Festus, the procurator of Judah, and the Jewish population of Jerusalem. No one from the Jewish assembly gathered in the temple seems to have taken offense at the sacrifice, which Neapolitanus attended "from a permitted place". Only a few weeks later, however, Eleazar, the son of the former High Priest Ananias and the captain of the Jerusalem temple, convinced his priestly colleagues to accept no more oblations or sacrifices from foreigners. This included the cessation of the daily sacrifices for the well-being of the emperor and the Roman people. According to the historian Josephus this decision was the main cause for the outbreak of the Jewish-Roman war (B.J. 2.409, 417).

How was it possible, that such a dramatic shift from cooperation to hostility in the course of some weeks could take place? Why did a member of the Sadducees, the priestly aristocrats of Jerusalem, who had pleaded for a cooperation with the Roman rulers for many decades, suddenly distance himself from the basic convictions of his group? Why could a cultic question of minor importance, whether foreigners and their sacrifices are allowed to enter the temple or not, gain such a significance that it split not only the family of the former High Priest Ananias but the entire priestly class?[2] Of course, there were many reasons for the Jewish-Roman war –

---

[1] The Greek Verb προσκυνέω used by Josephus does not only mean a reverent gesture or a prayer but also includes – at least in the given cultic context – suitable sacrificial offerings to the deity.

[2] Eleazar's father Ananias, who had been High Priest around 47–59 CE, his brother Simon, and his uncle Hiskia were leading members of the peace party (B.J. 2.418, 429) and were murdered during the following civil war (441). Eleazar also had several aristocrats among his followers (B.J. 2.451, 628); see Goodman, *Ruling Class*, 158–9, 218–21. The suggestion that Eleazar received his main support from the lower priests and Levites, which were exploited by the wealthy priestly families (Ant. 20.180–1, 206–7), as Baumbach, "Einheit", 104–6, emphasized, is possible, but this

political, economic, social – that cannot be dealt with here. But Josephus does not seem to be entirely wrong by emphasizing that religious and cultic reasons played a major role as well.[3] Obviously, the Jerusalem temple, which constituted an important identity marker for all Jewish groups, acquired central importance in the domestic and foreign policy struggles. And it seems that under the influence of the escalating political pressure some of those, who were responsible for the worship in the temple – i.e., the members of the priestly establishment and their clients – reformulated their own religious identity by defining the access to the temple in an exclusive way. The construction or reconstruction of religious identity in Judaism was never a result of merely political interests but was always dependent upon theological justifications.[4] In the Roman period, Jewish priests, especially the leading ones, had been educated theologians for a long time.[5] Therefore, the present study will investigate the cult-political and theological reasons that may have determined the religious identity of both parties: those who wanted to include the sacrificial offerings of foreigners in the temple cult of Jerusalem and those who wanted to exclude such offerings from there.[6]

1. Cult-Political and Theological Reasons for Permitting Offerings of Foreign Rulers

According to Josephus the peace party, which opposed Eleazar and his followers, consisted of influential laymen, respected Pharisees, and High Priests. His father Ananias belonged to this party as well. They tried hard to cancel Eleazar's decision and therefore gathered the people's assembly in the outer court of the temple (B.J. 2.411). The arguments that they put for-

---

view was not maintained by Josephus, who only mentioned that the reform priests constituted the majority (B.J. 2.410).

[3] Krieger, *Geschichtsschreibung*, 227–8, may be right that Josephus discussed the theological reasons of the Jewish-Roman war at length because he himself had probably been a member of the group around Eleazar before he did his about-face. But this insight rather supports the view that theological questions were of major importance among the reform priests.

[4] Thus a suggestion as made by Wellhausen, *Geschichte*, 345, for example, assuming that Eleazar may have hoped to become a leader of the insurgents, is not sufficient. The explanation that he may have been influenced by the lower priests, who have probably felt more sympathy with the rebels, as supposed by Hengel, *Zeloten*, 223, is possible but not satisfactory, since these priests were dependent on theological arguments as well.

[5] The statement of Wellhausen, *Geschichte*, 345, that the ruling priests of Jerusalem were no theologians may be true for the First Temple period but definitely not for the Second Temple period.

[6] Mell, "Ausbruch", 97–122, did a great deal in analyzing the theological background of the conflict. My study has to thank him for many insights and will try to advance the subject somewhat further.

ward against the decision, according to Josephus, included the following points. First, a long ritual practice of foreigners (ἀλλοφύλοι) adorning the Jerusalem temple with their dedicatory gifts had been established (412). Second, no one had ever been prevented from sacrificing at the temple (413); in fact, Jerusalem would garner a reputation of impiety (ἀσέβαια), should its temple be the only site where foreigners (ἀλλότριοι) were forbidden to sacrifice and to worship. Thus, Eleazar's reform introduced a strange ritual practice (θρησκεία ξένη; 414). Third, by rejecting sacrifices made for the benefit of the emperor and the Roman people, both – the emperor and the Roman people – would be placed beyond the pale (415); therefore, one had to fear that Jerusalem would be placed beyond the pale of the empire and that even Jewish sacrifices at the temple would become impossible (416).

Thus, Josephus – writing for a pagan audience – emphasized the issues of a long-standing ritual tradition, the Jewish reputation in the Roman-Hellenistic world, and the dangerous juridical and political consequences. He does not really reveal the theological reasons. Since he reported, however, that during the meeting several priestly experts on the ancient tradition confirmed that all the forefathers had accepted the sacrifices of foreigners (ἀλλογενεῖς; B.J. 2.417), Josephus indicated that there was an internal Jewish theological discussion about the topic. The reformers around Eleazar seem to have tired already of the arguments; they did not participate in the public meeting, which was a failure (418). We, however, who were not present in the Jerusalem assembly of the early summer 66 CE, have to reconstruct the probable theological arguments of the peace party from different sources.[7]

1.1 Oblations and Sacrifices of Foreign Rulers at the Jerusalem Temple

The argument of the peace party that sacrifices of foreign rulers in Jerusalem and their dedicatory gifts to the temple constituted a long-standing ritual practice seems to be correct.[8] There are no less than ten cases, where sacrifices or oblations of foreign rulers, their emissaries, or their relatives are reported, starting with Alexander (Ant. 11.336) and Ptolemy III Euergetes (C. Ap. 2.48), continuing with Seleukos IV (2 Macc 3:1–3) and Anti-

---

[7] The dispute between the two parties is mirrored by the Rabbinic tradition only in an indirect and legendary way; cf. Roth, "Debate", 95–7; Hengel, *Zeloten*, 367–8.

[8] See Schürer, *History*, 2:309–11. Because he wrote that "it is a well-attested fact that despite of the rigid barrier erected between Jews and Gentiles in regard of religious matters, gentiles participated in Temple worship at Jerusalem", he seems to have been astonished by this fact. But there is a broader theological foundation beneath this practice than he has realized.

ochos VII Sidetes (Ant. 13.242–3), and ending with Marcus Agrippa, the friend and son-in-law of Augustus (Ant. 16.14; Legat. 294–7), Vitellius, the legate of Syria under Tiberius (Ant. 18.122), and the emissary Neapolitanus already mentioned above (B.J. 2.341).[9] Of course, not all of these reports can be taken historically, since, for example, Alexander probably never visited Jerusalem. But these reports would not have been created, if such sacrifices and oblations of foreign rulers were not accepted or even appreciated by a majority of the Jewish population. These events are told with a touch of pride that Yhwh was honored and his sanctuary adorned even by the rulers of mighty empires. Furthermore they show a universalist view similar to that of the story about King Solomon's sermon in the newly founded temple, in which Solomon asked Yhwh to fulfill the prayers of all foreigners who had come to Jerusalem from distant countries to call on him, so that his great fame might be spread to all mankind (1 Kings 8:41–43).[10]

A closer look at these reports reveals that their authors were aware of the possible danger that the sacrifices of foreign rulers could perhaps defile the sanctuary. Thus, Josephus emphasizes that Alexander sacrificed "according to the instruction of the High Priest" (Ant. 11.336) and says that the sacrifices of Ptolemy III were performed "as it is customary (νόμινος) to us" (C. Ap. 2.48). Philo explicitly mentions that the dedicatory gifts of Marcus Agrippa to the temple "were permitted", that means, according to the Jewish law (Legat. 297). Josephus makes clear that the foreign rulers could not enter every part of the sanctuary. According to him, the bull sent by Antiochos VII for the sacrifice was taken by the guards at the gate, who took care of it in the temple (Ant. 13.242). And Neapolitanus celebrated his veneration in the sanctuary from a place "where it was permitted" (B.J. 2.341). Since foreigners were prohibited to enter the inner temple precinct of the Herodian temple, this place must have been a prominent location in the outer courtyard.[11] Thus, the sacrifices and dedicatory gifts of foreign rulers did not occur without any problems, but their Jewish advocates were confident that as long as the sacrifices conformed to the ritual rules of the Torah and were carried out under the control of Jewish priests they could not cause any damage.

---

[9] Cf. also the dedicatory gifts, which are ascribed to the old Antiochos IV Epiphanes (2 Macc 9:16), to the Roman ally of King Herod, Sosius (B.J. 1.357), and Caligula's grandmother, Julia Augusta (Legat. 319).

[10] That only prayers and not sacrifices are mentioned in this sermon probably has to do with the fact that it was written after the temple of Jerusalem had been destructed in 587 BCE, when the ruined sanctuary was reduced to lament services.

[11] Cf. the reconstruction of Busink, *Temple*, 2:1062–6, 1179, and Schürer, *History*, 2:284–7. Inscriptions fixed to the railings prohibited foreigners from entering the inner courtyards. The prominent place might have been in front of the eastern façade of the inner temple buildings.

1.2 Sacrifices for the Benefit of Foreign Rulers

The sacrifices for the benefit of foreign rulers constitute an important variant of the offerings discussed above, which are not restricted to specific visits of those rulers to a certain sanctuary, but are regularly celebrated by its local priesthood on their behalf.[12] At the Jerusalem temple, this kind of offering seems to have been continuously celebrated during the Persian, Ptolemaic, Seleucid, and Roman periods. According to the book of Ezra, King Darius I connected his permission for the reconstruction of the temple with the instruction that the offerings, which he was willing to dedicate to the "God of Heaven" should be used for sacrifices "for the life of the monarch and his sons" (Ezra 6:8–10). And in the view of Josephus, King Cyrus had already founded this ritual practice "for the salvation of the king, his family and the persistence of the empire", which was supposed to strictly follow the Mosaic ceremony (Ant. 11.17). Historically, however, the practice probably just took the place of the sacrifices of the Judean kings (2 Kings 16:15), which had included a holocaust, probably in the morning, and a grain offering, probably in the evening.[13] The ritual practice appears to have been continued under the reign of Ptolemy I (Aristeas 45) and even maintained during the Maccabean revolt (1 Macc 7:33). As far as we can determine, Augustus not only continued but also intensified the sacrifices "for the Caesar and the Roman people", because he equipped them with one bull and two lambs, which should be sacrificed as holocaust offerings twice every day (Legat. 157, 317). Philo is possibly right that these numerous sacrifices were carried out at the emperor's expense (Legat. 157), although Josephus claimed that they were paid for by the Jewish community (C. Ap. 2.77); but, of course, the money was probably taken from the provincial taxes raised from the Jewish population. In any case, the sacrifices for the well-being of the monarch and his empire were a long-lasting and accepted ritual practice in Jerusalem, indeed, as the peace party claimed. These daily sacrifices in the Jerusalem temple did not only demonstrate the loyalty of the Jews to their foreign overlords (Legat. 280; B.J. 2.197) but also helped to stabilize the empire and world order.

---

[12] Already Schürer, *History*, 2:311–12, regarded this kind of sacrifice as a special case of those offerings that were dedicated by foreigners; similarly Mell, "Ausbruch", 106–7.

[13] Since the two offerings of the king correspond to the two Tamid offerings in the morning and the evening mentioned before, they seem to have been sacrificed at the same time.

1.3 Normative and Theological Foundations from the Torah

It has been argued that the participation of foreigners in the temple cult had been merely a religious concession to the political conditions, to which the Jews and their temple were subjected for centuries under the rule of foreign powers.[14] However, this is not entirely true. The convictions of the peace party and the long-lasting ritual practice, to which they refer, have a legal and theological foundation in the Mosaic Torah. Since it contains no clear paragraph, however, in which the sacrifices of or for foreign rulers are permitted and regulated, this fact has almost been overlooked.[15]

Already the legislation of the book of Deuteronomy from the 7th century BCE has no problem of admitting the *gērîm*, that means the "resident aliens", to some of the Israelite pilgrimage feasts at the central sanctuary (Deut 16:9–15).[16] But these aliens were poor clients, who did not sacrifice themselves, and their inclusion in the cultic meals can rather be seen as an act of charity. In any case, the priestly legislators of the so called Holiness Code (Lev 17–27), who were at work in the first half of the 5th century BCE, opened the central temple cult to wealthy resident aliens of the Persian province Jehud, who were able to bring their own sacrifices, even expensive holocaust offerings.[17] In order to prevent the country from being defiled (18:24–30), they determined that all animal sacrifices, those of Judeans as well as of resident aliens, had to be performed at the central sanctuary (17:8–9), that means, at the Jerusalem temple.[18]

The priestly legislators of the book of Numbers, who may be located in the second half of the 5th century BCE, concluded their long paragraph about sacrifices containing their demand that all animal sacrifices should be accompanied by specific grain offerings and libations (Num 15:1–12) with the following statement:

> Num 15:13 Every native citizen shall do according to these (instructions), in order to perform a sacrifice by fire as a pleasant aroma for Yhwh.
>
> 14 When an alien, who resides among you, or anyone else, who may be among you in the course of your generations, wishes to perform a sacrifice by fire as a pleasant aroma for Yhwh, he shall perform (it) just as you perform.

---

[14] See, for example, Schwartz, "Sacrifice", 116; Mell, "Ausbruch", 120; cf. 106.

[15] Schürer, *History*, 2:309, mentioned only Lev 22:25 and 1 Kings 8:41–43, but the former reference should rather be interpreted in the opposite direction (see below p. 126); in addition, the latter speaks of prayers, not of sacrifices.

[16] For more details see Albertz, "Aliens", 54–65.

[17] That the social status of the *gērîm* in the Holiness Code differs from that shown in Deuteronomy has been clearly elaborated by Vieweger, "Fremdling", 276–8.

[18] Something similar is said concerning voluntary or pledged sacrifices in Lev 22:18, which played a central role in the later Rabbinic discussion; see Schwartz, "Sacrifice", 104–7.

The new ritual instructions are valid for every "native citizen" (*'ezraḥ*), that means all Jews. They are also valid for aliens (*gērîm*), who reside in the province of Jehud and who wish to sacrifice an animal at the temple according to the demand of Lev 17:8. No matter where they had come from and what they believed, the strangers in Jehud had to follow the same ritual norms as the Jews; that is the decisive criterion for the priests that made their sacrifice acceptable. In this way Num 15:14 is a clarification of Lev 17:8. The priestly legislators of the book of Numbers, however, intended to go a step further than those of the Holiness Code. They wanted to expand the circle of those who were permitted to sacrifice, but they had to overcome some terminological difficulties. The term *gēr*, on the one hand, was restricted to those aliens who resided in the province. The Hebrew term *nokrî* or *ben-nēkār*, which denotes foreigners without these restrictions, on the other hand, was inappropriate, because it often addresses – at least in the Torah – people who were definitely excluded from the Jewish community (Exod 12:43; Lev 22:25; Deut 14:21; 15:3; 23:21). Therefore, they created an uncommon and somewhat ambiguous expression "or anyone else, who may be among you in the course of your generations",[19] which is wide enough, to include any stranger, who might visit Jerusalem sometime in the future and wish to perform a sacrifice.[20] With this opening – from the viewpoint of the wanderings in the desert – of a wide future perspective, even later foreign kings or emissaries, who were not able to explicitly be addressed in the ideal past, could be included. Also, concerning these foreign visitors to the temple, it was of no consequence if they were of low or high rank; the correct ritual performance alone would be the decisive factor, rather than their belief. This perspective was similarly shared by Philo and Josephus' reports of such visits. Thus, the peace party had at their disposal a firm legal foundation for their position.

The unrestricted access to the Jerusalem Temple in the priestly legislation of the Torah is surprising. It cannot completely be explained by the priestly interest in increasing the sacrifices, for it can only be understood against the background of the theological concept of an inclusive monotheism, which earlier priests had developed in the books of Genesis and Exodus. According to this concept, there is only one God (*'ĕlōhîm*), who created the world and all mankind (Gen 1–9). Although he has revealed his proper name Yhwh only to Israel and thus created a very close relationship to this people (Exod 6:1–12), he still is related to all the other nations (Gen

---

[19] In Hebrew: אוֹ אֲשֶׁר־בְּתוֹכְכֶם לְדֹרֹתֵיכֶם; the expression can also include visits of proselytes from foreign countries such as the visit of the Queen from Adiabene reported in Ant. 20.49.

[20] For this interpretation see Baentsch, *Numeri*, 535; Milgrom, *Numbers*, 120–1; Seebass, *Numeri*, 2:140–1; as far as I see, Seebass is the only one who referred to B.J. 2.409–18.

10). Thus, Yhwh, the God of Israel, governs a universal realm and is present in the religions of all the people of the world in some way. If foreigners came to Jerusalem and dedicated their oblations and sacrifices to Yhwh, they venerated the only universal deity, who was not completely unknown to them. Therefore, the open ritual practice supported by the peace party was not just a concession to the political situation but deeply rooted in the universality of Yhwh himself according to the priestly concept of the Torah.[21]

2. Cult-Political and Theological Reasons for Prohibiting Offerings of Foreigners

Josephus does not mention any reasons why Eleazar and his priestly followers departed from the well-founded position described above and prohibited all offerings of foreigners, including the sacrifices of foreign rulers or those offered for their benefit.[22] From the long speech that he let King Agrippa II direct to the insurgents, one only can assume that the party favoring rebellion against Rome also founded its position on normative and theological arguments. Moreover, they appear to have been eager (σπουδή) to follow the Torah in a strict way and "preserve inviolate all the institutions" of their fathers (B.J. 2.393).[23] Thus, a direction for investigating their arguments opens up, although the reconstruction is even more hypothetical than before.

2.1 Steady Danger of Defilement of the Temple

Certainly one major reason for revoking the long-standing ritual practice was the experience of priests that the loyalty to foreign overlords, ritually manifested in the sacrifices for their well-being, implied an ever present danger that the temple would be defiled and the holiness of God would be

---

[21] This concept has its counterparts in the universal Zion theology attested in some Psalms (Ps 46; 48; 76; 84; 87), from which the eschatological concept of a future pilgrimage of all nations to Jerusalem and the glorification of Yhwh through their offerings was derived (Isa 60:6–7, 9b, 13–14); cf. also Isa 56:3–8.

[22] Josephus mentioned only Eleazar's "daring youth" as a possible reason. Since he was already in office under Albinus (62–4 CE), when his secretary was kidnapped by the *sicarii* (Ant. 20.208–10), this remark is probably not more than a polemical reproach.

[23] The conceptional relationship between Agrippa's speech (esp. B.J. 2.390–5) and the report of the controversy between the priestly parties (B.J. 2.409–17) was already recognized by Schwier, *Tempel*, 117–24.

violated, even if that danger had not always been fully appreciated. The lists of events where this danger became reality is long,[24] starting with intrusions into the holy chambers of the temple by the Persian governor Bagoses (Ant. 11.297–301),[25] Antiochos IV Epiphanes (1 Macc 1:21–25), and Pompey (B.J. 1.152–4), continuing with the installation of foreign symbols or statues attempted by Antiochos IV (Dan 11:31), Pilate (B.J. 2.169–74; Ant. 18.55–6), and Caligula (B.J. 2.184–203; Ant. 18.261–72), and ending with robberies of the temple treasury by Antiochos IV (1 Macc 1:24–25), Crassus (B.J. 1.179; Ant. 14.105–9), Sabinus (B.J. 2.45–50; Ant. 17.260–4), Pilate (B.J. 2.178; Ant. 18.60), and Gessius Florus (B.J. 2.293–6). Apart from these encroachments on the sanctuary there were steady conflicts about the Antonia, the stronghold at the northern side of the temple precinct and about the control over the High Priestly robe.[26] It may be that the last robbery of Gessius Florus, which provoked a series of Jewish uproars and Roman retaliatory strikes in Jerusalem, convinced Eleazar that the purity and holiness of the temple could only be secured if foreigners and their sacrifices were excluded from the temple area.[27]

2.2 Stifling Roman Presence in the Temple

Another cult-political reason may have to do how temple worship itself developed under Roman rule. It is highly probable that the two daily sacrifices for the well-being of the Emperor and the Roman people were performed together with the two Tamid offerings, which were sacrificed every day by the priests, accompanied by Levitical choirs, before sunrise and after sunset.[28] The Tamid was the usual offering on behalf of the people of Israel,

---

[24] Cf. the listing of Hengel, *Zeloten*, 211–15.

[25] For this important event, which has been often overlooked, see Albertz, "Controversy", 483–97. The Bagoses mentioned by Josephus can be identified with the Persian governor Bagohi from the Elephantine papyri.

[26] After his death, the stronghold extended by King Herod, became a Roman garrison, which controlled the temple, although it was regarded as unclean by the Jews (John 18:28). Consequently it is not terribly remarkable that the connecting buildings between the Antonia and the temple were destroyed during the uproars against Festus Gestus (B.J. 2.230–2). Herod deposited the precious and holy robe of the High Priest in the Antonia, where it came under control of the Romans, until Vitelius, the legate of Tiberius in Syria, unblocked the Antonia. The procurator Cuspius Fadus, however, forced the Jews to bring the holy robe back into the Antonia, though the Emperor Claudius decided to return it to the Jews (Ant. 15.403–20).

[27] That the decision of Eleazar aimed at restoring the purity of the temple is elaborated by Schwier, *Tempel*, 117, 124, 141; but the issue of holiness is likewise important.

[28] See Mell, "Ausbruch", 108. The suggestion can be supported by the fact that in 2 Kings 16:15 the Tamid and the king's offerings are already closely mentioned together and are of the very same sacrificial type.

normally paid from the temple tax (Exod 30:11–16; Neh 10:33), which was collected from the entire Jewish community inside and outside of Palestine. Consisting of a holocaust in the morning and a grain offering in the evening during the First Temple period (2 Kings 15:15), it was enlarged to two holocaust offerings and their accompanying grain offerings and libations during the Second Temple period (Exod 29:38–42a; Num 28:3–8). These two daily holocaust offerings for the benefit of the people of Israel consisted of one lamb each. The daily holocaust sacrifices for the benefit of the Caesar and the Roman people, however, had included one bull and two lambs since the days of Augustus (Legat. 317).[29] These items might have been meant as a gesture of generosity by the emperor towards his client and friend Herod, although it was paid from the provincial taxes, which had also been raised by the Jews. In the time of a continuous political conflict with the Roman overlords, however, the much more extensive sacrifices for the Emperor could pose severe psychological problems: Since the slaughter and offering of a bull compared to a lamb took much more time and was much more impressive, the priests and audience on hand for the daily services could get the impression that the cultic effort made for the Romans was greater than that put forth for the benefit of the Jewish people. In the face of this ritual expenditure for the foreign ruler that surpassed their own needs, critical priests could ask whether they were still Jewish functionaries in a Jewish institution or rather Roman puppets in a Roman theatre. Thus, because of the extensive sacrifices for foreign rulers the identity of the priests and the Jerusalem temple was at stake.

Another Roman custom might have intensified the problem of identity. During the great pilgrimage feasts the Roman cohort of Jerusalem, consisting entirely of men-at-arms, was accustomed to come across from the Antonia and to take up a position on the portico around the temple area (B.J. 2.224; 5.245). For the Romans, this was a security measure taken to prevent disorder and riots from arising among such a large gathering of people. In the eyes of the Jews, however, especially for the priests, who were responsible for the cultic service, this kind of surveillance by foreign forces was probably difficult to cope with. The Roman soldiers did not always succeed in showing a behavior appropriate to the holy rituals. For example, under the procurator Cumanus a soldier raised his robe, turned his backside to the Jews and let off a fart, which enraged the crowd of worshipers so much that many were crushed to death during the turmoil (B.J. 2.224–7). Thus, the responsible priests may have wondered whether they were still in control of

---

[29] Since the morning Tamid had been the recipient of greater expenditures in the past than the evening Tamid, the bull and one lamb were probably sacrificed in the morning, and the other lamb in the evening.

the temple worship or whether the massive presence of armed foreigners did not defile the holy worship itself. From this perspective, the decision of Eleazar and his priestly followers to reduce or even dispose of the presence of the foreigners can be understood as an attempt to protect their own Jewish identity and the Jewish identity of the temple against a stifling Roman presence, although such actions would reduce their personal income. In order to achieve this important target they were ready to risk the break with the Romans and join the insurgents.

2.3 Normative and Theological Foundations from the Torah and the Prophets

Although one might expect there to be a clear and normative basis for the position of the priests who wanted to reform temple worship by eliminating foreign sacrifices, it is difficult to find. Of course, there are many texts in the Pentateuch that emphasize the exclusive religious identity of the people of Israel,[30] especially in the Deuteronomistic layers. In the entire Torah, however, no commandment that explicitly prohibits oblations or sacrifices of foreigners to Yhwh can be found. Therefore, Hengel and others suggested that the reformers might have referred to the 18 decrees of the school of Shammai, which prohibited – among other things – the acceptance of "gifts" (מתנות) from gentiles.[31] But since this expression is not typical for sacrifices, nor for any other goods whose acceptance is prohibited by these decrees, the focus is rather on the private realm (i.e., special kinds of food), and it is highly improbable that any reference to public dedicatory gifts or sacrifices is intended. Moreover, it seems to be impossible to connect the legendary inauguration of these decrees with the Jewish revolt against Rome.[32]

In the Torah itself there are only two passages that could possibly be interpreted in the reformers' favor: The first is the so-called "community rule" of Deut 23:4–9, which originally prohibited members of specific neighboring nations – be it the Moabites and Ammonites forever, or the Edomites and Egyptians until the third generation – from gaining access to the assembly of Yhwh (בוא בקהל יהוה). This was probably aimed at the question of their complete political and cultic integration. But the regulation was soon interpreted in a way that foreigners should not have uncontrolled

---

[30] Cf. e.g. the Deuteronomic and Deuteronomistic concept of Israel as a holy people (*'am qādôš*) in Deut 7:6; 14:2, 21; 26:19; 28:9.

[31] Cf. Hengel, *Zeloten*, 203–11, following Graetz, *Geschichte*, 3:805–13.

[32] Cf. Stemberger, "Hananiah", 701–3, and already critical Krieger, *Geschichtsschreibung*, 225.

access to the temple (Lam 1:10).[33] With this understanding of the Pentateuchal text, the reformers could resume its enforcement. The second passage deals with a prohibition of buying sacrificial animals from foreigners
(Lev 22:25). In its original sense this regulation intended to prevent Israelites from buying such – perhaps cheaper – animals from foreign traders,
which later could turn out to be blemished.[34] In this sense, animal sacrifices
of Jews and not of foreigners are meant. But this regulation could perhaps
be interpreted in a more general sense that all animal sacrifices of foreigners must be suspected as unclean and thus be kept away.

It appears to me that the priestly reformers around Eleazar did not arrive
at their position simply from the Torah itself, but by reading and interpreting the Torah – diverting from the normal position of the Sadducees – in the
light of the future expectations that they may have found in the books of the
prophets. In the vision of Ezekiel, which described the ideal temple of the
future, they could read a clear regulation:

Ezek 44:9 These are the words of Adonay-Yhwh:
           No foreigner, uncircumcised in mind and body, shall enter my sanctu-
           ary, no one from all the foreigners, who live among the Israelites.

In its context this regulation prohibited temple slaves of foreign origin from
being employed at the temple anymore as they had been in the First Temple
period. Instead, the Levites are appointed to perform the lower services in
the future temple, for example, that of gatekeeper (Ezek 44:10–12). But of
course, it is possible to understand this prohibition in a more general sense:
that no foreigner at all should have access to the temple for any purpose,
because their presence would interfere with the increased degree of holiness
of that place.[35]

---

[33] Apart from that the "community rule" could be interpreted as a prohibition of mixed marriages (Neh 13:1–3). For the extensive inner-biblical exegesis of Deut 23:4–9 see Olyan, "Gemeinde", 178–82. Saul Olyan has developed his ideas during a lecture given within the Cluster of
Excellence at the University of Münster in May 2010.

[34] Schürer, *History*, 2:309 note 60, seems to have misunderstood this passage when he wrote:
"It is stated here that blemished animals may not be accepted even from Gentiles, which presupposes that in the ordinary course of events Gentile sacrifices was (!) lawful". He was possibly
following an interpretation of Rashi and Ibn Ezra. But the phrase at the end of the verse, "they (i.e.
the sacrifices) will not be accepted (by God) on your behalf", makes clear that the sacrifices not of
foreigners but of Israelites are meant. The animals simply came "from the hand of foreigners". The
phrase מיד "from the hand of" is also used in purchase transactions in Lev 25:14; cf. Milgrom,
Leviticus, 1881–2; Gerstenberger, *Leviticus*, 302.

[35] The possibility of such a general understanding has to do with the fact that Ezek 44:6–9
seems to constitute a prophetic application of the more general "community rule" in Deut 23:4–9
as shown by Schaper, "Rereading", 132–8, and Olyan, "Gemeinde", 183–4. This prophetic exegesis of the Torah, which provided itself with divine authority, was already part of an inner-biblical
legal exegesis, that led to an expanded scope of interpretation in the post-biblical period; see
Fishbane, *Interpretation*, 91–277.

It was especially the dreadful experience of seeing the temple and the city of Jerusalem destroyed and defiled by foreign powers in the past (Ps 74:7; 79:1) that provoked the hope that no foreigners would intrude into Jerusalem and its temple any longer, so that the city and the sanctuary would reach the status of complete and undisturbed holiness in the future. Such a prophecy already appears in the book of Deutero-Isaiah after the Babylonian exile:

> Isa 52:1   Awake, awake, put on your strength, O Zion,
> > put on your loveliest garments, holy city of Jerusalem;
> > for never shall the uncircumcised and the unclean enter you again.

The same expectation frames an earlier collection of the book of the Minor Prophets from the end of the 5th century BCE, probably responding to Bagoses' encroachment on the sanctuary:[36]

> Joel 4:17   Thus you shall know that I am Yhwh your God,
> > dwelling in Zion, my holy mountain;
> > Jerusalem will be holy,
> > and no foreigner will pass through her again.

> Zech 14:21   Every pot in Jerusalem and Judah shall be holy to Yhwh Sabaoth;
> > and all who sacrifice shall come and shall take some of them and boil
> > the flesh in them. Then, no Canaanite will again be seen in the house
> > of Yhwh Sabaoth.

The assumption that the reform priests around Eleazar really intended to fulfill such prophetic expectations is supported by the fact that the coins that were minted in Jerusalem during the years 66 and 67 CE likewise promoted the holiness of Jerusalem.[37] Against this prophetic background, the inscriptions ירשלם קדשה "Jerusalem is holy" of the first year, and ירשלם הקדושה "Jerusalem, the holy (one)" of the second year suggest a cult-political program. Thus, the decision of accepting no more oblations and sacrifices from foreigners has to be interpreted as a cult-political reform, aimed at providing the Jerusalem temple, which had been continuously threatened by defilement through foreign rulers in the past, with a higher degree of holiness in the future, according to the divine promises given by the prophets.[38]

---

[36] See Wöhrle, *Abschluss*, 150–65; Wöhrle calls this redactional layer "Fremdvölkerschicht I". Similar hopes were still upheld in later periods as can be seen, for example, from 4QFlor (4Q174 frag. 1 col. I:3–6).

[37] See, Meshorer, *Coins*, 154–8; idem, *Coinage*, 96–131; 259–63, plate 17–19.

[38] From a similarly strict point of view, the Qumran sectarians had already pleaded for prohibiting sacrifices – at least of sacrificial meals (*zĕbāḥîm*) – of the Gentiles at the Jerusalem temple; see 4QMMT B 8–9 (= 4Q394 frags. 3–7 col. I:11–12). They identified Jerusalem with the holy camp of the wilderness period (col. II:16–17; frag. 8 col. II:9–11), inspired as they were by pro-

3. The Liturgy of the Daily Temple Worship as
Support for either the One or the Other Position

Considering the paucity of direct sources that can reveal the theological motivations of the two quarreling parties of temple priests, the liturgy of the Tamid services may offer some additional insights. From the Septuagint and the Mishnah Tamid we have gained knowledge about those psalms that were sung by the Levitical choirs every day of the week during the Tamid services, which – until the decision of Eleazar – consisted of the sacrifices for the benefit of the people of Israel and the sacrifices for the benefit of the Emperor and the Roman people as well. From these seven Psalms and their sequence in the course of a week (Ps 24; 48; 82; 94; 81; 93; 92) one can reconstruct an outline of the theology that was common at the Jerusalem temple during the late Hellenistic and Roman periods and probably also shaped the theological thoughts of its priesthood in some way. A closer look at this theology reveals that both groups of priest, the peace party as well as the reform party, could feel corroborated by it.

3.1 Yhwh's Universal Rule from Zion

On three days of the week the universal kingship of Yhwh was celebrated in the Tamid worship. On the first day after the Sabbath, Ps 24 envisions how the creator of the world, to whom all its peoples belong (v. 1–2), entered the Jerusalem temple as the king of glory (v. 7–10). On the second day, Ps 48 praises Jerusalem as the one city with which this great heavenly king had identified himself (v. 2–4, 13–15) and from where he controlled the nations and protected his seat (v. 5–12). And on the sixth day, the pre-Sabbath, Ps 93 praises the eternal kingship of Yhwh, which he had demonstrated through his suppression of the chaos waters. As the reference to the chaos waters shows, the concept of Yhwh's worldwide kingship was also a profound influence behind the idea that Yhwh needed to defend and stabilize the threatened order of the world. Therefore, Ps 82, on the third day, asks Yhwh to judge the world (v. 8) by punishing those rulers who had divinized themselves and did not protect the poor and the weak (v. 2–4). Corresponding to this, Ps 94, on the fourth day, prays that Yhwh, as a god of vengeance, might punish the evildoers internal to the community who had oppressed his people. Finally Ps 92, on the Sabbath day praises Yhwh, because he eliminated the wicked and rescued the righteous (v. 10–16). Thus

---

phetic and psalmic perspectives (4Q398 frags. 14–21 col. I:10, 15); see also Schiffman, "Place", 89–92.

the eternal reign of Yhwh (v. 9) aimed at establishing justice both outside and inside of Israel.

The universal horizon of this theology clearly supports the position of the peace party, which pleaded for unrestricted access for all foreigners who wished to bring their oblations and sacrifices to this heavenly king, Yhwh, who ruled the world from Mount Zion. It paved the way for all kinds of cooperation. Nevertheless, this theology also supplied reasons for resisting the unjust measures and trouble-making interventions of the Roman government.[39] The task of carrying out revenge and establishing worldwide justice, however, was almost completely left to the competence of the divine king; it did not primarily belong to the realm of human responsibility. Thus, the peace party did not only have political but also good theological reasons of warning about any revolt against the Romans (B.J. 2.412).

3.2 Fighting for the Holiness of the Temple

Compared with the universality of Yhwh, the holiness of the Jerusalem temple is a less prominent topic in the Tamid psalms; it is mentioned only three times (Ps 24:3; 48:5; 93:5). In Ps 93:5, however, the text states that the establishment of Yhwh's kingship sought to bring about the reliability of his law and the eternal holiness of his temple. Thus the reform party could claim for itself that not only order and justice but also the law and the holiness of the temple were part of the major objectives of divine rule. The combination of holiness and law is important, because Ps 81, which was sung on the fifth day and thus preceded Ps 93 on the sixth, addressed the topic of the Mosaic law. In this Psalm the universal God reminded his people of their history of salvation and their specific relationship to him (v. 5–8). For Israel he had promulgated special ordinances, which included exclusive worship of Yhwh and excluded the veneration of any foreign deity (v. 10–11). Thus, seen from Israel's perspective, monotheism had an exclusive character. In this context Yhwh reminded Israel of its apostasy and his punishments in the past and admonished it to keep the law in the future (v. 9, 12–13). This admonition is connected with an important divine promise:

Ps 81:14 O that my people would listen to me,
    that Israel would walk in my ways,
  15 I would soon subdue their enemies
    and turn my hand against their foes.

---

[39] Thus the endeavors of the High Priests and their colleagues to resolve conflicts with the Romans, which are reported several times (e.g. Ant. 18.3–4; B.J. 2.243; Ant. 20.162, 189–96; B.J. 2.315–17, 320), accord with the theology of the daily temple worship practices.

According to these verses, Israel still lived under the rule of its enemies. But in the event that Israel followed God's admonition and became obedient to his law, Yhwh promised that he would subdue these enemies and intervene against them. On the basis of this promise the reform party of the priests was able to argue that the heavenly king would subdue the Romans, if they obeyed the Torah in such a strict way that the complete holiness of his earthly temple was restored. We learn from Josephus that the question of whether or not God could be won as an ally (σύμμαχος) in the rebellion against Rome was disputed extensively between the peace and the reform party (B.J. 2.390–2); in this context strict obedience in connection with ritual observances (θρησκεία) played a central role; this kind of obedience alone could give reasons for such a hope (391). It seems to me that the conditional promise of the Tamid Psalm 81:14–15 provides the proper basis of this debate.[40] Only because Eleazar and the priests around him believed in the divine promise that God would turn his hand against the Roman foes could they dare to introduce the rigorous ritual reform that excluded the Romans from the temple worship and assume the accompanying political risk. Moreover, they could refer to the fact that a radical commitment to the Torah and the temple – comparable with their own – had actually been honored by God during the successful Maccabean revolt (1 Macc 4:55; 2 Macc 8:24).

Conclusion

Both quarrelling priestly parties, on the eve of the Jewish-Roman War, determined their identity on the basis of holy scriptures, either the Tamid Psalms, the Torah, or the Prophets. The peace party emphasized the universality of God, the worldwide function of his temple, and an inclusive monotheism, based on the priestly concepts and legislation of the Pentateuch and the psalms centered on Zion and Yhwh's Kingship. The reform party stressed the holiness of God and his dwelling and an exclusive monotheism from an eschatological perspective, founded on instructions concerning exclusivity in the Pentateuch, Torah psalms, and prophetic promises. It is the wide range of different theologies and normative instructions collected in the Holy Scriptures of Judaism that made such differing cult-political options possible. In this connection, the scale of options was extended by the fact that the prophets became a second part of the canon next to the

---

[40] Mell, "Ausbruch", 116, already reconstructs the hopes of the reform party from the counter arguments of Agrippa's speech (B.J. 2.291). The text of Ps 81:14–15 helps these hopes to be understood more clearly.

Pentateuch at the end of the 3rd century BCE. While the position of the peace party was based on the Mosaic Torah alone, the rebellious party founded its divergent point of view on that Torah which could be interpreted in the light of prophetic expectations. Both positions, however, were indisputably Jewish ones; none of them could be designated as "apostasy" or excluded for theological reasons.[41]

Because of the fundamental hermeneutical differences and the inflamed political atmosphere, a theological understanding between the two priestly parties was not possible. Since the High Priests and the distinguished Pharisees did not succeed in changing Eleazar's mind and convincing the people's assembly by their arguments, they called for military support from Gessius Florus and King Agrippa II. While the former evaded his responsibility, the latter sent his cavalry of 2000 men (B.J. 2.418–21). A bloody civil war began, in which the reform priests, supported by the *sicarii* brigands, proved victorious (422–4). The members of the peace party were excluded from the temple service, and many of them were murdered in the turmoil (425, 441). Since the class of priestly aristocracy had split in half, the authority of those who would have been able to keep the potential religious violence under control was heavily undermined. Thus, the outbreak of religiously motivated violence became unavoidable.

References

Albertz, R., "From Aliens to Proselytes: Non-Priestly and Priestly Legislation Concerning Strangers", in R. Achenbach et al. (ed.), *The Foreigner and the Law: Perspectives from the Hebrew Bible and the Ancient Near East* (BZAR 16; Wiesbaden: Harrassowitz, 2011) 53–69.

–, "The Controversy about Judean versus Israelite Identity and the Persian Government: A New Interpretation of the Bagoses Story (Jewish Antiquities XI.297–301)", in O. Lipschits et al. (ed.), *Judah and the Judeans in the Achaemenid Period: Negotiating Identity in an International Context* (Winona Lake: Eisenbrauns, 2011) 483–504.

Baentsch, B., *Exodus – Leviticus – Numeri* (HAT 1,2; Göttingen: Vandenhoeck & Ruprecht, 1903).

Baumbach, G., "Einheit und Vielfalt der jüdischen Freiheitsbewegung im 1. Jh. n.Chr.", *EvT* 45 (1985) 93–107.

Busink, T.A., *Der Tempel von Jerusalem: Von Salomo bis Herodes – eine archäologisch-historische Studie unter Berücksichtigung des westsemitischen Tempelbaus* (2 vol.; Leiden: Brill, 1980).

Fishbane, M., *Biblical Interpretation in Ancient Israel* (Oxford: Clarendon, 1988).

García Martínez F./Tigchelaar, E.J.C. (ed.), *The Dead Sea Scrolls. Study Edition* (2 vol.; Leiden et al.: Brill, 1997–8).

Gerstenberger, E.S., *Das 3. Buch Mose: Leviticus* (ATD 6; Göttingen: Vandenhoeck & Ruprecht, 1993).

---

[41] In contrast to the position of the radical Hellenists during the Maccabean revolt, which was excluded from Judaism.

Goodman, M., *The Ruling Class of Judaea: The Origins of the Jewish Revolt against Rome A.D. 66–70* (Cambridge/New York: Cambridge University Press, 1987).

Graetz, H., *Geschichte der Judäer vom Tode Juda Makkabis bis zum Untergange des judäischen Staates* (Geschichte der Juden von der ältesten Zeit bis auf die Gegenwart; 3/1-2 vol.; Leipzig: Oskar Leiner, [5]1905).

Hengel, M., *Die Zeloten: Untersuchungen zur jüdischen Freiheitsbewegung in der Zeit von Herodes I. bis 70 n. Chr.* (Leiden/Köln: Brill, [2]1976).

Josephus, F., *De Bello Judaico: Der jüdische Krieg* (ed. O. Michel/O. Bauernfeind; 4 vol.; Darmstadt: Wissenschaftliche Buchgesellschaft, 1959–69).

–, *The Life – Against Apion* (ed. J.S.T. Thackery; Cambridge/London: Harvard University Press/ William Heinemann, 1926; reprinted 1961).

–, *The Jewish War: Books I-III* (ed. J.S.T. Thackery; Cambridge/London: Harvard University Press/William Heinemann, 1927; reprinted 1967).

–, *Jüdische Altertümer* (ed. H. Clementz; Halle: Hendel, 1899 = reprinted Wiesbaden: Matrix, 2004).

Krieger, K.-S., *Geschichtsschreibung als Apologetik bei Flavius Josephus* (TANZ 9; Tübingen/Basel: Francke, 1994).

Mell, U., "Der Ausbruch des jüdisch-römischen Krieges (66–70 n.Chr.) aus tempeltheologischer Perspektive", *ZRGG* 49 (1997) 97–122.

Meshorer, Y., *Jewish Coins of the Second Temple Period* (Tel Aviv: Am Hassefer, 1967).

–, *Ancient Jewish Coinage* (2 vol.; Jerusalem: Amphora, 1982).

Milgrom, J., *Numbers* (The JPS Torah Commentary; Philadelphia/New York: The Jewish Publication Society, 1990).

–, *Leviticus 17–22: A New Translation with Introduction and Commentary* (AB 3A; New Haven/London: Doubleday, 2000; reprinted 2008).

Olyan, S.M., "'Sie sollen nicht in die Gemeinde des Herrn kommen': Aspekte gesellschaftlicher Inklusion und Exklusion in Dtn 23,4–9 und seine frühen Auslegungen", in idem, *Social Inequality in the World of the Text: The Significance of Ritual and Social Distinctions in the Hebrew Bible* (JAJSup 4; Göttingen: Vandenhoeck & Ruprecht, 2011) 173–85.

Philo, *The Embassy to Gaius* (ed. F.H. Colson; London/Cambridge: William Heinemann/Harvard University Press, 1962; reprinted 1971).

Roth, C., "The Debate on the Loyal Sacrifices, A.D. 66", *HTR* 53 (1960) 93–7.

Schaper, J., "Rereading the Law: Inner-Biblical Exegesis of Divine Oracles in Ezekiel 44 and Isaiah 56", in B. Levinson/E. Otto (ed.), *Recht und Ethik im Alten Testament* (atm 13; Münster: Lit, 2004) 125–44.

Schiffman, L.H., "The Place of 4QMMT in the Corpus of Qumran Manuscripts", in J. Kampen/M.J. Bernstein (ed.), *Reading 4QMMT: New Perspectives on Qumran Law and History* (Symposium Series 2; Atlanta: Scholars Press, 1996) 81–98.

Schürer, E., *The History of the Jewish People in the Age of Jesus Christ (175 B.C.–A.D. 135)* (ed. G. Vermes et al.; 3 vol.; Edinburgh: Clark, 1973–87).

Schwartz, D.R., "On Sacrifice by Gentiles in the Temple of Jerusalem", in idem, *Studies in the Jewish Background of Christianity* (WUNT 60; Tübingen: Mohr Siebeck, 1992), 102–16.

Schwier, H., *Tempel und Tempelzerstörung: Untersuchungen zu den theologischen und ideologischen Faktoren im ersten jüdisch-römischen Krieg (66–74 n.Chr.)* (NTOA 11; Fribourg/Göttingen: Universitätsverlag/Vandenhoeck & Ruprecht, 1989).

Seebass, H., *Numeri: 2. Teilband: Numeri 10,11–22,1* (BKAT 4,2; Neukirchen-Vluyn: Neukirchener Verlag, 2003).

Stemberger, G., "Hananiah ben Hezekiah ben Garon, the Eighteen Decrees and the Outbreak of the War against Rome", in A. Hilhorst (ed.), *Flores Florentino* (Leiden: Brill, 2007) 691–703.

Vieweger, D., "Vom 'Fremdling' zum 'Proselyt': Zur sakralrechtlichen Definition des גר im späten 5. Jahrhundert v.Chr.", in idem/E. Waschke (ed.), *Von Gott reden: Beiträge zur Theologie und Exegese des Alten Testaments* (Neukirchen-Vluyn: Neukirchener Verlag, 1995) 271–84.

Wellhausen, J., *Israelitische und jüdische Geschichte* (Berlin/New York: de Gruyter, [9]1958; reprinted 2004).

Wöhrle, J., *Der Abschluss des Zwölfprophetenbuches. Buchübergreifende Redaktionsprozesse in den späten Sammlungen* (BZAW 389; Berlin/New York: de Gruyter, 2008).

Stefan Schorch

Martin-Luther-Universität Halle-Wittenberg

The Construction of Samari(t)an Identity
from the Inside and from the Outside

The period from the Persian to the Roman eras is characterized both by the emergence of multiple Jewish identities, and dramatic changes in the Jewish attitude(s) towards foreigners – ranging between cooperation and hostility. Whether and how these two facts are interrelated is an intriguing but rather unexplored question.[1] In the following, I would like to approach this problem from the perspective of the development of a distinct Samaritan identity. This process, as I will try to show, is part of the dramatic changes that occurred within Judaism during the 2nd century BCE.

My paper is divided into three parts: The first part will review in short the most common theories regarding the emergence of Samaritan identity proper, and it will substantiate my own view that we should not speak about Samaritans before the 2nd century BCE. The second part aims at a more detailed reconstruction of the processes that shaped Samaritan identity, both inside what was about to become the Samaritan community and outside it, from the perspective of the followers of Jerusalem. Finally, the third part will review how these developments interacted with the development of Jewish relationships toward foreign powers.

1. From Samarians to Samaritans

Samaritan identity as opposed to a general Jewish identity is characterized by especially and at least the following three points:
– The veneration of Mount Gerizim as the central place of worship.
– The use of a distinctive version of the Torah.
– The reference to an exclusive tradition, implying that their authenticity as "Israel" is true in both historical and religious terms.

---

[1] My thanks go to Rainer Albertz and Jakob Wöhrle, who raised this important question and organized the conference "Between Cooperation and Hostility" in Münster, June 2011, successfully creating a stimulating intellectual atmosphere for the discussion of this problem.

Regarding the time at which a distinctive Samaritan identity emerged, which comprised at least these three elements, the following suggestions have been made:

1) The irreversible break between Samaritans and Jews took place in early post-exilic times (early 5th century BCE – Menahem Mor).[2]

2) The break took place under the influence of Alexander's conquest of Palestine (second half of 4th century BCE – Matthias Delcor).[3]

3) The break took place in the Maccabean era (late 2nd century BCE – James D. Purvis).[4]

4) The break took place in the 3rd century CE (Alan David Crown).[5]

5) The break between Samaritans and Jews was not a single and dramatic event, but rather a gradual process (Richard James Coggins).[6]

As to the last suggestion, there is no doubt that the separation between Samaritans and Jews was part of a historical process extending over several centuries. This process, however, cannot be described solely in terms of evolution, as Coggins describes it, since it implies a fundamental change in the framework that served Jews and Samaritans as a means of defining their identity. Up to a certain point, the pre-Samaritans referred to and were regarded as part of a social, religious and ethnic framework that was common to Second Temple Judaism in general. From that point onward, however, the Samaritans became an independent group, and not just the population of Samaria but Samaritans proper, insofar as they defined themselves apart from Judaism in general within the boundaries of their own framework. This fundamental change must be datable, if the available sources allow it.

The general consensus in current research is that the break between Judaism and Samaritanism happened in the late 2nd century BCE. This consensus rests mainly on the following arguments:

– The Samaritan version of the Torah exhibits a harmonistic text-type, which is characterized by a strong tendency to avoid differences between parallel passages. Manuscripts with similar features are known from Qumran and date to the late 2nd century BCE. Therefore, the Samaritan Torah seems to have separated from the common textual tradition at that period of time.[7] While the Gerizim-followers participated in the general literary culture until the late 2nd century BCE, the Samaritan community did not share in the textual developments that began to occur in Judaism in the early 1st

---

[2] See Mor, "History", 2.

[3] See Delcor, "Hinweise".

[4] See Purvis, *Pentateuch*.

[5] See Crown, "Redating", 43–4.

[6] See Coggins, *Samaritans*, 163.

[7] Eshel/Eshel, "Dating", 227–40.

century BCE, and the formerly common literary culture disintegrated into two separate literal cultures, each largely independent from the other.

– Further evidence comes from the Book of Ben Sira. In ch. 50:25–26, the Hebrew text reads as follows:

בשני גוים קצה נפשי והשלישית איננו עם
יושבי שעיר ופלשת וגוי נבל הדר בשכם

Two nations my soul detests, and the third is not even a people: Those who live in Seir, and the Philistines, and the foolish people that live in Shechem.

The Greek translation of the same passage, however, contains significant differences:

ἐν δυσὶν ἔθνεσιν προσώχθισεν ἡ ψυχή μου καὶ τὸ τρίτον οὐκ ἔστιν ἔθνος
οἱ καθήμενοι ἐν ὄρει Σαμαρείας καὶ Φυλιστιιμ καὶ ὁ λαὸς ὁ μωρὸς ὁ κατοικῶν ἐν Σικιμοι

Two nations my soul detests, and the third is not even a people: Those who live in Samaria, and the Philistines, and the foolish people that live in Shechem.

Thus, within the Hebrew version, which dates to the early 2nd century BCE, the inhabitants of Shechem are not regarded as a people, they are not categorized at the same level as the Idumeans and the Philistines. According to the Greek translation, however, dating to the late 2nd century BCE, the Philistines are equaled to the Samarians, and the Shechemites become a subgroup of the Samarian people. The Idumeans, on the other hand, have been removed from the list, most probably as a result of a changed historical context, since they converted to Judaism in the 2nd century BCE. We have, therefore, in the Greek version of Sir 50:25–26 a very interesting source which mirrors a process of re-shaping identities.

The Idumeans disappeared from the list in Ben Sira 50, since they came to be regarded as Jewish in the meantime, while the attitude towards the Samaritans changed from distaste ("foolish people") into complete alienation: according to the Greek text of Ben Sira, they are no longer part of the Jewish people but have now become foreigners.

– The writings of Josephus Ant. 13 and the available archaeological evidence demonstrate that the sanctuary on Mount Gerizim and the town Shechem beneath it were destroyed by the Judean Johannes Hyrkanos in 129/128 and 112/111 BCE respectively.[8] Obviously, these drastic political and military events are further evidence that the break between Samaritans and Jews indeed took place at that time.

– After the separation between Jews and Samaritans, the language spoken by the forefathers of the Samaritans became a group-specific sociolect,

---

[8] See Barag, "Evidence", and Magen, *Excavations*, 13. Dexinger, "Ursprung", 135, and Zsengellér, *Gerizim*, 164, dated the destruction of Shechem to 108/107 BCE.

a linguistic marker of Samaritan identity. Samaritan Hebrew apparently goes back to the Hebrew dialect generally spoken in Samaria.[9] It has been demonstrated from a linguistic-historical point of view, that the interaction of this dialect with its linguistic environment came to an end in the 2nd or 1st century BCE;[10] this means that at that time Samaritan Hebrew emerged as part of Samaritan identity.

– In close connection with this process of shaping a distinctive Samaritan linguistic identity, the Samaritan reading tradition of the Torah started to emerge. Thus, the creation of the Samaritan community in the late 2nd century BCE went along with the emergence of a stable reading tradition. The written tradition of the Samaritan Torah was supplemented, therefore, by a firm and fixed oral tradition, connecting the written consonantal framework of the text with a certain way of pronunciation, vocalisation and phrasing.[11]

We should therefore conclude that Samaritans and Jews irrevocably separated towards the end of the 2nd century BCE. This date means that the Samaritans are to be considered the oldest distinctive group within the Israelite-Jewish tradition. However, while the separation had its roots in the past history of the conflict,[12] it also had a subsequent history of reception, during which Samaritan identity proper became set and developed its particular profile.

2. The Development of Samaritan and Jewish Identity
in the 2nd Century BCE

As mentioned before, Samaritan identity is characterized by at least three points:
– The veneration of Mount Gerizim as the central place of worship.
– The use of a distinctive version of the Torah.
– The reference to an exclusive tradition, implying the Samaritan's own authenticity as "Israel" in both historical and religious terms.

---

[9] "Das Konsonantengerüst der samaritanischen Tora bezeugt zwar eine sprachhistorisch frühere Stufe, aber denselben Dialekt wie die samaritanische Tora-Lesung" (Schorch, *Vokale*, 39, with further observations supporting this claim).

[10] For an account of Samaritan Hebrew from the perspective of the history of the Hebrew language, see Ben-Hayyim, *Grammar*, 335.

[11] See Schorch, *Vokale*, 61.

[12] This fact has been brought to light und underlined by Ferdinand Dexinger, "Ursprung", 82: "Die verschiedenen Vorschläge überblickend wird man jedoch sagen müssen, daß die Datierung der Trennung in die Makkabäer-Zeit eine vielseitige argumentative Absicherung erfahren hat. [...] Allerdings ist zu vermerken, daß durch diesen zeitlichen Ansatz der endgültigen Trennung nicht gleichzeitig die Frage beantwortet wird, woher jene Samaritaner eigentlich stammen, die sich in der Makkabäer-Zeit von Jerusalem lösten."

Most obviously, the third point, i.e. the Samaritan self-identification as the only true Israel, is historically dependent on the two preceding it in the list, and it is therefore most important to analyze these first two points in order to understand the development of the third.

2.1 Samaritan Identity and the Cultic Site on Mount Gerizim

The excavations carried out on the top of the hill in the years 1982–2005 under the direction of Yitzhak Magen uncovered a "sacred precinct", among the archeological remnants of which Magen identified "two main construction phases [...]: the first dates from the Persian period until the reign of Antiochus III (ca. 200 BCE); the second dates from the reign of Antiochus III until the conquest of Mount Gerizim by John Hyrcanus I (111–110 BCE)."[13] Magen dates the first temple, according to him the oldest building on Mount Gerizim, to the middle of the 5th century BCE.[14] Regarding possible earlier evidence from the Iron age, Magen writes: "So far, no firm evidence has been found on Mount Gerizim for the existence of a ritual site [...] dating from the Iron Age [...]."[15] However, this view does not seem to be entirely conclusive, even according to Magen's own excavations, which led *inter alia* to the discovery of three Proto-Ionic capitals. Capitals of this type date to the Iron age and "generally appear in temples".[16] Thus, although no foundations or walls from the Iron age seem to have been discovered so far, there is still some basis for the conclusion that there was an Iron age temple on Mount Gerizim.[17] We may therefore conclude that, since the Iron Age, different temples existed on the top of Mount Gerizim from at least the Persian period until 111–110 BCE, and maybe even centuries longer. Mount Gerizim was, in any case, not only a cultic site long before the emergence of the "Samaritans" proper but also housed a sanctuary for several centuries. One may even say that the Samaritans as an independent sect emerged only after the destruction of the temple on Mount Gerizim.

Thus, the first element of Samaritan identity proper (the veneration of a cultic site on Mount Gerizim) predates the emergence of the Samaritans, and the third element of Samaritan identity (the existence of an exclusive tradition of being "Israel") obviously depends on the second, the existence

---

[13] Magen, *Excavations*, 98.

[14] Magen, *Excavations*, 152.

[15] Magen, *Excavations*, 98.

[16] Magen, *Excavations*, 153.

[17] Magen considers these capitals as an imitation of the older type, used in the Persian temple; see Magen, *Excavations*, 153.

of a distinctive version of the Torah. Therefore, we will have to focus on the issue of the Torah in order to understand how Samaritan identity came into being.

2.2 The Samaritan Version of the Torah

It is well acknowledged that the Samaritan version of the Torah consists of a textual basis of the so-called pre-Samaritan type, on which a "thin layer" of "a few ideological elements" has been added.[18] As was already mentioned above, the pre-Samaritan basis of the Samaritan Torah is a harmonistic text, dating to the late 2nd century BCE.[19] As to the "ideological elements", the list usually provided comprises especially the following references:

1) The "Gerizim-commandment", an expansion of SP after Exod 20:13 and Deut 5:17.

2) The altar on Mount Gerizim (Deut 27:4).

3) בחר in the centralization formula.

2.2.1 The "Gerizim-Commandment"
The Samaritan Torah contains a lengthy expansion after both Exod 20:13 and Deut 5:17, establishing the special status of Mount Gerizim as part of the textual content of the Ten Commandments. However, it is only the insertion of these verses at this point in the Torah, and their combination in a *florilegium*, that is exclusive to the Samaritans, while the verses themselves that create this *florilegium* (= Deut 11:29a; 27:2b, 8a, 4a, 5–7; 11:30) have parallels in both the Masoretic and the Samaritan version of the Torah, as is indicated in the following translation of this passage:

[Deut 11:29a] When the LORD your God has brought you into the land +*of the Canaanites*+ that you are entering to occupy, [27:2b] you shall set up large stones and cover them with plaster [27:8a] and you shall write on the stones all the words of this law, [27:4a] so when you have crossed over the Jordan, you shall set up these stones, about which I am commanding you today, on Mount *Gerizim*, [27:5–7] and you shall build an altar there to the LORD your God, an altar of stones on which you have not used an iron tool. You must build the altar of the LORD your God of unhewn stones. Then offer up burnt offerings on it to the LORD your God, make sacrifices of well-being, and eat them there, rejoicing before the LORD your God. +*That mountain*+ [11:30] [–] beyond the Jordan, some distance to the west, in the land of the Canaanites who live in the Arabah, opposite Gilgal, beside the oak of Moreh, *opposite Shechem.*

---

[18] See Tov, *Criticism*, 80.
[19] See above, p. 136.

Textual Commentary:
The background coloring shows that the *florilegium* is basically a combination of Deut 11:29–30 and Deut 27:2–8, with the former passage framing the latter. The source of each part of the florilegium is printed before the respective verse in square brackets and elevated script. Textual pluses as against the source passage are indicated by a plus-sign before and after the respective passage; differences between MT and SP are marked in italics.

+*of the Canaanites*+: The text of the expansion contains ארץ הכנעני instead of הארץ which is in the source verse Deut 11:29a (both MT and SP).

Mount *Gerizim*: The Samaritan version of Deut 27:4 contains הרגריזים (always written as one word) instead of MT הר עיבל; see below, 2.2.2.

+*That mountain*+: The text of the expansion adds ההר ההוא in order to syntactically connect Deut 11:30 with the preceding passage, while the initial הלא המה of Deut 11:30 does not fit the new context of the *florilegium* and is therefore left out.

There is an obvious ideological aim in the creation of this *florilegium* about the altar on Mount Gerizim and the insertion of this passage at this prominent place of the Torah: The veneration of Mount Gerizim becomes part of the Ten Commandments. Thus, there is no question that the Samaritan Torah does contain textual changes that flow from ideological motivations. It seems important to make this conclusion, even though two further *loci classici* of the so-called "ideological corrections of the Samaritan Torah" will have to be removed from the list, as will be demonstrated in the following. Like the first instance (the Samaritan Gerizim-commandment), the latter two are occupied with the problem of the one and only holy place. However, regarding the latter two instances, the textual evidence is much more complicated than in the first case.

2.2.2 The Altar on Mount Gerizim (Deut 27:4)

In Deut 27:4–5, the people of Israel are commanded to build an altar after crossing the Jordan and entering the Holy Land. This altar is located on Mount Ebal, according to the Masoretic text, but on Mount Gerizim, according to the Samaritan version:

So when you have crossed over the Jordan, you shall set up these stones, about which I am commanding you today,
SP: *on Mount Gerizim* / **MT**: *on Mount Ebal*,
and you shall cover them with plaster. And you shall build an altar there to the LORD your God, an altar of stones on which you have not used an iron tool.

Most obviously, the altar of Deut 27:4–5 is of central importance within the narrative of Deuteronomy and the Torah as a whole, insofar as this is the first altar to be built by the Israelites after their entering the holy land. The Masoretic text implies that this altar is located on that mountain, which in

Deut 27:12–13 appears as the mountain of curses, while the Samaritan version locates it on the mountain of blessings.

As already mentioned, the textual difference between MT and SP was traditionally explained in scholarship as the result of a deliberate ideological change carried out by the Samaritans, supposedly aiming for the relocation of this first altar from Mount Ebal to Mount Gerizim.[20] However, it is now widely acknowledged in textual criticism that the evidence in the textual witnesses point to a different conclusion. Since the Old Greek translation, which was translated into Greek in the 3rd century BCE, seems to have contained the reading Mount Gerizim in Deut 27:4,[21] we have every reason to believe that the textual change was the reverse of what we previously thought – i.e. the older Hebrew text of Deuteronomy located the altar on Mount Gerizim, and the subsequent change into Mount Ebal was most probably carried out in order to delegitimize this altar by re-locating it onto the mountain of curses and, at the same time, to deprive Mount Gerizim of the altar. Thus, it is most probably not the Samaritan but the Masoretic text that is the result of an ideological textual change, carried out by followers of the temple of Jerusalem with an anti-Gerizim aim.

2.2.3 בחר in the Centralization Formula

According to the Masoretic text, the centralization formula, which appears 22 times in Deuteronomy, reads המקום אשר יבחר יהוה – "the place that the LORD will choose" (Deut 12:5 etc.). The Samaritan version, however, as is well known, contains the same phrase but with a somewhat different wording, namely המקום אשר בחר יהוה – "the place that the LORD has chosen". In order to evaluate these two readings, they ought to be read in their respective contexts:

Since the day that I brought my people out of the land of Egypt, I have not chosen a city (לא בחרתי בעיר) from any of the tribes of Israel in which to build a house, so that my name might be there, and I chose no one as ruler over my people Israel (לא בחרתי

---

[20] See Tov, *Criticism*, 95 note 67, and 266 note 37. One of the most influential scholars who favored counting Deut 27:4 as a Samaritan ideological change was Gesenius, the "first samaritanologist" (thus Tal, "Gesenius"), who in his seminal *De Pentateuchi Samaritani origine, indole et auctoritate commentatio philologico-critica* (1815) lists this case under the heading "Loca ad theologiam, hermeneuticam et cultum Samaritanorum domesticum conformata" ("Textual changes in accordance with Samaritan theology, hermeneutics, and cult"); see Gesenius, *Commentatio*, 58–61. For a short account of the influence of Gesenius' categorization of the textual differences, see Schorch, "Korrekturen", 4–9.

[21] For detailed support, see Schenker, "Seigneur", and idem, "Textgeschichtliches".

באיש); but I have chosen Jerusalem (ואבחר בירושלם) in order that my name may be there, and I have chosen David (ואבחר בדויד) to be over my people Israel. (2 Chron 6:5–6 // 1 Kings 8:16 LXX)

Thus, there is a clear textual link between the future tense יבחר of the Deuteronomic passages and the perfect בחרתי in Kings and Chronicles.

The Samaritan construction of this relationship is completely different from the Jewish one. Above all, the Samaritans acknowledge only the Pentateuch as their holy writ, and no further book beyond. Especially, they do not consider the so-called Deuteronomistic history or any other book of the Jewish Bible as part of their list of canonical books.[22] Thus, the identification of the chosen place with Jerusalem is, of course, not manifest in their sources, as is the case within the Jewish tradition. Nevertheless, the Samaritans, too, think of a very concrete place when they read their version of the Deuteronomic passages that speak of the central place of worship. This can be clearly seen when we look at the Samaritan version of these passages, with the Samaritan version of the centralization formula as our point of departure:

When you cross the Jordan to go in to occupy the land that the LORD your God is giving you, and when you occupy it and live in it, [...] you shall seek the place that the LORD your God has chosen (בחר) out of all your tribes as his habitation to put his name there. You shall go there. (Deut 11:31–12:5)

In Deut 27, this place is identified with the altar to be erected on Mount Gerizim:

So when you have crossed over the Jordan, you shall set up these stones, about which I am commanding you today, on Mount Gerizim, and you shall cover them with plaster. And you shall build an altar there to the LORD your God, an altar of stones on which you have not used an iron tool. (Deut 27:4–5 SP)

In light of how these texts are worded, it seems that the Samaritan claim that Mount Gerizim is the chosen place is well established in the book of Deuteronomy. Moreover, the use of the perfect tense indicates that the

---

[22] There is no sound basis for the claim that the Book of Joshua was once part of the Samaritan canon – a claim raided, for instance, by Zsengellér, "Canon". The Hebrew Samaritan Joshua, published by Gaster (see idem, "Josua"), is a manuscript produced in 1905, which was not copied from any ancient manuscript but was specifically made for the purpose of selling it to Gaster (fortunately enough, in this case there are sources to prove this manuscript a fake). It is thus not at all relevant to the question whether the Samaritans once had "Joshua", as was clearly shown by Paul Kahle in his short reaction to Gaster's publication; see idem, "Josua". Moshe Florentin, who analyzed the language of the Samaritan Hebrew Joshua, came to the same conclusion, i.e. that these texts were composed in modern times; see Florentin, *Hebrew*, 357–8. Therefore, what remains of the Samaritan "Josua" is a medieval chronicle, written in Arabic, which *inter alia* contains some Joshua material. That these passages resemble traditions found in the LXX and in Josephus simply seems to be due to the fact that it drew on those texts.

selection of this place has already occurred, and this expression creates a narrative link, connecting the altar on Mount Gerizim with the first altar built by Abraham, which, according to Gen 12:6–7, was erected at "She-chem, the oak of Moreh" (שכם אלון מרה). We thus have two textual versions of the selection of the chosen place, and this raises the question, whether the selection happened before Deuteronomy (= SP) or after it (= MT).

In this case as in the former, there is very strong textual evidence that the reading preserved in the Samaritan text is primary to that of the Masoretic text, the Masoretic text being the result of a secondary textual change. This can be seen from the fact that, again, the Old Greek translation, which is of Jewish origin and therefore anything but suspect of having a pro-Gerizim or even pro-Samaritan tendency, attests the perfect tense.

It even seems clear at which period of time the new reading was created, since 4QMMT, written around the middle of 2nd century BCE, attests the perfect tense, while the Temple Scroll, dating to the late 2nd century BCE, preserves the future tense:

4QMMT:

[... ישראל] ירושלים היאה מחנה הקדש היא מקום שבחר בו מכל שבטי [...]

For Jerusalem is the holy camp. It is the place that He chose from all the tribes of [Israel ...][23]

Temple Scroll:

לפני תאוכלנו שנה כשנה במקום אשר אבחר

You are to eat those before Me annually in the place that I shall choose. (11Q19 52:9)

ושמחתה לפני במקום אשר אבחר לשום שמי עליו

And rejoice before Me in the place that I will choose to establish My name. (11Q19 52:16)

Thus, the reading יבחר, which became part of the Masoretic *textus receptus*, entered the textual tradition most probably during the 2nd half of the 2nd century BCE.

At first glance, the reason behind this change appears enigmatic. Clearly, the reading בחר, as part of the older text that was current in both Samaria and Judah, had for centuries been understood in Judah and Jerusalem as referring to the primordial and eternal selection of Jerusalem. If so, why did scribes change the text so dramatically by making changes in the consonantal framework?

---

[23] 4Q394 f8 iv:9–11; compare Kratz, "Place", 72–3.

One of the reasons is certainly the situation of an increasing tension between the proto-Samaritans and the followers of the Jerusalem Temple, which developed throughout the 2nd century BCE, and which seems to have been caused by the Hasmonean rulers in Jerusalem.[24] Besides these historical and political circumstances, I tried to show elsewhere that the 2nd century BCE was a period of changes in the attitude toward scripture, focusing more and more on the textual surface instead on the textual deep structure, i.e. the specific wording instead of the internal narrative framework of the texts.[25] Thus, the textual change was certainly carried out in an atmosphere of hostility toward Mount Gerizim, and it may also have been partly motivated by a new way of reading the sacred texts, which took notice of every single detail in wording.

Nevertheless, looking at the long history that the reading בחר must have already had at this time in Judah, given that Deuteronomy was read in Judah long time before the textual changes were carried out, it seems improbable that the textual changes aimed primarily at the identification of the holy place, as the most common explanations hold. After all, as was argued above, the pro-Jerusalem elite were already convinced that their city had been eternally selected by the God of Israel,[26] and there is no doubt that they found justification for this view in the unchanged text of Deuteronomy, as well as afterwards in the "improved" version.

Therefore, we should look for another motivation for the textual change, and it seems to me that this motive can be found in the second of the two links that connect the Deuteronomic centralization passages to the continuation of the overall narrative in the Jewish canon, i.e. the election of the Davidic dynasty (compare 2 Chron 6:5–6 // 1 Kings 8:16 LXX).[27] Most noticeably, the textual change in the centralization passages of Deuteronomy from בחר to יבחר established the centralization formula as a textual parallel to the law of the king (Deut 17):

Deut 12:5 (MT)

המקום אשר יבחר יהוה אלהיכם מכל שבטיכם

the place that the LORD your God will choose out of all your tribes

Deut 17:5 (MT)

מלך אשר יבחר יהוה אלהיך בו מקרב אחיך

a king whom the LORD your God will choose, one of your own community

---

[24] See above, p. 137.
[25] See Schorch, "Libraries", 179–80.
[26] E.g., compare Ps 48:3.
[27] See above, 2.2.3.

With the establishment of this textual parallel between the centralization formula and Deut 17, the critical perspective on kingship, which characterizes the king's law in Deut 17, was softened if not removed from the text altogether, since the future election of the king is now *expressis verbis* in parallel with the future election of the place of the temple. Deut 17, therefore, now foreshadows David's election. It is only by this textual change of the centralization formula, from בחר to יבחר, that the Jerusalemite concept of a twofold election – place and dynasty – became firmly anchored in the written textual body of the Torah.

The development demonstrates that, at least on the textual level, a direct connection existed between the increasing tensions in the relationship with the proto-Samaritans, on the one hand, and the elaboration of explicit political claims during the Hasmonean age, on the other hand. Thus, what at first glance seems to have been primarily an internal conflict within the Israelite-Jewish tradition between followers of the temples at Mount Gerizim and in Jerusalem, respectively, a quarrel about the one legitimate place of cultic worship, was throughout the 2nd century BCE interconnected with a process of re-shaping Judean identity not only on the religious level, but on the political level, too.

3. Samarians, Samaritans, Judeans, and Foreigners

I tried to show in the preceding part that the textual development of Deuteronomy seems to reflect traces of important identity-shaping processes among the followers of both Jerusalem and Mount Gerizim during the Hasmonean era. In my final point, I would like to focus on the question of whether and how the process of re-shaping Jewish identity in relation to Samarian and Samaritan identity interplayed with changes in attitudes towards foreign powers. As a means of revealing these connections, I would like to proceed from some early traditions about the Samarians and Samaritans, preserved in Josephus' *Antiquitates*, and to analyze how they construct the relationship of Jews toward foreign powers.

It has long been observed that Josephus' account of the erection of a sanctuary on Mount Gerizim and its cult is far from coherent or even unequivocal in its judgments. Analyzing Josephus's descriptions, Ferdinand Dexinger demonstrated, largely successfully in my eyes, that this incoherence is mainly due to Josephus' use of different traditions, dating to different eras.[28] What is important here is less the exact date of these traditions, as suggested by Dexinger, but rather the observation that some of these tradi-

---

[28] See Dexinger, "Ursprung", and idem, "Limits", 97–9.

tions seem to antedate the final break between Gerizim followers and Jerusalem followers into Samaritans and Jews in the late 2nd century BCE. This is suggested, at least, when we look at a very basic difference. In some passages of the *Antiquitates* (especially in Book 9) the Samaritans are equated with the Kuthim, which means that they are of foreign descent. In large passages of Book 11, however, the followers of the Gerizim temple are considered as *homoethnoi* "compatriots", members of the same nation. If one takes into account the evidence from the Book of Ben Sira ch. 50 presented above,[29] this would mean that the latter passages predate the final break between the two sects.

According to this pre-break tradition, the sanctuary on Mount Gerizim was erected by the satrap Sanballat, who was a Kuthean – which here does not mean "Samaritan", as in later times, but "Samarian", i.e. someone who came from the area of Samaria. He did this as a favor for his Jewish stepson Manasse, brother of the high priest in Jerusalem. Moreover, the allowance to build the temple was provided by Alexander, whom Sanballat persuaded with the argument that the temple on Mount Gerizim supported his (i.e. Alexander's) imperial ambitions, since the forces of the Jews would thus become split and the unity of the Jews lost.

If the reconstruction that this tradition predates the break between Samaritans and Jews is right, as Dexinger and others believe (correctly, in my eyes), then this passage provides an important insight into a period when the tension between the followers of the two temples increased, although, at the time, it was still a quarrel within the people of the Israelite-Judean tradition. The Gerizim followers were still considered as compatriots, even though they were already on the threshold of becoming foreigners.

In this period of heated discussions the construction of attitudes toward and relationships with foreign powers seems to have been an important part of the argument and maybe even part of the concrete political strategies of the two sides.

On the one hand, foreign powers supported separatist movements, because this made it easier for them to rule over the Jewish people. Thus, according to the source referred to above, Alexander granted permission to build the temple on Mount Gerizim, because he hoped to weaken the influence and power of Jerusalem in the region of Palestine.

On the other hand, separatist movements used foreign powers in order to gain independence from Jerusalem. According to the source used by Josephus, it was the collaboration of a rebellious priest from Jerusalem with the Kuthean satrap from Samaria and with Alexander that endangered the unity of the Jewish people.

---

[29] See above, p. 137.

At least in the case of the Samarian followers of the Gerizim temple, who then became Samaritans, the only way out of this *circulus vitiousus* of factual or suspected collaboration, between heretics and foreign powers, seems to have been to create two new and separate identities: an exclusive Jewish identity and an exclusive Samaritan identity, emerging out of a formerly common and shared basis among the followers of the sanctuaries of Jerusalem and Mount Gerizim, respectively.

References

Barag, D., "New Evidence on the Foreign Policy of John Hircanus", *INJ* 12 (1992–3) 1–12.

Ben-Hayyim, Z., *A Grammar of Samaritan Hebrew: Based on the Recitation of the Law in Comparison with the Tiberian and Other Jewish Traditions* (revised edition in English with assistance from Abraham Tal; Jerusalem/Winona Lake: Magnes Press, Hebrew University/Eisenbrauns, 2000).

Coggins, R.J., *Samaritans and Jews: The Origins of Samaritanism Reconsidered* (Atlanta: John Knox Press, 1975).

Crown, A.D., "Redating the Schism between the Judaeans and the Samaritans", *JQR* 82 (1991) 17–50.

Delcor, M., "Hinweise auf das samaritanische Schisma im Alten Testament", *ZAW* 74 (1962) 281–91.

Dexinger, F., "Limits of Tolerance in Judaism: The Samaritan Example", in E.P. Sanders (ed.), *Jewish and Christian self-definition.* Vol. 2: *Aspects of Judaism in the Graeco-Roman Period* (London: SCM Press, 1981) 88–114.

–, "Der Ursprung der Samaritaner im Spiegel der frühen Quellen", in F. Dexinger/R. Pummer (ed.), *Die Samaritaner* (Wege der Forschung 604; Darmstadt: Wissenschaftliche Buchgesellschaft, 1992) 67–140.

Eshel, E./Eshel, H., "Dating the Samaritan Pentateuch's Compilation in Light of the Qumran Biblical Scrolls", in W.W. Fields et al. (ed.), *Emanuel: Studies in Hebrew Bible, Septuagint and Dead Sea Scrolls in Honor of Emanuel Tov* (FS E. Tov; Leiden/Boston: Brill, 2003) 215–40.

Florentin, M., *Late Samaritan Hebrew: A Linguistic Analysis of its Different Types* (Studies in Semitic Languages and Linguistics 43; Leiden/Boston: Brill, 2005).

Gaster, M., "Das Buch Josua in hebräisch-samaritanischer Rezension", *ZDMG* 62 (1908) 209–79; 494–549.

Gesenius, W., *De Pentateuchi Samaritani origine, indole et auctoritate commentatio philologico-critica* (Halle: Renger, 1815).

Kahle, P., "Zum hebräischen Buch Josua der Samaritaner", *ZDMG* 62 (1908) 550–1.

Kratz, R.G., "'The Place which He has Chosen': The Identification of the Cult Place of Deut. 12 and Lev. 17 in 4QMMT", *Meghillot* 5–6 (2007) 57–80.

Magen, Y. et al., *Mount Gerizim Excavations.* Vol. 1: *The Aramaic, Hebrew and Samaritan Inscriptions* (Judaea and Samaria Publications 2; Jerusalem: Israel Antiquities Authority, 2004).

Mor, M., "Samaritan History: 1. The Persian, Hellenistic and Hasmonaean Period", in A.D. Crown (ed.), *The Samaritans* (Tübingen: J.C.B. Mohr, 1989) 1–18.

Purvis, J.D., *The Samaritan Pentateuch and the Origin of the Samaritan Sect* (Harvard Semitic Monographs 2; Cambridge: Harvard University Press, 1968).

Schenker, A., "Le Seigneur choisira-t-il le lieu de son nom ou l'a-t-il choisi?: L'apport de la Bible grecque ancienne à l'histoire du texte samaritain et massorétique", in A. Voitila (ed.), *Scripture*

---

in transition: Essays on Septuagint, Hebrew Bible, and Dead Sea Scrolls in Honour of Raija Sollamo (FS R. Sollamo; Supplements to the Journal for the Study of Judaism 126; Leiden/Boston: Brill, 2008) 339–51.

–, "Textgeschichtliches zum Samaritanischen Pentateuch und Samareitikon", in M. Mor/F. Reiterer (ed.), *Samaritans Past and Present: Current Studies* (Studia Samaritana 5/Studia Judaica 53; Berlin/New York: de Gruyter, 2010) 105–21.

Schorch, S., "Die (sogenannten) anti-polytheistischen Korrekturen im samaritanischen Pentateuch", *Mitteilungen und Beiträge der Forschungsstelle Judentum, Theologische Fakultät Leipzig* 15/16 (1999) 4–21.

–, *Die Vokale des Gesetzes: Die samaritanische Lesetradition als Textzeugin der Tora.* Vol. 1: *Genesis* (BZAW 339; Berlin/New York: de Gruyter, 2004).

–, "The Libraries in 2 Macc 2:13–15", in G.G. Xeravits/J. Zsengellér (ed.), *The Books of the Maccabees: History, Theology, Ideology; Papers of the Second International Conference on the Deuterocanonical Books, Pápa, Hungary, 9–11 June, 2005* (Supplements to the Journal for the Study of Judaism 118; Leiden: Brill, 2007) 169–80.

Tal, A., "The First Samaritanologist: Wilhelm Gesenius", in S. Schorch/E.-J. Waschke (ed.), *Biblische Exegese und hebräische Lexikographie: Kontext und Wirkung des "Hebräischen Handwörterbuches" von Wilhelm Gesenius* (BZAW; Berlin/New York: de Gruyter, 2012; in print).

Tov, E., *Textual Criticism of the Hebrew Bible* (Minneapolis/Assen: Fortress Press/Royal Van Gorcum, ²2001).

Zsengellér, J., "Canon and the Samaritans", in A. van der Kooij/K. van der Toorn (ed.), *Canonization and Decanonization: Papers presented to the International Conference of the Leiden Institute for the Study of Religions (LISOR), held at Leiden 9–10 January 1997* (Studies in the History of Religions 82; Leiden et al.: Brill, 1998) 161–71.

–, *Gerizim as Israel: Northern Tradition of the Old Testament and the Early Traditions of the Samaritans* (Utrechtse Theologische Reeks 38; Utrecht: Universiteit Utrecht, 1998).

Andrea M. Berlin

Boston University

Manifest Identity: From *Ioudaios* to Jew

Household Judaism as Anti-Hellenization in the Late Hasmonean Era

Around 100 BCE, early in the reign of the Hasmonean king Alexander Jannaeus, two Levantine authors provide very similar descriptions of a contemporary cultural idea. The first is Meleager, a native of the city of Gadara. Writing in Greek, he asserts:

My birthplace was of Syria, the Attic haunt of Gadara;
My foster nurse was the island of Tyre, and Eukrates I own for sire ...
I am Meleager. Yes, and what if Syrian? Stranger, marvel not:
We inhabit a single homeland, the world.[1]

Meleager describes the cosmopolitan ideal – the world is our common home where more unites than divides us. He doesn't ignore the various identities by which people differentiated themselves; indeed he makes a point of listing his for three of his poem's four lines: his city of birth; his Attic cultural affiliation; the city where he moved to study; his family lineage; and his "nationality". But he asserts forthrightly that all are subordinate to a single larger identity, that of citizen of the world.

We do not know the name of the second author. He originally wrote in Hebrew, but his words come down to us only in Greek translation. This second author composed the work we know as 1 Maccabees. In it, he describes a decree formulated by the Seleucid king Antiochus IV, some sixty years earlier. He says that "the king wrote to all his kingdom for all to become one people (εἰς λαὸν ἕνα) and for each to abandon his own customs" (1 Macc. 1:41–42).[2] In contrast to Meleager's proud assertion of cosmopolitanism, our second author presents the notion of a single people as an indictment – an alien notion with baleful consequences.

---

[1] AP 7.417.1–5 = Gow/Page, *Greek Anthology*, Meleager epigr. II.1–5

[2] For a recent discussion of this decree in context see Mendels, "Memory", 52. I realize that the author of 1 Maccabees represents this statement as original to the time of the decree, meaning around 165 BCE. That may or not true, but in the event it is not verifiable. What is undeniable is that he wrote it down around 100 BCE, and that he clearly believed that its formulation would be understandable and persuasive to his audience. For this reason I think it is legitimate to offer it as a pendant to the epigram of Meleager.

For Meleager, cosmopolitanism is an easy add-on, a cultural win-win. He does not risk violating the essence of any of his various identities by adopting other ideas and practices. For the author of 1 Maccabbees, Israel's cultural practices are fundamentally compromised by other customs. Instead of win-win it's a zero-sum game, with difference as the trump card.

The wholly opposed attitudes of Meleager and the author of 1 Maccabees have been exhaustively analyzed. I admit great trepidation in joining this long-standing conversation. My goal is to provide a physical context for the period in which these authors write and a material template for thinking about the attitudes they express. My focus will be on the period leading up to the time of our authors' statements, the two generations or so after 142 BCE, when Simon captures the Akra and rids Jerusalem of its Seleucid garrison.

I begin by constructing a framework of chronological, geographic, and typological parameters, in other words situating the remains according to when, where, and what. The period is essentially the second half of the second century BCE. The areas to be examined are Judea and its immediate surroundings, meaning Idumea to the south, Samaria to the north, and the Mediterranean coast to the west and north. To the east, in ancient Perea, there are no datable remains from this time for us to consider. As for what to look at, I start with the admittedly scanty material evidence from Judea, and then move outwards to the remains from surrounding regions.

First, however, a larger question. What is at stake here? Despite the rich array of written sources, the intertwined character of political action and social response in Judea over several volatile centuries still confuses us. We want to pin down a few fixed points in a fast-moving story, so that we have a chance of understanding and yes, even learning something. Yet our written sources, though many and detailed, are insufficient. Each represents the point of view of an individual or a small group; when we take them together we have the notes and bars of a score but not the symphony. Material remains are the instruments of the orchestra – they provide the physical means for conveying the music. For us, those remains provide the physical surroundings in which Meleager, the author of 1 Maccabees, and their contemporaries compose, surroundings whose parameters necessarily inform but also limit their vision.

After 142 BCE:
Life in Jerusalem and Judea in the Early Days of Hasmonean Rule

In Jerusalem, a spate of recent excavation and publication now allows us to confidently assess the city's size, density, and character in the early decades of Hasmonean rule. The first thing to be said is that this is a time of population growth. Before this time, from the early third through the mid-second century BCE when the city was under Ptolemaic and Seleucid rule, people lived south of the Tem-ple Mount, on the long spur of the City of Da-vid. This is the only part of the city where datable remains in primary de-posits have been found. In the second half of the second century BCE, architectural and materi-al remains indicate that the Western Hill is reset-tled. A newly strength-ened fortification line is built, enclosing the en-tire area as far west as the Citadel. This newly protected area is not, however, densely occu-pied (fig. 1). The line of the wall follows clear topographic logic, with the builders taking ad-vantage of a shallow

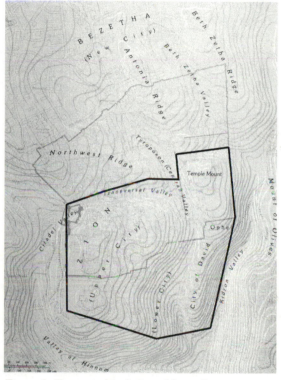

Figure 1: Topographical plan of Jerusalem.

east-west valley that demarcates the northern edge of the Upper City on the Western Hill. Their construction outlines a huge area that on present evi-dence is lightly occupied for another two generations or so, until the middle of the first century BCE.[3]

---

[3] On the City of David see Ariel, *Excavations*. On the Upper City see Geva, "Hellenistic Pot-tery", 148–50; Ariel, "Imported Greek Stamped Amphora Handles". On the Armenian Garden see Tushingham, *Excavations*. For a recent re-evaluation of the size of Jerusalem in the early Second Temple period, and especially the relationship between this modest and limited area and the more expansive description in the book of Nehemiah, see Finkelstein, "Archaeology" and "Territorial Extent".

The character of Jerusalem's later second century BCE occupation is consistent across the city, from the older and more densely built-up City of David to the newer, more sparse settlements on the Western Hill. Excavated remains from every zone tell a single story: people lived simply with only the most basic of household goods, all manufactured in the immediate environs of the city. The best representation of this lifestyle comes from the pottery found in the huge earth fills built up against the northern side of the newly constructed fortification around the Upper City. Thousands of vessels and fragments represent a household repertoire limited to the essentials: cooking pots, juglets for dispensing liquids such as cooking oil, small saucers and bowls for dining, lamps and perfume flasks, water pitchers and large jars for holding grain as well as wine and oil (fig. 2).[4] Imported, speciality, and luxury items do not appear at all. The picture provided here has been echoed everywhere in the city where levels of this period have been

recovered: the Armenian Garden, the Citadel, the Tyropean Valley, and the City of David.

Where did Jerusalem's new residents come from? Not, apparently, from villages in the surrounding countryside. The evidence of regional surveys shows

Figure 2. Pottery of the later second century BCE from Jerusalem.

clearly that in Judea as well as the region immediately north of Jerusalem the number of rural sites increases from the earlier to the later second century.[5] The Land of Benjamin survey found 75 sites with remains dating from the fifth through the third centuries BCE; by the end of the second century BCE the number is more than doubled, with over 175 sites (fig. 3). However, while the countryside is increasingly populated, almost all the sites are relatively small. Even previously substantial settlements, such as Beth Zur and Tell el-Fûl, are smaller in the later than the earlier second century. A telling reflection of this restructured countryside comes from the site of Ramat Rahel, a strategic, well-watered spot that dominates fertile surrounding valleys and also controls the main route that connects Jerusalem with

---

[4] These come from Upper City excavation Area W, strata 5–4, and Area X-2, strata 7–5; see Geva, "Hellenistic Pottery", 113–21.

[5] The most recent compilation of evidence is Tal, "Hellenism", 59–61 with further references there. For a summary of the region north of Jerusalem see Magen, "Land of Benjamin".

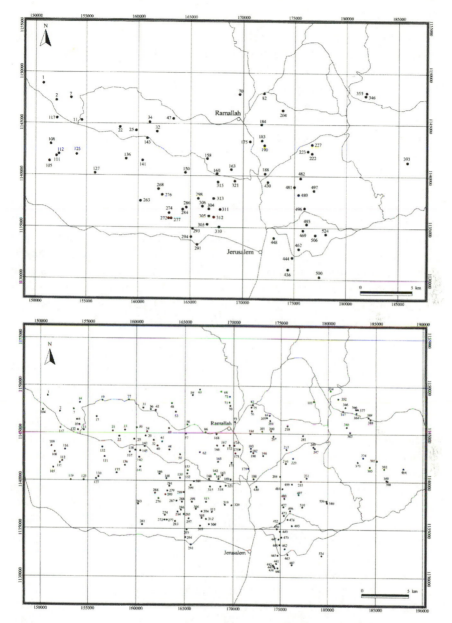

Figure 3. Top: Survey map of region immediately north of Jerusalem showing sites dating from the fifth through the third centuries BCE. Bottom: Survey map of region immediately north of Jerusalem showing sites dating from the third and second centuries BCE.

the coast. For several hundred years the site had housed an important administrative center linking Jerusalem to its agricultural hinterland. By early Hasmonean times that compound is at least partially dismantled and the settlement notably reduced in size.[6]

Qalandiyeh, one of the largest rural sites yet excavated, provides a view of life in the countryside. Qalandiyeh's inhabitants made wine and oil in quantity. Their compound includes a spacious production area with six wine presses, a large oil press, and smaller equipment perhaps for extracting perfumes. To one side stands a large main building with a central courtyard and surrounding rooms and storage areas. To the other is a second courtyard building with dwellings, workrooms, and storerooms. Construction is marked by well-dressed thresholds and doorjambs. The impression of comfortable country life is augmented by the 450 coins dating to the late Hellenistic and early Roman eras found at the site.[7] The coins testify to the inhabitants' ongoing commercial success as well as to the wider connections: 60 coins from Ptolemaic and Seleucid mints, Tyrian shekels, and even a Roman Republican denarius dating to 46 BCE. And yet, despite their contacts and monetary means, the finds show that Qalandiyeh's residents do not acquire luxury or imported goods. Instead, their houses hold the identical array of basic locally manufactured household goods as we see from houses in Jerusalem.[8]

The picture is the same at smaller sites throughout Judea. Typical is the small settlement of Umm el-Umdan, just outside Modein along one of the two natural routes connecting Jerusalem to the coast. Residents here live in simple houses with courtyards and open areas for gardens and animals. Their possessions are limited to the basic necessities of life – storage jars, cooking pots, small bowls and oil lamps – with nothing special or extra or foreign.

Thus in the first two generations of Hasmonean rule, Judea was a rural society. People lived dispersed throughout the region's hills and valleys, with Jerusalem the only place of significant size. In both city and countryside, people were self-sufficient and received no imported goods. Theirs is a culture of material simplicity, marked more by what is absent than what is present. This leads to a dificult question: how should we parse this absence? Is it inflected, by which I mean meaningful, or is it simply circumstantial?

We have two angles by which to assess this stripped-down lifestyle. One is to look back, to the material remains of the preceding several generations who lived under Ptolemaic and then Seleucid rule. The other is to look out,

---

[6] Lipschits et al., "Palace and Village", 37–8.
[7] Ariel, "Coins".
[8] Magen, "Qalandiyeh"; idem, "Qalandiya", especially pp. 83–4.

to the remains from sites in Idumea, Samaria, and along the coast during the decades contemporary with early Hasmonean rule. The evidence from both views, back in time as well as the present surroundings, shows that residents of Jerusalem and Judea had easy access to imported goods, both luxurious and mundane. This in turn suggests that the simple households of early Hasmonean times reflect peoples' purposeful choices.

I begin with Jerusalem in the years before Hasmonean rule.

Before 142 BCE:
Life in Jerusalem before Hasmonean Rule

In contrast to life in the early decades of Hasmonean rule, people living in Jerusalem under Ptolemaic and Seleucid rule could and did acquire imported goods. The most well-represented item was imported wine, primarily from Rhodes. Over a century of excavation has produced over 1000 stamped handles and many more unstamped amphora fragments (fig. 4, top). About 90% of the datable handles come from the later third through the middle of the second centuries BCE; the numbers drop abruptly after that point. Since local potters of this time were producing large storage jars for the region's wine and oil producers, the imported amphoras likely reflect some of the local population's taste for foreign wines.[9]

Figure 4. Top: stamped amphora handle found in Jerusalem, from a wine jar made in Rhodes, second century BCE. Bottom: Carved ivory box found in Jerusalem and depicting Zeus, in the guise of an eagle, carrying the youth Ganymede, second century BCE.

Residents set their tables with imported dishes. From several areas of the City of David excavations as well as from the pottery-laden fills in the Armenian Garden excavations are black slipped and painted plates, bowls, and drinking cups from Athens, Antioch, Alexandria, and other smaller producers in the eastern Mediterranean.[10] The specific forms and styles also occur at cities such as Tarsus in

---

[9] Ariel, *Excavations*, 12–25

[10] Tushingham, *Excavations*, 37, 41; Hayes, "Fine Wares", 183; Rosenthal-Heginbottom, "Hellenistic to Early Roman Fine Ware", 206–8; Berlin, personal study and forthcoming publication of

Cilicia, Paphos on Cyprus, Berenice in Libya – and, most notably, Samaria, just a day's journey north from Jerusalem itself.[11] The amounts found in Jerusalem are not large, but then again neither is the city's population dur-

---

Area G pottery – details: table vessels (figs. 51.2–5, 7–27, 52.13), four amphorae (figs. 53.1–4), and a few imported-type lamps, probably made in coastal workshops (figs. 53.5–12). The two earliest pieces are mid-late fourth century BCE Attic imports: an incurved rim bowl (fig. 51.13) and a bell krater (fig. 51.19). From the later fourth and third centuries BCE come three everted rim bowls (figs. 51.8, 10, 11), a thickened rim saucer (fig. 51.16), a rolled rim saucer (fig. 51.18), two West Slope painted dishes (figs. 51.20, 21), a West Slope painted hydria (fig. 51.23), two skyphoi (figs. 51.22, 25), two kantharoi, one with West Slope decoration (figs. 51.26, 52.13), and a cup foot with interior rouletting (fig. 51.27). For the small bowl with West Slope style laurel leaves on the interior (fig. 51.20) there are precise parallels at Paphos and Tarsus, and the decoration is quite common at Tarsus on other forms as well. Context dates range from the first half of the third century BCE through the middle of the first century BCE (though the later fills contain much residual material). The small skyphos covered in a mottled black to brownish-red slip (fig. 51.22) is also paralleled at Tarsus, as well as in Cyprus and at several Levantine sites. The ribbed skyphos (fig. 51.25) is paralleled at Tarsus. Both these latter forms appear in contexts ranging from the earlier third through the mid-second century BCE.

Other Area G vessels have fabrics that match descriptions of vessels found at both Antioch and Hama and described by the excavators as Antiochene (Waagé, "Tableware", 6; Christensen/Johansen, *Poteries*, 9); parallels for all occur at Antioch, and are otherwise confined to Levantine sites. The characteristics of inner full glaze and exterior upper half were noted as common at Tarsus (Jones, "Pottery", 153), Tell 'Arqa (Thalmann, "Tell 'Arqa", figs. 43.1–4 [incurved rim bowls], 43.16–18 [fish plates], 43.20 [everted rim bowl], all dated second century BCE), Samaria (Crowfoot, *Objects*, 223, on everted rim bowls in Hellenistic Fort Wall group, deposit closed c. 150 BCE). Parallels for these possibly Antiochene vessels are very largely found within the same sites and contexts: the third century BCE group at Antioch, the third and second century BCE level at Keisan, the mid to late second century BCE horizon at Pella, the Hellenistic Fort Wall deposit at Samaria, and the middle and upper levels of the Middle Hellenistic Unit at Tarsus, dating from the mid-third to the mid-second century BCE.

[11] The third century BCE imports from Antioch are all labelled as Attic (Waagé, "Tableware", 4), as are those from Tarsus (Jones, "Pottery", 158). At the latter site they are considered the impetus behind late third and second century BCE local production of lower-priced (and lower quality) imitations. Hayes identifies all early Hellenistic fine wares from the House of Dionysos at Paphos as Attic as well, and says they were replaced in the later third century by Aegean, Pergamene and Italic wares ("Paphos", 5–7). But see the cautionary articles by Clairmont ("Greek Pottery I"; "Greek Pottery II") in which he attempts to define vessels of Alexandrian and Cypriote manufacture; it was these centers, he believes, which supplied most if not all of the black wares found in the Hellenistic Near East. See also the discussion by Kenrick regarding the Benghazi (Berenice) ceramics, wherein a large group of black glaze vessels with a fine, hard, pinkish clay were isolated as Attic (Black-glazed B1 ware), but subsequent atomic absorption analysis showed that while many were indeed Attic, others were not, and that these latter were "not always visually distinguishable from the Attic" (*Excavations*, 31, 501). As for Samaria, all West Slope ware is considered Attic in origin, and is dated to the first half of the third century BCE (Crowfoot, "Hellenistic Pottery", 238). However Jones in the Tarsus publication ("Pottery", 262) had already noted that such plates were unlikely to be Attic. In the Samaria volume, Crowfoot quotes Homer Thompson as calling the profile "quite un-Attic" ("Hellenistic Pottery", 243). Hayes, *Paphos*, 6 note 15, and 7, has suggested a source in the southeastern quadrant of the Aegean, based on the finds from Paphos. The form may derive from earlier Attic West Slope plates, such as an example from Athens with a horizontal rim and crisply articulated ridges (Thompson, "Two Centuries", A38, figs. 6, 117, from a deposit closed c. 260 BCE).

ing these years. Archaeologists have also found a few luxury objects, such as a ivory box carved with a rendition of Zeus, in the guise of an eagle, and the youth Ganymede (fig. 4, bottom). It is true that remains of this period are frustratingly paltry. Occupation was confined to the City of David spur, an area with extensive later building. We can not point to a single intact house. But we do have large fills laden with household goods from this period. Thus while the nature of the evidence does not permit us to gauge real numbers or intensity of use, the simple fact of the appearance of imported wine and dishes and occasional luxury objects demonstrates that foreign goods as well as people could and did make their way to the city.

Such finds supply a material backdrop to the more vivid picture that written sources afford of Ptolemaic and early Seleucid Jerusalem. For example, the map in figure 5 shows the places where, in 259 BCE, Zenon, a Ptolemaic official, stopped for flour while on an inspection tour of royal lands. After landing at Strato's Tower, he journeys to Jerusalem, thus documenting both imperial contact and an easily accessed route inland from the coast (Edgar, Catalogue: P. Cairo Zen. I 59.004). Perhaps the most famous example of outside contact comes from the Letter of Aristeas, which describes Ptolemy II's summoning of 72 sages from Jerusalem to

Figure 5. Map showing places that the Ptolemaic official Zenon visited in 259 BCE according to P. Cairo Zenon I 59.004.

Alexandria in order to produce a Greek translation of the Hebrew Bible (Aristeas 32). As Lee Levine has pointed out, if the source is reliable one must conclude from this episode that there were at least that many scholars in the city with sufficient knowledge of Greek.[12] This evidence, taken to-

---

[12] L.I. Levine, *Jerusalem*, 58–9.

gether, evokes an image of Ptolemaic Jerusalem as a city with at least some sophisticated residents in close touch with and benefitting from Mediterraenean contact.[13]

After 142 BCE:
Life in the Surrounding Regions in the Early Days
of Hasmonean Rule

Before Hasmonean rule and also after it is established, Judea remains a rural society with Jerusalem the only place of significant size. But the array of foreign goods disappears, resulting in much plainer households. Though the population in both town and countryside increases under Hasmonean rule, that population's links with the world beyond Judea essentially disappear. Is this a general phenomenon? How do these early Hasmonean-era Judeans live in comparison to their contemporaries to the south, west, and north?

This question is readily answered: later second century BCE material remains from areas surrounding Judea reveal that people there live in a fundamentally different economic and social universe. Urbanized settlement patterns, Greek styles of house décor, Aegean wines and imported plates, figurines in Greek styles and subjects – the pervasiveness of all such goods demonstrates that at ground level, people were intimately connected to the wider Mediterranean world and its dominant Hellenizing culture. Typical are the array of remains from the Idumean city of Marisa, the coastal city of Dor, and the revitalized city of Samaria. I present these sites

---

[13] An important question that these scanty and residual fragments do not help answer is: who was actually living in Jerusalem prior to the conquest of the Akra? Was the city's population comprised largely of priests, their servants, and perhaps a small number of officials, with wealthy landholders and workers living on farms in the surrounding countryside? Or did the city also accommodate independent workers, a kind of middle class between peasant farmers and the wealthy? It should be remembered that people lived only in the City of David, since the Upper City was still unsettled in this period (Geva, "Hellenistic Pottery", 148–50). In this context it is interesting to consider the actions of Antiochus III after his conquest of the southern Levant, most significantly the remission of the punitive tax load that had been in place under the Ptolemies. According to Josephus Antiochus cancelled all personal and city taxes as well as promising a series of imperial dispensations so that citizens might "retrieve the condition of their city". These included: "for their sacrifices of animals, ... for wine and oil, and frankincense, the value of 20,000 pieces of silver, and [six] sacred artabrae of fine flour, with 1460 mendimni of wheat, and 375 mendimni of salt ... and for the materials of wood, let it be brought out of Judea itself, and out of the other countries, and out of Libanus, tax free; and the same I would have observed as to those other materials which will be necessary, in order to render the temple more glorious; and let all that nation live ... discharged from poll-money and the crown tax, and other taxes also ..." (Ant. 12.140–2).

because they have the widest excavation exposure and the broadest array of published material, but I emphasize that the same types and varieties of remains appear at tens and tens of other excavated sites, large and small, throughout these regions.

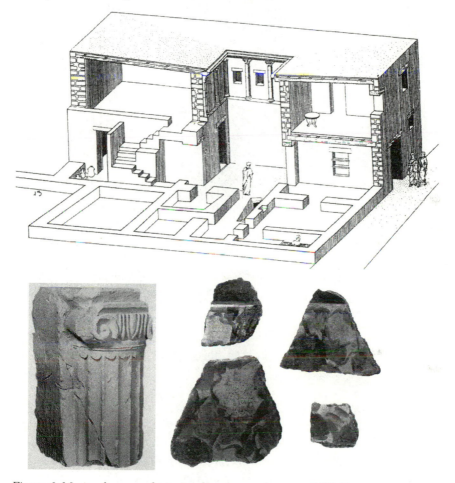

Figure 6. Marisa, house and interior décor, second century BCE. Top: axonometric reconstruction of House 53. Bottom: stuccoed Ionic pilaster and painted plaster wall decoration.

First Marisa, the largest city in Idumea. By the middle of the second century BCE the ancient tel is the acropolis of a large city, with blocks of houses covering the lower slopes and beyond. From these houses as well as from huge underground chambers beneath and around them, archaeologists have recovered literally thousands of objects that allow a detailed view of people's physical surroundings.

I adopt the point of view of a Judean invited into a home in Marisa. A narrow entrance off the street leads to a sheltered interior courtyard. Once

inside he is struck by interior adornment – painted walls and Greek-style columns affixed to the walls (fig. 6). When invited to sit down for a meal, he notices many things. First, in one corner, an array of foreign wine jars; from the later second century BCE alone there have been recovered at Marisa stamped handles and whole jars from Rhodes, Kos, and Knidos in the Aegean, Pamphylia in Anatolia, Brindisi in the Adriatic Sea, and North Africa.[14] He may drink that wine from a bowl of painted faience or clear glass or even from a rhyton decorated with the head of a horse or the Greek goddess Athena (fig. 7, top).[15] Turning to the table, he may

Figure 7. Marisa, tablewares, second century BCE. Top left: faience bowl. Top right: terracotta rhyton with head of Athena. Bottom: imported terracotta lamps.

notice that the legs take the form of Ionic columns, just as in the courtyard décor. On that table he will find an assortment of decorated dishes, including special jars for mixing and pouring wine along with an array of black and red slipped plates, bowls, and cups.[16] Each table in the dim room is illuminated by small but elaborately detailed lamps (fig. 7, bottom).[17] His host might open conversation with an explanation of the origins of these

---

[14] Ariel/Finkielsztejn, "Amphora Stamps". See also summary comments in Kloner, "Maresha".
[15] T. Levine, "Pottery", 124–6; Jackson-Tal, "Preliminary Survey"; Erlich/Kloner, *Terracotta Figurines*, 73–7.
[16] T. Levine, "Pottery", 74–92, 98–100, 106–8, 131, 134.
[17] T. Levine, "Pottery", 115–21.

various items, a wide arc from Ephesus to Rhodes, Antioch to Cyprus to Tyre, Alexandria to Carthage, and even as far west as Campania in the Italian peninsula.

On a shelf in the corner our Judean visitor's eye would surely be caught by colorfully painted molded vessels and figurines. Among the Greek heroes and gods found at Marisa are Herakles, the Dioskouri, Aphrodite, Athena, Artemis, anonymous musicians, dancers, and water-bearers, Herms and gorgons, and even theatre masks. This last might surprise since no built theatre has yet been found here, but in fact terracottas evoking Greek plays are common at sites from the Black Sea and central Anatolia through the southern Levant – in other words at places on the peripheries of Hellenistic society, where their presence likely refects peoples' desire to display cultural literacy and connections.[18]

Figure 8. Dor, imported decorated table ware, third century BCE.

A visitor to Dor would see the same general picture, though some of the specifics differ. Here too whole city

Figure 9. Dor, stone head of Hermes, second century BCE.

blocks have been uncovered and associated household goods retrieved. As at Marisa, Dor residents regularly enjoy wine from the Aegean islands of Rhodes, Knidos, and Thasos and eat off of black and red slipped dishes from eastern Mediterranean and Levantine producers (fig. 8).[19] Among the terracotta figurines are Herakles, Eros, Aphrodite, Cybele, and some well turned-out females.[20] Most impressive are two large stone sculptures of Greek subject and style – a winged Nike, goddess of victory, and a protective pillar topped with a head of Hermes (fig. 9).[21]

As at Dor and Marisa, so at Samaria: people live fully within the reach and ambit of the Hellenistic Mediterranean. They own terracotta and bronze figurines; identified subjects include Herakles, Eros, Aphrodite, Persephone, theatre masks, and

---

[18] Erlich/Kloner, *Terracotta Figurines*, especially p. 56 on theatre masks.

[19] Rosenthal-Heginbottom, "Pottery", 183–204 (amphoras) and 209–18, 222–33 (imported table wares); Stern, *Dor, Ruler of the Seas*, 226–52; idem, "Dor", 1700.

[20] Rosenthal-Heginbottom, "Teracottas"; Erlich, *Art*, 48–9.

[21] Stern, *Dor, Ruler of the Seas*, pl. VII.1; idem, "Dor", 1700; Erlich, *Art*, 22–3.

various offerants, dancers, and well-dressed ladies.[22] A dedicatory inscription to Isis and Serapis provides emphatic witness to a foreign cult.[23] As elsewhere, a variety of imported dishes and wine jars reveal that inhabitants partake of the Hellenistic good life. Again, the most compelling testimony are the several hundred Aegean wine jar fragments, because they can be precisely dated and sourced, and so demonstrate when and from where foreign goods arrived here: annually down to 110 BCE, from Sinope on the Black Sea; Thasos, Chios, and Paros in the northern Aegean; Kos, Knidos, and Rhodes in the southern Aegean; and Kourion on Cyprus.

A coin hoard dating to about 100 BCE discovered at the southern coastal city of Ashkelon complements and helps explain this dense array of Mediterranean goods.[24] The hoard includes one silver and 46 bronze coins. Most are small issues from cities in western and southern Asia Minor with the remainder from Paphos, Antioch, and Tyre. The coins were likely the ongoing collection of a member of merchantship's crew. Their origins reflect a route along the Asia Minor coast, then via Cyprus over and down along the eastern Mediterranean coast, with an eventual docking at Ashkelon.[25] The hoard's date of about 100 BCE is particularly striking, as it conforms so well with the pattern of Aegean wine jars. I have so far cited only the finds from Marisa, Dor, and Samaria – but as Gérald Finkielsztejn's studies at sites throughout Israel have shown, trade from Rhodes and the cities of western Asia Minor is widespread and even increases in the second half of the second century BCE.[26]

The monetary economy reflected in the array of coins collected by the Ashkelon merchantship crew member also exists in early Hasmonean Judea. By 100 BCE Hasmonean coins occur by the thousands. Indeed in Israel more coins of Alexander Jannaeus alone have been found than from all the Seleucid and Ptolemaic kings together with the coins of the newly independent Phoenician cities. At the single site of Gamla, archaeologists have found several hundred non-Hasmonean coins of various mints along with almost 4000 coins of John Hyrcanus and his sons Aristobolus and Alexander Jannaeus (fig. 10, left).[27] These coins are crucial testimony on two levels. First, their very existence reflects knowledge and acceptance of Mediterranean-wide cultural practice. This acceptance is further emphasized by the fact that Hasmonean coins display Greek as well as imperial Seleucid

---

[22] Reisner et al., *Excavations*, pl. 77; Crowfoot, "Teracottas", 83; Erlich, *Art*, 22, 34, 49.

[23] Lake, "Greco-Roman Inscriptions", 37 no. 13; Magness, "Cults".

[24] Gitler/Kahanov, "Late Hellenistic Coin Hoard".

[25] Gitler/Kahanov, "Late Hellenistic Coin Hoard", 392.

[26] Finkielsztejn, *Chronologie*; see also a summary of this argument in Gitler/Kahanov, "Late Hellenistic Coin Hoard", 394.

[27] Syon, "Coins", 34–6.

symbols such as the anchor (fig. 10, right). Second, the sheer quantities in which the coins appear demonstrate that people have a ready means of exchange. Coins are available, and are used.

Figure 10. Left: coin of the Hasmonean king Alexander Jannaeus, with anchor on reverse. Right: clay sealing depicting anchor, from the archive room of the Seleucid-era imperial administrative building at Kedesh, in northern Israel.

Their means notwithstanding, physical remains from early Hasmonean Judea reflect a largely rural society whose members live in an emphatically and deliberately simplified mode, devoid of foreign material affectations, culturally insular, traditional and inwardly oriented. Meanwhile, people living in Idumea, along the coast, and at Samaria are intimately connected to the wider Mediterranean world and its dominant Hellenizing culture. Two quotes, by men who knew this time and place well, capture the contradiction. The first is by a Jew possibly from Egypt whom Josephus called Aristeas. He writes: "Palestine possesses also harbors, well-situated, which supply its needs, that at Ascalon and Joppa, and Gaza as well as Ptolemais, founded by the king" (Letter of Aristeas 115). In contrast is Josephus himself, who says: "Well, ours is not a maritime country; neither commerce nor the intercourse which it promotes with the outside world has any attractions for us" (Contra Apionem 1.60).

There is one exception to the Mediterranean cultural universe surrounding Judea: the temple-city on Mount Gerizim, just 10 km southeast of Samaria. Excavations here have uncovered a monumental sanctuary and well-built town covering about 400 dunams (fig. 11, top). A plethora of inscriptions and historical references identify the population as Samaritans, a sect who follow the Torah and consider themselves descendents of biblical Israel. The architectural remains are grand and impressive, while jewelery, other metal finds, and especially thousands of second century BCE coins reflect prosperity.[28] Among the inscriptions found within the sacred precinct

---

[28] Magen, *Mount Gerizim Excavations*, pls. 10–12 and pp. 210–12.

are many that carry Greek names and a number written in Greek.[29] These
provide a context for two Samaritan inscriptions found on the Aegean island of Delos, one of which dates to the later second or early first century
BCE. Nevertheless, notwithstanding the sanctuary's size, importance, and
foreign connections, Samaritan households contain only and exactly the
same basic forms of locally made vessels found in Judean homes (fig. 11,
bottom).[30] Samaritans and Judeans appear united in their deliberate disa-
vowal of Mediterranean goods and likely also the culture they represent – a
point that incidentally begs the question of the motives that led John Hyrcanus to besiege and destroy the city in 110 BCE.[31]

I now return to the two witnesses with whom I opened. Meleager's description of this time and place as "an Attic haunt" and a "single world" are
readily understandable.

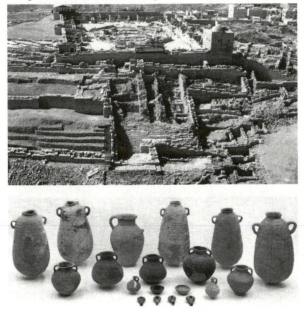

Mediterranean goods
coming largely from
the cities of the Aege-
an and Asia Minor
would obviously be
characterized as Greek,
and even though 350
years have passed
since the Parthenon
rose on the Acropolis
of Athens, that city
still stands as a cul-
tural exemplum. We
can also feel how this
time and place would
cause the author of 1
Maccabees to couch
his description of the
decree of Antiochus
IV as an imminent

*Figure 11. Mt. Gerizim. Top: view of sanctuary. Bottom:
pottery from temple and city, second century BCE.*

threat: "the king wrote to all his kingdom for all to become one people and
for each to abandon his own customs".[32]

---

[29] Magen, *Mount Gerizim Excavations*, 237–8.

[30] Magen, *Mount Gerizim Excavations*, 209–10.

[31] For recent discussion of this, see Magen, *Mount Gerizim Excavations*, 178; Magen, "Gerizim, Mount", 1742. Josephus recounts the event in Ant. 13.254–7 but his proffered date of 128
BCE has been countered by a wealth of datable remains extending to 110 BCE.

[32] For a somewhat different analysis of the impact of the dominant Mediterranean culture on
the authors of 1 and 2 Maccabees, see Mendels, "Memory", 44–53.

The intersection of chronology and aspect matters. In 142 BCE Simon captures the Akra and expells the Seleucid garrison. When he dies eight years later, his son John Hyrcanus takes over. This dynastic succession marks the transfomation of a small native rebellion into an independent polity. Five years later, in 129 BCE, the Seleucid king Antiochus VII Sidetes dies while on campaign in Parthia, an event that relieves the new ruler of his obligation to fund and supply troops on behalf of imperial Seleucid aims.[33]

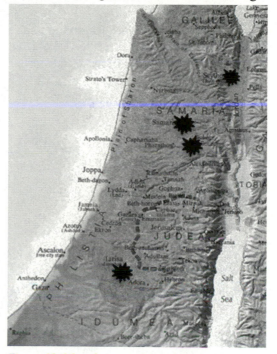

The manner in which Hyrcanus now chooses to deploy his resources is well reflected in the archaeological record: burned, damaged, and destroyed sites, large and small, throughout the region. These, in conjunction with a host of datable objects, allow us to

Figure 12. Map showing places destroyed by the Hasmonean king John Hyrcanus between 112 and 108/7 BCE. Dotted line indicates area controlled by Hasmoneans between 142 and 112 BCE.

chart his actions (fig. 12): in 112/11 BCE Marisa is destroyed and essentially abandoned, followed by Mt. Gerizim in 110, Samaria in 108 and Beth She'an-Scythopolis in 108/7.[34] By 103 BCE, when Hyrcanus' son Alexander Jannaeus takes the throne, the Hasmoneans control Idumea, Judea, Samaria, and Perea across the Jordan. This is the physical context of, and the political events leading up to, the moment of Meleager and the composition of 1 Maccabees.

---

[33] The best expression of the political opportunity of this moment remains that by the Roman historian Tacitus, who famously said: "The Macedonian power was now weak, while the Parthian had not yet reached its full strength, and, as the Romans were still far off, the Jews chose kings for themselves" (Histories 5.8).

[34] Kloner, "Maresha"; Avigad, "Samaria", 1302; Mazor, "Beth Shean", 1628.

Early First Century BCE:
Household Judaism Appears

This is also the immediate background to a new cultural practice, one that I
identified in a 2005 article as "household Judaism". The practice of household Judaism appears just now, in the early first century BCE, and continues to develop into the first century CE. Two physical aspects mark this
earliest stage. First, throughout the expanding Hasmonean kingdom, peo-

Figure 13. Storage jars from   *Figure 14. Cooking pots, first century BCE. Top*
Jerusalem (top) and Gamla   *left: from Jerusalem, Binyane Ha'Uma production*
(bottom), first century BCE.   *site. Top right: Beth Zur. Bottom: Gamla, Area B.*

ple's common household items are now manufactured with identical typological details such that they all look alike. For example, large storage jars,
whether found in a home in Judea or Gaulanitis, have a wide, flat band
around the mouth (fig. 13). Cooking pots now have a high, slightly canted
neck (fig. 14). The types of lamps and small bowls and saucers are now
made on identical models. Scientific analyses demonstrates that these basic
household goods are not products of a single manufacturing center. Instead
they are made of different clays, all local to the vicinities of the settlements
in which they are found. In other words, throughout the Hasmonean kingdom potters make and people use the same types of vessels.

Interestingly, while all these vessels remain undecorated and strictly util-
itarian, all are now made more carefully. In figure 15 are two water pitchers, one from early Has-
monean times (on the
left) and another from a
generation or so later
(on the right). The later
vessel has thinner walls,
a more carefully fin-
ished lip (better for pre-
venting dribbles), and a
shorter neck and higher
center of gravity, both
of which make it easier
to pour. Such attention

*Figure 15. Left: pitcher from Jerusalem, second
century BCE. Right: pitcher from Beth Zur, first
century BCE.*

to workmanship and detail characterizes all locally made household pottery
of the first century BCE.

Second, stepped plastered pools (*mikva'ot*) now appear – and in the same
settlements in Judea, the lower Galilee, and the Golan where the new array
of household goods show up (fig. 16).[35] *Mikva'ot* allow individuals to purify
themselves in connection with household-based events. Their sudden and
widespread appearance does not mean that the rite of immersion is new. But
it does mean that now across a broad spectrum of society people use *mikva'ot* regularly and so want them available. *Mikva'ot* are distinctive and
easily recognizable; both the installations and the practice they allow adver-
tise ethnic identity and proclaim cultural separation.[36]

To appreciate the message of both *mikva'ot* and the new vessels, one
must enter private household space – hence my term "household Judaism"
to describe this new phenomenon. Four points are worth noting. First, *this
is visible practice*, conscious, specific behavior carried out via material
objects. Second, *the specific objects are new*, first appearing in the early
years of the last century BCE but not before. Third, *the objects are basic
and domestic*; they represent the choices of private individuals. Finally,

---

[35] Netzer, *Palaces,* 39–43, 91, 102–5, 117–23, 160–2, 170–1; Reich, "Area A", 88–90; Magness, *Qumran,* 147–58; Reich, "Archaeological Evidence", 48–52; Gutmann, "Gamala", 463;
idem, *Gamla,* 118–22. Reich asserts that the earliest *mikva'ot* may be dated to the second part of
the second century BCE ("Synagogue", 289). His examples are the same as those I have listed
here. In fact, there is no positive evidence for so early a date from any of these locales; and further
all of these installations have a stratigraphic *terminus ante quem* of the later first century BCE. I
believe these *mikva'ot* most likely date from the time of Alexander Jannaeus.

[36] *Mikva'ot*, or at least installations that are physically identical to *mikva'ot*, first appear in
homes throughout Idumaea dating to the third and second centuries BCE. This is a fascinating
point, and one that deserves more detailed discussion.

none seem to be connected to or mandated by halakhah. In my original characterization I wrote that "household Judaism allowed Jews to infuse daily life with a religious sensibility, 'to advance the holy into the realm of the common' and thereby form a new cultural identity."[37]

Unlike the material lifestyle of early Hasmonean times, household Judaism is active: it depends on regular and widespread demand for and supply of specific goods as well as the construction of *mikva'ot*. Seth Schwartz has described Jewish identity in the last century BCE and first century CE as an "ideological complex" founded on "three pillars – the one God, the one Torah, and the one Temple".[38] I suggest that household Judaism comprises a fourth pillar, because it allows individuals to craft a discrete and distinct home and lifestyle. With its practice, Judeans live as one people – no matter where they actually reside within the Hasmonean kingdom. In effect, household Judaism is instrumental to the transformation from Judean to Jew.

Figure 16. Top: Mikve, Jerusalem Upper City, first century BCE. Bottom: Mikve, Gamla, Area B, first century BCE.

What is the impetus that leads to household Judaism? Might we see it as a reaction to Meleager's cosmopolitan world view? In 2005, I presented developments in chronological order but I did not study the era that led up to it. Instead, I

---

[37] Berlin, "Jewish Life", 425. The quote is from Milgrom, "Dynamics", 29. In a recent article Lee Levine asserts that "any discussion of Jewish identity in antiquity must recognize the fact that by the later Second Temple period Jews had developed a corporate identity with a significant degree of cultural and religious commonality as well as a degree of continuity from one generation to the next" ("Jewish Identities", 26–7). While I agree with this, I note that his discussion elides exactly where and how this common Judaism developed. That moment, with its attendant contingencies and experiments, is the crux of this study as well as Berlin "Identity", in which I study developments in the first century BCE in more detail.

[38] Schwartz, *Imperialism*, 49. See also L.I. Levine, "Jewish Identities", 26–7. David Goodblatt adds another layer with a thoughtful examination of differing nomenclature for Jews: Hebrew writers use "Israel"; non-Jews and Jews writing in Greek use "Judeans"; and official Hasmonean court writings refer to Judah ("Israelites", 82–6).

characterized household Judaism from the perspective of hindsight, looking back from a time several generations after it first developed. Here I present household Judaism as a development from an earlier material world and its political events. From this vantage point, it looks a bit different – less innocently empowering, more charged.[39]

In a recent study called "How Experiments End", Albert Baumgarten has examined the various modes by which the Romans related to and organized their rule over Jews in the land of Israel.[40] He argues for an historical understanding in which we acknowledge that successive historical stages create new realities. He encourages explanations that avoid a "neat and clear account that fits our sense of how events should happen" in favor of the "messy story ... [that avoids] teleological determinism ..."[41]

The paradigm of contingent historical processes is a useful one for thinking about the beginning and subsequent development of household Judaism. After all, in the early first century BCE, Jews find themselves in a new political world. Around them some foreign powers are receding while others act as agents furthering self-realization. This is a point of decision, a chance to choose a course. What is chosen depends on many factors: a leader's vision and authority; the attitudes and actions of surrounding peoples; but most significantly the group's sense of themselves, their proper place in the world and what they are owed. What do Jews choose now, and why?

At this point we are on the edge of knowing, balanced between evidence and the conclusions we draw from it. We need all of that evidence – both written and material, the notes of the score and the instruments of the orchestra – to understand this specific historical and cultural moment. For both written and material remains are products of and reactions to this time, a time when people choose to make their homes and possessions distinct, to preserve and edit older texts, and also to write new ones, new stories that show us how they understand their history and their destiny.[42]

And so the author of 1 Maccabees writes his story. He evokes the book of Joshua in order to recount the story of Judah Maccabee – only now, instead of territory, the children of Israel fight for a way of life. Our author

---

[39] I am indebted to an insight of Pierre Bourdieu (*Outline*, 164), as excerpted by Baumgarten ("Experiments", 161): "every established order tends to produce (to very different degrees and with very different means) the naturalization of its own arbitrariness".

[40] Baumgarten, "Experiments". Baumgarten credits his approach to Galison (*How Experiments End*) and the seminal study of Kuhn, *Structure*.

[41] Baumgarten, "Experiments", 160–1.

[42] Israel Finkelstein ("Jerusalem"; "Archaeology"; "Territorial Extent") has recently written a series of articles in which he argues strongly for a Hasmonean compositional date for certain sections of Nehemiah, specifically those that describe the size of Jerusalem and Yehud. Many aspects of his argument dovetail with points that I explore here.

takes an old theme and he composes a new score. When we study the material remains that his listeners leave behind we can almost hear them playing along.

References

Amiran, R./Eitan, A., "Excavations in the Courtyard of the Citadel, Jerusalem, 1968–1969 (Preliminary Report)", *IEJ* 20 (1970) 9–17.

Ariel, D.T., *Excavations at the City of David 1978–1985 Directed by Yigal Shiloh*. Vol. 2: *Imported Stamped Amphora Handles, Coins, Worked Bone and Ivory, and Glass* (Qedem 30; Jerusalem: Hebrew University, 1990).

–, "Imported Greek Stamped Amphora Handles", in H. Geva (ed.), *Jewish Quarter Excavations in the Old City of Jerusalem Conducted by Nahman Avigad, 1969–1982*. Vol. 1: *Architecture and Stratigraphy: Areas A, W and X-2. Final Report* (Jerusalem: Israel Exploration Society, 2000) 267–82.

–, "The Coins from Qalandiya", in Y. Magen et al. (ed.), *The Land of Benjamin* (JSP 3; Jerusalem: Israel Antiquities Authority, 2004) 145–77.

Ariel, D.T./Finkielsztejn, G., "Amphora Stamps and Imported Amphoras", in A. Kloner (ed.), *Maresha Excavations Final Report*. Vol. 1: *Subterranean Complexes 21, 44, 70* (IAA Reports 17; Jerusalem: Israel Antiquities Authority, 2003) 137–51.

Avigad, N., "Samaria (City)", in E. Stern (ed.), *The New Encyclopedia of Archaeological Excavations in the Holy Land* (4 vol.; Jerusalem: Israel Exploration Society, 1993) 1300–10.

Baumgarten, A.I., "How Experiments End", in L.I. Levine and D.R. Schwartz (ed.), *Jewish Identities in Antiquity* (Texts and Studies in Ancient Judaism 130; Tübingen: Mohr Siebeck, 2009) 147–61.

Berlin, A.M., "Jewish Life Before the Revolt: the Archaeological Evidence", *JSJ* 36 (2005) 417–70.

–, "Identity Politics in Early Roman Galilee", in M. Popović (ed.), *The Jewish Revolt Against Rome: Interdisciplinary Perspectives* (JSJSup 154; Leiden: Brill, 2012) 69–106.

Bourdieu, P., *Outline of a Theory of Practice* (Cambridge: Cambridge University Press, 1977).

Christensen, A.P./Johansen, C.F., *Hama: fouilles et recherches, 1931–1938*. Vol. 3.2: *Les poteries hellenistiques et les terres sigillees orientales* (Copenhagen: National Museum of Denmark, 1971).

Clairmont, C., "Greek Pottery from the Near East I", *Berytus* 11 (1955) 85–139.

–, "Greek Pottery from the Near East II", *Berytus* 12 (1956) 1–34.

Crowfoot, J.W., "Greco-Roman Terracottas", in J.W. Crowfoot et al. (ed.), *The Objects from Samaria* (London: Palestine Exploration Fund, 1957) 83–4.

–, "Hellenistic Pottery, General List", in J.W. Crowfoot et al. (ed.), *The Objects from Samaria* (London: Palestine Exploration Fund, 1957) 235–72.

– et al., *Samaria-Sebaste*. Vol. 3: *The Objects* (London: Palestine Exploration Fund, 1957).

Edgar, C.C., *Catalogue general des antiquités égyptiennes du Musée du Caire: Zenon Papyri* (vol. 79; Cairo: Institut français d'archéologie orientale, 1925).

Erlich, A., *The Art of Hellenistic Palestine* (BAR International Series 2010; Oxford: Hadrian Books, 2009).

Erlich, A./Kloner, A., *Maresha Excavations Final Report*. Vol. 2: *Hellenistic Terracotta Figurines from the 1989–1996 Seasons* (IAA Reports 35; Jerusalem: Israel Antiquities Authority, 2008).

Finkelstein, I., "Archaeology and the List of Returnees in the Books of Ezra and Nehemiah", *PEQ* 140 (2008) 1–10.

–, "Jerusalem in the Persian (and Early Hellenistic) Period and the Wall of Nehemiah", *JSOT* 32 (2008) 501–20.

–, "The Territorial Extent and Demography of Yehud/Judea in the Persian and Early Hellenistic Periods", *RB* 117 (2010) 39–54.

Finkielsztejn, G., *Chronologie detaillée et revisée des eponyms rhodiens de 270 à 108 av. J.–C. environ, premier bilan* (BAR International Series 990; Oxford: Archaeopress, 2001).

Galison, P., *How Experiments End* (Chicago: University of Chicago Press, 1987).

Geva, H., "Hellenistic Pottery from Areas W and X-2", in idem (ed.), *Jewish Quarter Excavations in the Old City of Jerusalem*. Vol. 2: *The Finds from Areas A, W and X-2. Final Report* (Jerusalem: Israel Exploration Society, 2003) 113–75.

–, "Stratigraphy and Architecture", in idem (ed.), *Jewish Quarter Excavations in the Old City of Jerusalem*. Vol. 3: *Area E and Other Studies. Final Report* (Jerusalem: Israel Exploration Society, 2006) 1–78.

Geva, H./Hershkovitz, M., "Local Pottery of the Hellenistic and Early Roman Periods", in H. Geva (ed.), *Jewish Quarter Excavations in the Old City of Jerusalem*. Vol. 3: *Area E and Other Studies. Final Report* (Jerusalem: Israel Exploration Society, 2006) 91–143.

Geva, H./Rosenthal-Heginbottom, R., "Local Pottery from Area A", in H. Geva (ed.), *Jewish Quarter Excavations in the Old City of Jerusalem*. Vol. 2: *The Finds from Areas A, W and X-2. Final Report* (Jerusalem: Israel Exploration Society, 2003) 176–91.

Gitler, H./Kahanov, Y., "A Late Hellenistic Coin Hoard", *Coin Hoards* 9 (2002) 259–68.

Goodblatt, D., "'The Israelites who reside in Judah' (Judith 4:1): On the Conflicted Identities of the Hasmonean State", in L.I. Levine/D.R. Schwartz (ed.), *Jewish Identities in Antiquity* (TSAJ 130; Tübingen: Mohr Siebeck, 2009) 74–89.

Gow, A.S.F./Page, D.L. (ed.), *The Greek Anthology: Hellenistic Epigrams* (Cambridge: Cambridge University Press, 1965).

Gutmann, S., "Gamala", in E. Stern (ed.), *The New Encyclopedia of Archaeological Excavations in the Holy Land* (Jerusalem: Israel Exploration Society, 1993) 459–63.

–, *Gamla: A City in Rebellion* (Jerusalem: Ministry of Defense, 1994) (Hebrew).

Hayes, J.W., "Hellenistic to Byzantine Fine Wares and Derivatives in the Jerusalem Corpus", in A.D. Tushingham (ed.), *Excavations in Jerusalem 1961–1967* (vol. 1; Toronto: Royal Ontario Museum, 1985) 181–96.

–, *Paphos 3: The Hellenistic and Roman Pottery* (Nicosia: Department of Antiquities of Cyprus, 1991).

Jackson-Tal, R., "A preliminary survey of the Late Hellenistic glass from Maresha (Marisa), Israel", in *Annales du 16ᵉ Congres de l'Association Internationale pour l'Histore du Verre* (Nottingham: AIHV, 2005) 49–53.

Jones, F.F., "The Pottery", in H. Goldman (ed.), *Excavations at Gözlü Kule, Tarsus*. Vol. 1: *The Hellenistic and Roman Periods* (Princeton: Princeton University Press, 1950) 149–296.

Kenrick, P.M., *Excavations at Sidi Khrebish Benghazi (Berenice)*. Vol. 3.1: *The Fine Pottery* (Supplements to Libya Antiqua 5, Tripoli: 1985).

Kloner, A., "Maresha (Marisa)", in E. Stern (ed.), *The New Encyclopedia of Archaeological Excavations in the Holy Land*. Vol. 5: *Supplementary Volume* (Jerusalem: Israel Exploration Society, 2008) 1918–25.

Kuhn, T., *The Structure of Scientific Revolutions* (Chicago: University of Chicago Press, ²1970).

Lake, S., "Greco-Roman Inscriptions", in J.W. Crowfoot et al., *The Objects from Samaria* (London: Palestine Exploration Fund, 1957) 35–42.

Levine, L.I., *Jerusalem: Portrait of the City in the Second Temple Period (538 B.C.E. – 70 C.E.)* (Philadelphia: Jewish Publication Society, 2002).

–, "Jewish Identities in Antiquity: An Introductory Essay", in L.I. Levine/ D.R. Schwartz (ed.), *Jewish Identities in Antiquity* (TSAJ 130; Tübingen: Mohr Siebeck, 2009) 12–40.

Levine, T., "Pottery and Small Finds from Subterranean Complexes 21 and 70, Pottery and Small Finds from Subterranean Complex 44", in A. Kloner (ed.), *Maresha Excavations Final Report*. Vol. 1: *Subterranean Complexes 21, 44, 70* (IAA Reports 17; Jerusalem: Israel Antiquities Authority, 2003) 73–136.

174 Andrea M. Berlin

Lipschits, O., et al., "Palace and Village, Paradise and Oblivion: Unraveling the Riddles of Ramat Rahel", *Near Eastern Archaeology* 74 (2011) 2–49.

Magen, Y., "Qalandiyeh", in E. Stern (ed.), *The New Encyclopedia of Archaeological Excavations in the Holy Land* (4 vol.; Jerusalem: Israel Exploration Society, 1993) 1197–200.

–, "Qalandiya – A Second Temple-period Viticulture and Wine-manufacturing Agricultural Settlement", in Y. Magen et al. (ed.), *The Land of Benjamin* (JSP 3; Jerusalem: Israel Antiquities Authority, 2004) 29–144.

–, "The Land of Benjamin in the Second Temple Period", in Y. Magen et al. (ed.), *The Land of Benjamin* (JSP 3; Jerusalem: Israel Antiquities Authority, 2004) 1–28.

–, "Gerizim, Mount", in E. Stern (ed.), *The New Encyclopedia of Archaeological Excavations in the Holy Land*. Vol. 5: *Supplementary Volume* (Jerusalem: Israel Exploration Society, 2008) 1742–8.

–, *Mount Gerizim Excavations*. Vol. 2: *A Temple City* (Jerusalem: Israel Antiquities Authority, 2008).

Magness, J., "The Cults of Isis and Kore at Samaria-Sebaste in the Hellenistic and Roman Periods", *Harvard Theological Review* 94.2 (2001) 157–77.

–, *The Archaeology of Qumran and the Dead Sea Scrolls* (Grand Rapids: Eerdmans, 2002).

Mazor, G., "Beth-Shean. The Hellenistic to Early Islamic Periods: The Israel Antiquities Authority Excavations", in E. Stern (ed.), *The New Encyclopedia of Archaeological Excavations in the Holy Land*. Vol. 5: *Supplementary Volume* (Jerusalem: Israel Exploration Society, 2008) 1623–36.

Mendels, D., "Memory and Memories: The Attitude of 1–2 Maccabees toward Hellenization and Hellenism", in L.I. Levine/D.R. Schwartz (ed.), *Jewish Identities in Antiquity* (TSAJ 130; Tübingen, Mohr Siebeck, 2009) 41–54.

Milgrom, J., "The Dynamics of Purity in the Priestly System", in M.J.H.M. Poorthuis/J. Schwartz (ed.), *Purity and Holiness. The Heritage of Leviticus* (Leiden: Brill, 2000) 29–32.

Netzer, E., *Hasmonean and Herodian Palaces at Jericho. Final Reports of the 1973 – 1987 Excavations* (Jerusalem: Israel Exploration Society, 2001).

Reich, R., "Archaeological Evidence of the Jewish Population at Hasmonean Gezer", *IEJ* 31 (1981) 48–52.

–, "The Synagogue and the *Miqweh* in Eretz-Israel in the Second-Temple, Mishnaic, and Talmudic Periods" in D. Urman/P.V.M. Flesher (ed.), *Ancient Synagogues. Historical Analysis and Archaeological Discovery* (vol. 1; Leiden: Brill, 1995).

–, "Area A – Stratigraphy and Architecture. Part IIc. Hellenistic to Medieval Strata 6 – 1", in H. Geva (ed.), *Jewish Quarter Excavations in the Old City of Jerusalem conducted by Nahman Avigad, 1969–1982*. Vol. 1: *Architecture and Stratigraphy. Areas A, W, and X-2. Final Report* (Jerusalem: Israel Exploration Society, 2000) 83–110.

Reisner, G.A. et al., *Harvard Excavations at Samaria, 1908–1910* (Cambridge: Harvard University Press, 1924).

Rosenthal-Heginbottom, R., "Imported Hellenistic and Roman Pottery", in E. Stern (ed.), *Excavations at Dor, Final Report*. Vol. 1B: *Areas A and C: The Finds* (Qedem Reports 2; Jerusalem: Hebrew University, 1995) 183–288.

–, "Terracottas from the Hellenistic Period", in E. Stern (ed.), *Excavations at Dor, Final Report*. Volume 1B: *Areas A and C: The Finds* (Qedem Reports 2; Jerusalem: Hebrew University, 1995) 455–6.

–, "Hellenistic and Early Roman Fine Ware and Lamps from Area A", in H. Geva (ed.), *Jewish Quarter Excavations in the Old City of Jerusalem*. Vol. 2: *The Finds from Areas A, W and X-2. Final Report* (Jerusalem: Israel Exploration Society, 2003) 192–223.

–, "Late Hellenistic and Early Roman Lamps and Fine Ware", in H. Geva (ed.), *Jewish Quarter Excavations in the Old City of Jerusalem*. Vol. 3: *Area E and Other Studies. Final Report* (Jerusalem: Israel Exploration Society, 2006) 144–67.

Schwartz, S., *Imperialism and Jewish Society 200 B.C.E. to 640 C.E.* (Princeton: Princeton University Press, 2001).

Stern, E., *Dor, Ruler of the Seas* (Jerusalem: Israel Exploration Society, 2000).

–, "Dor", in idem (ed.), *The New Encyclopedia of Archaeological Excavations in the Holy Land.* Vol. 5: *Supplementary Volume* (Jerusalem: Israel Exploration Society, 2008) 1695–703.

Syon, D., "The Coins from Gamla – Interim Report", *Israel Numismatic Journal* 12 (1992–3) 34–55.

Tal, O., "Hellenism in Transition from Empire to Kingdom: Changes in the Material Culture of Hellenistic Palestine", in L.I. Levine/D.R. Schwartz (ed.), *Jewish Identities in Antiquity* (TSAJ 130; Tübingen: Mohr Siebeck, 2009) 55–73.

Thalmann, J.P., "Tell 'Arqa (Liban nord) champagne I-III (1972–1974)", *Syria* 55 (1978) 1–153.

Thompson, H.A., "Two Centuries of Hellenistic Pottery", *Hesperia* 3 (1934) 311–480.

Tushingham, A.D., *Excavations in Jerusalem 1961–1967* (vol. 1; Toronto: Royal Ontario Museum, 1985).

Waagé, F.O., "Hellenistic and Roman Tableware of North Syria", in idem, *Antioch-on-the-Orontes.* Vol. 4.1: *Ceramics and Islamic Coins* (Princeton: Princeton University Press, 1948) 1–60.

Images

Figure 1. Used by permission of Carta, Jerusalem.
Figure 2. Photo courtesy of the Israel Exploration Society.
Figure 3. Maps courtesy of Yitzik Magen and the Israel Exploration Society.
Figure 4. Images courtesy of the Institute of Archaeology, Hebrew University.
Figure 5. Map courtesy of Oxford University Press.
Figure 6. Both photos courtesy of the Israel Exploration Society.
Figure 7. Images courtesy of the Israel Antiquities Authority.
Figure 8. Photo courtesy of Ephraim Stern and the Israel Exploration Society.
Figure 9. Photo courtesy of Ephraim Stern and the Israel Exploration Society.
Figure 10. Left photos (coin) courtesy of the Israel Exploration Authority.
           Right photo (sealing): Andrea Berlin and Sharon Herbert, Tel Kedesh Excavations.
Figure 11. Photos courtesy of Yitzik Magen and the Israel Exploration Society.
Figure 12. Map courtesy of Oxford University Press.
Figure 13. Top photo courtesy of the Israel Exploration Society.
           Bottom photo courtesy of the Israel Antiquities Authority.
Figure 14. Top left photo courtesy of the Journal of Roman Archaeology.
           Top right photo courtesy of the American Schools of Oriental Research.
           Bottom photo courtesy of the Israel Antiquities Authority.
Figure 15. Left photo courtesy of the Israel Exploration Society.
           Right photo courtesy of the American Schools of Oriental Research.
Figure 16. Top photo courtesy of the Israel Exploration Society.
           Bottom photo courtesy of Danny Syon and the Israel Antiquities Authority.

Doron Mendels

The Hebrew University of Jerusalem

Honor and Humiliation as a Factor in Hasmonean Politics according to the Narrator of 1 Maccabees[1]

The theme of *honor-humiliation* and *revenge* is one of those horizontal themes that appear in the Book of 1 Maccabees, mainly as an expression of the views of the book's narrator. The terms used by the translator of 1 Maccabees for depicting honor and revenge, such as *doxa*, *timē* and *ekdikēsis*, which also appear elsewhere in the Septuagint (i.e. in other biblical books) should be examined ad loc. and ad rem. They should be examined in the context of the particular book in which they appear. Certain terms in the Septuagint change their meaning from book to book, and this should be taken into account in particular when dealing with highly charged terms (as we have seen with the terms *domata* and *dora* which in 1 Maccabees clearly mean gifts but in the biblical corpus sometimes also mean bribery). Obviously, both the narrator and the translator made use of terms and phrases they found in the Old Testament but fitted them into the new context of the Book of 1 Maccabees. What matters for our purposes is not the use of one verse or another or a certain term but the Book of 1 Maccabees as a new creation, which differs considerably from any given book of the Old Testament.[2] Hence in this chapter we will deal with honor and its etiquette as they are presented by the narrator of 1 Maccabees, without comparing it, for instance, with 2 Maccabees.[3] Some preliminary comments would seem to be in order.

---

[1] See also Mendels, "Rejection". I wish to thank Christian Arlt in particular for his kind and efficient help during my stay at the Freie Universität Berlin as Mercator Professor (in the Seminar for Catholic Theology) during the spring semester of 2011. I extend my gratitude to Professor Rainer Kampling who was my host during this time and made my stay in Berlin pleasant and fruitful. This article is only one of several that I managed to work on during this wonderful time.

[2] This is contrary to the many scholars who wish to see the Book of 1 Maccabees as an imitation of other Old Testament books such as Joshua and Judges. There are no doubt influences, ideological as well as literary, but the book on the whole is an independent literary entity, and it seems that its narrator did not suffer overmuch from an "anxiety of influence" syndrome.

[3] The topic of honor and humiliation in the book of 2 Maccabees and Josephus' narratives are irrelevant for a discussion focusing on the presentation and views of the *narrator* of 1 Maccabees. Yet a detailed comparison will be undertaken by me in my commentary on 1 Maccabees, forthcoming in Hermeneia. Needless to say, I strongly believe in the unity of 1 Maccabees.

First and foremost, it is common knowledge that although systems of honor share some common ground, they *differ* from one society to another and should be distinguished from notions of honor found in the family of nations. Much of what we find in modern research is concerned with early modern history and the modern world; it should not be applied automatically to ancient societies. Thus I am not going to discuss here the sociological and anthropological history of honor but refer the reader to such books as those by Stewart, O'Neill and Bowman.[4] Neither am I planning to write here or anywhere else a comprehensive study on honor and shame in the Hellenistic period or in biblical and extra-biblical literature. Rather, I will focus on and go over the evidence narrated in the Book of 1 Maccabees in order to find out if and in what instances honor and humiliation played a role according to our narrator in the interactions of the Hasmoneans with other rulers in the Hellenistic Near East. Second, when dealing with societies that have systems of honor, one should clarify what *components* (or "assorted traits" according to O'Neill) of honor are embedded in these particular societies. In the case under survey here it will be difficult to do so in a consistent manner, since relationships between Hellenistic rulers suffer as it were from a lack of firm and enduring systems of honor. We shall see that the "operation" of honor comes to the fore mostly in etiquette (i.e. it is an external phenomenon). Third, by contrast, the Hasmonean rulers were imbued with a code of honor, probably as a result of their culture, where the sense of honor was very strong (as exemplified for instance in the Book of Ben Sira). Fourth, we should take into consideration that when the term "honor" is mentioned explicitly by the narrator of 1 Maccabees, e.g. X is honorable, or Y was received honorably by Z who is also honorable, it does not necessarily specify an objective condition (of being honorable), but an *interpretation* of the narrator (to be called here "descriptive honor"). He, no doubt, is writing about honor against the background of his own society. Hence when we study a case where the term is not mentioned (namely, when the narrator tells a story without the specific aim of saying something about honor), we can perhaps learn more about the reality. Fifth, the *rhetoric* used during encounters that involve honor and humiliation should be specified; some of the rhetoric probably reflects what the narrator thought about such encounters.

The narrative of the book concerning honor has two voices that are in dissonance with each other. On the one hand the narrator speaks constantly about the honor and esteem of the Jews in their own eyes, the eyes of their neighbors and his own (the narrator's). On the other, he depicts the Hellenistic rulers as the ones who disregard any firm systematic code or rules of

---

[4] See for instance Stewart, *Honor*; O'Neill, *Honor*; Bowman, *Honor*.

honor (because this code *as a well defined system* actually did not exist in reality). Frank Stewart, in his masterly book *Honor*, correctly claims that honor in the modern world is a *right*. According to him, such rights can be realized in vertical and horizontal systems of honor. The problem in Hellenistic international relations as reflected in the Book of 1 Maccabees (and elsewhere) is that although there are exhibitions of royal etiquette (e.g. honor and its rhetoric), decisions on the ground about crucial matters are not affected by rules of honor, and are almost solely based on power and personal interest. But the basic (primitive) feelings of humiliation and self-esteem (honor) are very strong and can sometimes become serious incentives for political action. Most of the Hellenistic rulers of the period under survey were megalomaniacs and viewed others as rivals or potential foes and hence their inferiors (pacts were anyhow breached all the time). There was no orderly and steady system of honor either horizontal or vertical, among the political rivals of the Hellenistic Near East.[5] However, among allies there was a vague kind of vertical system; a pinch of a "sense of honor" existed, but it usually did not last for long in relationships. When Alexander Balas recognizes that Ptolemy is powerful, he approaches him, and they make a pact in which the daughter of Ptolemy is wed to Alexander with great pomp. But this pact is quite quickly breached because both sides realize that there is another power elsewhere to be reckoned with and that they can gain more by acting alone (chapter 10). Since hardly any relationships between Hellenistic rulers were based on trust, the sense of honor was usually limited to etiquette. In short, power and weakness and their exhibition on the ground became the rule of the game.[6] *Integrity*, as we moderns understand it, in the context of international relations did not exist in the political arsenal of Hellenistic rulers, except for being implicitly mentioned in theoretical speculations concerning kingship (the *peri basileias* texts). This latter picture, which emerges from the Book of 1 Maccabees and accords with other external evidence, stands in sharp contrast to what the Jews themselves understood by honor. The narrator shows clearly that the Jews had a strong sense of honor (at least he shows that he himself had such a sense). This strong sense (embedded in the Jews from their biblical heritage and expressed very well in many of their books) frequently resulted in misunderstandings with their neighbors. The reason for this is that the Jews actually did not internalize the latter's cynical or non-existent sense of honor, and that no built-in system of honor really prevailed among these rulers.

---

[5] For these terms in relation to individual honor see Stewart, *Honor*, 54–63.

[6] See Eckstein, *Mediterranean Anarchy*, for power politics in the Hellenistic world.

In discussing these elements we will come to the conclusion that our narrator believes that friction within Jewish society and with the outside world
happened sometimes as a result of differing concepts of honor that could
not be accommodated to each other. Some of the episodes narrated in the
book will become clearer when seen against this background.[7]

The clash within Jewish society at the outset of the conflict with the Seleucids – which is not the subject of this essay – is an interesting case for
people who are interested in the formation of two systems of honor within
the same society (inside the Jewish society one can speak more easily about
"systems"). In reality, it may be stated here that the religious rift between
the so-called Hellenists and the "orthodox" Jews was not all that wide. But
they had a struggle that later in the century, in the early Hasmonean period,
led to bloodshed. The main issue at stake was the relationship with the
Seleucids, as I have shown in my *Rise and Fall of Jewish Nationalism*
(1992), and the competition over political issues (such as competition over
the High Priesthood). This resulted in a situation in which the pro-Seleucid
party adopted some of the methods of the Hellenistic empire, and the more
nationalistic (orthodox) group created a system of honor that exacerbated
the rift with the Seleucids. This becomes quite obvious during the wars with
the latter, since much that is done by the fighting Jews is beyond the "ethics" of war, not just in order to gain a victory on the battlefield but also to
insult the enemy. The abuse of honor is one of the reasons that much of the
war becomes a matter of revenge and humiliation (on both sides). To give
an example: to cut off the head and right hand of a Seleucid general and
even give the act "publicity" by carrying it out in a public place was sym-
bolically shameful for the Seleucids; thus the revenge that followed was
much more severe than might have been expected. Since the Seleucids did
not consider the Land of Israel high up on their scale of world priorities,
many of the battles were quite futile.[8] Thus much of what happened is *perceived* by the narrator as humiliation and its revenge. Let us start with the
more obvious aspects: When and why does our narrator use terms that denote honor and glory. The second part will discuss our own interpretation of
some examples.

---

[7] Such as the refusal of the people of Ephron to let Judah through (1 Macc 5:45–52), an incident that will be addressed later in the article. Even some of the so-called concessions granted by
Hellenistic rulers may have appeared as offensive to the Jews. Concessions and grants of his own
land and own offices could be seen as quite offensive by the recipient.

[8] See my *Memory*, 89–102.

The Narrator's View of Honor and Esteem

According to Hatch and Redpath, 1 Maccabees as against 2 Maccabees uses the terms *doxa* and *doxazein* 37 times (11 times in 2 Maccabees); *timē* is used 3 times in each book, and *endoxos* in its different forms appears 12 times. The term does not denote an objective trait but rather the state of mind of either the bearer (the person or institution that promotes the idea that he/she/it is highly esteemed) or a narrator who attributes it to a person or institution (the distinction between "external" and "internal" honor).[9] In our case the latter is the more frequent: *doxa* and *doxazein* are two key terms in the Book of 1 Maccabees. Once it is used in chapter 1 it has an uninterrupted resonance until it is mentioned again, and so on. The reader is aware of its presence (or "hears" its particular tone, to use a musical metaphor) throughout the book (like the terms "evil" and "arrogance"). It is thus no surprise to find that whereas these terms are used sporadically throughout the book they are mostly used when the narrator reaches chapter 14 (Simeon's regime), the climax, where they are used 13 times (out of 37 in the whole book). The term *doxa*, a typical narratorial term, becomes the main theme in chapter 14 where it turns into a vertical theme having been until then as it were a horizontal one. In which contexts of his narrative does our narrator use this term and what does it mean? First and foremost it is used as a contrast to the dishonor and disgrace that Israel underwent, according to the narrator, at the beginning of the book (1:40; also 2:9, 12). From then on it is embedded in our narrative memory. This theme of honor/glory and esteem as against disgrace and humiliation becomes part of the historical undercurrent and has a hermeneutical presence and dynamic until chapter 14 and beyond (as well as in the anticlimax of the book, chapters 15–16). In fact, the agenda is set by our narrator at the outset of the book in a poetic section, saying that Israel was glorious in the past, and he actually alludes to Israel's desired liberation from its foe which will restore its glory and honor.[10] The latter terms in fact mean that honor and esteem are relative concepts that can be judged against the glory and esteem of Israel's past (but also against its present neighbors). These expressions are not mere clichés used by the narrator;[11] they can be seen as a powerful statement (reminiscent of statements in Ben Sira). Henceforward the narrator moves step by step in his undercurrent of history until he reaches the ultimate

---

[9] Stewart, *Honor*, 9–29.

[10] For poetry in the book see Neuhaus, *Studien*.

[11] For instance Abel, *Livres*, 47, and Rappaport, *Commentary*, 27, 56–8, 60, 136, mention the terms denoting honor but do not have any systematic discussion on the subject.

"glory" (i.e. esteem), towards which he is striving throughout the whole book (i.e. the regime of Simeon and his covenant with Israel).

The book starts with the tale of the officers of the Seleucid king who offer Mattathias the chance to emerge from "distress" by taking gifts from the king – that is, by being "honored" by him (2:18). Mattathias refused as we saw in my gift article. To be honored by the king and yet reject this kind of honor was an abrasive move on the part of the Jews and caused a great deal of tension between Jews and Seleucids. The Jews according to this "old school" leader possess their own glory in the world. They do not need to be "honored" by gentiles. This concept will change later in the narrative. Be that as it may, at the end of the chapter, it is Mattathias who on his deathbed says that "great honor" (esteem) and "eternal good name" (renown) are inherent in the Jewish nation (2:51). It is not accidental that he attributes these traits not to one biblical ancestor or another (as he does with other traits) but collectively to "our fathers" ("which they performed in their generations"). The narrator begins the speech of Mattathias with the topic of glory and ends with this same topic connecting the glory to God and the belief in him among the nations. The source of glory is God ("through it you will be glorified", 2:62, 64). Our "mini" undercurrent of history continues in chapter 3, where Judah (even before he has done any of his great deeds) is praised in a poem inter alia mentioning that he "spread his people's glory far and wide" (3:3). This idea comes as a counterweight to the one mentioned a little further on in the chapter, where the narrator says that Seron the Seleucid general, before going to war in Judea says: "I will make a name for myself and be renowned in the kingdom" (v. 14). Glory and honor lurk constantly under the surface of the "real" history and give us some clue as to what the different sides to the conflict – or rather their narrator – were thinking about the motivations behind this struggle. The same theme of glory and good name will be mentioned again in a comment of the narrator apropos of the return of Judah and his brother Simeon for the rescue endeavor in the Bashan and the Galilee (respectively), and the suppression of the revolt of Joseph and Azariah. The narrator says in 5:63–64: "This man Judah and his brothers were highly esteemed in all Israel and among all the heathen wherever their name was mentioned and people gathered around them to extol them." This is a fulfillment as it were of what was said at the beginning of Judah's biography, and here his brothers are added. The narrator shows, as against the more declaratory statements about glory and good name up to now, that this honor or esteem had the approval of all Israel, and even of the heathen, whenever their name was mentioned. This so-called descriptive honor is important for our case. Glory and good name according to the concept of our narrator should be spread out in the world (not only among Jews but also among gentiles; this motif is found quite frequently in sections of the Bible such as the Psalter).[12] It even seems that glory and esteem of the Hasmonean leaders come instead of the acknowledgment of their God by the world. The Hasmonean brothers are extolled by all (Jews and pagans). It is quite clear that this is the narrator's view, since it is difficult to think that at the very beginning of their struggle the Maccabees wished to have any contact with the heathens (expressed by Mattathias' speech that honor and good name were inherent in the Jews themselves). Thus it is a comment of the narrator (or of the author of the poem that he chose for this place in the narrative) as a result of his hermeneutical approach. But let us go further with this survey. Chapters 4–8 of 1 Maccabees include only this one reference to honor and good name. The next occurrence is in 9:10, where we find the last words of Judah before he dies in battle. When his army wishes (justifiably) to avoid a clash with the Seleucid army, Judah says: "Far be it from me that I should do such a thing as to flee from them. If our time has come, let us die bravely for our brothers, and not leave an accusation against our honor." Throughout the chapters telling the story of Judah, we realize how he builds up his own glory. Dying in a futile war because the time has come (actually leaving the outcome to fate) shows what honor meant in Hasmonean Jewish circles. In this case Judah dies for the sake of honor, actually the most *elevated realization* of honor (certainly also in other cultures as has been shown by Stewart).[13] (The reader should note that the term is avoided by the narrator when he describes the Roman Empire in chapter 8.) Chapter 10 brings us back to a more practical meaning of *doxa*. The swift *transition*, from honor through the violent (almost suicidal) death of Judah to the ceremonial and somewhat more peaceful games of honor of his brother Jonathan, is one of the familiar literary strategies on which the narrative is based (the strategy of sharp twists and oppositions).[14]

In chapter 10 the narrator actually expresses the big change that the Hasmoneans underwent in their relationship with the Hellenistic powers (as I showed in the case of gift giving). The upgrading of the Hasmonean brothers within their Hellenistic environment is expressed by the use here of the word "honor" in a context of etiquette. Our narrator chose to use this expression in the context of the famous meeting between Alexander Balas and Ptolemy, the king of Egypt, when the latter weds his daughter Cleopat-

---

[12] Goldstein, *1 Maccabees*, presents many parallels from the Bible. See also recently Berthelot, "Biblical Conquest", and Hieke, "Role of Scripture". In spite of verbal and some ideological influences on the composition, the novelty of its wholeness is what matters. Beethoven in his piano sonatas here and there used motifs taken from the piano sonatas of Haydn, but this does not make the former an epigone of the latter (who was for a while his teacher).

[13] See Stewart, *Honor*, 34–5, 48.

[14] See my forthcoming commentary in Hermeneia (1 Maccabees).

ra to the former. The celebration is done *en doxē megalē* ("with great honor" or even better, "with great pomp", 10:58). Two verses later (10:60) it is Jonathan who goes to meet the two kings *meta doxēs* (this use, like the former reference, refers to aspects of ceremony that exemplify honor) and he "found favor in their sight". Here follows a relatively detailed description what it meant "to honor" someone in the Hellenistic court (probably a formal etiquette). In spite of some opposition against it (by Jewish opponents), Jonathan was clothed in purple (after being divested of his own garments by order of the king), and the king "made him sit beside him, and said to his officers, 'Go forth with him into the middle of the city. Proclaim that no one is to appeal against him for any reason. Let no one trouble him for any cause'." When those who were agitating against him saw the honor conferred on him, as the herald proclaimed, and saw him clothed in purple, they all fled. Thus the king showed him honor, placed him among his best friends and made him the general and civil governor of a province. Here the meaning of honor is twofold: ceremonial honor and declaratory honor, i.e. granting Jonathan some kind of immunity against verbal abuse or injury. Jonathan is honored by the king, but in his presence in this particular ritual he acknowledges the esteem and honor he feels for this king. Be that as it may, Jonathan returned to Jerusalem in peace (*eirēnē*) and good cheer (a term quite often used jointly with honor). This is in fact the narrative of a ritual granting of honor (a familiar ritual to be found also in the Book of Esther – the proclamation of Haman, where he is humiliated, verse 6:11). Physical *closeness* (or *nearness*) of the lower magistrate to a higher one is accentuated here.

Being as it were equipped with the honor granted by a Hellenistic king, Jonathan received respect (or honor, the terms used are again *doxē megalē*) from the people of Ashkelon who *out of fear* honored him: "they came forth to meet him with great acclaim" (10:86), and as a consequence "when King Alexander heard the news, he honored Jonathan still more" (10:88). The latter instance shows clearly the close link between power and respect. Here, according to our narrator, fear of his power brought about respect. Chapter 10 is subjected inter alia to notions of gifts and honor in Hellenistic courts and their etiquette. Until now we have seen that honor according to our narrator is associated with the following: reputation, good name (esteem), approved success in enterprises, courageous death, formal ceremonies such as state weddings and other rituals (etiquette), appointments by a king, fear that entails respect, etc. Let me now continue with the survey of the narrator's views of *doxa* (*timē* used much less).

In chapter 11:6 we find two further ceremonies/rituals that our narrator explains as being expressions of *doxa*: "Jonathan met the king at Joppa in honor (*meta doxēs*). They greeted each other and slept there. Jonathan accompanied the king as far as the river called Eleutherus." These gestures of etiquette show yet again the need for physical *closeness/nearness* in a hierarchical relationship between two rulers in the Hellenistic Near East (see Herod and Octavian, Josephus Ant. 15.218). If a *vertical* sort of honor *system* existed at all in Hellenistic courts, then it was a vague and non-settled system (between leaders; everyone thinking that he/she is the superior). In other words, since it was in any case an empty system, Hellenistic leaders frequently ignored it. Moreover, in a hierarchical system, the inferior has to respond positively to the superior when the latter asks for assistance. This we learn from 11:41–44. But from the continuation of the story we learn that although Jonathan sent three thousand men in response to the king's request, the king (Demetrius) was attacked by rioters in Antioch. Demetrius then asked again for Jonathan's help, and the latter helped him quell the riot. As a consequence "the Jews were held in *high esteem* before the king and before all the people of his kingdom" (11:51). Nevertheless the king proved false in all that he had promised; he became estranged from Jonathan and made no proper recompense for the favors done for him, but treated him *shamefully* (11:53). This is an interesting case for our study. It can be explained of course by a caprice on the part of the king. But this behavior is deeper than we have imagined so far. If we look closely at this affair against the background of the very basic feelings of humiliation and honor (as well as esteem) in the Hellenistic era, we can discover that what happened was that Jonathan, by going to help the king, twice demonstrated publicly the latter's *weakness* (once when the king sought his help because the army had deserted him and the other time to help him suppress a riot); he showed very openly how weak and vulnerable their king was. Our narrator stresses this fact: "When the inhabitants saw that the Jews controlled the city as they wished, their ardor weakened and they cried out to the king with supplication." In a way, the Jewish esteem by others ("external" honor mentioned above) could in this case be interpreted as a great humiliation for King Demetrius. Overly successful activity on the part of an inferior in an emerging vertical system of power (and honor) that requires acts of mutual honor can sometimes be disastrous.

The next reference on the part of the narrator is 12:12. This (probably fabricated) letter of Jonathan to the Spartans[15] mentions that the Jews "remembered the Spartans at every opportunity, incessantly on the festivals and on other appropriate days, in the sacrifices which we offer and in our prayers ... moreover we *rejoice* in your *esteem* (*tē doxē hymōn*)". Here we

---

[15] There exists a vast bibliography on this exchange of letters. See recently Bremmer, "Spartans and Jews", with some of the older literature. The masculine nature of Sparta may have attracted the Hasmoneans or rather their narrator (since the book deals only with men).

have yet another facet of *doxa*. The rhetoric of honoring another state or entity is here presented as part of a ritualistic relationship that has developed between two states (which in this case probably did not occur in reality). The Jews honor the Spartans by mentioning them in their prayers (this in itself seems unlikely), etc., and are "rejoicing" because of the *doxa* of the Spartans. This is not the first time that rejoicing for another's *doxa* is mentioned. Jonathan emphasized later in his letter that the Jews did not ask the Spartans for their help (because they rely on God), but I would go further, in line with what has just been said: Two states that believe in their self-esteem and honor (namely, think they are equals in the relationship) would be reluctant to ask for help if this is not needed urgently; it would put their esteem in jeopardy (because their weakness would be apparent to all). This is perhaps the reason that in the context of the treaty with Rome and in the description of Roman imperialism the word *doxa* was not mentioned. Let us move on to the climax of this whole work, chapter 14.[16]

Concerning the regime of Simeon, the narrator states that "the land of Judah was at peace during the entire life of Simeon. He sought the good of his nation, and his authority and reputation *pleased* them as long as he lived" (14:4). *Doxa* here has equal standing with other values and appears together with "pleased". Moreover, "among his many glories (*meta pasēs tēs doksēs autou*) was Joppa, which he took for a harbor" (14:5). In what follows, the hand of the narrator is again apparent, since we can find here a *summary* of most of the traits/values assigned during the narrative so far to the other Hasmonean brothers;[17] Simeon is presented as the epitome of most of the traits previously mentioned in the narrative of 1 Maccabees. Acquisition of the harbor has just been mentioned. Then, in verse 9, the youngsters are mentioned who "donned the glory and apparel of war"; and in verses 10, 15 we hear about Simeon's providing food for the cities and furnishing "them with means for defense, until his fame was proclaimed to the ends of the earth" and that he "glorified the sanctuary". Later the Spartans send to Simeon and say: "The ambassadors who were sent to our people told us about your fame [esteem] and honor, and we rejoiced at their coming" (again "rejoicing" associated with honor, v. 21); and in v. 23: "The people were pleased to receive the men honorably" (*endoxōs*). In the covenant between the people and Simeon the war for the Temple is mentioned (v. 29): "Simeon ... and his brothers endangered their lives, and withstood their nation's adversaries, so that their sanctuary and the Law might be upheld, thus bringing great glory to the nation." Finally, "when the people saw the

---

[16] See in general for this chapter commentaries by Dancy, Goldstein and Rappaport, ad loc., and van Henten, "Honorary Decree".

[17] For traits of honor, see O'Neill, *Honor*, 85–138.

trustworthiness of Simeon and the glory which he planned for his nation, they made him their leader and High Priest" (v. 35). And in verse 39 the great honor bestowed on Simeon by Demetrius is mentioned. All of this is an expression of a climax in the undercurrent history of the term "glory/honor," which has an independent existence linked here and there to the skeleton of facts. The one responsible for this concoction is none other than the narrator, since he summarizes here many of the notions about honor that he mentioned earlier (the so-called use of *descriptive honor*). In 15:9 it is Antiochus VII Sidetes who among other concessions says that he will greatly exalt Simeon, "your nation and the Temple, so that your glory [esteem] may be *manifest* throughout the world" (going back to former expressions of that nature in our text). The story of Antiochus VII at Dor is then adduced, a story that I discussed in the paper on gifts.

Since I have received some queries regarding this particular episode, I would like to clarify my intention there.[18] The order of events presented by the narrator is the following: Simeon comes to the aid of Tryphon in Dor and brings along soldiers and equipment as well as gold and silver as a gift (not meant as compensation for anything). Tryphon *rejects* the help of Simeon as well as the gifts he has brought. This in itself is a humiliating action on the part of the Seleucid king. Then Tryphon sends Athenobius to Simeon to present his own claims, saying inter alia that Simeon took Joppa and Gazara and territory in the land of Israel that belonged to Tryphon (15:28–31). He suggests that Simeon be given the option to compensate the latter with money (of course much more than the value of the original gifts; although the exact amount is not mentioned, it becomes clear from the text that it was much more). Athenobius is sent to the court of Simeon and is overwhelmed by the latter's wealth, and as a reaction Simeon utters his famous claim that the territory and cities that Tryphon is demanding are Jewish. When Athenobius returns to the king and tells him about his visit to Jerusalem, the king is angry. In other words, Simeon, when he comes to Tryphon's help at Dor, is thinking in terms of gifts (since according to him the land is anyhow Jewish and does not belong to the Seleucids), whereas Tryphon and Athenobius think of it as more than just a gift; they believe that Tryphon should have received either the territory or proper compensation. The subtext is quite clear: Simeon from the outset thinks in terms of gifting and seems sure that what he brought along as a gift was sufficient (since he had become accustomed to using gifts as an efficient diplomatic tool as used by Hellenistic rulers). Tryphon on the other hand is humiliated because Simeon failed to bring any substantial gift (since the gift he brought was undervalued by Tryphon and does not compare to what was

---

[18] Mendels, "Rejection", 254–5.

expected as compensation). We have here a very interesting case of a dialogue of the deaf.[19]

One more remark should be added about persons that are *endoxeis* in 1 Maccabees, a term that refers to the status of *people* (the illustrious retainers of the Macedonian king, 1:6). With an office comes "honor", as the Seleucid officer says to Mattathias: "You are a leader, a prominent (*endoxos*) and great man in this town" (2:17; in 2:8 Israel is compared in her distress to "a man without honor" [*adoxos*]). Lysias according to 3:32 is "a prominent man (*endoxon*) of royal lineage", as is Nicanor, one of the king's famous officers (*hena tōn archontōn autou tōn endoxōn*, 7:26); this term is used also in reference to a city, place or realm that is famous for its wealth (6:1 referring to Elymais, as in 5:32, 36 mentioned above). One can also be received with "honor" if considered an honorable person (*endoxos*), as the people of Ashkelon received Jonathan according to 11:60; and Onias received a Spartan envoy "honorably" because he was to be honored in the particular situation of the Jewish-Spartan pact (12:8). A reception "with honor" was apparently accompanied by etiquette: Tryphon received Jonathan "with honor, introducing him to all his friends, bestowing gifts upon him and briefing his friends and troops to obey him as they would himself" (12:43). This is an interesting case from our point of view: The intentions of Tryphon towards Jonathan were hostile, yet this did not deter him from showing honor and then capturing him treacherously. Etiquette here includes reception, introduction to other "friends" at the court and the bestowal of gifts. Here an additional grant has to be mentioned: The king orders his friends and troops to obey Jonathan as they would himself. In a former grant, as we have seen, the king grants Jonathan immunity from abuse and injury; here he elevates him to be his equal. This may be just ceremonial rhetoric, but it signifies the ritual of granting honor to an inferior ruler within a Hellenistic court. Also, the ambassadors of the Jews to Rome to renew the pact were received "honorably": "The people were pleased to receive the men honorably (*endoxos*)" (repeated in 14:40). These "definitions" of people as honorable in different situations are typical of our narrator and are expressions of his point of view. But it also shows that the concept of honor relating to people and things was known in the Hellenistic Near East, at least among the circles of our narrator. So far the discussion has been about esteem and honor as mentioned explicitly by the narrator. Let us now look briefly at some more complex examples: instances where honor is implied but the term is not mentioned; here we have to rely upon our *own interpretation* of the events.

---

[19] In 15:32 (and 36) the term *doxa* means the wealth of Simeon. In other societies as well, wealth is considered to be a reason for having honor; Stewart, *Honor*, 48–9.

Some Examples in 1 Maccabees and Our Interpretation

In this section I will deal with some examples of events that I interpret in terms of feelings of honor, humiliation and shame. We will see yet again that the clash of perceptions of honor in the Book of 1 Maccabees occurs quite frequently. The example of killing the person who went to sacrifice and the rejection of gifts (offered by a king who was otherwise generous in giving presents!) is a bad start for Mattathias and his movement; his actions were most probably interpreted by the Seleucid officer as being contrary to the expected behavior of an inferior to his superior. It is for this reason that the issue of obedience to the Seleucid king comes up so emphatically in chapter 2:29–38. The expression *poiēsate kata ton logon tou basileōs* (v. 33) recurs several times in our text and reveals the anger of the Seleucids, not necessarily for religious reasons but because of the mere fact of rejection of an *order* of the king (who is superior). When Judah "takes over" from Mattathias in chapter 3 and Apollonius attacks, Judah not only defeats him but takes his sword and "fights with it all his life". Taking the sword of the leader of the enemy is a humiliating gesture. Seron, as a reaction to this symbolic humiliation of a Seleucid general declares that he will *make a name for himself* and be renowned in the kingdom. He vows to fight Judah because he has "set at naught the command of the king" (verses 13–14). Such rhetoric is significant because it comes from the arsenal of terms probably used for describing strategies involving situations of honor and humiliation. What turns out to be central here is the rejection of the king's command (and gifts) and the humiliation of a Seleucid general on the battlefield. The greatest humiliations in history occur on the battlefield and in the aftermath of battles. This same Seron decides to take "revenge on the Israelites" (3:15), the narrator using here *ekdikēsin* (a crucial term that is repeated by the narrator many times in his description of the relationship between Jews and Seleucids). The narrator brings to the fore quite emphatically that this clash of Jews and Seleucids entailed an element of humiliation, shame and revenge. This is expressed also in the narrator's explanation that "then began the fear and dread of Judah and his brothers to fall upon the heathen around them. His fame reached even the king, and the heathen told about the military prowess of Judah" (3:25–26). In other words, fear and dread are feelings that result in respect and honor towards the powerful (instead of a code of rules accepted by all). The reaction of King Antiochus IV was *ōrgisthē thymō*, a narratorial comment meaning that he was angry and humiliated. Be that as it may, these feelings on both sides indicate, according to the narrator, that the clashes henceforward are not just because of the unwillingness of the Jews to adhere to the king's demands but even more because the Jews have actually humiliated him and his generals (the same king who had given presents with extravagance, "surpassing in this the kings who came before him", 3:30). One should not be misled: The Seleucid kings and other Diadochs were motivated by a drive for power, money and survival; for them, the only system of honor that existed was the total subordination of inferiors. (Thus later in the book we hear of Seleucid kings who, when they need the Jews for one task or another, grant them concessions. For the Seleucids this is a definite move towards a rebellious inferior. But for the Jews who were on the receiving end, parts of these documents may have had the effect of humiliation.) This time, as revenge, the king sent three generals (!), one of their aims being to sell the Jews as slaves after their victory (3:40–41). At the time this was seen as a humiliating move (see all the bas reliefs in the Ancient Near East where slavery is shown as the ultimate stage of humiliation of a conquered people).

Mourning is, I believe, one of the rituals associated with honor and shame. This is a kind of humiliation one takes upon *himself* before God. Since the Jews as compared to their rivals at that time have quite an elaborate sense of honor, and their system of honor is linked to God (a system can be godly as O'Neill and others have argued), they feel humiliated by their enemies, as they themselves say (3:42–44), and thus feel that self-humiliation will bring mercy and compassion (3:44). They gather at Mizpah and "that day they fasted, and donned sackcloth, put ashes on their heads, and tore their garments". Feelings (and rituals) of self-humiliation to fend off the humiliation that awaits them from outside are described here. (As in honor so also in humiliation: There is an internal one, that is, what one thinks of himself, and an external one, what others think of him.)[20] They say, inter alia: "What shall we do with these men, and where shall we take them away, now that Thy Temple is trodden down and profaned, and Thy priests are in sadness and humiliation" (*en penthei kai tapeinōsei*, v. 51)? In 1 Maccabees the feeling of sadness is linked to humiliation, whereas happiness and rejoicing are linked to glory and esteem.

Chapter 4 in its first part gives us yet another glimpse into the nature of the conflict between Maccabees and Seleucids. First there is a victory on the part of the Jews; but the battle seems not to have had a decisive ending.[21] After it, Lysias, the Seleucid general, assembles a bigger army, seeking revenge ("what he had wished to happen – i.e. the king – did not take place", v. 27), since the Seleucids did not achieve a victory. Also, the battle of Beth Zur has been won by the Jews (4:28–35). On the eve of the battle we find rhetoric that points to a struggle to gain honor and save face. Judah

---

[20] Stewart, *Honor*, 12.

[21] For the battles in general, see Bar-Kochva, *Judas Maccabaeus*, which is still the most detailed and reliable book on the military affairs of the Hasmoneans.

prays to God that, although the army of the Seleucids is strong, He should put them to "*shame* in spite of their army and their horsemen" (v. 31). He asks God to make the Seleucids "cowardly", to "melt the *boldness* of their strength. Let them quake at their destruction. Cast them down with the sword of those that love Thee, and let all who know Thy name praise Thee with hymns." Then (4:34–35) when Lysias "saw the growing rout of his army and in turn the increasing *boldness* of Judah, and how ready they were to either live or die *nobly* [which Judah indeed does later, in chapter 9], he marched away to Antioch". This is yet again a retreat of the Seleucid army probably without even fighting a real battle, much less fighting the battle to its bitter end. The narrator emphasizes here, as elsewhere, strength and boldness and the wish to fight honorably, as opposed to weakness, coward- ice and humiliation (through retreat from the battlefield). Such a humilia- tion incurred by the Seleucid army left the situation unsolved in a clash between two uneven powers where the superior one is constantly put to shame. According to this same unwritten code of rules, everyone could expect the Seleucids to return soon. And indeed the narrator says in 4:35: "There [in Antioch] he [Lysias] levied mercenary troops in greater numbers so that he might come back again against Judah." In between the military skirmishes with the enemy, Judah renovated the Temple and thereby caused "great joy among the people, and the *reproach* caused by the heathen was removed" (4:58).

The war of the Hasmoneans with the people of the Land of Israel, called the "heathen" (*ta ethnē*) in 1 Maccabees, has some interesting aspects from our point of view.[22] It is chapter 5 that concentrates on this war. We learn that Jews from the Bashan and Galilee were rescued by Judah and Jonathan and their brother Simeon and brought to Judea. The operation starts as an emergency call of the inhabitants of these areas; they fear annihilation by the heathen around them. They claim that the Jewish males of Tubias were killed and their wives, children and property carried off (5:13), an act hu- miliating in itself. The reaction of Judah is extremely fierce but also humili- ating (Simeon's reaction concerning the cities of the heathen in the Galilee is not mentioned). Judah does not limit himself to subduing the heathen, but as the heathen did to the Jews of Tubias, he humiliates them by *killing all the men* in certain cities (and even destroying others, in Idumea, complete- ly, 5:1–4). This is a practice we can find in the Bible (e.g. the males of Shechem after Dina's rape, Gen 34:25). It is doubtful that such a harsh act was still performed during the Hellenistic period. This is also to be seen as a typical, most primitive act of revenge for a treacherous act against one's

---

[22] For the hostile views of the narrator of 1 Maccabees towards the people of the Land, see Schwartz, "Israel".

honor: measure for measure (מידה כנגד מידה).[23] The Jews were humiliated
and their adversaries will be even more so. All of which shows that the
struggle is not just about territory and survival, but also about honor. The
Jews in the Bashan were humiliated, and Judah shows that he can "do better" and humiliate his adversaries in the most extreme manner (punishing
many cities as against one Jewish city). The story that ends this episode is
illuminating and exemplifies what we are discussing here.

Judah arrives at a city called Ephron (5:45–54). He requires passage
through the city but the inhabitants refuse. Suddenly it becomes a matter of
honor and saving face. Thus, as a reaction, Judah breaks into this gentile
city, kills all its males, plunders it and "passes the city over those who were
slain" (5:51; a procedure the Jews probably carried out also in Ashdod,
11:4–5). This story cannot be understood (unless we see it as a counter-
story to the one of Amalek in the Bible, who refused passage to the Israelites), unless we interpret it in line with the perception of honor of that time.
It actually transmits something like the following message: *Do not scorn a
leader who arrives at your city after being victorious everywhere. Do not
humiliate him.* Having been humiliated, Judah humiliated the city even
more, i.e. in a disproportionately fierce manner. (Interestingly, in 2 Maccabees this story is presented differently and does not have this meaning at
all.) When Judah later in this chapter goes to the land of the Philistines he
humiliates them in a different manner, by destroying their places of worship
and gods: In Ashdod he "pulled down their altars, burned up the carved
images of their gods, plundered the cities, and then returned to the land of
Judah" (5:65–68). This whole description shows that – as against the territorial message of the Book of Joshua – Judah actually relinquishes his hold
on the land on the eastern side of the Jordan River. But he wishes to rescue
the Jews and avenge their humiliation.[24] The evacuation of the Jews from

---

[23] For this notion in 2 Maccabees, cf. Ego, "Measure for Measure".

[24] Kathel Berthelot wishes to diminish the importance of the territorial aspect of the Hasmonean "ideology" by pointing out that Joshua is hardly present in 1 Maccabees ("Biblical Conquest").
Although I can readily agree with her that the ideology of Joshua's conquest of the Land does not
play a major role in Hasmonean politics, the conquest of the Land was a major concern of the
Hasmoneans, in particular the later ones (when 1 Maccabees was written). Berthelot does not take
into account that the borders of conquest of the Land as described in the Book of Joshua was only
one option for establishing the borders of the Land of Israel. There were other, more minimalistic
concepts (such as the one of the returnees after Cyrus' declaration; see my "Hecataues"). Be that
as it may, although the first Hasmoneans (or their narrator) did not establish any borders, they
nonetheless showed a great interest in the territorial dimension. This is the reason that Simeon in
his famous declaration about the Land (in spite of Berthelot's attempts at a different interpretation)
mentions the *klēronomia* which so clearly refers to the territory of the Land. (This is alluded to
already in chapter 2 of 1 Maccabees, in the Testament of Mattathias. There Kaleb is associated
with the *klēronomia*. This Testament is the ideological platform of the whole book of 1 Maccabees, as many scholars have argued; Hieke's article subsequent to Berthelot's in the same volume

these regions, along with the complete humiliation of the heathen there and in the city that symbolized re-entry into the western side of the Land of Israel, shows that honor and humiliation played a role in the power play in the Land of Israel. Relinquishing part of it means that neither the Jews nor the heathen will prevail there (the killing of all the males indicates that no continuity is expected in the heathen population). This is how the narrator presents it. Later the story will change somewhat when the Hasmoneans become more universalized. The narrator does not specify what happened in the Galilee except for the fact that the Jews there – or probably some of them – were taken by Simeon to Judea.

Now I should mention what might be called a *humiliating condition* of a famous person. In chapter 6 the narrator lingers on Antiochus IV's final illness and connects it to two shameful events in Antiochus' life previous to his illness. First mentioned is his great distress (*lupēs megalēs*) following his shameful retreat from Elymais, where he had wanted to plunder a temple (6:1–4). Second, the shameful flight of Lysias from Judea (6:5–8) overwhelmed the king and caused him to be greatly shaken (*lupēs ... enethymeitho*). Antiochus suffers terribly, and his physical and mental condition is narrated as typical of the moments of humiliation of a very inferior human being (such as Herod the Great at the end of his life).[25] The humiliating condition of the suffering king is followed by yet another invasion of the Seleucid army into Judea. In chapter 6 the narrator adduces the motif of honorable death, i.e. courageous behavior, as opposed to behavior that is base and dishonorable. The former is exemplified by the courageous fighting of the Jews and in particular the heroic death of Eleazar; the latter by the Seleucid general's breach of oath after an apparent victory of the Jews on the battlefield at Beth Zechariah. It is mentioned that the Jews fought courageously at Beth Zur (*epolemēsan andrōdōs*; 6:31). As noted earlier, courage is, according to our narrator, an important trait for earning esteem (see Stewart for courage's place in other societies). In this instance the narrator does not describe the battle itself – perhaps he had insufficient information – but says in just one verse that they fought "courageously". The death of Eleazar during the following battle in Beth Zechariah is also

---

rightly emphasizes this aspect.) It would be difficult to understand the fights of the Jews during the Hasmonean revolt if the territorial aspect were eliminated altogether. Even if Berthelot is right that certain chapters of the Book of Deuteronomy constituted the ideological base of the Book of 1 Maccabees (and not the Book of Joshua), other "non-Deuteronomistic" parts of 1 Maccabees express territorial considerations. In general, Berthelot's method, following other scholars, of drawing conclusions from biblical comparisons and expecting the Book of 1 Maccabees to be compatible with the biblical narratives can at times be misleading. Our book no doubt used biblical quotations and terms as building blocks, but the narrative and its comprehensive ideology are very different from any of the biblical books she mentions in her interesting survey.

[25] Josephus Ant. 17.168–72.

described as being "courageous" (6:45), thus "acquiring for himself ever-lasting fame" (*onoma aiōnion*; this is the utmost one can achieve and is a term rarely used by the narrator; even the Romans have just a "name" [*onoma*], 8:1, 12, and in v. 13 they are *hypsōthēsan*, not having *doxa*). Eleazar's death was a bitter disappointment since the king whom Eleazar was hoping to kill with his charge was not actually there. Nevertheless, it was considered by the narrator an honorable death symbolizing the heroic behavior of the Jews. Yet in the same chapter we hear about a truce first at Beth Zur and then a comprehensive one between the Seleucid army and the Jews. This latter truce ("peace") was accompanied by an *oath* that was very soon breached:

> 1 Macc 6:60   The king ... sent them a proposal to make peace, which they accepted.
>   61   The king and his officers gave them their oath. On these conditions they went forth from the stronghold.
>   62   But when the king entered Mount Zion, and saw the strength of the place, he rejected the oath that he had sworn, and gave orders to tear down the encircling wall.

This affair serves as an example of "formal" unfair and dishonorable conduct in the clashes narrated in the book between Jews and Seleucids. I will not enter here into the complex issue of oaths and swearing in the ancient Near East during the Hellenistic period, but merely comment that the so-called king (who was probably not there) breached a rule of any basic (or primitive) honor code (which can be found in many different societies): Oaths usually signify the *intention of the sides to honor/keep an agreement* (as well as *a situation*) that was agreed upon by two (or more) parties, such as a cessation of fire during a war. In these two chapters the narrator wished to show, in a condensed manner, that the clash between Seleucids and Jews can be seen also as a series of breaches of the word of honor given as it were by the Seleucids (according to the impression of the Jewish narrator). The so-called religious clashes become a matter of the past in this narrative (as is so nicely expressed in the words of Lysias to the king, probably a creation of the narrator himself in 6:59: "Let us make a treaty with them so that they can follow their own laws, as heretofore, for because of their laws which we abolished they became angry ...").

The new king, Demetrius I, sends Bacchides (with the impious Alcimus) to "take revenge" (using again the term *ekdikēsin*) on the Israelites. The king in fact continues the policy of the former king and his general Lysias, whom he murdered during a coup d'etat (7:1–4). It should be mentioned that Demetrius humiliates Antiochus and Lysias considerably when after they are captured he says to his troops: "Don't let me see them" (7:3), humiliating them even more by ignoring their former status and existence.

Bacchides, when he arrives in Palestine, kills sixty Hasidim to whom he had sworn that "we have no evil intentions either against you or your friends". They believed him, and he killed them. The narrator adds the reaction of their friends: "There is neither truth nor justice in them; they transgressed the covenant and the oath which they swore." (The Jews probably related to this oath as they themselves would have behaved in the case of an oath. But, as we shall see in a moment, the Seleucids would be bound by oaths only when it suited them.) When this same Bacchides arrives in Beth Zaith he kills those who have deserted to his army, which may have been a breach of oath as well (i.e. the promise to accept them and ensure their safety). Bacchides leaves and another Seleucid general, Nicanor, arrives. He tries to trap Judah, who comes to meet him (planning in fact to kidnap him and thus go back on his promise; this story has a nice elaboration in 2 Maccabees). Then this same Nicanor comes to the Temple and swears to demolish it if Judah is not handed over to him by the priests ("He swore [ōmosen] with rage, saying, 'Unless Judah and his army are delivered into my hands right now, it shall come to pass when I return in peace, that I will burn down this house.' He went away in great rage", 7:34–35). This feeling of rage is a typical expression of feelings of humiliation recurring in our book, as we have already seen. Nicanor, who wanted to take revenge, had revenge taken upon himself (a fulfillment of the prayer of the priests, 7:38); his army is crushed and he himself is punished with the ultimate humiliation; his head is cut off, as well as his right hand, and displayed near Jerusalem for the public to view (the King of Ai, Josh 8:29, and Saul, 1 Sam 31:9–10, are precedents). In all the cases mentioned it is the Seleucids who broke oaths, lost the battle and were treated in a humiliating manner. This gives us a clue as to our narrator's concept concerning this particular perception of honor: *Don't breach oaths taken by your enemy (even if you consider him inferior). It is not done. If you do, the other side will profit and be successful. The breach of a word of honor between states or leaders results in disaster for the one who breaches an oath (or a promise that was sworn).*

The pact between Judea and Rome narrated in chapter 8 is actually a formal written arrangement of the mutual agreement to respect each other's honor. In contrast to the behavior of Rome toward the conquered people in other regions of the world (by and large a relationship where Rome indulged in force and subjugated the others; I believe the term *doxa* and *timē* were avoided by the narrator in this case), in the pact between Rome and Judea the *antithesis* is narrated. Judea, unlike the nations described by Judah (i.e. the narrator) in his description of the Roman expansion, is *equal* to Rome in this pact. From the outset Judea, unlike some of the nations mentioned in Judah's speech, does not attack Rome, whose expansion is portrayed as resulting from Rome's needs for self-defense and resources; Judea is not conquered by Rome and does not have to pay tribute, etc. The pact, set by the narrator against the background of the description of Rome's power, in fact enhances the self-esteem of the Jews as seen by the narrator (since they become equal in *esteem* to Rome). The hand of the narrator is evident here as elsewhere in the book, since the narrative of Rome's expansion – quite a tendentious description – has a *dialogue* with both the negative narration of Macedonian imperialism presented in the first chapter of the book as well as with this pact. In any event, it is not accidental from a narratorial point of view that Judah is the one chosen by the narrator to tell the story of the expansion of Rome and also the one who concludes the pact with her. It is declared very clearly that the two worlds of honor, Judea and Rome, can "live" alongside each other without the one hampering the other or even destroying it as in the Seleucid case. The next chapter, chapter 9, narrates the death of Judah. He falls in battle because he did not want to run away and by that lose "honor" and exhibit cowardice. This was dealt with in an earlier passage, and there is no need to repeat it here; his stance expressed the point of view of the Jewish side, which can be formulated as follows: *When the army of the enemy challenges you directly on the battlefield, even if you are inferior in status, forces, etc., you should fight against all odds and save face.* Judah was conscious of the impossible odds facing him, but he fought and was killed so as to save his honor.

Whereas the war with the Seleucids became in many ways a long drawn out struggle for honor, there are instances when the time of *waiting for revenge* is short (as we saw above in the case of Nicanor's arrogance). We can detect in our narrative periods of humiliation and periods of satisfaction (i.e. revenge). This is one of the very important motifs that create the undercurrent of history in the Book – namely, connecting one episode to another. This is also why the periods in between the act of humiliation and the one of revenge (periods of "waiting") are somewhat "dead" periods for our narrator (in most instances not much happens in these periods, according to him). In other words he is mostly interested in examples of this motif when something "happens" (alongside other motifs). This is one of the reasons for the disproportionate linear description and distorted picture we as readers get about this period. Such an observation is important for understanding the narrative strategies of the book, but it also speaks to an aspect of the behavior of people and groups during the period when they are waiting for vindication after having been humiliated. This waiting period, which can be quite long at times, is crucial for understanding the position of the individual as well as of groups during the *vacuum* that ensues (in time and in feelings) between humiliation and vindication (revenge). An example, which appears in chapter 9, is typical in its narrative as well as in its terminology

of a very short passage of time between humiliation and revenge. The story
goes as follows: An Arab tribe promised to keep baggage for the Jews during the war with Bacchides. They then went back on their promise; they
stole the baggage and killed Jochanan, one of the Hasmonean brothers. The
Hasmoneans did not wait; they attacked the tribe during a wedding and
killed many, while others fled to the mountains. This was a measure-for-
measure act. The music and rejoicing of the wedding in the Arab tribe
turned into lamentation, says our narrator in his commentary. This means
(according to the codes of our narrator) that the Arabs were now the ones
humiliated (we have already mentioned the connection between rejoicing
and esteem, on the one hand, and lament and humiliation, on the other). The
story is presented as an independent unit within the general narrative, but it
had to be narrated because otherwise we would not have known how
Jochanan disappeared from the scene. He is the third of the Hasmonean
brothers, after Judah and Eleazar, to be killed. Shortly thereafter Jonathan
will be killed as well, and the last to be killed in the book will be Simeon.
Except for Judah and Eleazar who were killed in battle "honorably", the
three others were killed shamefully. The first two Hasmoneans died honorably because they were not yet part of the "club" of Hellenistic rulers and
acted according to their own code of honor, whereas the three later ones,
after they became part of the "club", died shamefully because they misin-
terpreted the intentions of the Hellenistic rulers and naively thought they
would be respecting the code of honor by keeping their promises; they
probably thought that their neighbors had the same codes of honor as they
themselves adhered to. Henceforward two not very harmonious voices are
"heard" simultaneously from the narrative. The one voice, the factual skeleton, conveys that the Jews are on a slightly better path after becoming play-
ers on the international scene (they are even getting gifts and reciprocating
as well as serving as the *philoi* of Seleucid kings and their governors; they
act as if they have become part of some sort of vertical honor scale). The
other voice, the undercurrent, reflects a negative perspective, since the three
last Hasmoneans (Simeon with some of his sons) died shamefully in the
unavoidable chain of humiliation and revenge. In reality the Hellenistic
rulers hardly possessed the virtue of honor, since honor and striving for
power do not always go hand in hand.

To get back to our narrative: When the realization dawned on both sides
that the power of the warring parties was *even* (and the death of the "wicked" Alcimus a fait accompli), a real ceasefire became possible between the
Jews and Seleucids. When Jonathan and Simeon exhibited their power very
forcefully and realized that Bacchides was in real trouble, only then did
Jonathan allow himself to propose peace to the Seleucid general, who took
an *oath* not to fight again, which he indeed kept. Only then was the oath

honored (as opposed to former incidents when the Seleucids felt that they did not have to honor an oath since in their eyes their foe at that time was so inferior and powerless):

1 Macc 9:70   When Jonathan heard about this [the weakness of Bacchides] he sent ambassadors to him to set before him a proposal of peace and to obtain the release of the prisoners.
71   He agreed and kept his word. He swore to him never to seek evil against him as long as he lived.
72   He gave back to him the prisoners whom he had taken before from the land of Judah. He went away and returned to his own land, nor did he ever again come to the land of Judea.
73   Thus the sword ceased from the people of Israel.

It is quite obvious that these latter words are but commentary of the narrator, who is actually transmitting this message: *that one can trust an oath given by the enemy only when this enemy feels that the other side is strong and equal in power.* With weaker enemies, when there is inequality between the rivals, an oath could be and in fact was worthless.

As we have already seen in the case of gifts and gifting, chapter 10 of the book is a real turning point and is presented as a transition period. Not only because gifts are given to Jonathan and he starts to be a player in this game of gifting, but also because the Hasmoneans, by becoming *philoi* and Seleucid officials, are recognized as "official members" in what Frank Stewart calls (concerning personal honor) *honor groups* of the Hellenistic rulers.[26] This means that subsequent to Bacchides' withdrawal the Jews became a power to be respected in the eyes of the Seleucids, and this acknowledgement received expression in the invitation of the Jews to what one should call the dubious "honor group". The latter comes to the fore also in what Alexander was told about the Jews before he approached them in order to have them as allies: "They [probably his *philoi*] told him about the battles and the brave exploits which he and his brothers had accomplished, and the sufferings which they had endured" (10:15). Courage and sufferings are values that are part of "external honor", i.e. what the society thinks of one who is imbued with these values. Courage and suffering also appear elsewhere in the book as traits that enhance one's esteem in the eyes of others (Sparta comes to mind). When Jonathan is offered the position of a *philos* of the king (by Alexander), which he later accepts, he automatically joins a group that is reckoned to be within the games and (minimal) gestures of honor. Although Alexander did not offer gifts, the acceptance of which would have made Jonathan a sort of vassal, Jonathan later agrees to Alexander's offer because the offer is to become part of a club (namely, to have

---

[26] Stewart, *Honor*, 54–63.

a rank that involves some external honor). Interestingly, Demetrius I, both in his first offer to Jonathan and in his second (where he offers to give concessions, gifts, etc.), does not mention the crucial words that Alexander, when he made his offer to Jonathan, wisely used (i.e. of the value of honor), but, as the narrator so masterfully discerned, Demetrius used only *words of flattery* (*megalynai auton*, v. 3, and in v. 24 *logous paraklēseōs kai hypsous*). The narrator is the one who makes this distinction between real honoring (in substantial terms) and mere flattery. This latter flattery is in addition to the fact that gifts and concessions were promised by Demetrius, but he gave no real acknowledgment of the Jews as part of an honor group in the Hellenistic Near East (e.g. no offering to be the *philos* in the king's court and no mention of words that would show the existence of "eternal honor" and esteem for the Jews; Demetrius offered flattery only in order to *supplement* his offer of material gifts). It was Alexander for whom Jonathan opted, and it was Alexander who later defeated Demetrius "fighting vigorously until the sun went down" (10:50), he himself earning esteem for his "vigor" (another expression that is used in our texts as part of the vocabulary for developing a "sense of honor"). Alexander, as mentioned above, formalized (even ritualized) the acceptance of Jonathan into the honor group (v. 61–66).

It has to be emphasized once again that although the "honor group" of Hellenistic rulers existed only as a vague concept, there was some "sense of honor", at least in the perception that our narrator had of the Hellenistic world. In any event, this joining of the Hasmoneans into one honor "club" perhaps explains the rhetoric of a general who acts on behalf of Demetrius II (who represents as it were another honor club). The latter claims the throne of his deceased father and wants to fight Jonathan because he was an ally of his foe Alexander. He sends Apollonius to Palestine, and when this general reaches Jamnia he sends to Jonathan saying: "You are quite alone in rising against us, but I have become a laughing-stock and a reproach because of you (*egō de egenēthēn eis katagelōta kai eis oneidismon dia se*). Why do you set up your authority (*exousia*) against us in the mountains?" (10:69–70). In the continuation of the narrative the reason for this humiliation becomes clear. Jonathan, he claims, avoided him on the battlefield. Apollonius sees humiliation in this move of avoidance and contempt on the part of Jonathan toward him. He hastens to tell Jonathan: "Ask and learn *who I am*, and who are the others who help us, and they will tell you. There is no chance of your making a successful stand against us, because twice your fathers have been put to flight in their own land" (i.e. we have twice humiliated your ancestors, v. 72). Jonathan's reaction was also swift. His "anger" was aroused; he went (together with his brother Simeon) to meet the Seleucid army and crushed it as well as some cities that had become the refuge of the escaping Seleucid army. Jonathan humiliates the cities he has conquered.

The reading of this passage should be done against the background of what we have claimed about Jonathan's acceptance into some sort of a vertical honor club of a Hellenistic *court*. Since he has been accepted into the vertical system of honor of one ruler, if such a system at all existed, certain rules of honor now have to be followed (at least according to our narrator). It is not that everyone adheres to them; as we have seen above some even breach them (by going back on their promises). Jonathan, acting within such a new status, is theoretically obliged to honor his superiors in this hierarchy of vertical honor, namely, the Hellenistic ruler with whom he had a pact. He honors both Alexander and Ptolemy but does not show honor to Demetrius II, their foe (Jonathan in fact looks upon Demetrius II as one who is outside the club, whereas the latter wishes to see Jonathan as part of his club of honor). From this incident with Demetrius II it seems that the refusal to fight or the escape of an army from the battlefield without a fight could be interpreted by the other side as a humiliation. A challenge to fight should be answered (we saw this in the case of Judah when he declares that he must fight what turns out to be his final battle or else he will lose his honor). Cowardice could be seen as a humiliation of one's rival (as in a duel where one of the rivals does not appear).[27] Thus the abstention of Jonathan at the beginning of this affair was a big blow to the honor of Demetrius II. He thought that as a Hellenistic prince he should be honored by his inferior; but Jonathan obviously did not recognize him as a legitimate member of the vertical honor club of which he was now a "member". When the Hasmonean brothers later crush the army of Apollonius, they earn their esteem in Alexander's vertical honor system (as is so nicely put by the narrator in v. 88: "When King Alexander heard the news, he honored [*doxasai*] Jonathan still more"). On the other hand when Apollonius was crushed, the cities that helped him were also crushed and fiercely humiliated by the Hasmoneans; they were seen as inferior to the Jews and should have behaved accordingly, i.e. with respect. This same Demetrius II, when Jonathan came to visit him later, received him with great honor and "elevated him in the sight of all his friends (*kai hypsōsen auton enantion tōn philōn autou pantōn*)". This expression means in practical terms that he promoted him in the hierarchy of vertical honor (i.e. rank) within his court. Be that as it may, Jonathan later helps Demetrius in Antioch, after having promised to honor him; but when the king is saved he turns his back on the Jews. I have dealt with this above.

---

[27] One allowable reason for not showing up is illness. See Frevert, *Ehrenmaenner*, 98, for this and for the Duellcodex of Hergsell (ibid., 53–62). In general see Stewart, *Honor*, 64–71 ("reflexive honor").

The narrator says as a commentary that Demetrius "became estranged from Jonathan and made no proper recompense for the favors which he had done for him, but treated him shamefully". A superior could despise an inferior, and the latter probably could hardly respond unless he broke with him and started a war, which is what happened in this case. It is Tryphon who then ensures that Jonathan is kept in the vertical honor system by confirming his high priesthood and appointing him as one of the king's *philoi* (11:57). Tryphon, i.e. Antiochus VI, even sent him gold plate and service and gave him permission to drink from gold goblets, dress in purple and wear a gold clasp (one component of etiquette in the Hellenistic courts). He appointed Jonathan's brother Simeon governor from the "Ladder of Tyre" to the borders of Egypt (11:58–59), thus enhancing both brothers in the hierarchy of the vertical honor system.

I will not linger further on this issue with additional examples but merely emphasize my comment on the strange story of Jonathan's death. During one of the wars of revenge of the Jews (13:6), Tryphon, on taking Jonathan captive, sends to Simeon his brother saying: "It is because your brother Jonathan owed money to the royal treasury, for offices that he held, that we are holding him. Send a hundred talents of silver and two of his sons as hostages, as assurance that he will not revolt against us when he is freed, and we will let him go" (13:15–16). The narrator, who knows what the end of the story is going to be (i.e. the death of Jonathan at the hands of Tryphon), comments: "Simeon knew that they were speaking to him treacherously", and adds, "He nevertheless sent to get the money and the children, that he should at no time incur hostility on the part of the people, who might say, 'Because I did not send the money and the children to him, he perished.'" (13:18). The end is known: Simeon sent whatever Tryphon asked for, but Tryphon while staying on the battlefield against Simeon, at Bascama, killed Jonathan and buried him there (13:23). If it is true that Jonathan paid for the right to be within the club of Antiochus VI (although he was killed by Tryphon), then, as in France before the French Revolution, in the Hellenistic era people could buy into the higher ranks within the Hellenistic courts. Yet the more important angle of our story is that in spite of his being part of this dubious honor club, and against all words of honor, he was killed and actually humiliated in the most shameful manner. Revenge in this case followed very fast. The behavior of Simeon, on the other hand, was noble and in accordance with the Jewish law of *pidion shevuyim*. But his own end would turn out to be as shameful as Jonathan's.

This survey should be concluded by showing the dichotomy between the narrator's perceptions and the factual skeleton. In part I of our survey we saw that the narrator, in particular in chapter 14, presents Simeon as the epitome of esteem achieved by the Hasmoneans. So it is somewhat ironic that in a following chapter, chapter 16, the factual skeleton shows that Simeon died shamefully, losing at a stroke all the esteem he had achieved. He is killed by a relative (probably of foreign descent, Abubus), in the shameful state of being drunk. If the reader has already become impressed with Simeon's esteem as described by the narrator, he now gets a slap in the face in this last chapter. There is no reason to doubt that the information about the murder of Simeon comes from the factual skeleton. Hence, were it not for the honorable behavior of his son John, the book would have ended on a most disappointing note concerning the Hasmoneans and their achievements. This is a typical example of a case where an honest narrator has to present an anticlimax that stands in dissonance with his own views and concepts – here, the aggrandizement of the Hasmonean brothers.

References

Abel, F.M., *Les livres des Maccabees* (Paris: Gabalda, 1949).

Bar-Kochva, B., *Judas Maccabaeus* (Cambridge: Cambridge University Press, 1989).

Berthelot, K., "The Biblical Conquest of the Promised Land and the Hasmonaean Wars according to 1 and 2 Maccabees", in G.G. Xeravits/J. Zsengeller (ed.), *The Books of the Maccabees: History, Theology, Ideology* (Leiden: Brill, 2007) 45–60.

Bowman, J., *Honor. A History* (New York: Encounter Books, 2006).

Bremmer, J.N., "Spartans and Jews: Abrahamic Cousins?", in M. Goodman et al. (ed.), *Abraham, the Nations, and the Hagarites* (Leiden: Brill, 2010) 47–59.

Dancy, J.C., *A Commentary on I Maccabees* (Oxford: Basil Blackwell, 1954).

Eckstein, A.M., *Mediterranean Anarchy, Interstate War, and the Rise of Rome* (Berkeley/Los Angeles: University of California Press, 2006).

Ego, B., "God's Justice. The 'Measure for Measure' principle in 2 Maccabees", in G.G. Xeravits/J. Zsengeller (ed.), *The Books of the Maccabees: History, Theology, Ideology* (Leiden: Brill, 2007) 141–54.

Frevert, U., *Ehrenmänner. Das Duell in der Bürgerlichen Gesellschaft* (Munich: C.H. Beck, 1991).

Goldstein, J.A., *I Maccabees* (AB; Garden City: Doubleday, 1976).

Hieke, T., "The Role of 'Scripture' in the last Words of Mattathias (1 Macc 2:49–70)", in G.G. Xeravits/J. Zsengeller (ed.), *The Books of the Maccabees: History, Theology, Ideology* (Leiden: Brill, 2007) 61–74.

Mendels, D., "Hecataeus of Abdera and a Jewish 'patrios politeia' of the Persian Period (Diodorus Siculus XL,3)", in idem, *Identity, Religion, and Historiography: Studies in Hellenistic History* (Sheffield: Sheffield Academic Press, 1998) 334–51.

–, *Memory in Jewish, Pagan and Christian Societies of the Graeco-Roman World* (London/New York: T&T Clark International, 2004).

–, "Was the Rejection of Gifts One of the Reasons for the Outbreak of the Maccabean Revolt? A Preliminary Note on the Role of Gifting in the Book of 1 Maccabees", *JSP* 20.4 (2011) 243–56.

Neuhaus, G.O., *Studien zu den poetischen Stücken im 1. Makkabäerbuch* (Würzburg: Echter Verlag, 1974).

O'Neill, B., *Honor, Symbols, and War* (Ann Arbor: University of Michigan Press, 1999).

Rappaport, U., *The First Book of Maccabees* (Jerusalem: Yad ben Zvi Press, 2004) (Hebrew).

Schwartz, S., "Israel and the Nations Roundabout: I Maccabees and the Hasmonean Expansion", *JJS* 42 (1991) 16–38.

Stewart, F.H., *Honor* (Chicago/London: University of Chicago Press, 1994).

van Henten, J.W., "The Honorary Decree for Simon the Maccabee (1 Macc. 14:25–49) in its Hellenistic Context", in J.J. Collins/G.E. Sterling (ed.), *Hellenism in the Land of Israel* (Christianity and Judaism in Antiquity series B; Notre Dame: University of Notre Dame Press, 2001) 116–45.

Johannes Schnocks

Westfälische Wilhelms-Universität Münster

From the "Master of the Elephants" to the "Most Ungracious Wretch"

The Image of Foreign Commanders in the Second Book of Maccabees

1. Introduction

The Books of Maccabees not only depict at great length the so-called Maccabean revolt itself, the events preceding it and the ensuing conflicts, but they also repeatedly deal with the relations between the antagonists. Thus they would seem to be a rewarding object of inquiry for the questions raised in this book. This first impression, however, should be qualified by the literary character of the books of Maccabees which are interested in depicting the enemy in quite different ways.

Robert Doran has already shown that the "attitude of the author of 1 Maccabees to Seleucid hegemony is clearly negative. All of Alexander's followers are suspect and treacherous, ever seeking plunder. From them the author wishes Judea to be independent."[1] It is not surprising therefore to find the Seleucids painted black in 1 Maccabees simply for reasons of narrative pragmatics.

In 2 Maccabees the situation is different and much more complex. The book seems to be a more promising object than 1 Maccabees for an inquiry not only about hostility against the Seleucids but also about cooperation with them both on a literary level and on the level of historical reconstruction. This means that we must enter into the current discussion of the literary character of the book and its value as a historical source – a discussion that has provoked many varied responses. In connection with this an almost ideological debate as to the correct way of interpreting 2 Maccabees and the possibility of determining the historical facts behind the text has ensued. It is to these issues that the present paper would like to contribute, concentrating on 2 Maccabees.

What I want to show here may be divided into two aspects. First, I consider 2 Maccabees to be quite an important historical source for the second century BCE; the historical information that it can provide is, however,

---

[1] Doran, "Independence", 102.

rather well hidden beneath thick layers of rhetoric. It is therefore not sufficient merely to determine the genre of 2 Maccabees or its general tendencies. Rather, the narrative patterns – especially if they refer back to the
Hebrew Bible – have to be recognized, subjected to a detailed analysis and
made part of the analysis of the book as an historical source. Second, I hold
that 2 Maccabees, aside from all its hostility to the Seleucids, permits the
conclusion that in at least two cases serious cooperation was attempted but
failed in the end.

2. The Character of 2 Maccabees

For the last one hundred years, since Benedikt Niese,[2] 2 Maccabees has
time and again been classified as "rhetorical", "pathetic" or "tragic" or else
as "mimetic historiography". The original reason for this lies in the attempt
to assign it a place within the context of Hellenistic literature. It goes without saying that such classifications demand discussion and correction.
Within some parts of recent scholarship this discussion has led to an extremely varied way of dealing with the text.[3] I cannot deal here with these
positions in any depth; nevertheless, they have to be briefly summarized
because, in some of them, the value of 2 Maccabees as a historical source is
flatly denied.

The following positions should be recognized.

1) As in Niese, "rhetorical" or "pathetic historiography" is used in the
sense of a certain style that shapes several passages in the text and that roots
the text in its Hellenistic surroundings. A recent convincing list of examples
that support this thesis for 2 Maccabees can be found in Daniel Schwartz's
commentary on 2 Maccabees.[4]

---

[2] Niese's "Kritik der beiden Makkabäerbücher" is a milestone in scholarship, especially on 2
Maccabees. He revises the notion that 2 Maccabees was a fanciful version of 1 Maccabees without
any historical value. After examining the narrative style with its emphasis on Jewish heroism and
pagan cruelty and with obvious inventions like the exaggerated numbers when it comes to armies
and killed soldiers he states: "All diese Dinge entsprechen der herrschenden Richtung der rhetori-
schen Geschichtsschreibung, wie wir sie in ihren hervorragendsten Vertretern, Theopomp, Kli-
tarch und Phylarch kennen, von der sich nur wenige auserlesene Geister wie Polybios frei gehalten
haben." (Niese, "Kritik", 300–1).

[3] It seems to me that this discussion reflects the very controversial debate within New Testament scholarship as to questions of form criticism in the gospels. Since recent Christian studies on
2 Maccabees are mainly by New Testament scholars this debate might have been superimposed on
the book. See Dormeyer, "Geschichtsschreibung"; idem, "Poesie"; Ebner, "Viten". Dormeyer
continuously mentions Josephus, Philo und 1–4 Macc as examples of early Jewish historiography
that, along with the narrative literature from the New Testament, belong to the genre of "mimetic
historiography" ("mimetische Geschichtsschreibung").

[4] Schwartz, 2 Maccabees, 78–80.

2) From a more form-critical point of view, "pathetic historiography" is used in the broad sense of a genre of Hellenistic literature. This categorization then serves as a starting point for further exegesis and therefore assumes a much greater weight than it does within the framework of stylistics, because it determines the narrative intention of 2 Maccabees: readers are to be involved emotionally in the action and, by means of this involvement, to become morally improved. Nothing has been said about the value of the text as a historical source, a question usually not in the center of studies working from this perspective.[5]

3) In contrast, Robert Doran wants to emphasize the historical value of 2 Maccabees and therefore rejects labels such as "pathetic" or "tragic" after examining their use in contemporary ancient sources: "In all this 'tragic history' is a term for history which one thinks is wrong. It is to give a work a backhanded compliment, but not to put it in a definite genre. One must therefore discard the classification of 2 Maccabees as 'tragic history'. One must rather attempt to assess the work of 2 Maccabees in itself, and attempt to grasp how the author is proceeding."[6] With an eye on other Greek works Doran concludes: "2 Maccabees, too, is the history of a city and its territory and its defense by its patron deity."[7]

4) The work of Tobias Nicklas, as well as other recent studies, also rejects the label "tragic historiography", the emphasis however lying on "historiography". 2 Maccabees should accordingly be read not as historiography but as a narrative that is best analyzed by narratological methods with no regard to historical facts.[8]

I myself hold to the first position: that the text is "pathetic" in terms of its historiographical style. The most important reason is that, even though it is quite obvious that 2 Maccabees is firmly rooted in Hellenistic literature, this should not be overstated, as has been pointed out by Daniel Schwartz: "True, our author was not a biblical author. But he was a Jewish author. Moreover, he was one of those happy people who was able to express a synthesis between two identities in a way that approaches an integrated whole. We term this synthesis 'Jewish-Hellenistic,' but for our author it was simply 'Judaism,' which was a legitimate and respected way to be Greek."[9]

Even if 2 Maccabees quotes to a much lesser degree from the Hebrew Bible than 1 Maccabees does, it still contains a great many ideas and narrative concepts that place it within the biblical tradition. For this reason, the

---

[5] See for example Dormeyer, "Poesie"; von Dobbeler, "Makkabäerbücher", esp. 6.1; and her commentary in idem, *Bücher.*

[6] Doran, "2 Maccabees", 110; cf. also Engel, "Bücher", 401.

[7] Doran, "2 Maccabees", 114.

[8] See Nicklas, "Geschichte"; idem, "Historiker"; idem, "Fratze"; Zwick, "Unterhaltung".

[9] Schwartz, *2 Maccabees*, 66.

latter position mentioned above is quite justified as far as a synchronic analysis of the narrative structure of 2 Maccabees is concerned. This analysis may lead to new insights. It can, however, only be a first step to be followed by others in order to understand the text on all its levels. These further levels include the question as to how the text relies on theological patterns from the Hebrew Bible and what clues there may be concerning its literary development. All of these analyses of the literary character of the text will ultimately help with a better evaluation of its historical reliability.

3. Between Recognition of God and Equivalent Retaliation: The Enemies and their Fate in the Psalms of Asaph and in 1/2 Maccabees

2 Maccabees is structured according to the motif of sin and atonement.[10] Thus Judas Maccabeus becomes active only after the extensive narration about the martyrs in 2 Macc 6–7. Chapter 8 then starts with a prayer of lamentation in 2 Macc 8:2–4, which is rendered in indirect speech. Those who know the biblical psalms and lamentations will presume that this lamentation is a prayer from the Hebrew Bible that has been adapted only superficially to a new context. This is not so. There are no verbal parallels. So where does this impression come from? I believe that the prayer is a new text written for 2 Maccabees, which, however, uses patterns of thought present in a few of the Psalms of Asaph. Some of these psalms deal with the catastrophe of 586 BCE, the fall of Jerusalem and the destruction of the Temple by the Babylonians. By transcending historical contexts, 586 could become a paradigm for all catastrophes befalling Jerusalem and Israel. As in many other instances in the Bible the woes of war and the attack by hostile powers could be interpreted as God's punishment for the sins of the people: God's wrath has been awakened so that he uses hostile armies as his instruments and no longer protects his people, the city of Jerusalem and even his temple from attack. In these Psalms of Asaph there is, however, a limit to divine wrath. If the enemies go too far with their attacks and, in turn, become blasphemous in their actions, God's wrath is turned against them – this at least being the expectation in the plea of Psalm 79. The Psalms of Asaph name two aims in God's actions against the enemies: they should either come to recognize the God of Israel, or they should be annihilated.

---

[10] See Engel, "Bücher", 403; and the contribution of Daniel Schwartz in this volume.

Both books of Maccabees refer to these psalms and to this pattern of thought. 1 Maccabees is very clear in this respect as it quotes from Ps 79. In 2 Maccabees the pattern is transferred to the Maccabeans' relation to their enemies as a general model as well as to the depiction of individuals, the latter being of much more interest to us than the first. Some examples may suffice to show this, even though the ground should be laid by a complete presentation of the Psalms of Asaph, namely Psalms 74, 75, 79 and 83. Instead I must restrict myself to the following verses:[11]

Ps 79:1　O God, the nations have come into your inheritance;
　　　　　they have defiled your holy temple;
　　　　　they have laid Jerusalem in ruins.
　　　2　They have given the bodies of your servants to the birds of the air
　　　　　　for food,
　　　　　the flesh of your faithful to the wild animals of the earth.
　　　3　They have poured out their blood like water
　　　　　all around Jerusalem, and there was no one to bury them.
　　　　　...
　　　6　Pour out your anger on the nations that do not know you,
　　　　　and on the kingdoms that do not call on your name.
　　　　　...
　　10　Why should the nations say, "Where is their God?"
　　　　　Let the avenging of the outpoured blood of your servants
　　　　　be known among the nations before our eyes.

Ps 74:18　Remember this, O LORD, how the enemy scoffs,
　　　　　and an impious people reviles your name.
　　　　　...
　　22　Rise up, O God, plead your cause;
　　　　　remember how the impious scoff at you all day long.
　　23　Do not forget the clamor of your foes,
　　　　　the uproar of your adversaries that goes up continually.

Ps 83:9　Do to them as you did to Midian,
　　　　　as to Sisera and Jabin at the Wadi Kishon,
　　10　who were destroyed at En-dor,
　　　　　who became dung for the ground.
　　　　　...
　　18　Let them know that you alone, whose name is the LORD,
　　　　　are the Most High over all the earth.

The psalms from which these verses come establish their own logic: The enemies' actions are not only lamented due to the suffering of Israel but depicted as an attack on God himself. The enemies' scoffing is of great

---

[11] All quotations from the Bible are from the NRSV.

importance, since the final question is always where God himself stands. The psalms seem to accept that God may turn against his own people in his wrath over their sins. If, on the other hand, atrocities of war, the extermination of the chosen people, the destruction of the Temple and the scoffing at God are at stake, God has to change sides because otherwise he would be denying the history he shares with his people. God's intervention, which the psalms hope for and want to provoke through prayer, should aim at two possible outcomes. The first aim is the annihilation of the enemies, which is clearly mentioned in Psalm 83:9–10. The second and ultimate aim, however, is conspicuously placed at the end of the psalm and has been formulated already in Psalm 79:10: the heathen are to recognize God and submit to him.

The psalms do not specify in what case exactly the enemies were to be exterminated, but Psalm 79:10, as well as the dynamics of the prayer in Psalm 83, clearly shows that the real aim is the recognition of the God of Israel. Thus this aim qualifies and reorients the psychologically understandable cry for vengeance. A dead enemy would not be able to recognize God. This implies that the unrestrained threats and pleas for annihilation could not have been meant quite literally. Apart from this it becomes quite clear that it is particularly important to these psalms that God does not tolerate blasphemy.

This concept of the enemy which we have seen here in the psalms lends itself quite easily to adaptation by the books of Maccabees because the enemies here again are explicitly characterized as non-believers in the God of Israel. Psalm 79 is one of the few texts in the Hebrew Bible where גוים may be translated correctly with "heathen".

The clearest case of reception of the Psalms of Asaph in the books of Maccabees is that of 1 Maccabees, which contains a literal quotation from Psalm 79.[12] It is situated within the episode of the slanderer and high priest Alcimos, who, according to 1 Macc 7:16, treacherously murdered a group of Hasideans. This is followed in v. 17 by the quotation from the psalm, "The flesh of your faithful ones and their blood they poured out all around Jerusalem, and there was no one to bury them." The quotation is triggered by the term חסידים ("Chassidim"), which in the Hebrew original may mean the pious of the psalms as well as the group of the Hasideans. Later it is said of Alcimos that he was worse than the heathen. If we believe 1 Macc 9:55–56, he suffered a stroke and, as befitted his slanders and perjuries, was struck dumb until he died a painful death. We encounter here a typical example of equivalent retaliation and of the turning of the divine wrath against the aggressor.

---

[12] For more detail, see Schnocks, "Gott", 154–6.

The same pattern can be observed in 2 Maccabees as Daniel Schwartz has shown in connection with the account of Antiochos' death in 2 Macc 9: "The author of 2 Maccabees is a great fan of tit-for-tat making the punishment fit the crime."[13] Beate Ego has compiled an inventory of this kind of punishment in 2 Maccabees.[14] As a result of her analysis "it becomes clear that in 2 Maccabees two differing concepts of God's righteousness are at work. The first, reflected in the 'measure for measure' principle, is seized upon in order to demonstrate God's definitive judgment over the Greek oppressors and prominent Hellenists like Jason or Menelaos. The second, in opposition to the first, makes clear that God's afflictions upon Israel are to be understood within the concept of pedagogical punishment, a punishment whose aim is to turn Israel from their sinful ways."[15]

Even more interesting in the context of this article is the fact that in 2 Maccabees there actually are instances where God's intervention against the Seleucids leads to a recognition of God on the part of the "heathen". The intention expressed in the psalms is thus transformed into narrative reality.

About Heliodor it is said in 2 Macc 3:36: "He bore testimony to all concerning the deeds of the supreme God, which he had seen with his own eyes." Also Nikanor, sent by Antiochos IV Epiphanes, returns in 2 Macc 8:36 as an ambassador of God to the king: "So he who had undertaken to secure tribute for the Romans by the capture of the people of Jerusalem proclaimed that the Jews had a Defender, and that therefore the Jews were invulnerable, because they followed the laws ordained by him." In a similar manner it is related of Lysias after his defeat in 2 Macc 11:13–14: "As he was not without intelligence, he pondered over the defeat that had befallen him, and realized that the Hebrews were invincible because the mighty God fought on their side. So he sent to them and persuaded them to settle everything on just terms, promising that he would persuade the king, constraining him to be their friend."[16]

So what may be gained by observing a conceptual proximity of 2 Maccabees to some of the Psalms of Asaph? It seems to be most important that one of the instruments used by the "author" of 2 Maccabees to paint a more complex picture of the enemies and the development of their characters now becomes visible. I believe that the depiction of the actions of the foreign rulers, which historically were certainly quite varied, was molded according to this pattern of interpretation borrowed from the Psalms of Asaph. The elements of this pattern are the following: a determination to

---

[13] Schwartz, "Antiochus", 264.

[14] See Ego, "Justice", esp. 146–8.

[15] Ego, "Justice", 153–4.

[16] Perhaps 2 Macc 13:23–24, where Antiochos V Eupator honors the temple, can be classified as a further example. A formal confession to the god of Israel however is absent here.

destroy the chosen people stereotypically ascribed to the enemies at the beginning of a conflict; a recognition of God if things went well; blasphemy and subsequent destruction if things went wrong. Recognizing this pattern in the text can even help the evaluation of 2 Maccabees as a historical source. We gain a tool to distinguish better between what might be attributed to the literary strategy employed by the author and what might shed some light on the historical events behind the text.

4. Seleucid Officials between Cooperation and Hostility in 2 Maccabees

4.1 Lysias (2 Macc 11; 13)

In 2 Maccabees Lysias does not at first appear as a Seleucid governor of Transeuphratene under Antiochos IV Epiphanes as in 1 Macc 3:32, but as the head of state (ἐπὶ τῶν πραγμάτων) under Antiochos V Eupator (2 Macc 10:11). In this capacity he leads an army against Jerusalem at the beginning of chapter 11 in order to hellenize the city thoroughly and to turn the Temple with its cult and high priest into a lucrative business. The episode ends with Lysias suffering a significant defeat after the attempt to conquer Beth Zur, a stronghold near Jerusalem. This defeat brings him to a recognition of God (2 Macc 11:13–14, see above). Afterwards he strives to reach a new contractual basis for cooperation between the Seleucids and Judah – an effort that seems to be documented with the four letters quoted verbatim in 2 Macc 11:16–38.

At the beginning of chapter 13 he counsels Antiochos V Eupator to remove the high priest and villain Menelaos and to have him executed. The author is anxious to relate that the execution in a tower full of ashes befits his crimes against the temple and the altar in a tit-for-tat way. Together with the king, Lysias then leads great armies in an unsuccessful campaign to Palestine which ends with the fruitless siege of Beth Zur and then negotiations and an agreement with the Jews.

It has repeatedly been recognized that the sequence of events related here cannot be historically accurate: the campaign of Lysias at the beginning of chapter 11 seems to be a doublet of the events told in chapter 13. Historically, Lysias (with Antiochos V Eupator at his side?) seems to have entered into quite promising negotiations with the rebels. When would that have been? In ch. 9 we are told that Antiochos IV Epiphanes himself led a lengthy campaign in the eastern provinces, in the course of which he died. He was accompanied by Philippos who escorted the corpse back to Antiochia (2 Macc 9:29), a procedure that now can be dated with the evidence from a Babylonian astronomical diary to the beginning of 163 BCE.[17] About Philippos we are told (1 Macc 6:55–63; 2 Macc 13:23–24) that he attempted a coup d'état and was able to force Lysias and Antiochos V Eupator to enter into negotiations in Jerusalem and then to return to Antiochia. It is probable that these events would have taken place very soon after his return from Mesopotamia, perhaps in the summer of 163 BCE.[18] Therefore 2 Macc 13:1, which dates the campaign of Lysias and Antiochos V Eupator to 163 BCE (the year 149 Seleucid Era), can be confirmed.[19] In 2 Macc 11:13–33, however, Lysias' peace negotiations are documented by some letters quoted verbatim.[20] Three of them are dated and show the year 148 Seleucid Era (autumn 165 BCE to autumn 164 BCE). That means that they were written before the death of Antiochos IV Epiphanes and refer to negotiations during his reign and not, as 2 Maccabees has it, during the reign of Eupator. These negotiations were undoubtedly hindered by Menelaos, who was apparently intolerable as high priest especially to the pious and at last even to the Seleucid authorities (cf. 2 Macc 13:4). He went to find Antiochos IV Epiphanes on his last campaign in Mesopotamia and persuaded him to give him further support (cf. the letter in 2 Macc 11:27–33). As Schwartz rightly observed,[21] the episode of his execution in 2 Macc 13:3–8 is only loosely connected to its context. It is therefore difficult to speculate when it happened. It seems, however, that it came too late to be the basis for cooperation on Seleucid terms. A number of further important victories had strengthened Judas Maccabaeus to an extent that led him to aspire to a position unacceptable to the Seleucids.

Even this short sketch of the relationship between the text of 2 Macc 9–13 and the historical events that seem to appear in the background of these stories shows how difficult it is to understand this relationship. More technical approaches to these difficulties can be helpful in demonstrating that the "author" used different sources or that he interchanged some chapters as compared to his *Vorlage*,[22] but they cannot explain the motivation to produce a text so enigmatic.

---

[17] See Gera/Horowitz, "Antiochus", 249–52; see also Schwartz, *2 Maccabees*, 30; and for the greater context of the historical problems imposed on readers by the events narrated in 2 Macc 9–13 and his suggestions to solve them, see ibid., 25–36.

[18] See Gera/Horowitz, "Antiochus", 251.

[19] This means that 1 Macc 6:20, which gives the year 150 Seleucid Era for Judas' siege of the Akra – an act that according to v. 28 triggered the same campaign – may reflect a source that counted the years according to the Macedonian reckoning (see Gera/Horowitz, "Antiochus", 252).

[20] For the historical sequence of the letters, see Habicht, *2. Makkabäerbuch*, 179–85.

[21] See Schwartz, *2 Maccabees*, 35–6.

[22] See, for example, Schwartz, *2 Maccabees*, 37, who argues convincingly that the "epitomator" – who in fact functions as an "author" in Schwartz's work on the text and should therefore,

A first step in achieving a satisfactory explanation might be found in combining the conceptual affinity of 2 Maccabees to some Psalms of Asaph with the oft-made observation that 2 Maccabees is structured in sections marked by a concluding sentence and that those sections correspond with phases of the narration.[23] The section of 2 Macc 4:1–10:9 ends with the sentence, "Such then was the end of Antiochus, who was called Epiphanes" (2 Macc 10:9). The section is characterized by massive violence, the desecration and subsequent new dedication of the temple and the hubris and blasphemy of Antiochos IV. There is no room for any kind of cooperation between Seleucids and Jews. The following section in 2 Macc 10:10–13:26,[24] however, has a more diversified character. It covers the reign of Antiochos V Eupator. Here we find the recognition of God and a good fate, on the one hand, and blasphemy and destruction, on the other. Moreover, we find both alternatives on the side of the enemies as well as on the side of Judas' warriors. Two examples may suffice. It is only in this section that we read about some Judean soldiers being killed in action (2 Macc 12:34). Some verses later we are told that the dead had "sacred tokens of the idols of Jamnia" (ἱερώματα τῶν ἀπὸ Ιαμνείας εἰδώλων) under their tunics (2 Macc 12:40). Their death in war is therefore interpreted as God's justice against idolaters, and Judas prays for the dead and makes every effort to atone for this sin by sending money to the temple to be used for atoning sacrifices. On the other hand we read about Lysias' attempts at building a lasting peace. Focusing on the temple, the section even ends with the statement that Antiochos V Eupator "honored the sanctuary and showed generosity to the holy place" (2 Macc 13:23).

What we find in this chapter about Lysias is most interesting in the context of the questions raised in this book. I believe that our author found Lysias in the historical accounts he had access to as one of the few Seleucids who acted as a true partner willing to make peace. Perhaps he even wanted to raise some kind of monument for him.[25] In his theological thinking, this cooperation must have been the result of Lysias' recognition of the God of Israel (2 Macc 11:13). Thus he was interested in Lysias not only for historical reasons but, more importantly for him, as an example of the con-

---

with Schwartz, be designated as such – used materials apart from Jason's in 2 Macc 10:10–11:38 and 13:3–8 and rearranged the original sequence of chapters 13, 12 and 9 into the present order. I am not sure, however, that the rearrangement of the material was due to the author's "mistaken impression that the letters of Chapter 11 showed Antiochus IV had died by 148" (ibid.).

[23] See the portrayal of the book's composition in Engel, "Bücher", 397–9.

[24] See the closing sentence in 2 Macc 13:26b.

[25] It is telling that Lysias' death (along with Eupator's) is narrated very briefly in 2 Macc 14:2 and that the same rare verb (ἐπαναιρέομαι) is used as for the planned murder of Judas in the same chapter (v. 13).

cept that he shared with the Psalms of Asaph: that the heathen may come to understand Israel's relationship to its God. On the one hand, then, the author was anxious to present all the material he found in order to show Lysias' contributions to peace negotiations; on the other hand, this material was not apt to fit into the literary strategy he used to narrate the reign of Antiochos IV Epiphanes. For this reason Lysias' early negotiations are all transferred into the early reign of Antiochos V Eupator. They are found, therefore, in a section of the book that is much more open to other perspectives and developments. If, for example, the letters from chapter 11 that stemmed from the era of Epiphanes had been incorporated into chapter 9 where they historically belong, they would have turned the chapter into a complicated moving back and forth between different perspectives. They would also have interfered with the logic connecting the king's blasphemy with God's judgment against him that was more relevant to our author. So, Lysias enters the scene in 2 Macc 10:11 as a still unknown character and is consequently referred to as *one* Lysias (Λυσίαν τινά). This rearrangement of the material had grave consequences, however. Lysias had to come to Jerusalem as an enemy after Epiphanes' death in order to conform to the pattern in the Psalms of Asaph – namely, to be able to experience God's actions and then to acknowledge him. This campaign to Jerusalem leads to promising negotiations. In order to be able to cite letter 3 in 2 Macc 11:27–33, Menelaos still had to be in office at the end of chapter 11. Then, in chapter 13 Lysias participates in a campaign against Judah that is cancelled in the end because of Philippos' coup d'état. Again, this second campaign could only have taken place very soon after the death of Epiphanes. It starts with the execution of Menelaos and ends again with promising negotiations and Antiochos V Eupator honoring the temple. We may connect 2 Macc 11 to Lysias' first campaign, recounted in 1 Macc 4:26–35, which is transferred to the era of Eupator, or recognize it as a doublet of 2 Macc 13 from a different source. The effect remains the same: our author put up with great inconsistencies in his story in order to tell us that Lysias turned from an enemy into a partner, who used his influence on the king to improve the situation and to get rid of troublemakers like Menelaos. We have no reason to doubt that there is at least an historical core to this picture.

4.2 Nicanor (2 Macc 14–15)

The last two chapters of 2 Maccabees present a well composed narrative full of action and suspense. After some years of relative stability under Lysias and Antiochos V Eupator, Demetrios I comes into power and with him a new schemer, the high priest Alcimos, who renders the situation once again uncertain. The most multifaceted figure is now Nicanor, who is introduced as the commander of the elephants (ἐλεφαντάρχης) and then promoted to Judean strategos.[26] He is at first sent to murder Judas in response to Alcimos' slanders, but then he signs a contract with Judas in spite of great initial distrust.

The text of 2 Macc 14:24–25 even states: "And he kept Judas always in his presence; he was warmly attached to the man. He urged him to marry and have children; so Judas married, settled down, and shared the common life." This idyll is, however, suddenly destroyed by Alcimos who again defames Nicanor and Judas before the king. Nicanor is therefore ordered to imprison Judas, who is, however, able to flee in time. Nicanor now tries to take the temple hostage, so to speak, by threatening to destroy it if Judas is not delivered to him. After that he tries to imprison the highly esteemed Razi who avoids this by committing suicide in the face of the soldiers, thus becoming a martyr. In chapter 15 Nicanor then turns into a blasphemer, preparing for battle against Judas and his army. In the night before the battle Judas dreams that he is given a golden sword by the prophet Jeremiah telling him: "Take this holy sword, a gift from God, with which you will strike down your adversaries" (2 Macc 15:16). About the battle itself it is said: "Nicanor and his troops advanced with trumpets and battle songs, but Judas and his troops met the enemy in battle with invocations to God and prayers. So, fighting with their hands and praying to God in their hearts, they laid low at least thirty-five thousand, and were greatly gladdened by God's manifestation" (2 Macc 15:25–27). Nicanor's body is dismembered as befits a blasphemer, and the day of the battle is named as a day of commemoration.

There is no question that this text is of a high narrative quality. In his narratological analysis, Tobias Nicklas argues regarding the Elephantarch: "In Abschnitt 14,12–15 als *Agent* gezeichnet, dessen Rolle nur in der Fortführung der Handlung besteht, wird Nikanor in VV 15–28 erzählerisch zum differenzierten *Character* 'ausgebaut'. Ab V 29 aber wird dieser wieder auf die Ebene des reinen *Type* zurückgefahren."[27] That is to say that Nicanor is again completely identified with the enemy. For Nicklas, this "nicht aufzulösende Widerspruch zwischen seiner Darstellung als 'Freund' des Judas und seiner Zeichnung geradezu als 'Fratze' des Judenhassers"[28] proves that the text is not a homogeneous composition, a thesis on which he does not elaborate, however. On the other hand, he assumes, in accordance with

---

[26] For the question of whether this Nikanor is the same historical figure as the one mentioned in 2 Macc 8:9, or is at least meant to be identified with him, see Schwartz, *2 Maccabees*, 473–4.

[27] Nicklas, "Fratze", 154.

[28] Nicklas, "Fratze", 155.

1 Maccabees, the historical Nicanor to have been a uniformly negative figure.[29]

I believe that we should take another look at Nicanor. What we know from every historical source about him is that he died in battle against Judas Maccabaeus. To the Seleucids, he was the most senior victim of the Maccabean revolt. 1 Maccabees therefore inevitably paints him as a profound scoundrel. 2 Maccabees is even more careful to show that he dies as an enemy of God, whereas Judas and his men are mere pious tools of the divine wrath. According to the Psalms of Asaph this fate awaits those strangers who sin against God by attacking the temple or the pious innocent or by blasphemy. Therefore none of Nicanor's actions that characterize him as an enemy of the Jews in 2 Maccabees are necessarily accurate historically. They are, on the other hand, not implausible and fit so well into the narrative strategy of 2 Maccabees that their historical accuracy cannot be either proven or denied without further independent source material apart from 1 Maccabees.

The friendship that 2 Maccabees claims to have existed between Nicanor and Judas, in contrast, is quite superfluous in terms of narrative consistency. The contrast between this friendship and the abominations that Nicanor commits, once he has turned into an enemy due to his king's orders, appear understandable if one considers that the text has to account for his terrible death. The peace treaty between the two generals – even 1 Macc 7:28–30 mentions negotiations! – may well have been historical. I therefore do not concur with Bar-Kochva who only sees "a literary invention intended to complicate the plot and make it more exciting in the manner of 'tragic' historiography".[30] This argument is weak. One could even ask in return what benefit in the sense of tragedy readers might have from a complication such as this. Rather, the extremely tense style of narration in 2 Macc 14:25 with an unmarked change of subject should be seen, as Doran has rightly argued,[31] as an indication that, here, the author condensed a longer passage from Jason's work into an asyndetical enumeration of three verbs: ἐγάμησεν εὐστάθησεν ἐκοινώνησεν.

If this is correct, it is quite probable that we see here an historically true case of real cooperation between Judas and Nicanor, even though, for reasons unknown, it turned out to be nothing more than a temporary interlude. What this cooperation exactly consisted of is hard to determine. Even the title that Judas supposedly bore has come to us in 2 Macc 14:26 only

---

[29] See Nicklas, "Fratze", 154 note 42.
[30] Bar-Kochva, *Judas Maccabaeus*, 355.
[31] See Doran, "Independence", 96–7.

through the mouth of Alcimos as an obvious slander – though attacking Nicanor rather than Judas.[32]

Whatever may have been the case here, everything we learn about it was written well after the attempt at cooperation had failed utterly and for good.

5. Conclusions

Three conclusions on the literary aspects of 2 Maccabees can be drawn from the considerations above.

1) 2 Maccabees can be shown to make use of the literary pattern of some Psalms of Asaph, and this, in turn, is significant for the book's narrative presentation of the Jews' relationship to foreign rulers.

2) This underpins the fact that 2 Maccabees was deeply rooted in the literary tradition of the Hebrew Bible as well as in that of Greek historiography.

3) By integrating a proper understanding of this pattern into our interpretation of the texts, we may understand somewhat better why the material concerning Lysias in 2 Macc 10–13 is arranged in a fashion that can inhibit attempts at historical inquiry as well as at comprehending the book's narrative logic.

With respect to the cooperation between the Seleucids and Judas Maccabaeus, this article's analysis sought to demonstrate the plausibility of serious attempts at cooperation both with Lysias in the era of Eupator (or even before) and with Nicanor in the time of Demetrios I Soter. The following three remarks try to outline what kind of cooperation this would have been.

1) A first step in that direction might have been, from the Seleucid point of view, to accept Judas as a partner for negotiations and therefore as a representative of the Judeans and not to dismiss him as a warlord any longer. 2 Macc 11:13–15 is quite explicit in this respect. If Lysias' first negotiations had fallen in the era of Epiphanes, they would have been wrecked by the king's decision, according to the letter in 2 Macc 11:27–33, to adhere to Menelaos as (the only?) representative of the people.

2) Eupator on the other hand is said in 2 Macc 13:24 to have received Judas. Even if he was forced into this by Philippos' coup d'état (2 Macc 13:23) and the necessity to cut short his campaign to Palestine, the author of 2 Maccabees is still anxious to convey that this development was a serious step toward cooperation, at least in the eyes of the hostile neighbors in Ptolemais who were upset about it (2 Macc 13:25–26).

---

[32] Thus, rightly, Schwartz, *2 Maccabees*, 552.

3) Even if little can be said about what historical conclusions can be drawn from the episode of the cooperation between Nicanor and Judas in 2 Macc 14, we can assume that at least some progress was achieved. Like Menelaos before, now Alcimos senses a rival and takes the opportunity to hatch his plot. Here again we are confronted with a situation where peace cannot be achieved against a hostile high priest. The story told in 2 Maccabees ends long before Jonathan is appointed high priest by Alexander Balas (1 Macc 10:20). Nevertheless, even if we subtract all polemics against Judas' antagonists, readers may well come to the conclusion that the text is hinting at the idea of the high priesthood for Judas or his brothers as a prerequisite of a lasting peace. Thus Schwartz might be right in suggesting that Judas Maccabaeus acted as a high priest after the conquest of Jerusalem.[33] Alcimos, who himself is introduced as a former high priest (2 Macc 14:3) and who brought Demetrios to restore him to this office, is said to have slandered Nicanor. According to him Nicanor should have appointed Judas as his successor (διάδοχος). If we follow Schwartz, this can only mean that Nicanor approved of Judas' high priesthood – and therefore violated the prerogative of the king.[34] On the other hand, this may be a lie of Alcimos the schemer. But perhaps we are entitled to guess that the unexpected cooperation of Nicanor and Judas might have consisted in the mutual agreement that Judas would not lead his rebels against the strategos as long as Nicanor would make no fuss about Judas lacking the king's appointment as high priest.

References

Bar-Kochva, B., *Judas Maccabaeus: The Jewish struggle against the Seleucids* (Cambridge/New York: Cambridge University Press, 1989).

Doran, R., "2 Maccabees and 'Tragic History'", *HUCA* 50 (1979) 107–14.

–, "Independence or co-existence: The responses of 1 and 2 Maccabees to Seleucid hegemony", *SBLSP* 38 (1999) 94–103.

Dormeyer, D., "Pragmatische und pathetische Geschichtsschreibung in der griechischen Historiographie, im Frühjudentum und im Neuen Testament", in T. Schmeller (ed.), *Historiographie und Biographie im Neuen Testament und seiner Umwelt* (Göttingen: Vandenhoeck & Ruprecht, 2009) 1–35.

–, "Poesie (NT)", *WiBiLex* (2010).

Ebner, M., "Von gefährlichen Viten und biographisch orientierten Geschichtswerken: Vitenliteratur im Verhältnis zur Historiographie in hellenistisch-römischer und urchristlicher Literatur", in T. Schmeller (ed.), *Historiographie und Biographie im Neuen Testament und seiner Umwelt* (Göttingen: Vandenhoeck & Ruprecht, 2009) 35–63.

---

[33] See Schwartz, *2 Maccabees*, 474–5.
[34] See Schwartz, *2 Maccabees*, 551–2.

Ego, B., "God's Justice: The 'Measure for Measure' Principle in 2 Maccabees", in G. Xeravits/J. Zsengellér (ed.), *The Books of Maccabees: History, Theology, Ideology* (JSJSup 118; Leiden/Boston: Brill, 2007) 141–54.

Engel, H., "Die Bücher der Makkabäer", in E. Zenger et al., *Einleitung in das Alte Testament* (Studienbücher Theologie 1,1; Stuttgart: Kohlhammer, [8]2012), 387–404.

Gera, D./Horowitz, W., "Antiochus IV in Life and Death: Evidence from the Babylonian Astronomical Diaries", *JAOS* 117 (1997) 240–52.

Habicht, C., *2. Makkabäerbuch* (JSHRZ I/3; Gütersloh: Gütersloher Verlagshaus Gerd Mohn, 1976).

Nicklas, T., "Aus erzählter Geschichte 'lernen'. Eine narrative Analyse von 2Makk 8", *JSJ* 32 (2001) 25–41.

–, "Der Historiker als Erzähler: Zur Zeichnung des Seleukidenkönigs Antiochius in 2 Makk 9", *VT* 52 (2002) 80–92.

–, "Die 'Fratze' des Feindes: Zur Zeichnung des 'Nikanor' in 2 Makk 14–15", *SJOT* 17 (2003) 141–55.

Niese, B., "Kritik der beiden Makkabäerbücher nebst Beiträgen zur Geschichte der makkabäischen Erhebung", *Hermes* 35 (1900) 268–307, 453–527.

Schnocks, J., "'Gott es kamen Völker in dein Erbe': Ps 79 und seine Rezeption in 1 Makk.", in U. Dahmen/J. Schnocks (ed.), *Juda und Jerusalem in der Seleukidenzeit. Herrschaft – Widerstand – Identität* (FS H.-J. Fabry; BBB 159; Göttingen: V & R Unipress, 2010) 147–60.

Schwartz, D.R., "Why did Antiochus have to fall (II Maccabees 9:7)", in L. LiDonnici/A. Lieber (ed.), *Heavenly Tabletts. Interpretation, Identity and Tradition in Ancient Judaism* (Leiden: Brill, 2007) 257–65.

–, *2 Maccabees* (CEJL; Berlin: de Gruyter, 2008).

von Dobbeler, S., *Die Bücher 1/2 Makkabäer* (NSK.AT 11; Stuttgart: Katholisches Bibelwerk, 1997).

–, "Makkabäerbücher 1–4", *WiBiLex* (2006).

Zwick, R., "Unterhaltung und Nutzen: zum literarischen Profil des 2. Buches der Makkabäer", in idem et al. (ed.), *Steht nicht geschrieben? Studien zur Bibel und ihrer Wirkungsgeschichte* (FS G. Schmuttermayr; Regensburg: Pustet, 2001) 125–49.

Catherine Hezser

University of London

Seduced by the Enemy or Wise Strategy?

The Presentation of Non-Violence and Accommodation with Foreign Powers in Ancient Jewish Literary Sources

Jesus' alleged pacifism has often been contrasted with ancient Jews' military actions and use of violence against their enemies.[1] The many wars of the Israelites against other nations and ethnic groups, described in the Hebrew Bible, as well as the Maccabean revolt and the first and second war against Rome are cited as examples of Jewish war-mongering, whereas Jesus' demand to love one's enemy and to turn the other cheek when slapped were seen as new and morally superior forms of conflict-resolution that were unprecedented in ancient Judaism.[2] Yet some scholars have questioned Jesus' alleged pacifism, and non-violent reactions to foreign rule are also found in ancient Judaism.[3] Ancient Judaism was far from homogeneous, and changing political circumstances provoked varying responses. The behavior of individual Jews and particular sets of people within Judaism toward foreign rulers, whether Hellenistic or Roman, must be understood as context-specific, multifaceted, and changing over time. At times some Jews seem to have considered it more advantageous to refrain from violent actions against the foreign rulers, to offer passive resistance, or to accommodate the authorities. The reasons why they preferred not to engage in fighting would have changed from one situation to another: becoming aware of the uselessness of military action; giving priority to Torah study over national independence; desiring to save human lives; or enhancing one's own status and/or economic position.

---

[1] For a recent emphasis on Jesus' pacifistic stance that was allegedly unprecedented in Judaism and other religions of that time see Brock, *History*, 9: "An unconditional rejection of war, so far as we know, arose first among the early Christians ... But nowhere else do we find pacificist [sic!] ideas leading to practical antimilitarism, to the refusal of military service as the ultimate expression of a principled repudiation of violence".

[2] This traditional juxtaposition has already been criticized by Laserstein at the time of the Weimar Republic; see idem, *Judentum*, 6–7.

[3] On non-violent reactions to foreign rule in ancient Judaism see especially Neher, "Adumbrations", 169–96; Kimelman, "Non-Violence", 316–34; Horsley, *Jesus*, 59–145; Zerbe, *Non-Retaliation*; idem, "'Pacifism'", 65–95; Broyde, "Fighting", 1–30; Schiffman, "Perspectives", 233–59.

Such restraint can hardly be called pacifism, however, at least as far as modern definitions and expressions of pacifism are concerned. Dictionaries define pacifism as "opposition to war and violence as a means of settling disputes, *specifically*: refusal to bear arms on moral or religious grounds" (Merriam-Webster); "a commitment to peace and opposition to war" (Stanford Encyclopedia of Philosophy). What these definitions share, and what makes them difficult to apply to ancient Judaism, is the theoretical element that they entail: pacifism is seen as a commitment to non-violence here, as a moral principle and theoretical standpoint that is held up irrespective of the concrete circumstances. Modern-day pacifists are against the use of arms because they oppose violence on moral and/or religious grounds. Military actions are considered incompatible with certain values and beliefs. Pacifists refuse to bear arms in whatever conflict they might be involved in and urge others to exercise a similar restraint. Such an all-encompassing commitment to non-violence can be found neither amongst ancient Jews nor in the Greek and Roman world in general. Military action against one's enemy was seen as a sometimes necessary part of life, even if a peaceful resolution to conflicts was the ideal.

Ancient Jews vacillated between hostility and cooperation, between military (re)action and accommodation with foreign rulers. Their respective behavior depended on the concrete political, social, and economic circumstances as well as on the specific values and attitudes held by particular individuals and groups.[4] Since ancient Judaism was not uniform, variant standpoints could be held at one and the same time. While some Jews were eager to restrain Hellenistic and Roman imperialism with military means, others opted for accommodation and compliance. The holders of both views considered their own solutions best for themselves and for the common good in the concrete circumstances they found themselves in. They did not develop theories of non-violence based on moral opposition to war in general.[5] In this regard they differed from modern-day conscientious objectors, who refuse to serve in the army on religious and moral grounds.

It should be noted that the Dalai Lama has already stressed the fundamental difference between pacifism and non-violence and emphasized that peace is more than the absence of war. In this vein, one may question the alleged opposition between hostility and cooperation, armed reactions and peaceful conflict resolutions: both are possible at one and the same time, and may even be advanced by the same set of people with the same goal in mind. The understanding of violence and non-violence is similarly ambiguous: not only military action but also structural exploitation and religious

---

[4] See also Schiffman, "Perspectives", 234; Horsley, *Jesus*, 62–5.
[5] See also Broyde, "Fighting", 17.

repression can be seen as forms of violence; non-violence takes many different forms and encompasses non-resistance as well as moral resistance,
active reconciliation and non-violent revolutionary actions.[6] It has been
stressed that "No one had ever thought of or preached the applicability of
total non-violence in social, political, and state affairs before Mohandas
Karamchand Ghandi."[7]

In the following we will examine a selection of literary texts that present
Jewish individuals and groups who refrained from fighting against Hellenistic and Roman rule, expressed their dissatisfaction in other ways, remained
neutral, or made accommodations to and even welcomed foreign rulership.
We will focus on the ways in which their non-violent stance is depicted:
what do the authors and editors of the texts tell us about the circumstances
of and reasons for their behavior? How do they judge it? We are particularly interested in the authors' and tradents' assessments of the respective
situations, in the values and prerogatives expressed in these accounts.

1. First and Second Maccabees:
Accommodation with the Enemy is Sinful

The books of First and Second Maccabees already show that the ways in
which non-violence or refraining from military action against a political
enemy is depicted in the sources depended on the ideological stance of the
authors and editors of the respective works and on their assessment of the
situation. It is interesting to see how First and Second Maccabees differ in
their depiction of such behavior. Let us first state the commonalities: for the
authors of both works religion and politics are closely interlinked; they
clearly support the Maccabees' revolt against Antiochus IV and the subsequent Hasmonean rulership.[8] Yet they differ in how they present the so-
called Hellenizers and those who refrained from joining the Maccabees in
their revolt. Since we are primarily interested in the literary and ideological
aspects of the depiction of non-violence and accommodation, the question
whether and to what extent the sequence of events put forth in these texts is
historically trustworthy does not concern us here.[9]

Already at the beginning of First Maccabees those Jews who were "saying: Let us go and make a covenant with the Gentiles all around us, for

---

[6] See Rinpoche, "Education", 456.

[7] Rinpoche, "Education", 455.

[8] See already Nickelsburg, *Literature*, 114–21.

[9] On this issue, which is widely disputed amongst scholars, see especially Tcherikover, *Civilization*; Bickerman, *God*.

since we separated from them many disasters have come upon us", are called "renegades" who "misled many" (1 Macc 1:11).[10] The identity of these people is not further specified here, nor do we learn how common this attitude was amongst Jews at that time (the note that they "misled many" may indicate that they had many followers). It seems that from the author's point of view, a "covenant with the Gentiles", whatever this might imply, was considered sinful, since it would lead to the dissolution of cultural, religious, and possibly also ethnic boundaries between Jews and non-Jews and constitute a threat to Jewish identity and the survival of Jews as a separate group. Whether the total merger of Jewish with gentile society was real and whether this was what the so-called Hellenizers actually wanted cannot be determined.[11] Their depiction here may well be exaggerated. The "horror scenario" serves to justify the Maccabees' opposition to collaboration with the Hellenistic ruler and their eventual decision to start a military revolt against him. The Hellenizers' cooperation with Antiochus is said to have led to his authorization "to observe the ordinances of the Gentiles" (ibid.), that is, to lead a gentile lifestyle, which the Hellenizers allegedly desired. It was not the king but the Hellenizers themselves who are said to have introduced gentile ways, after having received the king's approval. The gentile lifestyle is subsequently described in both negative and positive terms as the non-observance of certain Torah laws (esp. circumcision), the building (and attendance of) the institution of the gymnasium, and socializing with Gentiles.

The authors create an opposition between themselves, represented by the Maccabees as the guardians of Torah observance and of a Jewish identity that can be maintained only by preserving clear-cut boundaries between Jews and Gentiles, and other Jews who wished to cooperate more with Gentiles, a cooperation that involved giving up some traditional Jewish practices and adopting some gentile customs. The first position is presented as the right one from a religious point of view. An opposition between pietists and sinners ("renegades") is created, irrespective of the strategic or political implications of such moves. Antiochus and the Hellenizers seduced the people and this seduction is believed to have led to the desecration of the Temple, the destruction of buildings, and the death of women and children (cf. 1 Macc 1:29–32).

This dichotomy between quietism / cooperation / accommodation / sin versus opposition / fighting / rebellion / Torah-observance is visible

---

[10] The translation of 1 and 2 Maccabees, here and below, follows Coogan (ed.), *Apocrypha*, 201–78.

[11] The term "Hellenizers" is a modern term, based on Gustav Droysen's use of the term "Hellenism" as a merger between Greek and native Near Eastern cultures.

throughout First Maccabees. Without an active rebellion against the Seleucid king's measures, the author argues, the dissolution and disappearance of Judaism would have been the result (cf. 1 Macc 1:41–42: "Then the king wrote to his whole kingdom that all should be one people, and that all should give up their particular customs"). Jews would have been unable to maintain their particularity in religious observance and cultural practices. A polytheistic pagan culture into which some remaining Jewish habits could easily have been integrated is painted as the allegedly horrible future which only the Maccabees' active resistance was able to prevent (see 1 Macc 2). The entire work serves to justify that resistance, which allegedly saved Jews from losing their religious (and cultural and ethnic) identity, and is therefore highly critical of cooperation and accommodation.

The resistance of the Maccabees and their pious sympathizers is said to have started non-violently: Mattathias allegedly spoke out against the king's orders (1 Macc 2:19–22) and then fled to the hills, where he evidently established a resistance movement. The following example of the pietists (cf. 1 Macc 2:29: "many who were seeking righteousness and justice") is used to justify the Maccabees' move to active resistance against the pagan ruler. Hiding in the desert to continue Jewish practices against the king's orders, that is, practicing a form of non-violent resistance against the new order, the pietists are killed by the king's soldiers when they refrain from defending themselves on the Sabbath: "Then the enemy quickly attacked them. But they did not answer them or hurl a stone at them or block up their hiding places" (1 Macc 2:35–36), preferring to die (together with their wives and children) as innocent victims of the foreign ruler's violent oppression. Not so Mattathias and his sons, who learned a lesson from this event. The motto that subsequently guided them is expressed in the following words: "'If we all do as our kindred have done and refuse to fight with the Gentiles for our lives and for our ordinances, they will quickly destroy us from the earth.' So they made this decision that day: 'Let us fight against anyone who comes to attack us on the Sabbath day; let us not all die as our kindred died in their hiding places'" (1 Macc 2:40–41). The Maccabees' ensuing fight for the unobstructed continuation of what they considered proper Jewish religious observance did not distinguish between Jew and Gentile but rather between pietists (Torah observers) and Jewish and non-Jewish sinners (those who were accused of leading a gentile lifestyle). The killing, by Mattathias and his followers, of fellow Jews who obeyed the king's orders becomes justified in this scheme (cf. 1 Macc 2:23–24).

The author of Second Maccabees explicitly states that only "few in number ... fought bravely for Judaism" against "the barbarian hordes" (2 Macc 2:21). They are said to have been motivated by heavenly apparitions which, according to Daniel Schwartz, "are of great importance in our book, their occurrence turning into something of an axiom ...".[12] The focus of this passage is on the repossession of the Jerusalem Temple and the reestablishment of the laws (v. 22), both of which are said to have been brought about by divine intervention; that is, the Maccabees function as divine instruments here who liberated their fellow Jews from the foreign suppression of their cultic rites and religious practices. The juxtaposition between "Judaism" and a rejected Greek way of life, which is called "Hellenism" and "foreignism" in 4:13, seems to have been a particular concern of the author of 2 Maccabees.[13] At the same time, the author himself must have incorporated both Greek and Jewish culture: by calling his enemies "barbarians", "the author is attempting to present himself as a good Greek (of the Jewish type), hoping thereby to gain the sympathies of Greek readers".[14]

Before the outbreak of the revolt two different Jewish approaches to foreign rule are presented: on the one hand, a certain John the father of Eupolemus is said to have established "friendship and alliance with the Romans", which ensured the upkeep of "the existing royal concessions to the Jews". On the other hand, Jason the brother of Onias, who obtained the high priestly office illegitimately, allegedly "destroyed the lawful ways of living and introduced new customs, contrary to the law" (2 Macc 4:11). Like the author of 2 Maccabees, both John and Jason would have belonged to the educated upper strata of Jewish society who had enjoyed a certain amount of Greek education. Thus, they "must have been at home in Greek culture to some significant degree ...".[15]

According to this account, an alliance with foreign rulers does not necessarily go hand in hand with non-observance of the Torah but can lead to beneficial arrangements that ensure the preservation of Jewish practices. The "extreme" Hellenization [Schwartz: "Hellenism"] and increase in the adoption of foreign ways [Schwartz: "foreignism"] came about "because of the surpassing wickedness of Jason" (2 Macc 4:13) and later Menelaus (cf. 2 Macc 4:50), who did not represent their fellow Jews but were interested only in their own advancement and accumulation of wealth. The author is aware of the possibility that alliances with a foreign power might be a wise strategy. Yet he condemns both Jason's and Menelaus' embracing of foreign practices as stupid and selfish. Jason's "putting the highest honor upon Greek forms of prestige" eventually led to the opposite of what he intended: he brought total disaster upon the Jews and incurred divine punishment for "showing irreverence to the divine laws" (2 Macc 4:17).

---

[12] Schwartz, *2 Maccabees*, 172, with further references.
[13] See also Schwartz, *2 Maccabees*, 173.
[14] Schwartz, *2 Maccabees*, 174.
[15] See Schwartz, *2 Maccabees*, 221.

In 2 Maccabees Jason is accused of "relentlessly slaughtering his compatriots" (2 Macc 5:6) and driving many others into exile (5:9). His violence against his fellow Jews is said to have been continued by Antiochus, who killed young and old, women and infants (5:13–14), and desecrated the Temple, assisted by Menelaus (5:15–16). In order to evade them and continue traditional Torah observance Judah Maccabee and his sympathizers are said to have fled into the wilderness (2 Macc 5:27) like the pietists mentioned in 1 Macc (note that Mattathias and his sons are said to have fled to the hills there). Before their military resistance is mentioned, examples of various pious martyrs are presented: the scribe Eleazar (6:18–31) and the mother with her seven sons (ch. 7). Martyrdom is presented here as a legitimate and honorable way of resisting the king's commands and preserving one's integrity and Jewish identity.[16] The Maccabees' military resistance is seen as the more effective way of resistance, however, which was divinely legitimized and eventually successful.[17] Whereas martyrdom is presented as the individual choice of those who were particularly pious, only military resistance can solve the problem of foreign oppression on behalf of the Jewish community as a whole. Divine support for the Maccabees' war against Antiochus is continuously stressed here (cf. 2 Macc 8:2–4; 9:5, 13; 10:1; 15:34–35): the Maccabean revolt is presented as a holy war against the forces of evil at a time when non-violent resistance was considered honorable but would only lead to the death of the pious.[18]

2. Josephus:
The Necessity for Strategic Changes

Josephus' stance on submission to the enemy versus fighting and martyrdom is more complex than that of First and Second Maccabees due to his own change from military action to surrender during the first revolt against Rome. His assessment of the revolt was written from this later perspective and therefore does not necessarily reflect his earlier views as a rebel against Rome. Since we cannot examine his views on military action versus non-

---

[16] According to Broyde, "Fighting", 17, martyrdom "represents a form of pacifism in the face of violence". Schwartz, 2 Maccabees, 272, believes that "for our author it is martyrdom that works atonement and therefore allows for reconciliation and salvation".

[17] According to Schwartz, 2 Maccabees, 273, chapters 6–7, which deal with martyrdom, have a particular literary function in the structure of the book: they constitute a "turning point which will allow ... for the move from the downhill begun in Chapter 4 to the uphill that will begin in Chapter 8".

[18] See also Maier, Kriegsrecht, 48–50: the fight against the evil powers is considered one's sacred duty.

violence and submission in detail here, we shall concentrate on particular passages that focus on these issues.

In *Bellum* violence is usually associated with Herod (cf., e.g., B.J. 1.316; 1.437) and with the Romans (cf., e.g., 2.211–14; 2.310–12; 2.457; 3.426 etc.). Yet the Roman use of violence is said to have sparked popular violence amongst the Jewish masses who crowded together and reacted against their oppressors. A good example are the people who had gone to Jerusalem for the Sukkot festival, while Cestius Gallus destroyed Lydda and other cities. Although the day was a Sabbath, the crowd decided to defend itself against Gallus' anticipated attack: "... that rage which made them forget the religious observation [of the Sabbath] made them too hard for their enemies in their fight: with such violence therefore did they fall upon the Romans ... making a great slaughter as they went ..." (B.J. 2.29). The decision to transgress Sabbath observance in favor of fighting against the enemy is reminiscent of the Maccabees and the pietists who sympathized with them (see above). Like the author of 1 Maccabees, Josephus does not criticize this behavior but mentions it matter-of-factly, probably considering it legitimate in the given situation. As is well-known, Josephus supported the fight against Rome himself in the early stages of the war and actively contributed to it as a rebel leader.

Only at a later stage, when fighting against the Romans seemed futile and Vespasian proposed an armistice (cf. B.J. 3.344) did Josephus decide to give up the fight and surrender to the enemy. Against his co-combatants' accusations of betrayal and treason, Josephus justifies his move by reference to the changed circumstances that necessitated a change of strategy (cf. B.J. 3.362–86). While dying at the sword of the enemy is considered heroic in the context of war, when peace and mercy have been offered, the offer should be taken up to avoid further deaths (see his speech of self-defense in B.J. 3.381). He argues that in such a situation, to continue fighting would equal suicide:

"I confess freely that it is a brave thing to die for liberty; but still so that it be in war, and done by those who take that liberty from us; but in the present case our enemies do neither meet us in battle, nor do they kill us. Now he is equally a coward who will not die when he is obliged to die, and he who will die when he is not obliged so to do." (ibid.)

Surrender is presented as the strategically wise decision in this situation. If surrender to the enemy means enslavement – and this is an equation that is frequently made by both Josephus and Greco-Roman writers – the current state in which Josephus and his compatriots found themselves could not be called freedom either (ibid.).

An unnecessary death at the hands of Romans and suicide to avoid sur-render are seen as self-murder, which is called "unmanly", unnatural, and an act of impiety against God (see ibid.). Josephus elaborates on this latter point to justify his surrender as corresponding with the will of God. He claims that "the souls of those whose hands have acted madly against them-selves are received by the darkest place in Hades" (ibid.). By contrast, self-preservation is presented as the order of the day and the most pious act that a Jew could perform. Obviously, Josephus constructed the following parts of his narrative to show that his own decision was the right one, whereas those who continued fighting against the Romans or killed themselves in-stead of surrendering were foolish rather than brave and pious.

It is interesting to compare Josephus' justification of his own surrender at Jotapatha and preservation of his life with his presentation of the alleged mass suicide at Masada. The story of the mass suicide, irrespective of whether or not it actually happened,[19] presents a form of resistance in which violence is no longer directed against the enemy but against one's own body as a kind of replacement. Since violent resistance against the Romans seemed futile and surrender enslavement, the alternative suggested here was self-destruction, before the enemy could destroy oneself. The various argu-ments which eventually led to this decision are presented by Josephus in two speeches, which he attributed to Eleazar, the commander of the Sicarii at Masada (B.J. 7.323–88). The prospect of enslavement to the Romans features prominently here. Obviously, enslavement was a real danger, since prisoners of war were the main source of slaves in antiquity and the basis of Roman mass slavery. Yet the reference to enslavement also had a broader, more abstract meaning in that subjection to a foreign ruler was seen as enslavement of the conquered nation.[20]

In his first speech, which, in its present form, would have been formulat-ed by Josephus, Eleazar alludes to the Exodus experience, which should cause his fellow Jews never to accept another lord but God (see ibid.). To die as free men (and women and children), by suicide rather than being enslaved by the Romans, is proclaimed as both brave and pious. In contrast to Josephus himself, who argued that his surrender and survival would be in harmony with God's will, the opposite, namely self-destruction in re-sistance to the Romans, is proposed here as the most pious option. Once a continuation of fighting has proven to be futile, "to die after a glorious manner, together with our dearest friends", that is, suicide rather than slav-ery, is presented as the more honorable deed, whereas surrender to the ene-my is presented as the easier, "effeminate" and more popular option (see

---

[19] For a critical examination of the story see Ladouceur, "Josephus", 109.
[20] For the equation between surrender and enslavement see Hezser, *Slavery*, 222–5.

7.342–4). Eleazar allegedly concluded his second speech by emphasizing: "Let us die before we become slaves under our enemies, and let us go out of the world, together with our children and our wives, in a state of freedom. This it is that our laws command us to do ... God himself has brought this necessity upon us ..." (7.386).

Josephus presents this horrific deed as a possible alternative to his own surrender. Although this behavior was incongruent with his own, he admired "the courage of their resolution" and their "contempt of death", which he believes would have impressed the Romans (B.J. 7.389–90). Within *Bellum* the contrast between surrender to the Romans as a sign of fear and weakness (Masada) and surrender for the purpose of self-preservation (Jotapata) remains unresolved. Similarly unresolved is the contrast between suicide as heroic (Masada) and suicide as a sin before God (Jotapata). Ladouceur has suggested that Eleazar's speech at Masada, as formulated by Josephus, is based on Greek rhetorical conventions and philosophical arguments.[21] It may have been based on "the cult of the Republican Stoic martyr and suicide, Cato", which was "turned politically against the Roman emperors".[22] In the context of *Bellum*, Eleazar's arguments are presented as unpersuasive and opposed to his audience's hope for survival. One has to keep in mind that the entire narrative of *Bellum* served to justify Josephus' own decisions and actions and to present them as part of the most reasonable and morally defensible strategy that could have been taken under the given circumstances. In this context, "the historian's own speech becomes not only a moral rejection of suicide but also a pledge of allegiance to the new rulers; opponents of the regime, on the other hand, find their sentiments echoed by a Jewish fanatic".[23] Ladouceur sees the Masada incident as paradigmatic of Josephus' general argument: in their war against the Romans and at Masada, "Jews themselves have worked their own destruction", rather than choosing the more reasonable way of preserving themselves by giving in to the Romans.[24]

The model of peace for the price of submission is mentioned by Josephus several times in *Bellum*. When Hyrcanus was appointed high priest and Antipater procurator of Judaea, the latter advised the populace to submit to Hyrcanus in order to "live happily and peaceably, and enjoy what they possessed, and that with universal peace and quietness" (B.J. 1.201). Later, Florus is said to have deliberately destroyed the peace and instigated Jews to rebel against the Romans, in order to divert them from making personal

---

[21] Hezser, *Slavery*, 97–9.
[22] Hezser, *Slavery*, 100.
[23] Hezser, *Slavery*, 101.
[24] See Hezser, *Slavery*, 103.

accusations against him before the emperor (B.J. 2.280–3). Agrippa allegedly urged representatives of the Jews to maintain peaceful relations with
Rome: "So these great men, as of better understanding than the rest, and
desirous of peace, because of the possessions they had, understood that this
rebuke which the king gave them was intended for their good" (B.J. 2.338).
According to Josephus, both Antipater and Hyrcanus directed their appeals
toward the wealthy, alluding to their possessions, which could be maintained under peaceful conditions only. These wealthy aristocrats are distinguished from the common people. The common people are said to have
been favorably inclined toward rebellion against the Romans. The opposing
sides – Agrippa as well as the rebel leaders – allegedly tried to win over the
common people to their different strategies (see Agrippa's speech in B.J.
2.345–401). From hindsight we know that the rebel leaders were successful
in persuading at least part of the populace to rebel and that all participants
were eventually subdued by the Romans. From this later perspective of a
failed revolt Josephus advocates peace and submission to the victors.

3. Philo's *Legatio ad Gaium*:
The Diplomatic Route Towards Accommodation with Rome

The political situation in which Philo and his fellow-Jews found themselves
in Alexandria in the first century BCE was in many respects different from
Judaea in the first century CE. What was similar, though, was that both
Philo and Josephus belonged to the upper strata of Jewish society, had
enjoyed a Greek education, and were able to establish contacts with the
highest echelons of Roman society. At least as far as their own testimony is
concerned, both were in favor of accommodation with the enemy as long as
Jewish religious observance and civil rights were guaranteed. Whereas the
later Josephus appears as a lone figure, pursuing his own interests at vari-
ance with the rebelling masses, Philo was part of an official delegation; that
is, his intervention was backed by and conducted on behalf of his Alexandrian coreligionists. One or more written petitions are said to have preceded
the oral deliberations.[25] Letters of complaint and petitions sent to the responsible officials – usually much lower than the emperor, though – seem
to have been customary in the Roman world.[26]

---

[25] See the discussion in Schroedel, "Literature", 63–4.

[26] Haensch, "Administration", 80: "if one wanted to get the Roman administration involved in
one's problems, one had to directly approach the responsible officials". This phenomenon is also
reflected in later rabbinic sources; see GenR 49:9 and 64:10.

Obviously, Philo's starting point was different from Josephus': Alexandrian Jews had not rebelled against the Romans. They had suffered wrongs that Philo and his fellow-delegates hoped to rectify through their appeal to the highest authorities. In addition, they tried to ensure the maintenance of certain administrative structures and civil rights and prerogatives that Alexandrian Jews enjoyed.[27]

Philo, like Josephus, was well-aware of constant changes in the situation of Jews in Alexandria and the Roman Empire as a whole (see already Legat. 1). He stressed the necessity to adapt one's behavior and strategy to the respective circumstances and to reckon with the possibility that one's assessment and actions could be incorrect. The Roman emperor could be seen as a "savior and benefactor" at one time and then reveal himself to be a "hypocrite", "savage", and deceiver (Legat. 22) – and this changed perception required an adjustment of the actions on the part of the leading members of the Jewish community.

Philo maintains that Caligula saw Jews as his adversaries and was suspicious of them because they insisted on the exclusivity of their God while denying his own divinity, as they were exempted from emperor worship (Legat. 115–17). Like Josephus, he takes up slave metaphors to describe the relationship between the emperor and his subjects:

"Therefore a most terrible and irreconcilable war was prepared against our nation, for what could be a more terrible evil to a slave than a master who was an enemy? And his subjects are the slaves of the emperor, even if they were not so to any one of the former emperors, because they governed with gentleness and in accordance with the laws, but now that Gaius had eradicated all feelings of humanity from his soul, and had admired lawlessness (for looking upon himself as the law, he abrogated all the enactments of other lawgivers in every state and country as so many vain sentences), we were properly to be looked upon not only as slaves, but as the very lowest and most dishonored of slaves, now that our ruler was changed into our master." (Legat. 119)[28]

The master / enemy / emperor is contrasted with the (lowest) slaves / subjects / Jewish nation here. The behavior of the Roman emperor is said to have changed from being a gentle ruler to a hostile oppressor, with Caligula having initiated a "most terrible and irreconcilable war" against the Jews. The non-Jewish Alexandrian masses, most of them Egyptians (cf. Legat. 166), being aware of this enmity and the weak situation of their Jewish neighbors, are said to have used the opportunity to attack them, breaking into their houses, expelling them, and stealing their property (Legat. 122–4). The Roman governor refrained from intervening, so that the mob con-

---

[27] On this issue see Kasher, *Jews*, esp. 233ff.
[28] Translation with Yonge at www.earlyjewishwritings.com.

tinued and destroyed local synagogues (Legat. 133), not fearing any punishment from the Roman authorities.

Alexandrian Jews are said to have endured this persecution without fighting back or using any violence in their response to either the Alexandrian mob or the Romans. Community leaders seem to have chosen rather the diplomatic path of petitioning the emperor directly and asking him to intervene on their behalf: "For it appeared good to present to Gaius a memorial, containing a summary of what we had suffered, and of the way in which we considered that we deserved to be treated; and this memorial was nearly an abridgment of a longer petition which we had sent to him a short time before, by the hand of king Agrippa ..." (Legat. 178–9); that is, two letters seem to have preceded their visit to Rome. Philo reports on the delegation's visit retrospectively and, from that later perspective, thinks that it was based on self-deception: expecting Caligula to be a fair judge, they encountered "an irreconcilable enemy", who would not support them in any way (Legat. 180). When they heard that Caligula had ordered a statue of himself to be set up in the Jerusalem Temple, they did not decide to fight against the Romans, but "retired and shut ourselves up together and bewailed our individual and common miseries" (Legat. 190).[29]

Aware of the dangers involved in approaching the emperor and complaining about the offensiveness of his action, Philo considers whether it would be worthwhile to die in the course of their mission:

"And even if we were allowed free access to him, what else could we expect but an inexorable sentence of death? But be it so; we will perish. For, indeed, a glorious death in defense of and for the sake of the preservation of our laws, is a kind of life. But, indeed, if no advantage is derived from our death, would it not be insanity to perish in addition to what we now have to endure, and this too, while we appear to be ambassadors, so that the calamity appears rather to affect those who have sent us than those who remain?" (Legat. 192)

The arguments and options put forth here are reminiscent of Josephus' deliberations: on the one hand, it is considered honorable to die for the preservation of Torah observance (cf. Eleazar's speech, although the circumstances are different); on the other hand, this self-sacrifice might not benefit anyone and therefore be futile. It would merely increase the number of Jews already killed by the Romans and increase the misery that the community is enduring. This latter line of argumentation resembles Josephus' reasoning and eventual decision to submit to the Romans: the preservation of Jewish life may be more important than a vain attempt to contend

---

[29] On the non-violent response to Caligula's plan see also Gendler, "Pursuit", 40–2. He calls the Jewish popular response a "striking instance of the actual application of nonviolence in a conflict with the Roman troops" (42). Cf. Josephus Ant. 18.277.

with the Romans, whether with military force or verbal indictment. Philo is pulled back and forth: the nobleness of acting on behalf of the community and the necessity to keep up hope for a more peaceful situation are mentioned as arguments in favor of action (Legat. 195–6).

In ch. 32 Philo describes the encounter between representatives of Judean Jews, who tried to avert the erection of the emperor's statue in the Jerusalem Temple, and the Roman governor Petronius in Phoenicia. He emphasizes the Jews' peaceful intentions and total lack of means to attack the Romans:

"Then the body of the old men, standing before him, addressed him in the following terms: 'We are, as you see, without any arms, but yet as we passed along some persons have accused us as being enemies, but even the very weapons of defense with which nature has provided each individual, namely our hands, we have averted from you, and placed in a position where they can do nothing, offering our bodies freely an easy aim to any one who desires to put us to death'." (Legat. 229)

Offering to sacrifice themselves and their families for the preservation of the Temple and the observance of their laws, they allegedly stressed that "we are a peaceful nation, both by our natural disposition and by our determined intentions, and the education which has been industriously and carefully instilled into us has taught us this lesson from our very earliest infancy" (Legat. 230). Philo's account presents a formidable example of a nonviolent resistance movement, which is willing to endure harm on behalf of its principles rather than taking up arms:

"We willingly and readily submit ourselves to be put to death; let your troops slay us, let them sacrifice us, let them cut us to pieces unresisting and uncontending, let them treat us with every species of cruelty that conquerers can possibly practice, but what need is there of any army? ... And when we are dead, let this commandment be inscribed over us as an epitaph, 'Let not even God blame us, who have had a due regard to both considerations, pious loyalty towards the emperor and the reverential preservation of our established holy laws'." (Legat. 233–6)

The ideal disposition, according to Philo, is a combination of loyalty towards the emperor and Torah observance (see also Legat. 301: "The honor of the emperor is not identical with dishonor to the ancient laws"). Previous Roman emperors seem to have been satisfied with the loyalty shown by the conquered nation and permitted Jews to continue living according to their own laws. Under Caligula, however, this equilibrium was threatened by the emperor's demand of a reverence that Jews could show toward God only. Monotheism, which formed the very basis of the Jewish religion, was threatened by Caligula's actions. In such a situation, an armed uprising would have been the only alternative to the peaceful resistance that Philo describes. In retrospect we know that in Palestine continued Roman provocations would eventually lead to the violent struggle of various Jewish rebel groups and the Roman destruction of the Temple. Philo's *Legatio ad Gaium* shows other, more peaceful options that were still considered feasible in the Diaspora at the end of the Second Temple period.[30] In advocating non-violent resistance and self-restraint rather than violent anger, Philo represents a philosophical tradition reminiscent of Stoicism. Anger and "most ferocious passions" are associated with Pilate (Legat. 303),[31] whereas the Jewish elders are able to control their emotions and thereby reveal themselves to be wise men.

4. Synoptic Gospels:
Persistence in Persecutions

The synoptic gospels do not allow us to reconstruct Jesus' position on violent or non-violent resistance to Rome. The references are too sparse and incidental. They cannot be added up cumulatively to reveal Jesus' pacifistic stance, as Peter Brock has claimed.[32] Since the sayings always appear in specific literary contexts and relate to particular situations, they cannot be blended into a coherent theoretical system. In addition, they may reflect the views of the later tradents and editors, who (re-)formulated them, even if they are attributed to Jesus. All three synoptics seem to have been written after the destruction of the Temple (cf. Mark 13:2, par. Matt. 24:2 and Luke 21:6; Mark 13:14; Luke 19:41–44) and therefore reflect a political situation that was quite different from that of Jesus' lifetime. At least some aspects of the praise of non-violence and passive resistance may have been attributed to Jesus retrospectively, reflecting the attitudes and circumstances of later Christian leaders and communities.

In fact, references to any kind of political stance are rare in the earliest gospel of Mark. The only statement that may imply a political view is the well-known saying, "Give to the emperor the things that are the emperor's, and to God the things that are God's", attributed to Jesus in Mark 12:17 (par. Matt 22:21 and Luke 20:25). If seen in isolation from its context, the saying might be interpreted to suggest a separation between religion and politics as independent spheres with their own laws, regulations, and duties. Each individual would then be advised to follow the rules of both the political and the religious authorities. Such a stance would resemble that of Philo

---

[30] On Philo's stance see also Zerbe, *Non-Retaliation*, 58. He calls Philo a "political realist" whose response was "pragmatic".

[31] See also Harris, *Rage*, 241.

[32] See Brock, *History*, 9.

outlined above: a combination of loyalty towards the emperor combined with Torah observance. This pragmatic view seems to have been shared by Paul who advised Roman Christians to "pay to all what is due to them – taxes to whom taxes are due, revenue to whom revenue is due, respect to whom respect is due, honor to whom honor is due" (Rom 13:7).

In Mark the saying appears at the end of a pronouncement story about an encounter between Jesus and his alleged opponents, Pharisees and Herodians (Mark 12:13–17). These opponents are said to have asked Jesus whether it was lawful to pay taxes to the emperor. The question is formulated as a challenge meant to reveal Jesus' disloyalty to Rome. Obviously, the author of the story associated political loyalty with the Pharisees (the post-70 rabbis of his own times?) and the Herodians (the Jewish aristocracy?), whereas Jesus (later Christians?) was suspicious in this regard. The story was probably meant to avert such suspicions and to confirm later Christians' willingness to pay the dues requested by the political power. The tenor of the story is that of accommodation with Rome as long as religious freedom was guaranteed, a view that seems to have been shared by educated (upperclass) Jews such as Philo, Josephus, and the later rabbis.

The main text that may thematize a pacifistic stance and recommend passive resistance is the beginning of the Sermon on the Mount (Matt 5, par. Luke 6), parts of which may have originated in the Q sayings-collection before the texts were enhanced and reformulated by the respective gospel editors.[33] Matthew's version is more detailed than Luke's, a phenomenon that has caused some scholars to see Luke's version as more original.[34] More important and interesting than originality, which cannot be ascertained, is the respective editorial rendering of the text. In particular, the saying that seems to propagate active pacifism, "Blessed are the peacemakers (*hoi eirēnopoioi*), for they will be called children of God" (Matt 5:9), is missing in Luke.[35] The following portion, in which those who are persecuted are blessed, appears in both Matthew and Luke, but with interesting differences. Matthew's blessing of "those who are persecuted for righteousness' sake (*dikaiosynēs*)" (Matt 5:10) has no equivalent in Luke. If *dikaiosynē* is understood as Torah observance here, the sentence would fit well

---

[33] Betz, "Sermon", esp. 33–4: The versions of Matthew and Luke "are two substantially different elaborations of basically similar materials ...". Both versions "have an integrity of their own, compositionally, functionally, and theologically" which may have preceded the respective gospel writers' editorial changes.

[34] According to Lachs, *Commentary*, 70, Matthew's version is "more studied, theologically worked out" and eschatological than Luke's.

[35] Hendrickx, *Sermon*, 31, notes that the noun *eirēnopoios* appears only here within the entire Greek Bible. For the verb *eirēnopoiein* see Col 1:20 and Prov 10:10 in the Septuagint. For further literature on this verse see Betz, *Sermon*, 137 note 359.

into the context of ancient Jewish writings, where persecution for the sake of the Torah is frequently thematized (see 1 and 2 Macc, Philo and Josephus above). In contrast to Matt 5:9, where active peacemaking efforts are praised, the endurance of – and possible resistance to – evil is valued here. Peace and righteousness are often associated in rabbinic texts (see the discussion below). Both sayings express notions that were shared by ancient Jewish authors who favored accommodation and peacemaking in contrast to quarrels and rebellion, even if one's own suffering, and that of one's community, was involved.

Davies, following Selwyn, assumes that these and similar verses were "formulated by teachers and prophets in the early Church, in times of persecution when Christians especially needed exhortation and support".[36] While Matt 5:10 refers to persecution on behalf of righteousness, the following verse (Matt 5:11, par. Luke 6:22) mentions persecution as a consequence of one's association with Jesus, whatever that may mean. The formulation "on my account" (*heneken emou*) is very general and unspecific: it might refer to the transmission of Jesus' teachings and stories about his miracles and not necessarily imply belief in Jesus as the messiah or Christ.[37] The term "lying" (*pseudomenoi*), which some textual witnesses lack, renders the reasons for the alleged persecution of those who sympathize with Jesus even more enigmatic. Davies assumes that these verses refer "to the condition of the Church face to face with Judaism", and he puts a lot of emphasis on the undefined "they" ("the Synagogue") in contrast to Luke's generalized "people" here, but his interpretation is based on his belief in the contrast between the "old" and "new" Israel as the context for the Sermon on the Mount.[38]

In the Lukan version the accusations are explicitly said to have been christological: those who are defamed "on account of the Son of Man" (*heneka tou hyiou tou anthrōpou*) are blessed. That such accusations may have been made falsely is not even envisioned there. While both Matthew's version and Luke's version of the blessing would have had their "Sitz im Leben" amongst the followers of Jesus, only Luke's version was formulated by those who held christological beliefs that saw in Jesus the divine "Son of

---

[36] Davies, *Setting*, 376, with reference to Selwyn, *Epistle*, 451, who detected similar notions in 1 Pet 3:11, 15.

[37] See also Betz, *Sermon*, 147: "Notably, these presuppositions do not contain a trace of a higher christology. The phrase 'because of me' says no more than that the reason for the persecution is Jesus' teaching, which is dedicated to righteousness."

[38] Davies, *Setting*, 289–90. See also Betz, *Essays*, 10, who argues that the Sermon on the Mount "belongs to early Jewish Christianity, a product of the mid-first century, when the Jewish Christian community was still part of Judaism". The Jewish Christians who formulated it were aware of "a strained relationship to their mother faith" and considered themselves the "true" Judaism.

Man".[39] Matthew's version can be understood in the context of Jewish Christian groups who had adopted Jesus as their teacher and continued to follow many Jewish practices. Both versions bless those who suffer evil without thematizing possible actions they might have taken to resist or avoid it. Instead, they promise a future heavenly reward to those who suffer for their beliefs (Matt 5:12; Lk. 6:23). The reference to the persecution of "the prophets who were before you" (Matt 5:12, cf. Luke 6:23) seems to connect these blessings with biblical history: just as the ancient prophets had to suffer for uttering truth, the new prophets, that is, the followers of Jesus, have to suffer for their convictions.[40] The element of "passive resistance" implied here would have consisted of persistence and faithfulness to one's ideals in situations of external oppression, whatever forms it might take.

In a later part of the so-called "Sermon on the Mount", passive resistance or the endurance of evil and oppression without retaliating is advocated more explicitly. Again, characteristic distinctions between the versions in Matthew and Luke are noticeable. In Matt 5:38–39 a contrast is created between two possible reactions to being harassed by others: responding in an equal manner ("An eye for an eye and a tooth for a tooth", cf. Exod 21:24 and Lev 24:20) or not reacting at all but rather embracing one's victimhood ("... if anyone strikes you on the right cheek, turn the other also"). The biblical *lex talionis*, which was no longer practiced in Roman times, was meant to limit the revenge and punishment of crimes within the community of Israelites.[41] The contexts and circumstances envisioned in the Hebrew Bible and in Matthew's gospel are quite different. Matthew uses the biblical saying in separation from its context in order to form a background that contrasts with the behavior he advocates: non-retaliation and passive endurance. The reference to also turn the other cheek (Matt 5:39) was probably not meant to invite lashes but to emphasize the necessity to endure suffering and harassment for one's beliefs (see also the continuation in v. 40–42).[42]

While Luke shares the saying about turning the other cheek (Luke 6:29), this version lacks Matthew's contrast between the biblical rule of equal retaliation and the recommended passive endurance. What is merely stressed in Luke is love of and support for one's enemies (Luke 6:27), a notion that Matthew again set in contrast to a biblical rule that he para-

---

[39] On this form of christology see Teeple, "Origin", 213–50, with the bibliographical references ibid., 213 note 1.

[40] On this tradition see Steck, *Israel*.

[41] See Hendrickx, *Sermon*, 84; for bibliographical references see Betz, *Sermon*, 276–7.

[42] For alternative interpretations see Betz, *Sermon*, 290.

phrases and even extends (Matt 5:43–44, cf. Lev 19:18).[43] The recommendations to turn the other cheek and to love one's enemies are presented as Christian innovations here. Although neither of these recommendations has a direct parallel in ancient Judaism, the support of one's enemies is also occasionally mentioned in biblical and rabbinic texts.[44] Davies believes that Matthew's contrasting statement was directed against the Qumran sectarians who separated themselves as the "sons of light" from other Jews whom they saw as the "sons of darkness".[45] Such an interpretation may be supported by liturgical texts from Qumran, which express a dualistic outlook "apparent in the blessing of peace upon the righteous and the denial of peace to the wicked", in contrast to the priestly blessing which was "pronounced for the sake of all Israel".[46] The fact that the fight against the "sons of darkness" is an eschatological expectation[47] and that there is also evidence of the inclusive priestly blessing at Qumran indicates, however, that the Matthean charge, if directed against the sectarians, would have been one-sided and overstated, perhaps for rhetorical reasons.

Neither Matthew nor Luke state what the advantages of the seemingly strange behaviors they advocate would be. Perhaps the implication is that retaliation would lead to the continuation of violence whereas passive endurance, and even friendly behavior towards one's enemies, would eventually end it.[48] The simple psychological insight that one's own behavior evokes a similar behavior in others (e.g., friendliness reinforces positive behavior and aggression invites aggression) may have formed the basis of these counsels.[49] In a situation of social and political inequality, when one's enemies are more powerful than oneself, the advice to intercept the circle of violence with non-retaliation may have been much wiser than open rebel-

---

[43] According to Konradt, "Deutung", 230–1, the Matthean admonition to love one's enemies (Matt 5:43–48) may be interpreted as criticism against the expectation of a military-oriented Davidic messiah, an expectation that allegedly ceased with the unsuccessful revolt against Rome ("implizite Kritik an der im jüdisch-römischen Krieg gescheiterten Erwartung eines kriegerischen davidischen Messias ..."). That such expectations survived the first Jewish revolt, however, is indicated by the Bar-Kokhba revolt and Bar Kokhba's messianic connotations.

[44] Hendrickx, Sermon, 91, refers to Prov 25:21–22; see also Lachs, Commentary, 108, with reference to rabbinic examples; Betz, Sermon, 310–11; Kimelman, "Non-Violence", 317; Zerbe, Non-Retaliation, 51–5.

[45] Davies, Setting, 245–9.

[46] Nitzan, "Prayers", 129 and 132. On war and peace in the Qumran documents see Martone, "Guerra", 83–93.

[47] See Zerbe, Non-Retaliation, 106. On the idea of war in Jewish apocalyptic thought with special reference to Qumran texts see Schiffman, "War", 484–7.

[48] See also Kimelman, "Non-Violence", 328, in connection with rabbinic analogies: "The insight again is that the means one chooses to respond to an assailant will largely determine his reaction".

[49] On behavior and its consequences see Hargie et al., Skills, 65–8.

lion and violent resistance.[50] It is inappropriate to take these sayings out of
their textual and historical contexts and view them as expressions of Christian moral superiority over biblical or ancient Jewish social practices. They
should rather be seen as recommendations in response to day-to-day harassments of Christians by popular mobs or Roman authorities.[51] The exact
nature and extent of these "persecutions" or social rejections cannot be
reconstructed on the basis of the unspecific evidence.[52] Perhaps the gospel
writers' formulations were deliberately unspecific to allow Christians in a
variety of situations to feel addressed by their words.

Harassments and persecutions are also thematized in Matt 10:17–18, 22–
23 (par. Luke 21:12, 16–17). It is not entirely clear who the envisioned
victims and victimizers are. Should all Christians known to the respective
authors be considered the victims or only the leaders or missionaries? A
number of different people and institutions are blamed for the harassments:
the populace, courts, synagogues, governors, kings, prisons (Matt 10:17–
18; Luke 21:12), and even relatives and friends (Luke 21:16); in other
words, both Jews and Romans are presented as the "other" who allegedly
victimized Christians.[53] Again perseverance is recommended as the proper
behavior in such a situation (Matt 10:22; Luke 21:19).

5. Palestinian Rabbinic Literature:
Peace as a Moral Value and Messianic Ideal

Rabbinic literature was composed after the two revolts against Rome, at a
time when Palestinian Jews were forced to accommodate themselves to
Roman rule. Their religious practices and civil institutions were tolerated by
the Romans, and they generally enjoyed a peaceful and flourishing time.
Increased urbanization and mobility benefitted the development of the

---

[50] See the chapter on aggression in Sabini, *Psychology*, 473–518.

[51] Cf. Hendrickx, *Sermon*, 35: the term "persecuted" (*diokein*) is "a verb often used in the New
Testament to describe all kinds of maltreatment suffered by Christians because of their faith (Mt
10:23, 23:34 etc.; compare Mt 13:21)".

[52] Lachs, *Commentary*, 78, refers to the exclusion of the *minim* (*birkat ha-minim*) in the Amidah as possibly indicative of a social and ideological setting, but scholars have rejected the idea
that this blessing was directed primarily or exclusively against Christians. In addition, the time
period in which it was introduced into the Amidah remains uncertain. On the *birkat ha-minim* see
Kimelman, *"Birkat Ha-Minim"*, 226–44; Horbury, "Benediction", 19–61; Instone-Brewer, "Benedictions", 25–44; Marcus, "'Birkat Ha-Minim'", 523–51.

[53] Luz, *Matthew*, 89, believes that Matt 10:17–18 deals "with experiences that the church had
in the past mission to Israel", but he admits that "the logion does not absolutely have to be interpreted from the Palestinian situation". He refers (ibid., note 38) to Hare, *Theme*, 108, who interprets v. 17 to refer to Jewish and v. 18 to refer to gentile persecutions of Christians.

rabbinic network with its increasing presence in some of the major cities of the Galilee and coastal plain. Rabbis who lived in or visited the cities, whether Caesarea and Bet Shean or Tiberias and Sepphoris, would have entered an environment that was distinctly Roman, with theatres, amphitheatres, bathhouses, temples, statues, Greek script and language everywhere they went. In cities such as Caesarea and Bet Shean, which were modeled on Roman cities, the ubiquity of Roman culture and paganism would have been only gradually smaller than in the Galilean centers of Torah scholarship. In such environments, rabbis had to constantly reconsider and adjust their attitudes and behaviors to maintain a rabbinically defined Jewish identity while, at the same time, participating in the surrounding culture and daily life. They developed various strategies to cope with what they perceived as pagan. Issues they discussed ranged from visits to Roman baths and theatres to business contacts with non-Jews. While they maintained a generally negative attitude toward Roman imperialism, on a day-to-day basis accommodation was the rule.

The story about R. Yochanan b. Zakkai's escape from Jerusalem ('Abot de Rabbi Nathan A 4, B 6 and 13, b. Giṭ. 56b, LamR 1:31), which can be considered the foundation-story of the rabbinic movement, already indicates the general rabbinic attitude towards Rome: Yochanan allegedly predicted Vespasian's kingship and was granted the right to move to Yavneh and teach his students there.[54] Loyalty towards Roman emperorship is associated with toleration, and perhaps even support of rabbinic scholarship here. Obviously, the story in its various versions cannot be taken as historical evidence of an actual encounter between the rabbi and the Roman general. The prophecy seems to be based on Jeremiah, a model that Josephus also used to describe his own behavior in the besieged city.[55] The rabbinic story serves as a foundation myth that explains rabbinic settlement in Yavneh, a place where Romans relocated provincial loyalists after 70 CE.[56] It indicates that rabbis acknowledged Roman authority as long as they were allowed to conduct their Torah study and teaching without Roman intervention. This situation seems to have prevailed during the following centuries. In Roman Palestine rabbis were free to deal with various internal Jewish civil-law issues alongside other judges and courts, whether Jewish or Roman.[57]

Rabbis of the late second to fifth centuries CE were not interested in the outbreak of another war. They preferred to maintain the *status quo*. Günter Stemberger has shown that rabbinic references to war mostly refer to the

---

[54] On this story see Saldarini, "Escape", 189–204; Schäfer, "Flucht", 43–101.

[55] Josephus B.J. 5.391–4; cf. Cohen, "Josephus", 366–81.

[56] See Josephus B.J. 4.444: Vespasian "settled there the worthy citizens from the cities that had surrendered to him earlier".

[57] See Harries, "Courts", esp. 90–2 on rabbinic arbitration.

past or to future eschatological times. The discussion of wars mainly appears in rabbinic biblical exegesis but had no real significance for the rabbis' own times.[58] When talking about necessary wars, rabbis tried to exclude as many Jews as possible from the obligation to participate in them. Obviously, the two revolts against Rome had taught them a lesson: although "the biblical texts did not permit a clearly pacifist stance, ... in daily reality rabbis did not want to be involved in wars which were always the wars of others".[59]

The term "peace" (*shalom*) appears thousands of times in rabbinic literary sources,[60] was used in early Jewish prayer,[61] is a feature of ancient Jewish burial inscriptions,[62] and served as a common greeting in antiquity as nowadays.[63] The very phenomenon of its abundance in so many different contexts in Roman Palestine indicates the importance of the concept of peace amongst Palestinian Jews of the first centuries CE. At the same time, the term *shalom* has many different meanings in rabbinic literature. Peace in the military sense of an absence of war was only one of these meanings and not the most prominent amongst them.[64]

In rabbinic literature, the term *shalom* generally refers to interpersonal harmony. It is used most frequently for relations amongst fellow-Jews and, less often, for relations between Jews and Gentiles. Peace is presented as one of the highest moral values humans should strive for in imitation of God. Rabbis viewed God as the ultimate peace-maker as far as peace amongst political entities and ethnic groups was concerned. At the same time, they urged Jews to strive for peace in their local and familiar surroundings, in contexts in which their own behavior would have had an immediate impact. Even in a situation of political powerlessness, rabbis believed that individuals could make a difference by implementing peace amongst themselves. Their propagation of peace as a condition of social harmony must be seen in the context of rabbinic theology and anthropology: humans must work together with God in mending the world; they must

---

[58] Stemberger, "Guerra", 138–9.

[59] Stemberger, "Guerra", 139 (my translation from the Italian).

[60] No comprehensive study of the use of this term in rabbinic sources exists.

[61] See Reif, "Peace", 113–32.

[62] The Hebrew *shalom* already appears in some ossuary inscriptions from Herodian times; see Rahmani, *Catalogue*, nos. 217, 226, 286(?), 682(?), 694(?); "shlm" in 3 and 66(?). In the later Greek inscriptions from Caesarea, Jaffa, and Bet She'arim the Hebrew element is often limited to the term *shalom* or *shalom al Yisrael*; see Hezser, *Literacy*, 374 and 374–5 note 150, 378–80. This Hebrew word and phrase seem to be used to indicate the Jewishness of the buried person.

[63] See, e.g., m. Šeb. 5:9; m. 'Abot 4:15.

[64] See also Maier, *Kriegsrecht*, 90–1. Hendrickx, *Sermon*, 31, notes that in the Hebrew Bible the term *shalom* is also "very rich in content", and the LXX used more than twenty-five different terms to translate it.

strive to implement the messianic ideal of world-wide peace in the here and now. This idea is expressed in the late antique Midrash Leviticus Rabbah (amongst other texts):

"R. Shimon b. Yohai said: Great is peace, since all blessings are comprised therein, as it is written: 'The Lord will give strength unto His people; the Lord will bless His people with peace' (Ps 29:11). Hezekiah said two things. Hezekiah said: Great is peace, for in connection with all other precepts it is written, 'if you see' (Exod 23:5), 'if you meet' (Exod 23:4), 'if it happens' (Deut 22:6): if a precept comes to your hand, you are required to perform it; if not, you are not required to perform it. But here [it says]: 'Seek peace and pursue it' (Ps 34:15) – seek it for your own place and follow it from another place. Hezekiah said another thing: Great is peace, for with regard to all the journeys it is written: 'And they [the children of Israel] journeyed [pl.] ... and encamped [pl.] (Num 33:6), [the plural implying that] they journeyed in dissension [*machloqet*], and they encamped in dissension. When they came before Mount Sinai, they all became one encampment." (LevR 9:9)

Peace is seen as the greatest blessing here whose ultimate source is God. Nevertheless humans are urged to implement peace in all situations in which they find themselves. Therefore peace is also presented as the greatest precept, which each individual Jew is required to perform, both in his or her immediate surroundings (that is, the family, village, and home-town) as well as in the broader social context, wherever one may go. Various biblical texts are used in support of the rabbinic emphasis on peace here. The focus is on peace amongst fellow Israelites ("one encampment"), that is, internal social harmony within the smaller or larger Jewish collectivity. After the two revolts rabbis would have considered the wider political sphere out of their reach and therefore focused on what was closer to them. Nevertheless, their perspective included other locations ("follow it from another place") to which their "journeys" might eventually lead them. Interestingly, the term *machloqet* is used as the opposite of *shalom*, a term which rabbis also applied to their own halakhic disputes. They were aware of the fact that *machloqet* characterized their contemporary reality; nevertheless, *shalom* was held up as an ideal and the ultimate goal.

That the rabbinic ideal of peace also concerned the wider political sphere is evident from another text in the same midrashic context:

"R. Yose the Galilean said: Great is peace, since even in a time of war one should begin with peace, as it is written: 'When you draw near unto a city to fight against it, then proclaim peace unto it' (Deut 20:10). R. Yudan b. R. Yose said: Great is peace, seeing that the Holy One, blessed be He, is called Peace, as it says, And he called Him Lord, Peace! (Judg 2:24). R. Tanhum b. Yudan said: From this we derive the rule that a person may not offer his fellow the greeting 'Peace' in a place of filth." (LevR 9:9)

The statement attributed to R. Yose the Galilean is based on similar notions in the Hebrew Bible, of which Deut 20:20 is quoted as an example here: before engaging in military action against another nation, the possibility of a peaceful solution should be sought. Only if there is no chance of peace is military action considered legitimate. In the following statement attributed to R. Yudan b. R. Yose God is even equated with peace. Peace is thereby elevated to a higher sphere and associated with holiness, so much so that using the greeting *shalom* in a filthy place is considered inappropriate.

Peace is also mentioned frequently in tannaitic texts and mostly refers to creating a harmonious relationship between one person and another. According to m. Pe'ah 1:1, "creating peace between one person and another" is one of the "things which have no measure", that is, which should be practiced in abundance. This notion is very reminiscent of the praise of peace-makers in the Sermon on the Mount (Matt 5:9), discussed above. Peace-making is equated to honoring one's parents and charitable work. All three activities are seen as moral ideals that equal only the study of Torah in their religious value. A similar notion is expressed in a saying attributed to Hillel in m. 'Abot 1:12: "Hillel says: Be like the disciples of Aaron: a lover of peace and a pursuer of peace." Again, the active element is stressed: the love of peace, that is, propagating peace as an ideal, is not sufficient. Pursuing peace or actively striving after peace is demanded here.

The high value of peace-making is also stressed in an amoraic story tradition transmitted in LevR 9:3. The story relates that R. Yannai was hospitably received in the house of a non-rabbi and offered food and drink. During the meal the rabbi allegedly tested his host's religious learning and found him deficient in this regard. Thereupon he treated him disrespectfully and called him a dog ("A dog has eaten of Jannai's bread"), regretting the table fellowship he had accepted. The man became angry and claimed that Yannai and his fellow rabbis maintained a monopoly on Torah knowledge ("You have my inheritance, which you are withholding from me!"). The story ends with the following dialogue between the rabbi and his non-rabbinic host:

"R. Yannai said to him: How have you merited to eat at a table with me? The man said: Never in my life have I, after hearing evil talk, repeated it to the person spoken of, nor have I ever seen two persons quarrelling without bringing peace between them. He [R. Yannai] said to him: You possess such good breeding [*derekh eretz*], and I called you a dog!"

Again, the active element in peace-making is stressed and equated to Torah learning in its value. Moreover, making peace between individuals is presented as an example of good breeding, *derekh eretz*.

In the Mishnah tractate Avot and other rabbinic sources the close connection between peace and justice or righteousness is stressed – e.g., "Rabban Shimon b. Gamliel says: on three things does the world stand: on justice, and on truth, and on peace, as it is said: 'Truth and a judgment of peace judge in your gates' [Zech 8:16]" (m. 'Abot 1:18); "... the more righteousness, the more peace" (m. 'Abot 2:7). As we have seen above, the connection between righteousness and peace also appears in Matt 5:9–10, where the blessing of the peacemakers is followed by the blessing of "those who are persecuted for righteousness' sake", a notion that does not have a parallel in Luke. This association is based on the fundamental idea that righteousness and justice should govern interpersonal relationships. Again, the theological concept of *imitatio Dei* plays a role here: since God is believed to be righteous and just, humans should strive for righteousness and justice and behave towards each other in a just way. Only on the basis of just rules and interpersonal obligations can peace – both in social and political terms – be created and maintained.

Rabbis believed that lasting peace could ultimately be granted by God only, that it was a condition of messianic times, whereas the reality of everyday life was governed by the lack of peace amongst individuals. This is expressed in an exegetical story attributed to R. Simon in GenR 8:5. The biblical story of the creation of Adam is associated with Ps 85:11 here, which is not understood in its literal sense, though. Whereas the literal translation of the text is: "Lovingkindness and truth met each other, justice and peace kissed each other", the rabbinic authors of the story understood the relationships negatively: "Lovingkindness and truth encountered each other [in battle], justice and peace have taken up arms against each other", deriving *nishqo* from *nesheq*, "weapon", "armor". These personified values are said to have fought against each other, trying to influence God when Adam was about to be created. "Peace said: Let him not be created, because he is full of strife." Yet despite the fact that human beings engage in disputes amongst each other, God decided to create them. The condition of lack of peace and quarrels amongst humans is seen here as part of the world's reality. God created an imperfect world, whereas peace and perfection are to be expected only of the world to come. This text is another expression of the pragmatism with which rabbis saw the world: actively striving for peace is propagated as a value but will always remain imperfect until God grants peace to humans, whether in this world or the next. Peace is a blessing promulgated by God (cf. m. 'Uq. 3:12; ExR 15:26; 52:5; LevR 3:6).

At the end of our discussion, another aspect of the rabbis' pragmatic attitude toward the reality of everyday life should be mentioned briefly: regulations enacted "for the good order of the world". This expression appears numerous times in the Mishnah already, especially in tractate Gittin chapters 4 and 5. Most of these regulations are meant to create stability within the Jewish community itself. For example, m. Giṭ. 4:2 states that R. Gamliel the Elder ruled "for the good order of the world", that is, in the public interest, that a husband should not be allowed to set up a court at another locale and cancel a *get* (divorce document) without his wife or her agent being present; if this is done, the wife might consider the *get* valid, marry another man, and produce illegitimate children with him (being married to two husbands); or she might become an *agunah*, deserted by her husband but unable to remarry. Similarly, the same *mishnah* rules that all possible names of the husband and wife and their places of residence should be included in the *get*, again to prevent misunderstandings and their possibly disastrous consequences. Similarly, the house of Shammai is said to have ruled that a half-slave, whom one of his masters had released, should also be released by his second master, "for the good order of the world", to prevent the confusions that his unclear status would bring about (m. Giṭ. 4:5).[65]

While most of the contexts in which the formula is used concern inner-Jewish relationships, sometimes relations between Jews and non-Jews are envisioned. Thus, m. Giṭ. 4:6 rules that "one should not ransom captives for more than their value [i.e., their purchase price], for the good order of the world". Although rabbis generally encouraged the redemption of enslaved Jews (cf. t. Giṭ. 4:2; t. Mo'ed Qaṭ. 1:12), the caution against redeeming war captives for large amounts of money is based on the notion that a high ransom price would motivate Romans to enslave even more Jews. A good deed applied to an individual could lead to a social evil if looked at from a broader perspective, especially in terms of its possible social and political consequences. The general public interest and relations between Jews and Romans are the motivating factors behind this ruling.

6. Conclusions

In the Hellenistic and Roman periods both Jews and Christians seem to have preferred non-violent conflict resolutions whenever they were possible, even if they would lead to a loss of human life. John H. Yoder has already emphasized that the non-violent stance in early Christianity, which is sometimes called "pacifism", "was a part of the common Jewish legacy".[66] With the exception of the Hasmonean and Herodian periods, Jews were directly subjugated to foreign rule and lacked political authority. In

---

[65] See also m. Giṭ. 4:3–4, 7, 9; 5:3; 9:4; m. 'Ed. 1:13.
[66] Yoder, "Charge", 77.

this situation of "not being in charge" a non-violent stance was often con-sidered wiser than a violent uprising, even in situations of provocation from the foreign rulers and their subsidiaries. On that basis, the two revolts against Rome seem to have been exceptions rather than the rule.

While peaceful conflict resolutions were the ideal, ancient Jews were not principally opposed to military pursuits, should they be necessary to pre-serve Jewish religious observance and cultural identity. In this regard Jews resembled Greeks and Romans who also lacked a pacifistic stance in the modern understanding of the term. Whether Jesus and early Christians were generally opposed to military action remains doubtful. In situations of pow-erlessness and persecution, "turning the other cheek" would have been wiser than engaging in useless battle, as Josephus had already argued. Pre-serving one's own life and those of one's fellow believers was sometimes valued higher than a heroic defeat that might have equaled suicide. By blessing peace-making and non-violence early Christians seem to have turned a necessity into an ideal.

First and Second Maccabees as well as rabbinic literature stress that Jew-ish identity is based on Torah observance with all that it implies (e.g., Sab-bath observance, circumcision, monotheism etc.). If Torah observance is threatened and observant Jews are killed by a foreign military, a violent rebellion may be the only means to restore the possibility of living a Jewish life, as the example of the Maccabees indicates. If Torah observance is guaranteed, as it was in Roman times after the two revolts, Jewish religious leaders seem to have tolerated foreign rule, even if they did not like it (see also Philo). At the time of the first revolt against Rome the situation was ambiguous and Jewish reactions mixed: there were provocations by Roman officials but no general prohibition of Jewish religious observance; some Jews opted for rebellion whereas others decided to give in to the Romans. With his own shifting stance Josephus embodied this uncertainty.

Sometimes choices had to be made between Torah observance (and po-litical independence), on the one hand, and the preservation of Jewish life, on the other. Those who fought against Antiochus and the Romans risked being killed in battle; others chose to kill themselves rather than to become subservient to the Romans (Masada). If there was at least a glimpse of hope that traditional ways could be maintained, surrender (Josephus) and ac-commodation (rabbis) were often preferred. How ancient Jews reacted to foreign rule would have ultimately depended on each individual's values and preferences, as well as on his or her assessment of the situation. A general pacifistic stance, on the other hand, is not recognizable in ancient Jewish literary sources.

References

Betz, H.D., *Essays on the Sermon on the Mount* (Philadelphia: Fortress, 1985).

–, "The Sermon on the Mount and Q: Some Aspects of the Problem", in J.E. Goehring et al. (ed.), *Gospel Origins and Christian Beginnings: In Honor of James M. Robinson* (Sonoma: Polebridge Press, 1990) 19–34.

–, *The Sermon on the Mount: A Commentary on the Sermon on the Mount, including the Sermon on the Plain (Matthew 5:3–7:27 and Luke 6:20–49)* (Minneapolis: Fortress Press, 1995).

Bickerman, E., *The God of the Maccabees* (Leiden: Brill, 1979).

Brock, P., *A Brief History of Pacifism from Jesus to Tolstoy* (Toronto: Syracuse University Press, 1992).

Broyde, M.J., "Fighting the War and the Peace: Battlefield Ethics, Peace Talks, Treaties and Pacifism in the Jewish Tradition", in J.P. Burns (ed.), *War and Its Discontents: Pacifism and Quietism in the Abrahamic Traditions* (Washington: Georgetown University Press, 1996) 1–30.

Cohen, S.J.D., "Josephus, Jeremiah, and Polybius", *History & Theory* 21 (1982) 366–81.

Coogan M.D. (ed.), *The New Oxford Annotated Apocrypha* (Oxford: Oxford University Press, ³2001).

Davies, W.D., *The Setting of the Sermon on the Mount* (Cambridge: Cambridge University Press, 1966).

Elssner, T.R. "Antiquity and the Idea of Peace", in: *Deuterocanonical and Cognate Literature Yearbook* (Berlin/New York: de Gruyter, 2010) 353–70.

Gendler, E.R., "The Pursuit of Peace: A Singular Commandment", in J.P. Burns (ed.), *War and Its Discontents: Pacifism and Quietism in the Abrahamic Traditions* (Washington: Georgetown University Press, 1996) 31–46.

Haensch, R., "The Roman Provincial Administration", in C. Hezser (ed.), *The Oxford Handbook of Jewish Daily Life in Roman Palestine* (Oxford: Oxford University Press, 2010) 71–84.

Hare, D.R.A., *The Theme of Jewish Persecution of Christians in the Gospel According to St. Matthew* (SNTSMS 6, Cambridge: Cambridge University Press, 1967).

Hargie, O. et al., *Social Skills in Interpersonal Communication* (London: Routledge, ³1994).

Harries, J., "Courts and the Judicial System", in C. Hezser (ed.), *The Oxford Handbook of Jewish Daily Life in Roman Palestine* (Oxford: Oxford University Press, 2010) 85–101.

Harris, W.V., *Restraining Rage: The Ideology of Anger Control in Classical Antiquity* (Cambridge/London: Harvard University Press, 2001).

Hendrickx, H., *The Sermon on the Mount* (London: Geoffrey Chapman, 1984).

Hezser, C., *Jewish Literacy in Roman Palestine* (TSAJ 81; Tübingen: Mohr Siebeck, 2001).

–, *Jewish Slavery in Antiquity* (Oxford: Oxford University Press, 2005).

Horbury, W., "The Benediction of the 'Minim' and Early Jewish-Christian Controversy", *JTS* 33 (1982) 19–61.

Horsley, R.A., *Jesus and the Spiral of Violence: Popular Jewish Resistance in Roman Palestine* (San Francisco: Harper and Row, 1987).

Instone-Brewer, D., "The Eighteen Benedictions and the 'Minim' Before 70 CE", *JTS* 54 (2003) 25–44.

Kasher, A., *The Jews in Hellenistic and Roman Egypt: The Struggle for Equal Rights* (Tübingen: Mohr Siebeck, 1985).

Kimelman, R., "Non-Violence in the Talmud", *Judaism* 17 (1968) 316–34.

–, "*Birkat Ha-Minim* and the Lack of Evidence for an Anti-Christian Jewish Prayer in Antiquity", in E.P. Sanders (ed.), *Jewish and Christian Self-Definition* (2 vol.; Philadelphia: Fortress, 1981) 226–44.

Konradt, M., "Die Deutung der Zerstörung Jerusalems und des Tempels im Matthäusevangelium", in C. Böttrich/J. Herzer (ed.), *Josephus und das Neue Testament: Wechselseitige Wahrnehmungen* (WUNT 209; Tübingen: Mohr Siebeck, 2007) 195–232.

Lachs, S.T., *A Rabbinic Commentary on the New Testament: The Gospels of Matthew, Mark, and Luke* (Hoboken/New York: Ktav Publishing House/Anti-Defamation League, 1987).

Ladouceur, D.J., "Josephus and Masada", in L.H. Feldman/G. Hata (ed.), *Josephus, Judaism, and Christianity* (Detroit: Gohei Hata Books, 1987) 95–113.

Laserstein, B., *Das Judentum ist der Friede! Dokumente der Friedensbewegung* (Berlin: Zehl & Koch Verlag, 1926).

Luz, U., *Matthew 8–20: A Commentary* (Hermeneia; Minneapolis: Fortress Press, 2001).

Maier, J., *Kriegsrecht und Friedensordnung in jüdischer Tradition* (Stuttgart: Kohlhammer, 2000).

Marcus, J., "'Birkat Ha-Minim' Revisited", *NTS* 55 (2009) 523–51.

Martone, C., "Guerra e pace a Qumran e nei Testi Apocalittici", in M. Perani (ed.), *Guerra santa, guerra e pace dal Vicino Oriente antico alle tradizioni ebraica, cristiana e islamica* (Florence: Giuntina, 2005) 83–93.

Neher, A., "Rabbinic Adumbrations of Non-Violence: Israel and Canaan", in R. Loewe (ed.), *Studies in Rationalism, Judaism & Universalism* (London/New York: Routledge/The Humanities Press, 1966) 169–96.

Nickelsburg, G.W.E., *Jewish Literature Between the Bible and the Mishnah. A Historical and Literary Introduction* (Philadelphia: Fortress Press, 1987).

Nitzan, B., "Prayers for Peace in the Dead Sea Scrolls and the Traditional Jewish Liturgy", in E.G. Chazon (ed.), *Liturgical Perspectives: Prayer and Poetry in Light of the Dead Sea Scrolls* (Proceedings of the Fifth International Symposium of the Orion Center for the Study of the Dead Sea Scrolls and Associated Literature, 19–23 January, 2000; Studies on the Texts of the Desert of Judah 48; Leiden: Brill, 2003) 113–32.

Rahmani, L.Y., *A Catalogue of Jewish Ossuaries in the Collections of the State of Israel* (Jerusalem: Israel Antiquities Authority, 1994).

Reif, S., "Peace in Early Jewish Prayer", in: *Deuterocanonical and Cognate Literature Yearbook* (Berlin/New York: de Gruyter, 2010) 377–99.

Rinpoche, S., "Education for Non-Violence", in D. Bernstorff/H. von Welck (ed.), *Exile as Challenge: The Tibetan Diaspora* (Hyderabad: Orient Longman, 2003) 454–70.

Sabini, J., *Social Psychology* (New York/London: W.W. Norton Company, 1992).

Saldarini, A.J., "Jochanan Ben Zakkai's Escape from Jerusalem. Origin and Development of a Rabbinic Story", *JSJ* 6 (1975) 189–204.

Schäfer, P., "Die Flucht Johanan b. Zakkais aus Jerusalem und die Gründung des 'Lehrhauses' in Jabne", *ANRW* II.19.2 (1979) 43–101.

Schiffman, L.H., "Historical Perspectives on Dissent and Disobedience: Jews Against Jews in Late Antiquity", in M. Sokol (ed.), *Tolerance, Dissent, and Democracy: Philosophical, Historical, and Halakhic Perspectives* (Northvale/Jerusalem: Jason Aronson, 2002) 233–59.

–, "War in Jewish Apocalyptic Thought", in L.H. Schiffman/J.B. Wolowelski (ed.), *War and Peace in the Jewish Tradition* (New York: Yeshiva University Press, 2007) 477–95.

Schroedel, W.R., "Apologetic Literature and Ambassadorial Activities", *HTR* 82 (1989) 55–78.

Schwartz, D.R., *2 Maccabees* (CEJL; Berlin/New York: de Gruyter, 2008).

Selwyn, E.G., *The First Epistle of St. Peter* (London: Macmillan, 1946).

Steck, O.H., *Israel und das gewaltsame Geschick der Propheten: Untersuchungen zur Überlieferung des deuteronomistischen Geschichtsbildes im Alten Testament, Spätjudentum und Urchristentum* (WMANT 23; Neukirchen-Vluyn: Neukirchener Verlag, 1967).

Stemberger,G., "La guerra nella Mišnah e nei Midrašim halakici", in: M. Perani (ed.), *Guerra santa, guerra e pace dal Vicino Oriente antico alle tradizioni ebraica, cristiana e islamica* (Florence: Giuntina, 2005) 131–9.

Tcherikover, V., *Hellenistic Civilization and the Jews* (Philadelphia: Jewish Publication Society, 1961).

Teeple, H.M., "The Origin of the Son of Man Christology", *JBL* 84 (1965) 213–50.

Yoder, J.H., "On Not Being in Charge", in J.P. Burns (ed.), *War and Its Discontents: Pacifism and Quietism in the Abrahamic Traditions* (Washington: Georgetown University Press, 1996) 74–90.

Zerbe, G.M., *Non-Retaliation in Early Jewish and New Testament Texts: Ethical Themes in Social Contexts* (JSP Supplement Series 13; Sheffield: JSOT Press, 1993).

–, "'Pacifism' and 'Passive Resistance' in Apocalyptic Writings: A Critical Evaluation", in J.H. Charlesworth/C.A. Evans (ed.), *The Pseudepigrapha and Early Biblical Interpretation* (Sheffield: Sheffield Academic Press, 1993) 65–95.

Kai Trampedach

Ruprecht-Karls-Universität Heidelberg

The High Priests and Rome

Why Cooperation Failed[1]

Flavius Josephus attempted to define the peculiarity and political demands of the Mosaic Law with the neologism "theocracy". In his *contra Apionem*, Josephus explains to his non-Jewish audience that the unique nature of the order founded by Moses could not be explained in conventional constitutional terms. Instead, it would be better to speak of *theokratia* since the lawgiver had dedicated the legal order completely to God and his rule (*archē*) and power (*kratos*). The constitution of the Jews, according to Josephus, did not revolve around the dominion of one person, a small group or even a state over others, but on the rule of God over humanity in general and over his chosen people in particular. Democracy, oligarchy or monarchy can therefore be subsumed under the term *theocracy* if they fulfill theocratic claims – i.e., if they ensure that the life of the community can be aligned with the will of God. Josephus understands Jewish theocracy, therefore, as an absolute norm that precedes constitutional and institutional configuration and that itself is subject to certain conditions. It is the binding standard for any (political and social as well as individual) activity in this world.[2]

Did Josephus therefore think that the constitutional realization of a theocracy was arbitrary? Not at all. Rather, in his view, Jewish tradition laid out the way in which this had to be done. "What could be finer or more just", he asks in *contra Apionem*, "than [a structure] that has made God governor of the universe, that commits to the priests in concert the management of the most important matters and, in turn, has entrusted to the high priest of all the governance of the other priests? ... So, what regime could be more holy than this? What honor could be more fitting to God, where the whole mass [of people] is equipped for piety, the priests are entrusted with special

---

[1] Some topics discussed in this paper are also dealt with in Trampedach, "Schwierigkeiten" (forthcoming). I thank the Konstanz Cluster of Excellence "Cultural Foundations of Integration" and its Institute for Advanced Study for the translation of my text and for the fellowship which allowed me *inter alia* to work on this article.

[2] Josephus C. Ap. 2.164–5. See Gerber, *Bild*, 338–59; Barclay, *Against Apion*, 262; Trampedach, "Hasmonäer", 61–5.

supervision, and the whole constitution is organized like some rite of consecration?"[3] There is no doubt: If the state is like a permanent form of worship, then the priests must set the tone. For Josephus, the scion of an old Jerusalem family of priests, hierocracy is the given constitutional form of theocracy. He is trying to bring the pagan addressees of his text closer to the idea that the Jewish priesthood is a particularly worthy expression of aristocracy.[4] Originally, the priests were simply the best, as Josephus makes clear: "These the legislator initially appointed to their office not for their wealth nor because they were superior by any other fortuitous advantage; but whoever of his generation surpassed others in persuasiveness and moderation, these were the people to whom he entrusted, in particular, the worship of God."[5] At the time of Josephus it was tradition that qualified the priests for their leadership role. Josephus refers to Mosaic legislation granting the priests a special position. Against the backdrop of numerous constitutional changes, he presents an almost uninterrupted series of high priests over the course of two thousand years. After all, Jewish autonomy after the return from Babylonian exile was reorganized as a temple state under the leadership of the high priest and the other priests.[6]

Apart from the apologetic intentions that Josephus is pursuing in *contra Apionem*, with his thoughts focused especially on theocracy and hierocracy, I believe that his ideal concept has heuristic value. In the following, I would like to attempt to articulate the limits and possibilities of his concept as applied to the history of Judea, particularly in the period of direct Roman administration between 6 and 66 CE. At the same time, I will also account for the two conditions outlined by my title, specifically: 1) that the relationship between the Judean high priests[7] and the Roman occupying power can

---

[3] Josephus C. Ap. 2.185–8 (translation: Barclay, *Against Apion*, 273–5); cf. C. Ap. 2.193–4.

[4] Schwartz, "Josephus", 31–40, shows that Josephus does not use the term "aristocracy" in a consistent way; in B.J. and Ant., Judean "aristocracy" does not denote hierocracy "but rather government by council" (34). Nevertheless, in Josephus aristocracy and priestly leadership are closely associated, and the councils Josephus is thinking of are certainly dominated by wealthy priests.

[5] Josephus C. Ap. 2.186.

[6] Josephus Ant. 20.224–51. Hengel/Deines, "Common Judaism", 67, pointed out, that Josephus, in advertising the Judean constitution as hierocracy, could hope to convince his non-Jewish readers: "ancient priestly wisdom from the Orient had something especially honorable about it for the Romans and Greeks". Even before Josephus, Pseudo-Hekataios (in Josephus C. Ap. 1.187–8) and Strabo (16.2.36–7) emphasized the leading position of the priests in Judea: "both seem influenced by the presumption the priestly administration of power and justice would guarantee superior government" (Barclay, *Against Apion*, 274). See also Diod. 40.3; Just. 36.2.16; Mason, *Flavius Josephus*, 191–2, 195–7.

[7] By the term "high priest" I mean, as Josephus and the New Testament do, the actual incumbent as well as someone who belonged to the group of ex-high priests; in its plural form, the expression was also used, as Smallwood, "High Priests", 16, put it, "loosely to denote members of the High Priestly families who did not actually hold office".

be characterized as a cooperation (albeit an asymmetric one); and 2) that this cooperation failed.

As the Roman general Pompey was holding court in the spring of 63 BCE in Damascus, three Jewish factions presented themselves to him, asking him to support their respective claims. While the brothers Aristobulus II and Hyrcanus II were there competing for the monarchy, a third group appeared before Pompey. According to Diodorus, the faction consisted of more than two hundred of the most respected men (*hoi epiphanestatoi*), and according to Josephus, they represented the *ethnos*. This group asked Pompey to free the Jews completely from monarchic rule and in its place to reinstate the high priest and the (priestly) aristocracy to their former (rightful) positions. According to Diodorus and Josephus, this delegation justified its concerns with a general and a special argument: 1) a monarchy would run counter to the traditions of their people, as it was customary for them to obey the priests of their god; and 2) the present kings had ignored their fathers' laws and enslaved citizens unfairly, for they had acquired the kingdom by means of mercenary troops, criminal acts, and a number of gratuitous murders.[8]

Nearly 60 years later, after the death of King Herod (in 4 BCE), this set of circumstances was repeated. Only this time it was in Rome and in front of Emperor Augustus: While the brothers Archelaus and Antipas were contending for the inheritance of their father, a third delegation appeared, representing – as Josephus pointed out – the *ethnos*. The delegation, consisting of 50 envoys and joined by 8.000 Jews from the city of Rome, asked the emperor for autonomy, calling for the dissolution of the monarchy and the inclusion of the Herodian regime in the province of Syria. To make a fundamental argument against monarchy and for hierocracy would have been inappropriate before the imperial court. It is therefore not surprising that the Judean envoys only made use of the second argument that had been presented decades before to Pompey. In their speech to the emperor, therefore, they described the attacks by Herod and Archelaus. As is well-known, Augustus did not agree with the Judean envoys and their Roman supporters at first. Rather, he divided up Herod's kingdom among his sons Archelaus, Antipas and Philip. Ten years later, however, the circles hostile to the monarchy – Josephus calls them the leaders (*hoi prōtoi*) of the Judeans and Samarians – succeeded in bringing down Herod's despised son. After hearing their complaints, Augustus chose to put Archelaus' territory (Judea, Samaria and Idumea) under direct Roman rule; this meant adding it to the

---

[8] Diod. 40.2; Josephus Ant. 14.41.

province of Syria and assigning it to a knight-prefect, who in turn was under the authority of the emperor's senatorial legate in Antioch.[9]

As was customary in such cases, the Romans were on the lookout for wealthy local and regional elites who might serve them as associates or collaborators in exchange for privileges and wide-ranging opportunities for advancement.[10] In Judea they had no choice: it was not simply some *polis* but the temple that was the focus of Jewish identity. Furthermore, it was the only Judean institution that had survived the reign of Herod more or less undamaged.[11] Tradition, ritual (monitoring the daily sacrifice) and wealth pointed the Romans inevitably to the priestly elite in Jerusalem. In addition, the high priests alone seemed to be in a position to ensure peace, order, and the uninterrupted exploitation of the country. In other words, they could administer justice among the Judeans and collect tribute for the Romans. Josephus confirms this a priori assumption when he says that, after Herod and Archelaus, the Judean "constitution became an aristocracy, and the high priests were entrusted with the leadership of the nation" (Ant. 20.251). The two delegations in Rome calling for the removal of Archelaus and asking for autonomy in the province of Syria could not have had anything else in mind. Autonomy in this respect could only mean a temple-based state and priestly rule.

Who belonged to this specifically Jewish aristocracy besides the acting high priest? Unfortunately, the source material available does not provide a precise answer. It is clear that this "nobility" included the former high priests, the main temple officials and their families – all of whom were themselves members of the Sanhedrin. The nineteen holders of the high priesthood between 6 and 66 CE stemmed only from four clans in whom power and influence were concentrated.[12] For the most part, the Romans assigned them responsibility for the internal affairs of Judea. As in other

---

[9] Josephus B.J. 2.80–100, 111, 117; Ant. 17.299–323, 342–4; 18.1–2; Smallwood, *Jews*, 107–10; Eck, *Rom*, 23–7, and Bernett, *Kaiserkult*, 173–5, 187–8. The doubts that Goodman, *Ruling Class*, 39, has raised against the importance of the delegations from Judea do not seem convincing to me.

[10] *Exempli gratias*: Garnsey/Saller, *Roman Empire*, 26; Jacques/Scheid, *Rom*, 367–9, esp. 368: "Weil die Römer ihre Besitzungen nicht direkt militärisch kontrollieren und verwaltungsmäßig erfassen konnten, begünstigten sie schon seit republikanischer Zeit lokale Honoratioren als Garanten der Stabilität und nahmen sie sogar allmählich in ihre eigene Führungsschicht auf. Außerdem suchten die Kaiser im Namen der offiziell propagierten Eintracht gewöhnlich die Akzeptanz der verschiedenen Eliten."

[11] Goodman, *Ruling Class*, 111; cf. ibid., 43: "In the case of Judaea the obvious institution which might be expected to provide the desired impression of peace and continuity within the country was the Temple and its priesthood." Goodman adds, however, that because of Herod's autocratic policy the high priests were "weak men who lacked local prestige which might have enabled them to carry the people with them on behalf of Rome". I will come back to this below.

[12] Schürer, *History*, 2:227–36.

provinces, the Romans also encouraged competition between the leading families. Since there were neither elections nor offices in Judea that might encourage such competition, the Romans (like Herod and Archelaus before them) ensured relatively frequent changes in the office of high priest. The fact that the high priests were chosen only from a limited number of families shows that the Romans did not wish to weaken the position but to create a ruling class. The frequent changes were intended, in my view, to counteract monarchical tendencies and to prevent an excessive accumulation of power by individual persons or clans.

Hence, the Romans – completely in the spirit of Josephus – accepted the priority of the high priesthood of Jerusalem in that part of the province of Syria formerly ruled by Archelaus. In the following decades until the revolt, they supported their Jewish provincial elite in numerous ways, as I will now demonstrate.

Even the way in which provincialization proceeded betrays the fact that the emperor of the Roman administration – in my view – desired to keep a low profile in this troubled region. The prefect resided in Caesarea and only came to Jerusalem when it was necessary to ensure public order, as was regularly the case at major pilgrimage festivals. He only had about 3.500 men available as auxiliary troops, for the Roman legions were stationed in relatively remote locations in northern Syria and Egypt.[13] In addition, there was the far-reaching autonomy of the temple administration, which was nothing special *per se*, except if we consider the Jerusalem temple's broad scope in terms of its authority. With regard to the internal administration of justice, this autonomy may have encompassed (although the matter is disputed) even the power of the high priest and Sanhedrin (a competence granted to very few cities in the early imperial period) to implement capital penalties, albeit of course only in religious matters.[14] In addition, the Jerusalem temple was the only institution besides the imperial treasury that was permitted to collect regular contributions throughout the empire. In the process, it accumulated a great deal of wealth. Few took pleasure in the constant flow of money to Jerusalem. As one can imagine, this was espe-

---

[13] According to Eck, *Rom*, 39, the choice of Caesarea should not be interpreted as having been made out of Rome's respect for the holiness of Jerusalem but simply as a continuation of the residence of the former monarch. There are, however, other factors that have to be taken into account. First, the main residence of the Herodians had always been Jerusalem with its Hasmonean Palace, the Antonia, and the large palace of Herod. Second, Jerusalem was unquestionably the center of Judean (and Jewish) life. When the emperor decided that his prefect should regularly stay at a place some distance from Jerusalem, he underlined Judean autonomy. Other strategic and political reasons that recommended Caesarea to the Romans are discussed by Beebe, "Caesarea", 195–207. See also Smallwood, *Jews*, 145–6, and Haensch, *Capita provinciarum*, 232–4.

[14] Smallwood, *Jews*, 149–50.

cially the feeling in those towns where there were larger Jewish communities.[15]

In many respects, the Roman administration accommodated the religious sensitivities of the Jews. Hence, the Jewish population was released from participating in the imperial cult. Instead, as Philo and Josephus document, they offered twice daily a sacrifice "for Caesar and the Roman people".[16] Even more serious was the religious moderation that the Romans imposed on themselves in their province. As shown by the activities of Prefect Pontius Pilate in Jerusalem, who tried otherwise but finally gave in, the Romans could not even hoist standards in their barracks or dedicated shields in the praetorium that were decorated with images of the Emperor or inscriptions to him.[17] Rather, whenever they were in Jerusalem, they were required to abandon any open religious activity of their own, even in private. This, too, was the case for the soldiers in their service, from the prefect and his staff on down to the cohort stationed in the Antonia.[18] Even outside of Jerusalem, the Romans refrained from displaying any images. In 37 CE, when the Syrian governor Vitellius took up arms with two legions and auxiliary forces against the Nabatean king Aretas, a Jewish delegation in Ptolemais (Acre), whom Josephus calls *andres hoi prōtoi* (Ant. 18.121), asked him to change his marching route so as not to advance with their standards through Judea. Indeed, Vitellius gave his army orders to make a large detour around Judea.[19] Accordingly, the prefects refrained from putting the portrait of the emperor on coins minted in Caesarea.[20] Similarly, there was no presentation of Roman rule in the form of victory monuments or other material symbols. The epigraphy confirms this observation. To my knowledge, no one has yet found, outside of the Syro-Hellenistic towns, any milestones or other monumental inscriptions from the period before 70 CE.[21]

Nonetheless, there were also provocateurs on the Roman side who contributed to the poisoning of the atmosphere. Those who distinguished them-

---

[15] At the same time, Roman provincial governors like Flaccus, the late-Republican propraetor of Asia who confiscated Jewish money (Cicero pro Flacco 66–9), may have grumbled occasionally about this privilege.

[16] Philo Legat. 157, 232, 317; Josephus C. Ap. 2.77; B.J. 2.197, 409; Smallwood, *Jews*, 83, 147–8; Mason, *Judean War 2*, 164 (with a refutation of Bernett, *Kaiserkult*, esp. 194–9, who argues that the Romans never really accepted the sacrifice as a substitute for direct emperor worship).

[17] Josephus B.J. 2.169–74; Ant. 18.55–9; Philo Legat. 299–305. See Eck, *Rom*, 53–9; Wilker, *Jerusalem*, 93–103.

[18] For a telling example of how far the Roman prefect could go in considering the religious sensitivity of the Judean high priests, cf. John 18:28–29.

[19] Josephus Ant. 18.120–2.

[20] Smallwood, *Jews*, 148; Eck, *Rom*, 58–9. Pontius Pilate, however, issued coins with representations of symbols that were used in the imperial cult (Bernett, *Kaiserkult*, 202–5).

[21] Compare Isaac, *Limits*, 427–35 (App. I).

selves in this were primarily soldiers from auxiliary units, who came from the country but were not themselves Jews. But it is significant to note how the Roman administration reacted in such cases. One soldier who had taken a Torah scroll in a raid and thrown it into a fire was led to his execution through the ranks of his Jewish accusers in Caesarea.[22] In another case, the Emperor Claudius himself condemned the tribune of the Jerusalem cohort to be handed over in chains to the Jews in Jerusalem. They in turn dragged him through the city and ultimately decapitated him.[23] When he made this decision, Claudius was issuing a verdict in favor of a delegation from Jerusalem sent to Rome by the governor of Syria, Ummidius Quadratus. At the same time, he relieved Prefect Cumanus of his duties and sent him into exile. This leads us to a final point, something Paul McKechnie pointed out in an article a few years ago. In the years 44 to 66, we hear of seven Jewish delegations from Palestine who presented their concerns in Rome to the emperors Claudius and Nero. The emperors decided six of those cases in favor of the Jews. To put it differently, in each case, the emperor sided with the Jerusalem priesthood – even when it meant having to snub his own officials. The only defeat the Jews had to accept concerned the struggle for supremacy in Caesarea.[24]

However, especially in the twenty years preceding the rebellion, the high priests were less and less successful at ensuring peaceful conditions in Jerusalem, not to mention of the rest of the country. The rebellion finally broke out when a group of radical priests led by Eleazar, son of the high priest Anania, prevailed in rejecting the sacrifices of non-Jews. Josephus explains: "This was the foundation of war against the Romans, for they cast aside the sacrifice on behalf of these [the Romans] and Caesar."[25] The leaders of the ruling class, as we know, were not able to reverse this symbolic declaration of war that had emerged from their ranks, for they themselves were overtaken by the momentum of the uprising. Many of the leading insurgents (including Josephus) came from the ranks of the higher priesthood.[26]

---

[22] Josephus B.J. 2.228–31; Ant. 20.113–17.

[23] Josephus B.J. 2.244–6; Ant. 20.136. Mason, *Judean War 2*, 199, comments that "this beheading, after torture and humiliation by foreigners, following the months-long journey back to Judea in anticipation, would be an extreme form of degradation for the tribune".

[24] McKechnie, "Judean Embassies", 340–61, with summary on 361: "In order to rule in favour of the Jerusalem priests in the middle decades of the first century, the emperors ruled against three procurators of Judaea, a legate of Syria, and Claudius' personal friend Agrippa II. Over about two decades the political priority which was accorded to giving judgments favourable to the Jerusalem priests appears to have been consistently high."

[25] Josephus B.J. 2.409–10 (translation: Mason, *Judean War 2*, 313–14).

[26] Goodman, *Ruling Class*, 167–70; Price, *Jerusalem*, 31–8, 40–3.

This raises the question: Why in the end did the cooperation of the Roman provincial administration and the indigenous local elites fail in Judea? And why had it proven to be so weak even before that? Several answers come to mind.

1) The Jerusalem priesthood could and would not accept the types of integration that the Roman Empire made available for the provincial elite. Against the backdrop of Roman rule in other provinces, it is striking that Judea did not produce any knights, senators, governors, or military commanders – and only very few Roman citizens. Purity strictures, to which the priests were particularly subject, prevented social communication and interaction with the prefects and officers of the Roman army stationed in the country. Moreover, the priests could not offer any of the qualities, like military achievement or rhetorical expertise, that garnered respect in the eyes of the Roman administrators. It is no surprise, under these circumstances, that the Roman provincial administrators and the Jewish provincial elites could not develop relationships of trust.[27] Even more serious was the fact that the auxiliary units stationed in Palestine were for the most part (as elsewhere in the empire) recruited from within the province itself but not from among the Jewish population. As a result, the Roman army in Judea was perceived more as an occupying power than as a guarantor of the peace. Nonetheless, the high priests could feel fortunate that the Herodians in Rome took over the lobbying for the Jewish temple-state. From their Roman citizenship to their proximity to the Emperor, they possessed those qualities that gave them influence in Rome.[28] However, they had little leverage in Judea, and their relationship to the priestly elites – a subject I will return to – was by no means free of conflict. Class interest by itself was not sufficient in the long run for establishing firm ties with Rome. Resistance, whether overt or covert, therefore remained a constant temptation, as demonstrated in the end by the theocratic stance taken by Eleazar and his followers in their declaration of war in the temple.[29]

2) As one analyzes a number of conflicts that arose, it becomes clear that the priestly elite did not have sufficient authority. In serious cases, they could not restrain young "hotheads" (a term that is virtually a *topos* in Josephus) or the masses once they were agitated.[30] Despite its privileged posi-

---

[27] Goodman, *Ruling Class*, 47–9.

[28] Wilker, *Rom*, esp. 144–6, 284–9.

[29] Smallwood, "High Priests", esp. 28–9. The suggestion of Horsley, "High Priests", 55, "that the [Judean] aristocracy remained consistently pro-Roman" is derived from an uncritical reading of Josephus, harmonizing the contradictions of his narrative. Moreover, the fruitless question of whether the high priests were pro- or anti-Roman does not help to explain why the initial cooperation failed.

[30] Mason, *Judean War 2*, 186.

tion, then, the priesthood contributed little to the acceptance of Roman rule. Why did the high priests and the ruling class gain so little authority and prestige despite their efforts? If we follow Martin Goodman, who has studied this question most thoroughly, it was "because they could not claim a monopoly of any of the crucial marks of distinction generally accepted as worthy of respect by their fellow Jews".[31] The chief priests shared the same ancestry as thousands of other priests who were excluded from power. Instead, their wealth was most certainly what marked the ruling class and qualified them for their role in the eyes of the Romans. Yet such wealth – reflected in the magnificent houses of Jerusalem's Upper City excavated by archeologists –[32] did not translate into authority in the context of Jewish culture. It was instead considered meaningless, or even an obstacle, on the pathway to salvation, especially because this wealth had so often been acquired at the expense of the poor rural population. Because wealth did not procure anyone social prestige in Judean society, it could also not be transformed by way of *euergetism* into social capital. Could the Jewish *zedaqah* or *caritas*, i.e. the obligation to provide for the poor, perhaps give the priestly elite the credibility and authority that their wealth could not? This is unlikely, since gifts to the poor were supposed to be distributed randomly and anonymously, and there was no social convention obligating the poor to be grateful. Rather, Jewish *caritas* is primarily an obligation vis-à-vis God; in contrast to Roman clientelism, charitable giving did not create social ties.[33]

3) The priesthood itself was divided in many respects. Intensified competition for the office of high priest, particularly since about 59 CE led to increasing tensions within the priestly elite.[34] Adding to that circumstance were the stark divisions between the higher priests (or *kohanim*), on the one hand, and the lower priests (or Levites), on the other. Each of the various factions had armed gangs that sought to intimidate or terrorize their opponents on the streets.[35] In a state of outrage, Josephus reports that the Levites, aided by King Agrippa II (the temple superintendent appointed by the Romans), obtained the right to wear linen garments like the priests.[36] As this episode suggests, the higher priests had also had a falling out with Agrippa. When Judea was re-provincialized after the death of Agrippa I in 44 CE, the Emperor Claudius assigned the supervision of the temple (*exousia tou naou*) to the head of the Herodians, thereby giving them the right to appoint

[31] Goodman, *Ruling Class*, 117.
[32] Avigad, *Discovering Jerusalem*, 81–165; Berlin, "Jewish Life", 441–2, 446, 450, 453.
[33] Goodman, *Ruling Class*, 117–30.
[34] For one particularly illuminating episode cf. McLaren, "Ananus", 1–25.
[35] Josephus Ant. 20.179–81, 213–14.
[36] Josephus Ant. 20.216–18.

and remove high priests.[37] I understand this measure, too, as a type of *detente*, an attempt to place temple affairs completely in Jewish hands – in addition to the autonomy that had already been conceded and in the process reducing a particularly explosive source of friction. However, this calculation ended up backfiring inasmuch as, in the eyes of the higher priests, the Herodians were no better than the Romans. Starting in the late 50s, Agrippa II fought a running battle with the priests, a struggle that now forced the Romans to intervene more than ever.[38] Consequently, anarchy began to spread at the start of the sixties: "Real influence could be gained only by acquiring the support of the Roman administrators, particularly the procurator, or by appealing by popular measures to the mass support of the people."[39] In other words, the warring parties in Jerusalem had two options: they could try either to outdo each other in bribing the procurator or to improve their image as spokesmen for their people against the Roman occupiers. As conflicting as these two options were, they nonetheless had to collide at some point.

In this final section of my article, I would like to return to Josephus' conceptions of theocracy and hierocracy. Roman provincial rule allowed for the hierocratic expression of theocracy, which Josephus thought was the ideal constitution for the Jews, an ideal that was both nostalgic and apologetic. But the dynamic that had seized Judean society since the Maccabean Revolt was expressed as little by this concept as the fact that the high-priestly class could not play the role of a Greco-Roman aristocracy – despite how much Josephus repeatedly tries to suggest otherwise in his historiographical works. Josephus overlooks the fact that the leadership of the priests and especially the high priest already appeared questionable under the Hasmoneans and Herod.[40] In the wake of this damage, other groups stepped forward. Josephus also overlooks the fact that the priestly elite did not possess the necessary standing – either in relation to the Romans or in relation to the Judeans – to maintain law and order or to preclude the catastrophe of a war against Rome. At the same time, it was not possible for an alternative to a temple-based state or priestly rule to develop. To understand why that

---

[37] The *exousia tou naou* exercised by the Herodians between 44 and 66 CE is thoroughly treated by Wilker, *Rom*, 205–52.

[38] Wilker, *Rom*, 310–16.

[39] Goodman, *Ruling Class*, 147.

[40] Goodman, *Ruling Class*, 111: "The prestige of the High Priest's office had been drastically diminished after 37 B.C., and no Jewish sources from the years after A.D. 70 regret the complete disappearance of these 'leaders of the nation'." In my opinion, the high priest's loss of authority started even earlier, when the Hasmoneans occupied the high priesthood in 152 BCE as a result of military success and subjected it to their political and military ambitions; consequently, their claim to high priesthood was contested right from the beginning (cf. Trampedach, "Hasmonäer", 51–6).

was the case, I would like to return to the term "theocracy". In my opinion, Josephus succeeded with this train of thought in characterizing well the unique religious, political, social concept that dominated the thinking of all Judeans – albeit in many varieties. Regardless of Josephus' intentions, the term "theocracy" has a descriptive value that I find productive for the considerations to follow.

Theocracy, of course, requires mediation. God does not rule in person – or at least not yet. In the Jewish context, there are two mediating authorities that precede the traditional priesthood both historically and systematically: the law and the prophets. In such circumstances, power is possessed by whoever can establish himself as a prophet or whoever can be heard as an exegete and interpreter of the Torah and the acknowledged prophets.

A range of apologetic interests prevents Josephus from developing these options. Power and influence in a theocracy are mediated not by traditional honorary privileges or everyday acts of worship, but by means of divine revelation. Thus, there was no shortage of prophets in the period under consideration. They were often very popular, and, regardless of the actual danger they posed, they could not be utilized for political purposes. For they were opposed by other Jewish groups as heretics and by the Romans as troublemakers.[41] Other charismatic-ascetics such as Josephus' teacher Bannus or John the Baptist were characterized by "the power ascribed to them precisely because of their lack of institutional authority or social status".[42]

A more important group with a permanent presence, whom the Romans never apparently had in their sights, were the Scribes and Pharisees. The social composition of this group, to my knowledge, cannot be determined.[43] It was probably fairly diverse and did not play much of a role. Since in any event it was not a clearly defined group, and since everyone, including priests such as Josephus himself, was in principle able to participate in processes of exegesis and interpretation, it did not represent a constitutional alternative to hierocracy. As a result, exegesis – like prophecy – was not consolidated within the standard political structures and, therefore, lay outside the bounds of political control.[44] Whether the eagle on the facade of the Herodian temple violated the commandments of the Torah was not a

---

[41] Examples apart from Jesus: Josephus B.J. 2.258–63; Ant. 20.97–9, 169–72; Acts 5:36; 21:38; Josephus B.J. 6.285.

[42] Goodman, *Ruling Class*, 78.

[43] Schwartz, "Scribes", 89–101, argues convincingly that the scribes mentioned in the New Testament are to be identified with Levites who saw themselves as representatives of priestly law. In any case, like most Pharisees, the scribes were certainly not part of the ruling class.

[44] Hengel/Deines, "Common Judaism", 38–40, emphasize, on the one hand, the self-understanding of the Pharisees "as heirs of the prophets so that the competence which legitimated the prophets also characterized them", and, on the other hand, the "Pharisaic diversity" which did not allow for "any unified political position".

matter that could be decided in a generally binding way; instead, it was a matter of opinion. Hence, to cite one extreme example, radical scribes could claim, with reference to the Torah, that this was indeed a violation and could thereby incite their zealous disciples to destroy the eagle – despite the terrible consequences of such an act (and not just for the perpetrators).[45]

Although the Scribes and Pharisees, particularly in political terms, did not follow a united party line, they influenced popular attitudes toward Roman rule much more than the leading priests.[46] They promoted practices of purity that were becoming increasingly strict, especially as reflected in the archaeological record (food, household utensils, ritual baths). Andrea Berlin has termed these practices "household Judaism".[47] The increasing rejection of foreign luxury goods and other commodities, along with the associated tendency toward economic isolation, shows that the aversion to foreign rule had increasingly broader repercussions. These phenomena also explain why the idea of an originally small group – sanctifying itself by loosening the Gentile yoke – fell on such fertile ground.

But how did they believe they could stand up to the Romans? One answer is provided by the theocratic philosophy of history. Its foundational texts demonstrate that God's activities in history are at all times comprehensible. Having entered into a covenant with the people of Israel that commits Israel to abiding by the law, God must in return protect Israel. In line with this thinking, political setbacks have to be understood as God's punishment for sin or degeneration. Yet that cannot be the last word. For in the end, God will always save and raise up his people. The Exodus story, with the flight through the Red Sea, contains the original model that is allegedly confirmed time and again in the course of history. However, these biblical examples were less consequential in this case than the Maccabean revolt. In that event, Jewish resistance triumphed against the (initially) far superior Seleucid occupying forces. Even the death of Caligula, which saved the temple in Jerusalem from desecration, was also understood as divine intervention.[48] Nothing about the fundamental situation had changed, however. Foreign rule was a constant stumbling block. When reality lags too far behind what is believed to be the norm, when the godless appear to rule and oppress the righteous, then the apocalypse comes to serve as a

---

[45] Josephus B.J. 1.648–50.

[46] Schürer, *History*, 2:402.

[47] Berlin, "Jewish Life", 417–70; cf. Hengel/Deines, "Common Judaism", 41–51.

[48] For example, the speeches Josephus put in the mouth of Agrippa shortly before the outbreak of the revolt and of himself at the beginning of the siege indicate in an inversive manner, that the people of Jerusalem hoped for God's assistance (*symmachia tou theou*) and based their confidence on the well-known "historical" (i.e. biblical and post-biblical) analogies: Josephus B.J. 2.390–5; 5.375–419.

response that can rescue the credibility of a theocratic philosophy of history. From such a perspective, God will come and establish his dominion over the entire world. Yet, how might the establishment of the long-awaited kingdom of God be accelerated? While (generally speaking) quietistic circles sought salvation in prayer and daily rituals, the Zealots sought to provoke the intervention of God through active struggle. In any event, numerous sources indicate that the expectation was widespread – indeed, it was the prevailing mood among the Jewish population in Palestine – that the hoped-for redemption was close at hand. The destruction of Rome and of idolatry more generally was seen as a necessary precondition for realizing the kingdom of God.[49]

Sensing the appeal of a "liberation theology", the young priestly avant-garde that halted the sacrifices for the emperor and began to mint new silver coins (the *shekel* of Israel) believed themselves to be ushering in a new era of freedom and independence.[50] By setting itself up all at once at the forefront of the movement, this group underscored its claim to leadership over the various competing groups.

In conclusion: The cooperation between Rome and the Judean priestly elite failed essentially for two reasons.

1) The God of the Torah conceived of Israel as a fundamentally egalitarian community based on a social ethics of solidarity. He thereby created an inevitable norm to which malcontents of all kinds could appeal. The emphatic presence of this norm explains not only why adverse socio-economic conditions (in contrast to other Roman provinces in which these were also present) could ignite the willingness of the larger population to undertake a rebellion but also why an aristocracy on the Greco-Roman model was not able to develop in Judea.

2) In the Jewish theocracy, power could be derived only from divine revelation. The need to interpret divine revelation became a problem because it was not channeled through an uncontested and united exegetical authority but instead resulted in multiple, conflicting interpretations and the formation of sects. Under such conditions, it was not possible to restrict (or to institutionalize) governmental power or political authority to a particular group of individuals. This explains why Judea had an elite that was traditional in many respects but was not capable of governing – and why the Romans did not manage to create one. Moreover, the lack of legitimacy for this-worldly (i.e., non-divine) rule also explains why the revolt after initial

---

[49] Hengel, *Zeloten*, esp. 181–8, 315–18.

[50] McLaren, "Coinage", 149–52; "the priestly pedigree of anti-Roman ideologies" is emphasized also by Goodblatt, "Priestly Ideologies", esp. 241–2, 248–9. Probable theological justifications for the cessation of the daily sacrifices for the well-being of the emperor and the Roman people are discussed by Albertz, "Foreign Rulers", pp. 115–133, in this volume.

successes led to a civil war. Only in the face of the Roman siege of Jerusalem did it once again turn into a revolt. And as such, it ended in uncompromising ruin.

References

Avigad, N., *Discovering Jerusalem* (Nashville et al.: Thomas Nelson Publishers, 1983).

Barclay, J.M.G., *Against Apion: Translation and Commentary* (Flavius Josephus. Translation and Commentary 10; Leiden/Boston: Brill, 2007).

Beebe, H.K., "Caesarea Maritima: Its Strategic and Political Significance to Rome", *JNES* 42 (1983) 195–207.

Berlin, A.M., "Jewish Life Before the Revolt: the Archaeological Evidence", *JSJ* 36 (2005) 417–70.

Bernett, M., *Der Kaiserkult in Judäa unter den Herodiern und Römern* (Tübingen: Mohr Siebeck, 2007).

Eck, W., *Rom und Judaea: Fünf Vorträge zur römischen Herrschaft in Palaestina* (Tübingen: Mohr Siebeck, 2007).

Garnsey, P./Saller, R., *The Roman Empire: Economy, Society and Culture* (London: Duckworth, 1987).

Gerber, C., *Ein Bild des Judentums für Nichtjuden von Flavius Josephus: Untersuchungen zu seiner Schrift Contra Apionem* (Leiden/Boston: Brill, 1997).

Goodblatt, D., "Priestly Ideologies in the Judean Resistance", *JSQ* 3 (1996) 225–49.

Goodman, M., *The Ruling Class of Judaea: The Origins of the Revolt against Rome A.D. 66–70* (Cambridge: Cambridge University Press, 1987).

Haensch, R., *Capita provinciarum. Statthaltersitze und Provinzialverwaltung in der römischen Kaiserzeit* (Mainz: Philipp von Zabern, 1997).

Hengel, M., *Die Zeloten. Untersuchungen zur Jüdischen Freiheitsbewegung in der Zeit von Herodes I. bis 70 n. Chr.* (Leiden/Köln: Brill, [2]1976).

–/Deines, R., "E.P. Sanders 'Common Judaism', Jesus, and the Pharisees", *JTS* 46 (1995) 1–70.

Horsley, R.A., "High Priests and the Politics of Roman Palestine: A Contextual Analysis of the Evidence in Josephus", *JSJ* 17 (1986) 23–55.

Isaac, B., *The Limits of Empire: The Roman Army in the East* (Oxford: Clarendon Press, 1990).

Jacques, F./Scheid, J., *Rom und das Reich in der Hohen Kaiserzeit 44 v. Chr. – 260 n. Chr.* Vol 1: *Die Struktur des Reiches* (Stuttgart/Leipzig: B.G. Teubner, 1998).

Mason, S., *Flavius Josephus und das Neue Testament* (Tübingen/Basel: Francke Verlag, 2000).

–, *Judean War 2: Translation and Commentary* (Flavius Josephus. Translation and Commentary 1B; Leiden/Boston: Brill, 2008).

McKechnie, P., "Judean Embassies and Cases before Roman Emperors", *JTS* 56 (2005) 339–61.

McLaren, J.S., "Ananus, James, and Earliest Christianity: Josephus' Account on the Death of James", *JTS* 52 (2001) 3–25.

–, "The Coinage of the First Year as Point of Reference for the Jewish Revolt", *SCI* 22 (2003) 135–52.

Price, J.J., *Jerusalem under Siege. The Collapse of the Jewish State 66–70 C.E.* (Leiden et al.: Brill, 1992).

Schürer, E., *The History of the Jewish People in the Age of Jesus Christ (175 B.C.-A.D. 135)* (A new English Version revised and edited by G. Vermes/F. Millar; 3 vol.; Edinburgh: T&T Clark, 1973–87).

Schwartz, D.R., "Josephus on the Jewish Constitutions and Communities", *SCI* 7 (1983–4) 30–52.

–, "'Scribes and Pharisees, Hypocrites': Who are the 'Scribes' in the New Testament?", in idem, *Studies in the Jewish Background of Christianity* (Tübingen: J.C.B. Mohr, 1992) 89–101.

Smallwood, E.M., "High Priests and Politics in Roman Palestine", *JTS* 13 (1962) 14–34.

–, *The Jews under Roman Rule: From Pompey to Diocletian: A Study in Political Relations* (Leiden: Brill, 1976).

Trampedach, K., "Die Hasmonäer und das Problem der Theokratie", in A. Pečar/idem (ed.), *Die Bibel als politisches Argument: Voraussetzungen und Folgen biblizistischer Herrschaftslegitimation in der Vormoderne* (HZ-Beiheft 43; München: R. Oldenbourg, 2007) 37–65.

–, "Schwierigkeiten mit der Theokratie: Warum die römische Herrschaft in Judäa scheiterte", in idem/A. Pečar (ed.), *Theokratie und theokratischer Diskurs: Die Rede von der Gottesherrschaft und ihre politisch-sozialen Auswirkungen im interkulturellen Vergleich* (Tübingen: Mohr Siebeck, 2012) 117–142.

Wilker, J., *Für Rom und Jerusalem: Die herodianische Dynastie im 1. Jahrhundert n. Chr.* (Frankfurt am Main: Verlag Antike, 2007).

Index of Ancient Sources

Hebrew Bible/Old Testament

Genesis
1–9	121
2:1–4	45
5:22–24	63
10	121–2
11:27–32	45
12:6–7	144
17	45
17:8	44
28:4	44
34:25	191
37–50	39, 57
37:3–50:21	55
37:28	55 n.8
37:36	55 n.8
39	57–9, 61, 65–6, 69
39:3–4	58
39:14	58
39:19–20	58, 59 n.18
39:20–23	58 n.17
40	59 n.18
41:40	39
41:42	39
45:7	56
45:11	56
46:1–5	59–61, 68–9
47:4	56
49:15	64 n.34
50:1–14	60 n.22
50:25–26	63

Exodus
1:10	90
1:22	90
6:1–12	121
6:2–8	44–5
12	46
12:43	121
13:19	63
16	45
20:13	140
21:24	238
23:4–5	243
29:38–42	124
30:11–16	124

Leviticus
9	44
16	44
17–27	120
17:8–9	120–1
18:24–30	120
19:18	239
22:18	120 n.18
22:25	120 n.15, 121, 126
24:20	238
25:14	126 n.34
25:33	44

Numbers
11	48
12:6–8	48
15:1–12	120
15:13–14	120–1
28:3–8	124
31:11–12	105 n.62
31:21–24	105 n.62
33:6	243

Deuteronomy
4:7–8	100
5:17	140
7:1–6	89
7:1	73 n.4
11:29–30	140–1
11:31–12:5	143
12:5	142, 145
13:18	40 n.17
14:21	121
15:3	121
16:9–15	120
17	145–6
17:5	145
17:14–20	48
19:16–19	101
20–24	90
20:10	243
20:20	244
21:22–23	103
22:6	243
23:4–9	125, 126 n.33.35

23:4	73 n.4
23:21	121
27:2–8	140–1
27:4–5	141–3
27:12–13	142
28:53	65 n.40
28:55	65 n.40
28:57	65 n.40
30:3	40
34	44, 47

Joshua

7	40 n.17
8:29	195
18:1	44
19:51	44
24	46
24:32	63

Judges

2:24	243

1 Samuel

8–12	48
31:9–10	195

2 Samuel

13:18–19	55 n.7
14:7	102 n.53

1 Kings

3–10	48
8:16	143, 145
8:41–43	118, 120 n.15
8:50	40

2 Kings

13:23	40 n.17
15:15	124
16:15	119, 123 n.28
17:24–34	76
17:24–28	74
18	36
22–23	40
24:3	39
24:20	39
25	49
25:21	41
25:27–30	39–40

Isaiah

10:7	89
30:6	65 n.40

40–55	36, 43
43:16–21	37
44:3	48
44:28	37
45:1–3	37
45:5	91 n.8
45:13	37
47:6	36
51:1–3	43
51:11	43
52:1	127
54:7–8	36

Jeremiah

40–42	41

Ezekiel

11:14–18	42
33:23–29	41–3
35:10	42 n.26
36:2–3	42 n.26
36:5	42 n.26
36:27	48
39:29	48
44:6–9	126 n.35
44:9–12	126

Joel

3:1–2	48
4:17	127

Amos

1:3–2:3	91

Haggai

2:23	83

Zechariah

8:16	245
14:21	127

Psalms

24	128–9
29:11	243
34:15	243
48	128–9
74	209
74:7	127
75	209
79	208–10
79:1	127
79:10	210
81	128–9

81:14–15	129–130		*Daniel*	
82	128		2–6	39
83	209–10		2:48	39
83:9–10	210		3:3–13	99
85:11	245		5:29	39
92	128			
93	128–9		*Ezra*	
94	128		1–6	77
118	85 n.55		1:2	77
			1:8	76
Proverbs			4–6	73
10:10	236 n.35		4:1–10	75
25:21–22	239 n.44		4:1–5	74–6, 85
			4:6–24	74–6
Lamentations			4:6–11	75
1:10	126		4:11–23	78, 80
			4:11–13	75
Esther			4:16	75
2:5	96		4:24	74
2:15	96		5–6	77–8
2:20	108		5:1–4	77
2:21–23	98		5:5	77
3:1–7	97		5:9	77
3:7	99		6:1–5	77
3:8–11	100		6:7–8	77
3:8	93–4		6:8–10	119
3:12–15	101–2		6:14	77
3:12–14	93		7:23	34
3:13	92, 102, 104–5		7:28	34
6:1	108		9–10	73
6:10–11	39		9:1	73 n.4
6:11	184		9:2	21
6:13	21		9:4	73 n.4
7:4	102		10:3	73 n.4
7:7–10	103			
8:4–5	104		*Nehemiah*	
8:10–12	104–5		1:1–7:5	79
8:11	102		1–6	73
8:15	39		2–6	79
9:1–16	105		2–4	83–5
9:1–2	108		2:1–6	79
9:1	103		2:9–10	79–80
9:2	106		2:17–20	79
9:5	106		2:19	80, 83
9:7–10	106		3:33–37	79–81
9:14	106		3:34	85
9:15	106		3:38–4:3	79
9:16	106, 108		3:38	79
9:20–32	99		4:1	80, 85
9:20–28	92		4:17	79
9:22	103		5	79, 85
10:3	39		5:7	84

5:13	84		10:33	124
6	83, 85		13	73, 85–6
6:1–14	84		13:1–3	126 n.33
6:1–9	79–80, 83		13:4–9	79, 82, 84–5
6:6–8	83		13:28–29	79, 85
6:10–14	83		13:28	81
6:15–16	79			
6:15	79, 84		*2 Chronicles*	
6:17–19	83–4		6:5–6	143, 145
9	21		36:23	33

Apocrypha and Pseudepigrapha

Ben Sira			3	182, 189
44–49	62		3:3	182
45:3	63 n.30		3:11–12	24
45:18	63 n.30		3:13–14	1893:14 182
49:14–16	63–4		3:15	189
49:15	62 n.29		3:25–26	189
50:25–26	137		3:25	19
50:26	62 n.29		3:30	190
			3:31	108 n.72
1 Maccabees			3:32	188, 212
1	18, 181		3:35–36	22
1:1–10	18 n.16		3:37	108 n.72
1:6	188		3:40–41	190
1:11	19, 224		3:42–44	190
1:29–32	224		3:51	190
1:40	181		4–8	183
1:41–42	151, 225		4	190
2–16	18		4:27	190
2	21, 65–6		4:28–35	190–1
2:8	188		4:55	130
2:9	181		4:58	191
2:12	181		5	20, 24, 25 n.35, 191
2:17	188		5:1–4	191
2:18	182		5:1	19
2:19–22	225		5:10	19
2:23–24	225		5:13	191
2:29–38	19 n.19, 189		5:32	188
2:29	225		5:36	188
2:35–36	225		5:45–54	192
2:40–41	225		5:45–52	180 n.7
2:46	22		5:57	20
2:49–68	65		5:62	20
2:51	182		5:63–64	182
2:53	65		5:65–68	192
2:62	182		6	193
2:64	182		6:1–16	108–9
2:67–68	66		6:1–8	193

6:1	188		12:21	20
6:20	213 n.19		12:43	188
6:31	193		12:53	20
6:45	194		13:3	65 n.40
6:55–63	213		13:6	201
6:59	194		13:15–16	201
6:60–62	194		13:18	201
7	17		13:23	201
7:1–4	194		13:42	107
7:13–16	19 n.19		14	21, 181, 186, 202
7:16	210		14:4	186
7:17	210		14:5	186
7:26–43	107 n.68		14:9	186
7:26	188		14:10	186
7:28–30	217		14:15	186
7:33	119		14:21	186
7:34–35	195		14:23	186
7:38	195		14:29	186
7:48–50	107 n.68		14:35	187
7:49	107		14:39	187
8–16	17		14:40	188
8	195		15–16	181
8:1	194		15:9	187
8:12–13	194		15:16–24	21 n.22
9	191, 196		15:28–31	187
9:10	25, 183		15:32	188 n.19
9:55–56	210		15:33–34	25
9:70–73	198		15:36	188 n.19
9:72–73	22		16	202
10	179, 183–4, 198			
10:3	199		*2 Maccabees*	
10:15	198		2:21	22, 225
10:20	219		2:23	17
10:24	199		3–8	18
10:50	199		3	22
10:58	184		3:1–3	18 n.16, 117
10:60	184		3:25–26	24
10:61–66	199		3:36–39	25 n.33
10:69–70	199		3:36	211
10:72	199		3:39	27
10:86	184		4:1–10:9	214
10:88	184, 200		4:11	226
11:4–5	192		4:13	226
11:6	184		4:17	18, 226
11:41–44	185		4:26–35	215
11:51	185		4:42	24
11:53	185		4:50	226
11:57	201		5:2–4	24
11:58–59	201		5:6	227
11:60	188		5:9	24, 227
12:1	25		5:13–14	227
12:8	188		5:15–16	227
12:12	185		5:21	109 n.75

5:27	227		12:40–41	24
6–7	208		12:40	214
6:6	23		13	212, 214 n.22, 215
6:18–31	227		13:1	213
7	227		13:3–8	213
7:37–38	19 n.18		13:4	213
8:1	22–3		13:7–8	24
8:2–4	208, 227		13:23–24	211 n.16, 213–14
8:5	18–19		13:23	218
8:9	216 n.26		13:24	218
8:24	130		13:25–26	218
8:36	25 n.33, 211		14	219
9–13	213		14:2	214 n.25
9	19, 211–12, 214 n.22, 215		14:3	219
9:1–2	108 n.72		14:11–15	107 n.68
9:4–7	109		14:12–29	216
9:5	227		14:24–25	216
9:6	24		14:25	217
9:8	109		14:26	217
9:11–17	25 n.33		14:28	107 n.68
9:12	109		14:31–37	107 n.68
9:13	227		14:34–35	27
9:16	118 n.9		14:38	23
9:28	109		15	19
9:29	213		15:12–16	24
10–13	218		15:16	216
10	19		15:25–27	216
10:1	227		15:34–35	227
10:9	214		15:36	108
10:10–13:26	214		15:37	22
10:11	212, 215			
10:29–30	24		*3 Maccabees*	
11	212, 215		3	99
11:8	24			
11:13–33	213		*Testament of Joseph*	
11:13–15	218		1:3–10:4	67
11:13–14	211–14		1:3–7	67
11:13	25 n.33		2:1–10:4	67
11:16–38	212		2:4–7	67
11:27–33	213, 215, 218		2:8–9:5	67
12	214 n.22		10:1–4	68
12:34	214			

New Testament

Matthew			5:12	238
5:9–10	245		5:38–39	238
5:9	236–7, 244		5:39–42	238
5:10	236–7		5:43–48	239 n.43
5:11	237		5:43–44	239

10:17–18   240
10:22–23   240
13:21   240 n.51
22:21   235
23:34   240 n.51
24:2   235

Mark
12:13–17   236
12:17   235
13:2   235
13:14   235

Luke
6:22   237
6:23   238
6:27   238
6:29   238
19:41–44   235
20:25   235
21:6   235
21:12   240

21:16–17   240
21:19   240

John
18:28–29   256 n.18
18:28   123 n.26

Acts
5:17   27 n.38
5:36   261 n.41
21:38   261 n.41

Romans
13:7   236

Colossians
1:20   236 n.35

1 Peter
3:11   237 n.36
3:15   237 n.36

Rabbinic Works

ABOT DE RABBI NATHAN
A 4   241
B 6   241
B 13   241

BABYLONIAN TALMUD
Baba Batra
12b   34 n.3

Sanhedrin
11a   34 n.3

Giṭṭin
56b   241

MIDRASH
Genesis Rabbah
8:5   245
49:9   231 n.26
64:10   231 n.26

Exodus Rabbah
15:26   245
52:5   245

Leviticus Rabbah
3:6   245
9:3   244
9:9   243

Lamentations Rabbah
1:31   241

MISHNAH
'Abot
1:12   244
1:18   245
2:7   245
4:15   242 n.63

'Eduyyot
1:13   246 n.65

Giṭṭin
4:2   246
4:3–4   246 n.65
4:5   246
4:6   246
4:7   246 n.65

4:9	246 n.65
5:3	246 n.65
9:4	246 n.65

'Uqṣin

| 3:12 | 245 |

TOSEFTA

Pe'ah

Giṭṭin

| 1:1 | 244 |

| 4:2 | 246 |

Šebi'it

Mo'ed Qaṭan

| 5:9 | 242 n.63 |

| 1:12 | 246 |

Latin and Greek Writings

AESCHYLUS
Persians
| 1.584–90 | 98 |

APPIAN
Syriaca
| 66 | 108 n.72 |

ARRIAN
Alexandri Anabasis
| 4.11.8–9 | 99 n.40 |

DIODORUS
Library of History
| 40.2 | 253 n.8 |
| 40.3 | 252 n.6 |

HERODOTUS
Histories
1.79	95 n.25
1.106	95 n.24
1.134	97 n.33
3.79	95
3.159	103 n.60
4.43	103 n.60
7.136	98
7.238	103 n.60

JOSEPHUS
Antiquitates
11	96
11.17	119
11.297–301	95
11.302ff	81 n.37
11.309	81
11.324	81
11.336	117–18
12.140–2	160 n.13
12.160	82
12.354–5	108 n.72

13.242–3	118
13.254–7	166 n.31
13.296–7	28 n.40
13.296	27 n.38
13.401	27 n.38
13.408	28 n.40
14.41	253 n.8
14.63	28
14.65	28
14.67	28
14.390–1	29
14.462	29
15.218	185
15.403–20	123 n.26
16.14	118
17.149	29
17.151	29
17.168–72	193 n.25
17.168	29
17.299–323	254 n.9
17.342–4	254 n.9
18.1–2	254 n.9
18.3–4	129 n.39
18.55–9	256 n.17
18.120–2	256 n.19
18.121	256
18.122	118
18.196	15
18.255	29
18.257	15
18.277	233 n.29
19.278ff	15
20.49	121 n.19
20.97–9	261 n.41
20.113–17	257 n.22
20.136	257 n.23
20.162	129 n.39
20.169–72	261 n.41
20.179–81	259 n.35
20.180–1	115 n.2

20.189–96	129 n.39
20.206–7	115 n.2
20.208–10	122 n.22
20.213–14	259 n.35
20.216–18	259 n.36
20.224–51	252 n.6
20.251	254

Bellum Judaicum
1.146	28
1.148	28
1.150	28
1.201	230
1.287	29
1.316	228
1.340–1	29
1.357	118 n.9
1.437	228
1.648–50	262 n.45
1.648	29
1.650	29
1.656	29
2.29	228
2.80–100	254 n.9
2.111	254 n.9
2.117	254 n.9
2.169–74	256 n.17
2.183	29
2.197	119, 256 n.16
2.211–14	228
2.224–7	124
2.228–31	257 n.22
2.230–2	123 n.26
2.243	129 n.39
2.244–6	257 n.23
2.258–63	261 n.41
2.280–3	231
2.291	130 n.40
2.310–12	228
2.315–17	129 n.39
2.320	129 n.39
2.338	231
2.341	115, 118
2.345–401	231
2.390–5	122 n.23, 262 n.48
2.390–2	130
2.393	122
2.409–18	121 n.20, 122 n.23
2.409–10	257 n.25
2.409	115, 256 n.16
2.410	116 n.2
2.411–418	116–17
2.412	129

2.417	115
2.418–21	131
2.418	115 n.2
2.422–4	131
2.425	131
2.429	115 n.2
2.441	115 n.2, 131
2.451	115 n.2
2.457	228
2.487	15
2.628	115 n.2
3.344	228
3.362–86	228
3.381	228
3.426	228
4.444	241 n.56
5.245	124
5.375–419	262 n.48
5.391–4	241 n.55
6.285	261 n.41
7.323–88	229
7.342–4	230
7.386	230
7.389–90	230

Contra Apionem
1.60	165
1.187–8	252 n.6
2.48	117–18
2.77	119, 256 n.16
2.164–5	251 n.2
2.185–8	252 n.3
2.186	252 n.5
2.193–4	252 n.3

JUSTINUS
Phillipic History
36.2.16	252 n.6

LETTER OF ARISTEAS
32	159
45	119
115	165

PHILO
In Flaccum
115	24 n.29
170	25 n.33
170–4	24 n.29
189	24 n.29

Hypothetica
7.6	28 n.40

Legatio ad Gaium

1	232
22	232
115–17	232
119	232
122–4	232
133	233
157	119, 256 n.16
166	232
178–9	233
180	233
190	233
192	233
195–6	234
229	234
230	234
232	256 n.16
233–6	234
280	119
294–7	118
299–305	256 n.17
301	234
303	235
317	119, 124, 256 n.16
319	118 n.9

PLATO
Laws

7.793	28 n.40

POLYBIOS
Histories

3.30.4	25 n.34
18.22.8	25 n.34
31.9	108 n.72
31.14.4	107 n.68

QUINTUS CURTIUS RUFUS
Histories of Alexander the Great

8.5–13	98 n.35

TACITUS
Histories

5.8	167 n.33

THUCYDIDES
Peleponnesian War

5.84–116	90

XENOPHON
Anabasis

3.2.13	98 n.35, 99 n.39

Ancient Near Eastern Sources

CYRUS CYLINDER

12	37
13	37
15	37
32	37

ELEPHANTINE PAPYRI

TAD A4.7	78
TAD A4.7,29	81
TAD A4.8	78
TAD A4.8,28	81

MESHA STELE

KAI 181.17	89

PERSIAN INSCRIPTIONS

DB 4.33–43	101
DNa 10–11	101
DSe 9–10	101
DZc 5	101
XPh 46–56	101

WADI ED-DALIYEH PAPYRI

WD 22	81
WDSP 11r	81

Index of Authors

Abel, F.M. 181
Achenbach, R. 89–90, 96, 106
Albertz, R. 41, 46, 54–7, 59–60, 120, 123
Ariel, D.T. 153, 156–7, 162
Assmann, J. 89
Avigad, N. 167, 259

Baden, J.S. 44
Baentsch, B. 121
Bar-Kochva, B. 190, 217
Barag, D. 137
Barclay, J.M.G. 251–2
Bardtke, H. 93–4
Barstad, H.M. 41
Barton, J. 91
Bauks, M. 44
Baumbach, G. 115
Baumgarten, A.I. 171
Becker, J. 66–8
Bederman, D.J. 90
Beebe, H.K. 255
Beentjes, P.C. 62
Ben-Hayyim, Z. 138
Berlin, A. 92, 94, 98
Berlin, A.M. 157, 170, 259, 262
Berman, J. 100
Bernett, M. 254, 256
Berthelot, K. 183, 192–3
Betz, H.D. 236–9
Bevenot, H. 99
Bickerman, E. 223
Blenkinsopp, J. 44, 75–6, 78–9, 85
Blum, E. 54–6, 60
Böhler, D. 76
Bourdieu, P. 171
Bowman, J. 178
Boyarin, D. 16, 23
Brann, M. 13
Bremmer, J.N. 185
Brettler, M.Z. 47
Brock, P. 221, 235
Broyde, M.J. 221–2, 227
Bush, F.W. 93
Busink, T.A. 118

Carroll, R.P. 83
Caskel, W. 82

Cerfaux, L. 99
Christensen, A.P. 158
Clairmont, C. 158
Clines, D.J.A. 99
Coats, G.W. 54
Coggins, R.J. 136
Cohen, S.J.D. 23, 241
Collins, J.J. 62–3, 66–7
Coogan, M.D. 224
Crowfoot, J.W. 158, 164
Crown, A.D. 136
Crüsemann, F. 46, 55–6, 93
Cuffari, A. 95, 97

Dancy, J.C. 186
Danker, F.W. 29
Daube, D. 94, 98
Davies, W.D. 237, 239
de Jonge, M. 66
Deines, R. 252, 261–2
Delcor, M. 136
Delling, G. 25
Dexinger, F. 137–8, 146
Dietrich, W. 54–8
Dihle, A. 90
Docherty, S. 61
Dommershausen, W. 65
Donner, H. 54, 59
Doran, R. 53, 205, 207, 217
Dormeyer, D. 206–7
Drosdowski, G. 15
Dušek, J. 81

Ebach, J. 53–5, 57–9
Ebner, M. 206
Eck, W. 254–6
Eckstein, A.M. 179
Eerdmans, B.D. 57
Egger-Wenzel, R. 65
Ego, B. 94, 99, 110, 192, 211
Engel, H. 64, 207–8, 214
Erlich, A. 162–4
Eshel, E. 136
Eshel, H. 136

Finkelstein, A. 25
Finkelstein, I. 41, 153, 171

Finkielsztejn, G. 162, 164
Fishbane, M. 126
Florentin, M. 143
Fox, M.V. 94
Frevel, C. 44
Frevert, U. 200
Fried, L.S. 74

Galison, P. 171
Garnsey, P. 254
Garscha, J. 42
Gaster, M. 143
Geller, M.J. 27
Gendler, E.R. 233
Gera, D. 213
Gerber, C. 251
Gerhards, G. 90
Gerleman, G. 93–4
Gerstenberger, E.S. 126
Gertz, J.C. 54, 60
Gesenius, W. 142
Geva, H. 153–4, 160
Gilbert, M. 62
Gitler, H. 164
Godley, A.D. 97
Goldstein, J.A. 64–5, 183, 186
Goodblatt, D. 170, 263
Goodman, M. 27, 115, 254, 257–61
Gow, A.S.F. 151
Grabbe, L.L. 73
Graetz, H. 125
Grätz, S. 34, 73–4, 77
Grove, P.B. 14
Gruen, E. 20, 61
Gunkel, H. 55, 57–8, 60
Gunneweg, A.H.J. 75, 77, 83, 85
Gutmann, S. 169

Habicht, C. 99, 213
Haensch, R. 231, 255
Hagedorn, A.C. 94, 96, 99
Haller, M. 93
Hare, D.R.A. 240
Hargie, O. 239
Harries, J. 241
Harris, W.V. 235
Hayes, J.W. 157–8
Heltzer, M. 94
Hengel, M. 62, 82, 116–17, 123, 125, 252,
    261–3
Hendrickx, H. 236, 238–40, 242
Hettlage, R. 99
Hezser, C. 229–30, 242

Hieke, T. 65, 183, 192
Hollander, H.W. 61, 66, 68
Horbury, W. 240
Horowitz, W. 213
Horsley, R.A. 221–2, 258
Huttenbach, H.R. 92
Hutter, M. 94

Instone-Brewer, D. 240
Isaac, B. 256

Jackson-Tal, R. 162
Jacob, B. 55, 58–9
Jacques, F. 254
Jenni, E. 106
Johansen, C.F. 158
Jones, F.F. 158

Kahanov, Y. 164
Kahle, P. 143
Kaiser, O. 64
Karrer, C. 77, 80, 84
Kasher, A. 232
Katz, S.T. 92
Kebekus, N. 54–6
Kee, H.C. 66–7
Keel, O. 91
Kellermann, U. 82
Kenrick, P.M. 158
Kent, R.G. 100–1
Kimelman, R. 221, 239–40
Kloner, A. 162–3, 167
Knauf, E.A. 44, 82
Koch, K. 101
Köckert, M. 43–4
Konradt, M. 239
Korošec, D. 92
Kottsieper, I. 96, 108
Kratz, R.G. 53–4, 81, 104, 144
Krieger, K.-S. 116, 125
Kugler, R.A. 66–7
Kuhn, T. 171
Kuhrt, A. 90

Lachs, S.T. 236, 239–40
Ladouceur, D.J. 229
Lake, S. 164
Laserstein, B. 221
Lee, T.R. 62
Lemaire, A. 82
Lemkin, R. 92
Levenson, J.D. 94, 96, 99
Levin, C. 54, 60

Levine, L.I. 159, 170
Levine, T. 162
Lewis, B. 90
Lichtenberger, H. 47
Lipschits, O. 41, 156
Lisewski, K.D. 61–3
Littman, R.L. 94
Loader, J.A. 93
Luther, M. 93
Lux, R. 53, 57–9, 83
Luz, U. 240

Macchi, J.-D. 37, 94, 110
Mack, B.L. 63
Magen, Y. 47, 137, 139, 154, 156, 165–6
Magness, J. 164, 169
Maier, J. 227, 242
Marböck, J. 62
Marcus, J. 240
Martone, C. 239
Mason, S. 14, 16, 23, 252, 256–8
Mazor, G. 167
McKechnie, P. 257
McLaren, J.S. 259, 263
Meinhold, A. 53, 56–7, 59, 93–4, 96, 100, 105
Mell, U. 116, 119–20, 123, 130
Mendels, D. 21, 67, 151, 166, 177, 180, 183, 187, 192
Meshorer, Y. 127
Middendorp, T. 63
Milgrom, J. 121, 126, 170
Mittag, P.F. 108
Modrzejewski, J.M. 15
Momigliano, A. 26
Mooren, L. 99
Mor, M. 136
Mørkholm, O. 108
Mulder, O. 64

Neher, A. 221
Netzer, E. 169
Neuhaus, G.O. 65, 181
Nickelsburg, G.W.E. 17, 223
Nicklas, T. 207, 216–17
Niditch, S. 53
Niehoff, M. 61
Niese, B. 206
Nihan, C. 44, 47
Nitzan, B. 239
Noth, M. 38–9

O'Neill, B. 178, 186
Oded, B. 77

Olyan, S.M. 126
Otto, E. 89–91

Page, D.L. 151
Parpola, S. 36
Paton, L.B. 92–3, 98
Pervo, R.I. 68
Pohlmann, K.-F. 42
Porten, B. 96
Price, J.J. 257
Purvis, J.D. 136

Rahmani, L.Y. 242
Rappaport, U. 181, 186
Redford, D.B. 54, 57, 59–60
Reich, R. 169
Reif, S. 242
Reisner, G.A. 164
Reiterer, F.V. 62, 65
Rengstorf, K.H. 67–8
Reuter, H.-R. 91
Rinpoche, S. 223
Römer, T. 35, 38, 40, 46–8, 53–4, 56–7, 59–60
Rooke, D.W. 96
Rosenthal-Heginbottom, R. 157, 163
Roth, C. 117

Sabini, J. 240
Saldarini, A.J. 241
Saller, R. 254
Sauer, G. 62–3
Schabas, W.A. 91
Schäfer, P. 241
Schaper, J. 126
Scheid, J. 254
Schenker, A. 142
Schiffman, L.H. 128, 221–2, 239
Schmid, K. 49, 53–5, 57, 60
Schmidt, L. 44
Schmitt, H.-C. 54, 57
Schmitt, H.H. 99
Schnocks, J. 210
Schorch, S. 138, 142, 145
Schroedel, W.R. 231
Schunck, K.D. 81
Schürer, E. 117–20, 126, 254, 262
Schwartz, D.R. 16, 19, 22–3, 26, 108–9, 120, 206–7, 211, 213–14, 216, 218–19, 226–7, 252, 261
Schwartz, S. 19, 170, 191
Schwiderski, D. 75, 82
Schwier, H. 122–3
Seebass, H. 121

Selbmann, F. 92
Selwyn, E.G. 237
Shectman, S. 44
Simpson, J.A. 14
Smallwood, E.M. 252, 254–6, 258
Smyth, F. 40
Smyth, H.W. 98
Sonnet, J.-P. 40
Steck, O.H. 33, 238
Steil, A. 35
Stein, J. 14–15
Stemberger, G. 125, 242
Stern, E. 47, 163
Stewart, F.H. 178–9, 181, 183, 188, 190, 198, 200
Syon, D. 164

Taeger, F. 99
Tal, A. 142
Tal, O. 154
Talmon, S. 94, 103
Tcherikover, V. 223
Teeple, H.M. 238
Thalmann, J.P. 158
Thomas, J. 67
Thompson, H.A. 158
Thornton, T.C.G. 103
Tilly, M. 66–7
Tondriau, J. 99
Tov, E. 140, 142
Trampedach, K. 251, 260
Tushingham, A.D. 153, 157

Ulrichsen, J.H. 67

VanderKam, J.C. 96
van Henten, J.W. 19, 186

van Oorschot, J. 43
van Unnik, W.C. 21
Veijola, T. 90
Vieweger, D. 120
von der Way, T. 89
von Dobbeler, S. 64–5, 207

Waagé, F.O. 158
Wacker, M.-T. 106
Wahl, H.M. 53, 94, 103
Walbank, F.W. 99
Weimar, P. 54–5, 57
Weiner, E.S.C. 14
Wellhausen, J. 38, 116
Welten, P. 33
Westermann, C. 55, 59–60
Wiemer, H.-U. 99
Wiesehöfer, J. 98, 107
Wilker, J. 256, 258, 260
Willi, T. 33
Willi-Plein, I. 99
Williamson, H.G.M. 96
Witte, M. 63–4
Wöhrle, J. 54, 60, 127
Wright, J. 73, 78, 81, 83–4
Würthwein, E. 93

Yamauchi, E.M. 94
Yavetz, Z. 95–6
Yoder, J.H. 246

Zadok, R. 96
Zenger, E. 44, 89, 94
Zerbe, G.M. 221, 235, 239
Zimmerli, W. 41–2
Zsengellér, J. 137, 143
Zwick, R. 207